EAST EUROPEAN MONOGRAPHS, NO. XII

LJUDEVIT GAJ AND THE ILLYRIAN MOVEMENT

ELINOR MURRAY DESPALATOVIĆ

EAST EUROPEAN QUARTERLY, BOULDER
DISTRIBUTED BY COLUMBIA UNIVERSITY PRESS
NEW YORK AND LONDON
1975

DB
378.5
.G34
D47

Elinor Murray Despalatović is Associate Professor of History
at Connecticut College

Copyright © 1975 by East European Quarterly
Library of Congress Catalog Card Number 75-6228
ISBN 0-914710-05-2

Printed in the United States of America

EAST EUROPEAN MONOGRAPHS

The East European Monographs comprise scholarly books devoted to the history and civilization of Eastern Europe. The studies are published by the *East European Quarterly* in the belief that they contribute to knowledge of the area and stimulate research and scholarship.

1. Political Ideas and the Enlightenment in the Romanian Principalities, 1750-1831. By Vlad Georgescu. 1971.

2. America, Italy and the Birth of Yugoslavia, 1917-1919. By Dragan R. Zivojinovic. 1972.

3. Jewish Nobles and Geniuses in Modern Hungary. By William O. McCagg, Jr. 1972.

4. Mixail Soloxov in Yugoslavia: Reception and Literary Impact. By Robert F. Price. 1973.

5. The Historical and Nationalistic Thought of Nicolae Iorga. By William O. Oldson. 1973.

6. Guide to Polish Libraries and Archives. By Richard C. Lewanski. 1974.

7. Vienna Broadcasts to Slovakia, 1938-1939: A Case Study in Subversion. By Henry Delfiner. 1974.

8. The 1917 Revolution in Latvia. By Andrew Ezergailis. 1974.

9. The Ukraine in the United Nations Organization: A Study in Soviet Foreign Policy, 1944-1950. By Konstantyn Sawczuk. 1975.

10. The Bosnian Church: A New Interpretation. By John V.A. Fine, Jr. 1975.

11. Intellectual and Social Developments in the Habsburg Empire From Maria Theresa to World War I. Edited by Stanley B. Winters and Joseph Held. 1975.

12. Ljudevit Gaj and the Illyrian Movement. By Elinor Murray Despalatovic. 1975.

TO MARIJAN, PAVICA AND MIRNA

PREFACE

This is a study of the relationship between Ljudevit Gaj and the Illyrian Movement. In most works in Western European languages which touch upon the Illyrian Movement, Gaj is identified as its spokesman and leader. This is certainly true for the early years of the Movement, 1835-1842, but less so for the years between 1843 and 1848. Ljudevit Gaj was a journalist, editor, publisher, and, sometimes, politician. A man of common birth in a land in which the nobility dominated social and political life, he could play a key role in the Movement when it was in its predominantly cultural phase, but when it became politicized after 1841, he was gradually pushed into a secondary role.

The first two-thirds of this work is based upon my dissertation for Columbia University, which carried the career of Gaj and the development of the Illyrian Movement up to 1843. It seemed a logical place to end, as leadership of the Movement had passed to others by that time and Gaj's papers contain little information on his political activities after 1843. This is due to the fact that he destroyed many letters and papers in the early 1850's, much of this material relating to his secret politics in the *Vormärz* years. As I prepared my dissertation for publication, it became obvious that it would be necessary to carry the story up to 1848, for Gaj rose to power once more in the early months of the revolution — he therefore could not have been all that minor a figure after 1843 — and because the period between 1843 and 1848 saw the fruition of many of the reforms Gaj had proposed in 1835 and 1836. This leads however to a difference in emphasis in the two parts: the first is primarily about Gaj and his impact on the Movement; the second about the growing strength of the Movement and Gaj's varied attempts to retain a position of leadership within it.

Very little has been written about Ljudevit Gaj in the English language or indeed in any Western European language. There is no adequate published biography of Gaj in any language. He is mentioned in Croatian literary or political histories, usually with a brief biographical sketch, or treated in some detail in articles or monographs which deal with one aspect of his life or with the Illyrian Movement. Certain years have brought forth a whole series of publications on Gaj and the Illyrian Movement: 1872, the year of Gaj's death; 1885, the fiftieth anniversary of the commencement of the Illyrian Movement; 1909, the centenary of Gaj's birth; 1935, the centenary of the Illyrian Movement; and 1972, the centenary of Gaj's death. Many of these gloss over the less attractive aspects of Gaj's life. The late Josip Horvat's recent biography of Gaj is the only balanced study. Unfortunately he died before it was put into final form, and it remains today in manuscript.

The sparsity of critical works on Gaj cannot be explained away by lack of archival material, especially for the years before 1843. It seems to me that the reason Gaj has remained a central but relatively unknown figure in Croatian history is because his life contained so many contradictions. Ideologist of the Illyrian Movement in its early years, gifted organizer and agitator, idolized by the educated youth of Croatia in the 1830's and early 1840's, he fell from power in 1848 due to a political scandal, and lived the rest of his life as an embittered and somewhat shabby figure. He can be viewed as a national hero, victim or opportunist, and one is torn between admiration, sympathy and distrust.

The focus of my study is Ljudevit Gaj. For that reason I have dealt with other important Illyrians only when their lives and thoughts touched Gaj in some significant way. This is no way implies that they were not important, or that Gaj did everything alone. One of the aspects I examine is the exact role Gaj played once he was recognized as leader, and we shall see that the others did the bulk of the day-to-day work in the organizations of the Movement.

Ljudevit Gaj was not an original thinker. He was a practical man who took ideas and adapted them to his purpose — the awakening of a feeling of national identity in his homeland. He was influenced by the works of Herder, Kollar, P.J. Šafařik, Kopitar, Janko Drašković, Karadžić, Vitezović, and probably many others. I have identified influences only when I have been able to prove them from documents. Certain of the Croatian studies about Gaj dating from the late 1930's, especially those of F. Fancev, attribute influences much too easily and without sufficient evidence. In the end, where Gaj found his ideas, is not as important as what he did with them.

In the course of my research I encountered a problem familiar to most students of Eastern European history; some of the interesting leads could simply not be followed up because I lacked training in the languages in which the sources were written. This is true of the Czech and Slovak materials, and of all primary source material in Slovene or Hungarian.

The first two chapters form an introduction to the problems facing Croatia in the early nineteenth century. This seemed necessary due to the complexity of the material, and the lack of information on these subjects in the English language.

I am deeply indebted to the late Josip Horvat for his interest in my work and his generosity in sharing with me the fruit of many years of research. During the two years I spent in Zagreb doing research on Gaj and the Illyrian Movement, I met with Mr. Horvat many times. Before I left he gave me a copy of his Gaj manuscript and some of his notes, telling me that he did not expect to live to see the biography published, and hoped that it would in some way become known through my work. I hope his Gaj biography will be published one day. It needs much editorial work, but it is insightful, well-written, and based upon many years of archival research. I have used the Horvat manuscript mainly as a chronological guide to Gaj's activities and as a source for attempting to understand Gaj's motivations. My work is not at all a duplication of Horvat's study, but it is in many ways a continuation of it.

I am also indebted to Professor Jaroslav Šidak of the University of Zagreb. Josip Horvat helped me to understand Gaj, and Professor Šidak to understand Croatian history in the Illyrian period. I have deep respect for him as a historian and have relied many times in this study on his various works.

If I were to thank all of the people who in one way or another aided me in my research, the list would be many pages in length. I would especially like to mention the late Professor Rudolf Bićanić, Professor Ljudevit Jonke, Professor Mirjana Gros, Dr. Branko Hanž, and Dr. Miroslava Despot — all of Zagreb, and thank them for their kind assistance. I could never have found my way through the manuscript collections without the aid of Mr. Lazlo Nemeth, archivist of the *Haus-Hof- u. Staatsarchiv* in Vienna, and Mr. Šime Jurić, Custodian of the Manuscripts Collection of the Zagreb University Library. The generosity of the Ford Foundation enabled me to spend almost two years in Zagreb in research for this book. I would like to thank Professor Rado Lenček for his most useful criticism, and Professors István Deák, Vojtech Mastny and the late Professor Philip Mosely for their helpful suggestions for adapting the dissertation to book form. Mrs. Patricia Minucci was my major typist and I thank her for her help.

In conclusion I would like to thank the late Professor Henry L. Roberts, my dissertation adviser, for his faith in my work and his patience and wise direction in seeing the major part of this project through.

CONTENTS

CHAPTER I

INTRODUCTION

This is a study of Ljudevit Gaj and, through him, of Croatian nationalism. The terms *nation, nationality* and *nationalism* will appear many times in these pages. We use them every day, but with different shadings and meanings. Historians, sociologists, psychologists, political scientists and others have described and defined nationalism, yet the constant appearance of new books on the subject indicates that we are still unsatisfied with the definitions we have. Perhaps it is too early to arrive at a clear definition of nationalism, since it is so much a part of our world and our consciousness. In order to avoid misunderstandings and confusions in terminology, I have drawn up working definitions of nationality, nation, and nationalism, which will be applied consistently within the pages of this study.(1)

A nationality is a community of men who share all or most of the following characteristics: language, customs, religion, myth, territory, historical experience, and institutions. A nation is a nationality which has a territory and a state organization of its own.

Nationalism is the self-awareness of the nationality, manifested most frequently as the desire to protect its interests against any encroachment in cultural, economic, or political life by another nationality or outside power. It is a feeling of belonging, a loyalty to a group larger than the immediate family, clan, village or region. It is the belief, not always articulated in the first phase of national self-awareness, that the nation state is the best form of political organization, and the most efficient way for the nationality to protect its interests.

This study will examine the rise of nationalism in Croatia (the Kingdom of Croatia, Slavonia and Dalmatia) in the early nineteenth century, through an analysis of the Illyrian Movement and its leader Ljudevit Gaj.

The Croatian Kingdom had been in existence for nine centuries: first as an independent medieval state, then as a historic unit within Hungary and, later, the Habsburg Empire. Yet one of the major problems before Ljudevit Gaj and other concerned Croats in the early nineteenth century, was to define the nationality to which the Croats belonged. The Kingdom of Croatia, Slavonia and Dalmatia was small and weak, a shabby remnant of the medieval Croatian state. Croats formed the majority of the population of the Kingdom, and represented substantial minorities in the bordering territories. They were part of a larger ethnic group — the Southern Slavs — and of one of the major European peoples — the Slavs. The Illyrian Movement attempted to fuse all of these allegiances into one.

The Illyrian Movement, or Croatian national awakening, had three major aspects. It was a cultural renaissance in which the Croatian vernacular was made into a modern literary language. It was a political movement which strove to uphold the traditional privileges of Croatia within the Hungarian Kingdom, and it was an attempt to establish cultural unity among all the Southern Slavs. Ljudevit Gaj expressed these three concepts succinctly in the motto he introduced in 1841: "God preserve the Hungarian Constitution, the Croatian Kingdom, and the Illyrian Nationality." Daily political life was to take place within the framework of the Habsburg Empire, the Hungarian Kingdom and the Kingdom of Croatia. However, the nationality to which the Croats belonged, according to this definition, was not the Croatian but the "Illyrian," or Southern Slav nationality.

The Croatian national awakening was at the same time part of a Pan-Slav movement which began in the early nineteenth century among the Slavs of the Habsburg Empire. This movement(2) has been called by various names: Pan-Slavism, Slavism and Allslavism. We shall use the term Pan-Slavism in this study, for it was the name most frequently used by Gaj and his contemporaries. The Pan-Slavs of the early nineteenth century, whose leaders were P. J. Šafárik and Jan Kollár, believed that the Slavs belonged to a single nationality, and that the Slavic languages were actually dialects of one great Slavic language. They were not interested in creating a Slavic state but, instead, in building a cultural community among all the Slavic peoples. This is quite different from the politically-oriented, Russian-dominated Pan-Slavism of the late nineteenth century.

From the beginning the Illyrian Movement was, therefore, ideologically both conservative and radical. It worked toward the preservation of Croatian tradition while creating the basis for modern Croatian and Southern Slav nationalism. In order to understand the implications and goals of the Illyrian Movement, we must first examine the history of the term "Illyrian," the historic position of Croatia, and conditions within the Kingdom of Croatia, Slavonia and Dalmatia on the eve of the national awakening.

Our knowledge of the history of the ancient Illyrians is still extremely fragmentary. A tribe of Illyrians lived along the northern frontier of classicial Greece. Later, the name Illyrian began to denote a number of ethnically related Indo-European tribes inhabiting the northeastern part of the Balkan peninsula, the Danubian basin and large areas of Central Europe, and the southeastern coast of the Appenine peninsula. The tribes which settled on the territory of present-day Jugoslavia represented the cultural and ethnic core of the widely dispersed Illyrians.(3)

In the third century B.C., Rome began its conquest of the Illyrian lands. After almost two and a half centuries of bitter resistance the Illyrians were subjugated, and Rome established the Province, later Prefecture, of *Illyricum,* a political and administrative unit which expanded and contracted in size over the centuries.(4)

The Slavic invasions of the sixth and seventh centuries A.D. completely changed the ethnic character of Illyria-*Illyricum.* A great many native Illyrians died resisting the intruders, others fled, and the rest were absorbed by the flood of Slavic settlers who largely destroyed the Roman and Christian civilization of *Illyricum.* In the following two centuries the Slavs were converted to Christianity, which divided them into Roman Catholic and Orthodox religious communities. At roughly the same time the first medieval Southern Slavic states began to emerge.(5)

The name Illyria was revived in the fifteenth century by Croatian humanists. They knew little of the history of this area in the period between the decline of Rome and Byzantium and the rise of the medieval Slavic states, hence they assumed that the contemporary inhabitants of *Illyricum* were descendants of the ancient Illyrians, and that the language which they spoke was the "Illyrian language." The terms "Croat," "Slav" and "Illyrian" began to be used interchangeably.(6)

In the late eighteenth and early nineteenth centuries, the term "Illyrian" began to be used more frequently albeit no less ambiguously. The Illyrian National Congress which met in 1790 at Temesvar was a gathering of Hungarian Serbs. In 1808 Jernej Kopitar, the Slovene philologist, identified "Illyrian" as the Slavic "dialect" spoken by all of the Southern Slavs except the Croats and Slovenes.(7) However, the Illyrian Provinces established by Napoleon in 1809 were made up of Dalmatia, conquered portions of Civil and Military Croatia, and three Slovene provinces — Istria, Carniola and Carinthia. In 1816, after the break-up of the Napoleonic Empire, the predominantly Slovene areas of the former Illyrian Provinces were made into a new Austrian administrative unit which was called the Kingdom of Illyria.

Therefore we see that by 1825, "Illyria" had been the name for a number of political and administrative entities: ancient Illyria, Roman-

Byzantine *Illyricum,* Napoleonic or Habsburg Illyria. "Illyrian" could mean Southern Slav, Serb, Croat or Slovene.

Medieval Croatia was once a strong and independent kingdom. In the tenth and eleventh centuries it had stretched from the Adriatic Sea to the Drava and Mura rivers, and into Bosnia. The political capital of the Croatian Kingdom was Biograd na moru, a town on the Adriatic coast, and the center of state power lay between the Gvozd (Kapela) mountains and the sea. Croatia, therefore, was an Adriatic kingdom with far-reaching hinterlands. In 1089, the former Byzantine theme of Dalmatia was added to the Kingdom, giving it control of the northern and central Adriatic coast.

The Croats had been converted to Christianity by the Roman church. Their ethnic brothers and neighbors to the east, the Serbs, had been converted by Byzantium. To the north was Hungary, a Roman Catholic kingdom. To the west lay Ostmark, also Catholic.

Although Croatia was an elective Kingdom, the crown had gone almost without interruption to a member of the Trpimir dynasty. In 1074, King Petar Krešimir died without issue. The last remaining Trpimir was his sickly nephew Stephen. Before his death Krešimir had strengthened the position of his most trusted follower, Zvonimir, who was married to Helen of Hungary, daughter of King Bela I. Zvonimir, with the aid of the Pope, was elected King in 1076. In 1089, Zvonimir died without issue. Stephen Trpimir was elected King in 1089 and died in 1090.

For more than twelve years the Croatian throne was contested. Civil war and anarchy swept the land. The major bids for the throne were made by Helen of Hungary, for her brother Ladislas King of Hungary, and by Petar Svačić, the candidate of the Croatian nobility.

The problem of succession was finally settled by force and compromise. The Hungarian claim to the throne was reinforced by the presence of Hungarian troops, but the agreement reached, the *Pacta Conventa,*(8) was that between a legal successor to the throne and his subjects, rather than between a conqueror and the conquered. In 1102, King Koloman, who had succeeded his uncle to the throne of Hungary in 1095, met with representatives of the twelve Croatian clans. The Croats agreed to recognize Koloman as their King, and his successors as their future kings. He, in turn, promised to respect the privileges and property of the Croatian nobility. Later the same year he was formally elected and crowned. He pledged that he and his successors would respect the laws of the Croatian Kingdom, come to Croatia to be crowned, and negotiate matters of state with the Assembly of Croatian nobles.(9)

The Union of Croatia with Hungary in 1102, a union through the person of the king, represented the end of Croatian independence. From 1102 to 1918, Croatia was a part of the Hungarian Kingdom with special rights due to the fact that she was *partes adnexae* (annexed lands) rather than *partes subiugate* (conquered lands). Although the Kingdom of Croatia was not absorbed by its larger partner, its fate was now linked to that of another state, and its king was a foreigner. Through the succeeding centuries Croatia lost most of her territory. By 1825 all that remained of the lands of medieval Croatia were six small counties in the northern and central part of the original hinterlands.

The lands beyond the Gvozd mountains, which had come to be known as Slavonia, were lost first. From the mid-thirteenth to the mid-sixteenth centuries, Slavonia formed a separate political unit within the Kingdom of Hungary. It lay between the heartland of the old Croatian Kingdom and Hungary. During this period Slavonia had its own *Ban* (Governor) and its own local *Sabor* (meeting of the Estates).

The next major territorial loss involved the Croatian territories on the Adriatic coast. Croatia was forced back from the coast first by Venice, then by the Turks, and, finally, by Austria. By 1420 Dalmatia had fallen into the hands of the Republic of Venice which was soon in control of the northern Adriatic coast as well. The Turks, pushing up the Balkan peninsula in a steady wave of invasions, soon moved toward the coast. For the next two centuries the Adriatic coast, save for a small strip of territory in the northwest and the independent Republic of Ragusa (Dubrovnik), was controlled by these two powers. Most of the coastal cities and the islands were under Venetian rule. The Turks held the hinterlands. Large migrations of Croats moved inland to Slavonia. The name Croatia came with them, and the center of the Kingdom of Croatia came to rest in the former Slavonian county of Zagreb.

In 1526, after the Turkish victory at Mohacs, the Hungarian nobles elected Ferdinand of Austria as their King. In the following year the Croatian nobles acting independently also chose Ferdinand of Austria as King of Croatia. They sent him a formal delegation with the message:

> Let it be known to Your Majesty that no ruler has ever subjugated Croatia by force, rather, after the death of our last King, Zvonimir, we of our own free will attached ourselves to the Crown of the Hungarian Kingdom, as we at this time join ourselves to Your Majesty.(10)

Thus the Croats reasserted their independence of action and in return received assurances that their special rights and privileges would be respected. Until the collapse of the Empire in 1918, the history of Croatia would be linked not only to that of Hungary, but also to the sprawling complex domains of the Habsburgs.

After the accession of Ferdinand of Austria to the thrones of Hungary and Croatia, Slavonia was again put under the jurisdiction of the Croatian *ban,* and the Slavonian and Croatian Estates once more met jointly. In 1089, with the acquisition of Dalmatia, the title "the Kingdom of Croatia" had been expanded to "the Kingdom of Dalmatia and Croatia." After the reincorporation of Slavonia this was changed to "the Kingdom of Croatia, Slavonia and Dalmatia," or, as it was later called, "the Triune Kingdom." This formal title lasted until 1918. However the inflation in title should not disguise the fact that in the mid-sixteenth century only the northwesternmost part of the Kingdom of Croatia, Slavonia, and Dalmatia remained free.

Even this territory was divided. Croatia lay on the border of the Moslem and Christian worlds. The Turks were held back from further conquest in Europe by a wall of Habsburg territory. The Habsburgs, faced with the problem of defending this vast frontier, had resorted to a solution much like that of Imperial Rome. They established a cordon of fortresses and fortified villages along the length of the frontier, staffed by mercenary troops and settled by peasant soldiers.(11) The parts of Croatia which bordered on Ottoman territory were organized in this manner. This area, known as the Croatian Military Frontier, was no longer under the jurisdiction of the Croatian *Ban* and the Croatian *Sabor.*

The Croatian migration from the Adriatic coast to Slavonia was only one of a complex series of migrations set in motion by the Turkish armies. Serbs, Southern Slavs of Orthodox faith who had lived within medieval Serbia, began to move into what had been Croatian territory. Many were settled in the Military Frontier. This was the first of two major waves of migration. The second came when the Serbs moved into the devastated areas left by the Turks as they were pushed south again in the late seventeenth and early eighteenth centuries.(12) These migrations left the lands actually under the jurisdiction of the *Ban* of Croatia and areas claimed by the Kingdom (Dalmatia, the Military Frontier) with a sizable Serbian minority.

In the course of the late seventeenth and eighteenth centuries, most of the lands which had formerly belonged to the Triune Kingdom were freed from the Turks and from Venice. Croatia was too small, and perhaps too passive, to demand her rights effectively. In fact with the passage of centuries the claims of medieval Croatia had been overlaid by other claims: Venice had more recently controlled Dalmatia, Hungary had ruled Slavonia, and the central Habsburg power could detach or annex areas for reasons of military necessity. For these reasons, Turkish Dalmatia was given to Venice, Slavonia was divided between Croatia, the Military Frontier and Hungary, and the Military Frontier remained under Austria.

Austria received Dalmatia in 1797 after the fall of the Republic of Venice, and lost it again only a few years later to Napoleon, who added to it the Republic of Ragusa. From 1814, when Austria regained control of Dalmatia, to 1918, despite Dalmatia's historic ties to the Kingdom of Croatia, it remained an Austrian province.

The fate of Slavonia was somewhat different. The northwestern section of old Slavonia was now known as Croatia. The rest of Slavonia, after the liberation from the Turks, remained under Austrian rule for several decades. The land was thinly populated and had suffered much devastation. In 1745, only three Slavonian counties were returned to Croatia, although in theory all of Slavonia belonged under the jurisdiction of the Triune Kingdom. A large part of Slavonia was made into additional Military Frontier territory, and another section was given to Hungary.

The three Slavonian counties were known as Civil Slavonia. The three counties already within the Triune Kingdom were known as Civil Croatia. The parts of the Military Frontier which had been created from the former territory of the Kingdom were known as the Croatian and Slavonian Military Frontiers.(13)

The remaining bit of Croatian territory on the Adriatic coast which was neither within Dalmatia nor part of the Military Frontier, Rijeka and the former county of Severin, was also under joint Hungarian-Croatian jurisdiction in 1825. This territory was known as the Hungarian Littoral. In matters of justice and education the Littoral was considered part of the Triune Kingdom. In all other matters it was directly under Hungary. Representatives from the Hungarian Littoral were sent to both the Croatian *Sabor* and the Hungarian Parliament.(14)

Croatia still lay on the border between the Ottoman Empire and the West in the early nineteenth century. Bosnia remained under the Turks. The part of Bosnia which had been included within medieval Croatia was known as "Turkish Croatia." In the eighteenth and nineteenth centuries the Triune Kingdom continually demanded the return of the medieval Croatian lands: Dalmatia, the Military Frontier, and Turkish Croatia.

Let us now examine the statistics of area and population for both the Triune Kingdom, and the Croatian and Slavonian Military Frontier. The Military Frontier returned in the 1870's, and was the one part of the old Croatian territory not permanently lost to the Triune Kingdom. Many of the decisions made by the leaders of the Illyrian Movement regarding the national language and the creation of a feeling of national identity, were made with future return of the Military Frontier in mind. Perhaps the best symbol of the interrelatedness of the two areas is that the leader chosen to head the Revolutionary Government of Croatia in 1848, Ban Jelačić, was an officer from the Croatian Military Frontier.

The lands of the Triune Kingdom were made up of the counties of Civil Croatia (Varaždin, Zagreb and Križevci), and those of Civil Slavonia (Požega, Srijem, and Virovitica). The six counties of the Triune Kingdom did not even form a compact geographical unit, for a strip of the Croatian Military Frontier separated Civil Croatia from Civil Slavonia.

The total area of the Triune Kingdom comprised 334.8 geographical square miles. It was smaller than the Military Frontier which had 373.7 geographical square miles.(15) The Triune Kingdom, however, had a larger population.(16)

TABLE 1

POPULATION OF THE TRIUNE KINGDOM AND OF THE CROATIAN AND SLAVONIAN MILITARY FRONTIER, 1785-1846(a)

	1785	*1805*	*1846*
Triune Kingdom	649,075	656,519	854,502
Croatian and Slavonian Military Frontier	523,326(b)	629,729(c)	785,887

a. For 1782, 1785 and 1805: Vrbanić, *op. cit.*, p. 39. For 1815: Carl B. Hietzinger, *Statistik der Militargrenze der osterreichischen Kaiserthums* (Wien: Carl Gerold, 1817-1823), I, p. 65. For 1846: Alexius Fényes, *Ungarn im Vormärz* (Leipzig: Friedrich Ludwig Herbig, 1851), pp. 33-34, 40-42.
b. 1782.
c. 1815.

If we examine the figures for 1846 more closely, we see that there was a large Serbian minority concentrated in the Military Frontier and Civil Slavonia. Information on nationality was not included in the census until 1880, but we do have figures for religious affiliation. Religion is the most commonly accepted distinction between a Serb and a Croat; Croats are Catholic, and Serbs are Orthodox.

TABLE 2

POPULATION BY RELIGION IN 1846(a)

	Roman Catholic	Orthodox	Other
Triune Kingdom			
a. Civil Croatia	484,251	4,320	1,709
b. Civil Slavonia	218,746	137,756	7,720
TOTAL	702,997	142,076	9,429
Croatian and Slavonian Military Frontier	420,789	359,856	5,242

a. Fényes, *op. cit.*, pp. 49-52.

Therefore we see that in 1846, people of Orthodox faith constituted forty-five per cent (45%) of the population of the Military Frontier, thirty-seven percent (37%) of Civil Slavonia, and only eight per cent (8%) of Civil Croatia.(17) In addition, people of Orthodox faith represented nineteen percent (19%) of the population of Dalmatia.(18)

The Triune Kingdom had an agrarian economy in 1825. The land was owned by the Church and the nobility, and worked by serfs, who formed the vast majority of the population.(19) The serfs were personally free, but tied to their landlords by three kinds of obligations: labor *(robot)*, produce, and money payments. These obligations had been defined most recently in the *urbars* of Maria Theresa and her son, Joseph II, in 1756 for Civil Slavonia and in 1789 for Civil Croatia. The serfs also had to pay a tithe to the Church. The conditions of the Croatian serfs appear to have been somewhat harsher than those of the Slavonian serfs.(20)

The nobility was divided into two groups: the magnates and the gentry. This distinction was both economic and political. The Church and the magnates owned the large estates. Prelates and magnates participated directly in the meetings of the Croatian *Sabor* (Parliament), while the lessor nobility had only indirect representation in the *Sabor.*

The income of magnates in Civil Croatia went as high as 60,000 forints a year, and in Civil Slavonia to 100,000 forints, whereas some of the smaller holdings of the gentry averaged as little as 400 forints income a year.(21) The majority of the noble landholdings in Civil Slavonia were quite large and the nobility was of mixed ethnic origin.(22) In Civil Croatia, where the old Croatian nobility had fled during the Turkish invasions leaving their family estates behind, the average noble landholding was small, with the exception of the estates of the few magnates.(23) Most of the magnate families were of foreign origin as can be seen in their names: Nugent, Sermage, Gyulay, Bathyany, Erdödy, Rauch and Kulmer. There were a few Croatian magnates left: the Oršić, Drašković and Bedeković families, but they were the exception to the rule. Many of the magnates lived abroad, in Vienna, Buda and Paris.

The gentry in Civil Croatia were numerous, including the owners of small estates and men who possessed only their titles. There were also communities of peasant nobles in Civil Croatia who had been granted their noble status during the Turkish wars of the early 15th century.(24) The largest peasant noble community was that of Turopolje. The peasant nobles continued to live as peasants, paying reduced taxes and sharing political rights not as individuals but as a community.(25) In 1785 there were 8,946 male nobles of all gradations of rank in Civil Croatia, and 314 male nobles in Civil Slavonia.(26) The Croatian nobles were predominantly of Croatian ethnic origin and possessed an unbroken tradition of participation in the political life of the Kingdom.

Although land was the major source of wealth it was not the only one. A network of good roads, navigable rivers and canals tied the interior to the coast, bringing the grain and other produce from the rich lands of Southern Hungary and Slavonia to Rijeka and other Adriatic ports. Towns began to spring up along this route. The Triune Kingdom was now tied to the world economy, its grain and other goods competed on the world market, and fluctuations in the world price of grain could have serious internal economic effects.(27)

There were a few industries, but they were small and scattered. This was due in great part to the mercantile policies of the Habsburgs which treated Hungary as the source of raw materials and encouraged industry in the Austrian provinces.(28) Most of the local industry of the Triune Kingdom dealt with the processing of raw materials: lumber, foodstuffs, tobacco, and leather. There were some mines and shipyards, and a few small glass and ceramic factories. The textile industry was poorly developed except in the manufacture of silk.(29)

The middle class was small, predominantly foreign, and concentrated in the Royal Free Towns and smaller market towns. The towns of the Triune Kingdom served many functions. They were administrative, military, religious, cultural, and economic centers. The largest town in 1787 was the Royal Free Town of Varaždin, with a population of 4,814.(30) The towns began to grow more rapidly in the early nineteenth century, and by 1829 the largest was Osijek with a population of 9,242, then came Zagreb with 8,175 and Varaždin which now had 7,787.(31) The inhabitants of the towns included merchants, artisans, and members of the free professions. Nobles also kept houses in the major towns, which were the county seats. Osijek was predominantly a Magyar town, while Varaždin and Zagreb had large German populations. Karlovac, which had a population of about 4,000 in 1829, was an exception.(32) It was a Croatian town, and the middle point of the commerce between the coast and the interior.

As the territory of the Triune Kingdom had diminished, the traditional institutions of Croatian autonomy had become weaker. The Croatian Estates had asserted their independence in 1527 with their separate election of Ferdinand of Austria, and again in 1712 when they adopted the Pragmatic Sanction eleven years before Hungary, but by 1712 the tone of the declaration had become somewhat sharper:

> . . . According to law we are a land affiliated with Hungary, and in no way a subject people of Hungary. At one time we had our own national non-Hungarian kings. No force or slavery made us subordinate to Hungary, but we through our own free will became subjects not of the Hungarian Kingdom, but of the Hungarian King. We are free and not slaves . . .(33)

Until the mid-eighteenth century the administration of the Triune Kingdom had been headed in theory and fact by the *Ban* of Croatia (Viceroy) and the Croatian *Sabor* (Parliament). As the Habsburg rulers set out to consolidate their scattered lands and rule them more efficiently, the *Ban* and the *Sabor* found themselves increasingly limited in their spheres of action.(34) In 1767 Maria Theresa established the *Consilium regium* (Council of the Kingdom) for Croatia. It was designed to serve the same function for Croatia as the Hungarian Court Chancellery did for Hungary: to be the direct link between the person of the sovereign and the Kingdom.(35) The *Consilium* took over some of the political, economic and military matters previously under the jurisdiction of the *Ban* and *Sabor*. In 1779 Maria Theresa abolished the *Consilium* and instead of returning the duties it had performed to the Croatian authorities, she transferred them to the Hungarian Court

Chancellery. Now, in certain key administrative matters, Croatia was subject not only to the King but to Hungary, through the Hungarian Court Chancellery.(36)

The Ban, the King's representative in Croatia, was chosen by the King, and in the eighteenth and early nineteenth centuries was usually a Hungarian magnate. The Ban chose his assistant, the *vicebanus.* If the Ban died or retired, the *vicebanus* lost his position as well and the King would appoint a *locumtenens,* most often the Zagreb Bishop, to serve until a new Ban was chosen.(37)

The Croatian *Sabor* was unicameral, made up of the Catholic prelates, the magnates, representatives of the nobility elected by the county assemblies, representatives of the *kaptol* (Zagreb Cathedral Chapter), the Royal Free Towns and, from 1776, the Governor of Rijeka.(38) The Ban and the *Sabor* stood at the head of the administrative apparatus of the Kingdom, although, after 1767 their competence was somewhat limited. The decisions of the *Sabor* could not become law without the King's approval. The *Sabor* elected the other high administrative officials, the most important being the *protonotar* (Keeper of the Seal).

From the mid-sixteenth century on the Croatian *Sabor* regularly sent delegates to the Hungarian Parliament: three to the Lower House (the *protonotar* and two delegates elected by the *Sabor),* and one to the Upper House.(39) The Croatian deputies were not seated with the representatives of the Hungarian counties, but were given a special place to the right of the podium.(40) The three counties of Civil Slavonia sent representatives both to the Croatian *Sabor* and to the Hungarian Parliament and at the Parliament the Slavonian deputies sat with the deputies from the Hungarian counties.

The Croatian *Sabor* gave detailed instructions to its deputies. One of their major tasks was to defend the *Jura municipalia* (Municipal Rights) of Croatia, a special body of laws and privileges which had evolved over many centuries and which defined Croatia's position within the Kingdom of Hungary. The most important of these ancient rights were: jurisdiction in internal affairs, reduced taxes, special representation at the meetings of the Hungarian Parliament, maintenance of an independent military force, and independence of Hungary in decisions concerning religion and language.(41)

The *Sabor* deputies were not the only Croats to attend the Hungarian Parliament. Every *veliki župan* (high sheriff), the highest county official, was entitled to participate in the meetings of the Lower House, and the diocesan bishops and magnates attended in their own right, as members of the Upper House.(42)

The counties of Civil Croatia were the true center of Croatian political life. The titular head of the county administration, the *veliki župan* (high sheriff) was appointed by the King and chosen from among the magnates of the Kingdom. The *pod-župan* (deputy high sheriff) — the real county executive — and the other county officials, were elected by the county assemblies every three years. All nobles of the county could participate in the County Assembly which in addition to its function of electing county officials also chose representatives to the *Sabor.* The county assemblies could meet whenever they wished, were the bodies which approved and implemented the decisions of higher political and administrative organs within their own boundaries and could, in theory, refuse to carry out an order if it were judged to be illegal or harmful.(43) The Slavonian counties had the same formal structure, as did all of the counties of the Hungarian Kingdom, but they did not enjoy the protection of the *Jura municipalia,* which applied only to Civil Croatia. They paid the same tax rate as the Hungarian counties, twice that of the counties of Civil Croatia,(44) and, as we have seen, were represented both at the *Sabor* and the Hungarian Parliament. Their legal status was, at best, ambiguous and would become a major issue in the struggle between the Croats and the Magyars in the 1840's.

Although steps toward the modernization of the Habsburg Empire were taken by Maria Theresa in the areas of taxation, centralization of the administrative apparatus, protection of the serfs, and educational reforms, the reforms of her son, Joseph II, struck at the very roots of Croatian autonomy. His radical reorganization of the administrative divisions of the Kingdom of Hungary, his disregard for the traditional institutions of government, his attempt to introduce German as the administrative language of Hungary, taxation of nobles, freeing of the serfs from personal bondage — all challenged the jealously-guarded privileges of the Croatian nobles. His attack on the privileged position of the Catholic Church and dissolution of some of the religious orders, brought him the disfavor of the Croatian clergy. Although most of Joseph's reforms were revoked before his death, the Croatian nobility and prelates were determined to protect themselves against any possible recurrence.

For this reason the Croatian nobles joined in a common front with the Hungarian nobles, and in 1790 and 1791, the Croatian *Sabor* in fear of another such break with tradition by a Habsburg ruler, surrendered a good part of its traditional autonomy to Hungary:

> . . . until those parts of Croatia presently under the Turks and Venice are acquired, and until a sufficient number of counties to constitute a viable political unit are assembled — the six remaining counties will receive orders from the Regent's Council.(45)

In effect the decisions of the Croatian *Sabor* in 1790 and 1791 meant that the administrative apparatus of the Triune Kingdom would no longer be subject to the Ban and the *Sabor,* but would come directly under the Hungarian administrative authorities. The *Sabor's* jurisdiction was thus limited to strictly internal matters, such as education and justice. All other legislation was made by the Joint Parliament (Meeting of the Hungarian Parliament with Croatian deputies present).

The Ban remained the formal head of government, but his actual power was sharply abridged. No attempt was made to broaden the Croatian representation at the Joint Parliament in order to make certain that the Croatian deputies had a strong, rather than a special, position within that body.

Between 1790 and 1845, the Croatian *Sabor* came to meet only before and after the sessions of the Joint Parliament, for it was in Hungary now that laws were made. The *Sabor* met to choose and instruct its deputies, and upon their return to hear their reports and pass upon the decisions of the Joint Parliament. The Croatian nobles would soon realize that they had made a mistake in 1790, and that their Hungarian allies against Germanization and centralization would present an even greater threat to Croatian autonomy than had the reforms of Joseph II.

CHAPTER II

NEED FOR A CROATIAN NATIONAL RENAISSANCE

The *Sabor's* decision of 1790, to surrender to Hungary a good part of what remained of Croatian autonomy, was accompanied by a burst of enthusiasm for all things Hungarian.(46) However, this feeling of Croatian-Hungarian solidarity was threatened from the outset. The Magyars were no longer interested in preserving the *status quo*. They were in the midst of a national cultural renaissance which would soon be politicized and, in its new form, pose a direct threat to the political and cultural traditions of the Triune Kingdom.

The last quarter of the eighteenth century was a period of cultural renaissance in Hungary. Linguists and lexicographers pruned the Magyar language of clumsy and obsolete expressions. Playwrights, poets and novelists demonstrated through their use of the language that it was capable of expressing delicate nuances of feeling, while scholars demonstrated its adaptability to precise expression. The first Magyar language newspaper, *Magyar Hirmondó* (Hungarian News), began publication in 1780, and was soon followed by other newspapers, pamphlets, and learned and literary journals in the Magyar tongue.(47) There was a renewed interest in the history of Hungary and in her folk tales and poetry.(48)

The goal of the leaders of the Hungarian cultural renaissance — Kazinczy, Bessenyei and Révai — was to have the Magyar language become the medium of Hungarian cultural life. Implicit in this was the belief that a nationality cannot reach intellectual maturity in a language other than its mother tongue. The scholars and writers of the late eighteenth century who chided their fellow Magyars for neglect of their national language were expressing an underlying fear that the Magyar language might disappear altogether, and with it the Magyar nationality.(49) Their concern was echoed and sharpened by the German philosopher J.G. Herder who in his *Ideen zur Philosophie der Geschichte der Menschheit* (1784-1791), foresaw a bright future for the Slavs, but predicted the demise of the Magyar language.(50)

It must be remembered that the Magyars constitute an isolated ethnic group in East Central Europe. Their national renaissance could not draw upon the reforms and literary traditions of close ethnic brothers, as could the Slavs. While the Magyars were the dominant nationality in the Hungarian Kingdom, they did not even form a numerical majority of the population. In 1846 there were 4,774,899 Magyars in a total population of 11,895,796.(51) Among the other nationalities were Croats, Serbs, Slovaks, Rumanians, Ruthenians and Germans. The nobility, with the exception of the Croats, was Magyar either by birth or by assimilation.(52) There was almost no native bourgeoisie. The peasants, still serfs, represented all of the nationalities.

Latin had long served as the language of the Hungarian Kingdom. When Joseph II attempted to substitute German for Latin, he provoked a violent reaction. It was not so much the attack on Latin which sparked Magyar resentment, but the substitution of a foreign modern language for it. Latin had served Hungary well. It masked the ethnic diversity of the Kingdom and allowed the elite, regardless of nationality, to communicate with each other, receive an education, debate and govern in a neutral tongue. Latin would one day have to be replaced by the vernacular, as it had been in other European states, but German was not the vernacular of Hungary.

Herder had watched Joseph's reforms with interest. He viewed the attempt to impose German as an unwitting attack on the most important possession of the non-German peoples within the Empire. He wrote:

> Does a nationality *(Volk),* especially a backward nationality, have anything more precious than the language of its fathers? In this language lives a whole world of tradition, history, religion and principles of life, all of a nationality's heart and soul. To take this language away from such a people, or to degrade this language, means that you are taking away its one immortal possession, that has passed from generation to generation . . .(53)

A good Emperor, continued Herder, should not only tolerate but respect all the languages of his Empire. The best culture of any nationality springs from its own national soil and finds expression in the national language.(54) Herder's views on the importance of the national language were shared by other German philosophers of the time, among them Fichte and Schleiermacher,(55) and their writings were to lay the philosophical foundations for the ideology of nationalism which in an almost chain reaction would sweep East Central Europe in the nineteenth century.

Emperor Joseph II's clumsy attempts at Germanization gave new meaning to the Hungarian cultural renaissance.(56) Why should

Magyar not become the administrative language of Hungary? It was now a modern language of proven worth and adaptability.

In 1790 at the same session of the Joint Parliament in which the Croatian deputies asked politely that their autonomy be limited, several Magyar deputies proposed that Magyar be made the official language of the Hungarian Kingdom.(57) The Croatian deputies fought this proposal vigorously. Croatia, they said, was not a province of Hungary but a Kingdom with special rights and privileges under the Hungarian Crown. It would be just as unfair to the Croats to make Magyar the official language of Hungary, as it would be to the Magyars to make German the official language. Latin, not Magyar, was the language of the Constitution and tradition.(58)

The Croatian deputies did not yet realize the magnitude of the threat and their response was basically conservative. The immediate problems were obvious. Few Croats spoke Hungarian. As long as the business of the Joint Parliament was carried out in Latin, all deputies had to speak in a foreign language. Were Magyar to become the language of debate, the Croatian deputies would be at a definite disadvantage. If Magyar became the language of the Hungarian Civil Service, would the sons of Croatian nobles be able to qualify for it, would the Croats already in the Service be retained? Most serious of all was the assumption that a modern Hungary would be a Magyar Hungary. What place would Croatia and its *Jura municipalia* have in a Magyar nation state?

The Joint Parliament decided in 1791 to retain Latin, at least for a while, as the official language of Hungary. However, in preparation for the future transition to Magyar, it was decided that the Magyar language would become a required subject in the schools of Hungary proper and an elective subject in the schools of the Triune Kingdom.

The language question was brought up again in 1805 and 1811. No decision was reached. There were more pressing issues in those years: the French Revolutionary Wars, the defeat of Austria by Napoleon, the Congress of Vienna. The Parliament was not called into session between 1811 and 1825. The 1825 session went forward in the familiar way. The Croats demanded the return of their lost territories and the Magyars again proposed that the Magyar language become the administrative language of the Hungarian Kingdom. Latin was, again, retained, but the Croatian deputies promised in return for this that the study of Hungarian would be encouraged in the Triune Kingdom, and in 1827 the Croatian *Sabor* made Hungarian a required subject in all the schools of the Triune Kingdom.

There was no accepted Croatian literary language in 1825,(59) there were, instead, three Croatian dialects each with its own literary tradition. These are known as *štokavski, kajkavski,* and *čakavski, što, kaj* and *ča* being the word in each dialect for "what". Although a person speaking *kajkavski* could be understood by a speaker of *štokavski* or *čakavski,* it would be with some difficulty due to phonetic, syntactic, morphological and lexical differences.(60) Let us illustrate this by taking a short verse from a *kajkavski* poem and "translating" it into the other two dialects:

Kajkavski	Kak je, tak je, tak je navek bilo, Kak bu tak bu, a bu vre nekak kak bu!
Štokavski	Što je, je; tako je uvijek bilo, Što će biti, bit' će, a nekako već će biti!
Čakavski	Ča je, je, tako je navik bilo, Ča će bit', će bit', a nekako će već bit'!(61)

Kajkavski was the dialect traditionally associated with Civil Croatia. The *kajkavski* word for Croatia is "Horvatska," and for the dialect itself "Horvatski" (Croatian). It was the dialect of the county of Varaždin and of a large number of the inhabitants of the other two counties. *Kajkavski* had once been the dialect of a large part of Slavonia as well, but warfare, depopulation, foreign occupation and migrations had pushed the southern boundaries of the dialect much further north. *Kajkavski* is closely related to the Slovene language and may once have been a Slovene dialect. It is the transitional dialect between Slovene and *štokavski.*(62)

Čakavski had originally been the dialect of a much larger area too. It had been spoken as far south as the river Cetina and had formed the western boundary of the *štokavski* dialect. But by 1825, as far as it is possible to ascertain, the *čakavski* area had shrunk to Istria, the Croatian Littoral, part of Gorski Kotar, narrow strips of land around the towns of Zadar, Trogir, Šibenik and Split, and all the islands except Lastovo.(63)

From the earliest period of the Southern Slav settlement on the Balkan peninsula, *štokavski* had been spoken over the largest area. It had been spoken along with *kajkavski* in Eastern Slavonia, and with *čakavski* in Bosnia-Hercegovina and Dalmatia. *Štokavski* was the dialect of medieval Serbia. The Turkish invasions and accompanying migrations had pushed the boundaries of the *štokavski* dialect much further north and northwest, to the loss of the other two dialects. In 1825, *štokavski* was spoken in the Military Frontier, in Civil Slavonia and in Dalmatia.(64)

The *štokavski* dialect has three sub-dialects, based upon divergent treatment of the common Slavic vowel "jat" (Ѣ). These are known as *ekavski, ijekavski* and *ikavski.* The difference between the three sub-dialects can be seen in the following illustration;

Ekavski: Rekao sam detetu da mi da mleka.
Ijekavski: Rekao sam djetetu da mi da mlijeka.
Ikavski: Reka' san ditetu da mi dal mlika.(65)

Roughly, *ekavski* was spoken in the eastern part of the *štokavski* dialect area, *ijekavski* in the south and *ikavski* in the north.

Not only did the Croats not all speak the same dialect or write in the same literary language, but they did not even write the sounds of their language in the same way. There was no standard orthography. The Croats used the Latin alphabet, as did the Slovenes, while the Orthodox Southern Slavs, the Serbs and Bulgarians, used the Cyrillic graphic system (alphabet). The Latin graphic system used by the Croats in 1825 did not have special letters or diacritical marks to modify letters for typically Slavic sounds, such as *c, č, š, ž, ć.* By tradition, different combinations of letters were used to represent these sounds according to the patterns of non-Slavic literary languages. At this time at least three orthographical "norms" governed the use of the Latin alphabet: Hungarian, German and Italian; e.g. *czar, tsar,* or *zar* for today's *car* (emperor); *czast, zhast,* or *chast* for today's *čast* (honor).(66)

A visitor to Zagreb in 1825 might have found it difficult to believe that he was in the political and cultural capital of a Southern Slav Kingdom. Latin was the language of the government offices, the law courts, the *Sabor,* the secondary schools and the Zagreb Academy. German was spoken in the streets, in the smart shops, cafes and restaurants. The only local paper was the newly established *Agramer Zeitung.* The local theatre produced German plays and the local musical society sang German songs. The visitor would have heard *kajkavski* spoken only if he had taken the trouble to look behind the facade of the capital, in the marketplace full of brightly clad peasants, in the servants' quarters of the nobles' town houses, in small shops and perhaps among the priests.

An educated Croat was expected to speak Latin and German in addition to his mother tongue. He might also know Italian or Hungarian. The language of instruction in all schools he attended beyond the primary level was Latin.(67) In 1825 the Triune Kingdom had six *gimnazije* (secondary schools), four theological seminaries and the two-year Zagreb Academy, a partial University which offered courses in law and philosophy.(68) Few Croats attended primary school. In 1805 there were only fifty-five primary schools in the entire Kingdom; some of these had only a few students, other lacked regular teachers.(69) It was only here in the pitifully few primary schools that the Croatian dialects were studied and used as the language of instruction.

In 1818 Anton Nagy, censor of books in Buda, formerly professor at the Zagreb Academy, complained that not one Croatian manuscript had been submitted to his office that year.(70) The censors in Vienna, Venice and Milan, he said, had had much the same experience. Yet was Croatian not potentially as beautiful as any other European language?:

> With sadness in the hearts of those of us who do not hesitate to tell the truth, we must admit that *in the efforts to improve orthography, to enhance the strength and beauty of the mother tongue, as well as in the publication of books and manuscripts, no nation is so far behind as the nation of the Croats, Slavonians and Dalmatians.*(71)

By 1818 there had already been three abortive attempts to publish a newspaper in the Croatian language.(72) The reasons for the failure of the first two newspapers, one planned for publication in 1792 and the other in 1814, are still unclear, but the third newspaper, which was supposed to appear in 1818, failed to publish because the editor could not find a single subscriber.(73)

Nagy's concern for the Croatian language was shared by a few patriots. The most influential among them was Bishop Vrhovac (1752-1827), the highest official of the Catholic Church in the Triune Kingdom during the first decades of the nineteenth century. Bishop Vrhovac did his best to awaken support for a national renaissance.(74) He planned a new Croatian translation of the Bible, collected many books and manuscripts about the Croatian past, attempted to establish a printing press which would publish books in the national language, and urged patriots to draw up proposals for orthographic reform. In a letter to the clergy of the Zagreb Bishopric in 1813, he asked the clerics to gather folk proverbs, tales and poems, and even to collect the everyday words and phrases of the common people. He asked them to look into local libraries and archives for material which would enrich the study of Croatian literature and history. The clergy did not respond.

Croatia's neighbors, the Slovenes, the Hungarians, the Germans, the Italians, and the Serbs of the Voivodina, had already begun their period of national renaissance. Croatian students attending the Universities of Vienna, Pest, and Graz came in contact with these movements. Civil servants, such as Nagy, living in Pest and other Hungarian towns could observe the Hungarian national awakening at first hand and contrast it with the passive mood of the Croats. Educated Croats read the works of the German romantic writers and philosophers. Herder's ideas on the importance of the national language awoke in some of them an awareness of the beauty and potential of their own mother tongue.(75) In 1815 Antun Mihanović, a Croatian student at the University of Vienna, published a pamphlet in which he urged the Croats to discard use of the "dead" Latin language and, instead, to cultivate their own "living" Croatian language.(76)

The debates in the Joint Parliament over compulsory study of Magyar in the schools of the Kingdom of Hungary and the use of Magyar as the official language of Hungary, brought forth some interesting, though unsuccessful, reform proposals directed at the Croatian language by Croatian nobles and educators. In 1790 the Križevci County Estates came out with a plan to have Croatian studied in all of the schools of the Triune Kingdom.(77) It found little support. In the same year the Faculty of the Zagreb Academy drew up a petition to raise the Zagreb Academy to rank of a full University. The Croatian *Sabor* supported the petition, but it was rejected at the meeting of the Joint Parliament.(78) The petition cited the need for a university to serve not only the youth of the Triune Kingdom and Military Frontier, but students from Bosnia and Serbia as well. The Academy Faculty seem to have been considering the use of Croatian (dialect unspecified) as the language of instruction, since, unlike Latin, it could be understood by all Southern Slavs.(79)

In 1813 Josip Sermage, Superintendant of Schools for the Triune Kingdom, and Ladislav Žužić, professor of history at the Zagreb Academy, attempted to arouse support for the establishment of a national library and national museum. The only practical result of their efforts was the enlargement and opening to the public of the Zagreb Academy library.

In 1809, at the Peace of Schönbrunn, Austria surrendered a part of Civil Croatia, much of the Croatian Military Frontier, and the heart of her Slovene lands to Napoleon. He joined them with Dalmatia, which had been under French rule since 1806, and created a new political unit, the Illyrian Provinces. The Illyrian Provinces cut across traditional boundaries and for the first time brought together Serbs from the Military Frontier and Dalmatia, Slovenes from the Austrial Littoral, Carniola and Carinthia, and Croats from the Military Frontier, Istria, Dalmatia and Civil Croatia.

The Illyrian Provinces had only a brief existence, from 1809 to 1813. The capital of the Provinces was Ljubljana, a Slovene town. Marshal Marmont, the French Governor General, hoped to introduce the *štokavski* dialect of Dubrovnik which he called "Illyrian," as the official language of the local administration, while French was to be used for the highest offices and foreign affairs.(80) This was opposed by the Slovenes who did not consider "Illyrian" their language, and a compromise was reached in 1810 whereby two Southern Slavic literary languages were to be cultivated in the Illyrian Provinces, Slovene in the north and "Illyrian" in the south.(81)

The creation of the Illyrian Provinces has been viewed by some historians as a major step toward the Illyrian Movement.(82) There is little to substantiate this claim. Croats, Serbs and Slovenes did live together in a political unit for four years, and the name used for the Province was the same as that chosen by the Croats for their national awakening. But here the similarities end.(83) It is perhaps more significant that the national consciousness of the Slovenes was already developed enough by 1810 for them to reject the adoption of a Southern Slav literary language based on the *štokavski* dialect, and that the *kajkavski* or *čakavski* dialects spoken by many of the Croatian inhabitants of the Provinces were neither considered by Marmont nor defended by the Croats for use in the place of *štokavski.* The Southern Slav cultural unity fostered somewhat naively by the French was to fall prey to many of the same stresses that plagued the Illyrian Movement of Ljudevit Gaj. Perhaps in this way they are related.(84)

The Illyrian Provinces were ceded to Austria in 1815 at the Congress of Vienna. The Habsburgs then divided the non-military parts of the territory into three sections: the predominantly Slovene Kingdom of Illyria (which was a legal fiction), Civil Croatia and Rijeka which were returned to the Triune Kingdom in 1822, and the Austrian province of Dalmatia.

The Croatian political and educated elite were slowly beginning to realize by 1825 that their national culture and traditional rights were in danger. Creation of a modern literary language would give them a valuable weapon in the emerging struggle. But how did one go about making a modern language? Much could be learned from observing the developments among the other Southern Slavs.

In 1825 almost all of the Southern Slavs lived within two Empires: the Habsburg Empire and Ottoman Empire. There was no universally accepted Southern Slavic literary language to bind them together, no tradition of an all-encompassing Southern Slavic state, no clear awareness of "Southern Slavness." There were, instead, Croats, Serbs, Slovenes and Bulgarians.

The Croats and Slovenes were Roman Catholics, the Serbs and Bulgarians were Orthodox. There were as well many Moslem Southern Slavs in Bosnia and Macedonia. All but the Slovenes had had independent medieval states for a time. The Croats and Slovenes considered themselves part of the Western civilization, while the Serbs and Bulgarians belonged to the Byzantine-Ottoman cultural and political tradition. The Southern Slavs of the Habsburg Empire had to deal with problems quite different from those demanding the attention of the Southern Slavs in the Ottoman Empire. Hence, work on the formation of a Southern Slav (Yugoslav) nationality could begin in earnest only after each of the separate nationalities had achieved a clear awareness of its own unique being.

Although the Habsburg Empire contained Slovenes, Croats, and some Serbs, each national group had its own specific problems and a different historical relationship to the Empire.(85) The territory in which the Slovenes lived — the Austrian provinces of Styria, Carinthia, Carniola and the Austrian Littoral — came under Habsburg control in the fourteenth and fifteenth centuries. Only Carniola was predominantly Slovene in nationality; Germans formed the national majority in Styria and Carinthia, and in the Littoral (Istria, Gorizia and Gradiska) Italians were the largest national group (Slovenes were second and Croats third).(86) Dalmatia, in theory still a part of the Triune Kingdom, had recently become an Austrian province and was now being subjected to an intense period of Italianization. Civil servants from the Italian Provinces of the Habsburg Empire filled the provincial administration. They considered service in Dalmatia, which was poor, sparsely populated and backward, as a kind of exile and a common quip was that "Dalmatia is the Siberia of Austria."(87) Italian was the language of the schools, of the majority of the educated class, of the government and of the towns. The Croatian dialects were spoken in the countryside.(88) The Military Frontier was administered by the Austrian Military Authorities. The six counties of the Triune Kingdom and the Hungarian Littoral were part of the Kingdom of Hungary. There was also a large community of Serbs in the Vojvodina, who had migrated to this area in the late seventeenth century and enjoyed certain rights and privileges as a religious community.(89)

The vast majority of the Serbs, the Croats of Bosnia-Hercegovina, the Macedonian Slavs and the Bulgarians, lived in the European provinces of the Ottoman Empire.(90) There was a small semi-independent Serbian Principality, which had been born out of the Serbian uprisings of the first two decades of the nineteenth century. Although the Principality was still garrisoned by Turkish troops in 1825, the civil government was Serbian. This small state, which as yet included only the Pašaluk of Beograd, was to serve as the nucleus of the future Kingdom of Serbia and the center of Serbian expansionism.

The only independent Southern Slav state in 1825 was the tiny mountain principality of Montenegro. A loose confederation of Serbian tribes, ruled by a hereditary Prince-Bishop, involved in intermittent wars with the Turks, Montenegro was a warrior society which eked its meager living from the rocky soil.

The first movement for political independence came from the Southern Slavs of the Ottoman Empire, the Montenegrins and the Serbs, but the cultural awakening began among the Southern Slavs of the Habsburg Empire.

Although each Southern Slav nationality had its own period of national awakening, the movements were actually part of a larger Slavic renaissance, and of a general European stirring of nationalities. By 1825, cultural renaissance among the Slovenes and the Serbs had already begun.

Perhaps because the Slovenes could not draw upon the traditions of an independent Slovene state to spark a feeling of national consciousness, they laid special stress at the beginning of their national awakening on the fact that they were members of a larger community — the Slavs.(91) This is well demonstrated in Jernej Kopitar's introduction to his *Grammatik der Slavischen Sprache in Krain, Kärnten und Steyermark* (1808) in which he says:

> The millions of Slavs of Inner Austria, with whose grammar the present work concerns itself, are a small, old, but not unimportant . . . branch of the most widely spread family of peoples on God's earth (The Slavs).(92)

By 1825 the Slovenes had already taken the first steps toward the creation of a modern literary language. In 1817 a chair for the Slovene language was established at the Ljubljana *lyceum.* Philologists and other interested scholars and patriots had begun to publish grammars, compile dictionaries and offer proposals for orthographic reform. Educated Slovenes, especially the younger generation, were becoming interested in the problems of language in ever-increasing numbers.

One of the major problems in the development of the Slovene literary language was that no one Slovene dialect was dominant enough in geographical extent or literary tradition to serve as the vehicle of the new all-Slovene language. Each province had its dialect, its body of literature in the vernacular, and its grammarians and language reformers.(93) In addition, the Slovenes, like the Croats, experienced difficulties caused by an unsystematic Latin orthography.

Jernej Kopitar (1780-1844), a scholar of the first order and a man of strong opinions, was one of the most interesting figures of the Slovene renaissance. Kopitar believed that in order to create a modern literary language which should, of course, be based upon the vernacular, the vernacular should first be cleansed of foreign words, reformed and simplified. Only then, after the basic linguistic reforms had been made, should literature be written in this new literary language.(94) Yet though no agreement had been reached on orthographic or other reforms, the body of literature in the Slovene vernacular grew year by year. Kopitar became Censor for Slavic and Modern Greek books in Vienna in 1808. He attempted, without success, to direct the Slovene literary movement from a distance. But when he came in contact in Vienna with a young Serb, Vuk Karadžić, Kopitar was at last able to guide the development of a modern literary language — Serbian.

The Serbian renaissance took a somewhat different form. The dialect spoken almost universally by the Serbs of the Vojvodina and of the Ottoman Empire was *štokavski.* Yet the language used in the first part of the Serbian renaissance was *Slavenosrpski,* an artificial and archaic literary language,(95) known only to the educated classes. The renaissance began in the Vojvodina in the second half of the eighteenth century. By 1825, volumes of religious literature, secular prose and poetry had been published in *Slavenosrpski.*

The use of *Slavenosrpski* was challenged in the last decades of the eighteenth century by Dositej Obradović (1740-1811). Obradović believed that the Serbian literary language should be based upon the vernacular, and he set out to prove this by writing many secular books in his own version of the vernacular, a *štokavski* mixed with some elements of *Slavenosrpski.*

Apart from the Vojvodina, there were two other centers of Serbian literary activity, Vienna and Pest. The chief magnet in each case was a printing press. It was in Vienna, that the Serbian vernacular was finally molded into a modern literary language by Vuk Karadžić.

Vuk Karadžić (1787-1864)(96) had been born in Turkish Serbia. He took part in the first Serbian uprising and came to Vienna in 1813 after the revolt had been crushed. Through the circle of Serbian patriots gathered around *Novine serbske* he met Jernej Kopitar. With Kopitar's advice and encouragement, Karadžić began to publish works in the Serbian vernacular: first a volume of Serbian folk poetry and a grammar in 1814, then another book of folk poetry in 1815. In 1818 Karadžić published a Serbian dictionary with grammar which proposed essential reforms of the Serbian literary language. Three more volumes of folk poetry appeared in 1828, and a fourth in 1833.

Vuk Karadžić's collections of folk poetry demonstrated the beauty of the Serbian vernacular *(štokavski).* His dictionary, grammar and orthographic reform became models for others to follow. He based the new literary language on the vernacular as it was spoken, favored the *ijekavski* variant of *štokavski,* and introduced a phonetic orthography. Karadžić's reforms aroused much controversy. They were opposed by the hierarchy of the Serbian Orthodox Church and by the writers of the Vojvodina, who were dedicated to the preservation of *Slavenosrpski.* Although decades would pass before the Serbs of the Vojvodina and the Principality would accept Karadžić's language reforms. the battle between the two Serbian literary languages was now well under way.

The Croats badly needed a national renaissance and the first step in this renaissance would be the creation of a modern literary language. The alternatives facing the Croats in the choice of the dialect upon which to base their literary language were sharply drawn by 1825. Although *kajkavski* was the dialect traditionally associated with Croatia, *štokavski* was spoken by the greatest number of people in Civil Slavonia, the Military Frontier, and Dalmatia. If the *kajkavski* dialect were chosen as the basis of the new literary language, it would link the Croats more closely to the Slovenes, but this would be of little use either linguistically or politically, for the Slovenes did not yet have a standard literary language, they were in the Austrian part of the Empire, not the Kingdom of Hungary, and they had never been part of the Croatian Kingdom.

If *štokavski* were chosen, it would not only provide linguistic unity for the Croats past and present, but would also bring the Croats closer to the Serbs. With Karadžić's language reforms, the Serbian vernacular was now becoming a modern literary language. The practical solution today seems so obvious that one wonders why the choice of *štokavski* for the Croatian literary language presented a problem, but, as we shall see, traditions die slowly.

CHAPTER III

LJUDEVIT GAJ — YOUTH (1809-1826)

The Croatian Zagorje lies north of Zagreb. Zagorje (za-gorje) literally means "behind the mountain ridge," the ridge made up of the Žumberačke mountains and Medvednica, which stretches like a wall from Slovenia to a point northeast of Zagreb. The name Zagorje is a local and traditional one. The administrative and political unit with which it was synonymous, from the fifteenth to twentieth centuries, was the county of Varaždin.

Zagorje, thanks to its geographical position, enjoyed a cultural and social continuity rare in the lands inhabited by the Southern Slavs. It belonged to that small part of Croatia which was neither in the fore front of Turkish attack nor under Turkish rule. The mountain ridge acted as a natural fortress of sorts, and the marshy plains and string of defenses along the Sava river deflected the Turkish armies.

Although sparsely settled during the period prior to the Turkish invasions, the population of Zagorje was increased by a continual stream of immigrants until, by the early nineteenth century, it was the most densely populated part of the Triune Kingdom.(97) Sheltered from Turkish domination, constantly under Hungarian, then Hungarian and Habsburg rule, the social structure of the Croatian Zagorje remained relatively unchanged. The Hungarian King, the Catholic Church and the local nobility were the sources of authority. Although migration was continuous, the newcomers were quickly absorbed by the native population. While Orthodox Serbs formed a minority in the other counties of Civil Croatia and a majority in some parts of Civil Slavonia and the Military Frontier, the population of the Croatian Zagorje remained Catholic and Croatian.(98)

The town of Krapina, the birthplace of Ljudevit Gaj, lies in a narrow river valley. It was an important market town in the early nineteenth century, attracting many skilled artisans. It also had coal mines and a small but flourishing pottery industry.(99) Krapina enjoyed certain of the privileges of a free town: the right to elect local officials and judges, the right to hold markets on certain days, and the right of free trade. It also served as a cultural center for the surrounding area, for it possessed both an elementary school and a Franciscan monastery. The land surrounding the town belonged to the Church or to the local nobles, a continual succession of Croatian and Hungarian families. The artisans and professional people of the town, constantly renewed by immigration from Austria and Hungary, usually stayed in Krapina for one or two generations.(100) The peasants were the unchanging element in the population.

Three small hills rise above the town of Krapina, each capped with the ruins of an old castle. These castles, built by local nobles in the middle ages, were endowed with a more illustrious past by the local inhabitants, who believed that they dated back to the Roman Empire when Krapina was part of the Province of Illyria. It is assumed in the tale that the Illyrians were Slavs. According to the legend the castles belonged to three brothers, Čeh, Leh and Meh, scions of a distinguished Illyrian family. The brothers organized a plot to oust the Romans from Illyria, but they were betrayed by their sister, and forced to flee. Accompanied by their fellow conspirators, each brother led a group of refugees in a different direction. Čeh traveled north and founded the Kingdom of Bohemia, Meh went northeast and established the Kingdom of Poland, and Leh, or Rus as he is sometimes called, set off to the east to found Russia.(101) Therefore Krapina was much more than a bustling little market town in the Croatian Zagorje, it was the legendary home of the Slavs.

Ivan (Johann) Gaj, the father of Ljudevit, was born in 1754 in Cepanović, a small Slovak town at the foot of the Tatra mountains.(102) Ivan Gaj must have come from a family of some means, for immediately after completing a long and expensive period of professional training, he came to Krapina with enough capital to purchase the local pharmacy.(103) We do not know why Ivan Gaj chose Krapina. It may have been at the suggestion of his sister who was living in Varaždin at the time;(104) the Krapina pharmacy was a branch of the Halter pharmacy in Varaždin. Ivan's choice may also have been influenced by the role the Krapina pharmacy played in the newly-organized medical services of the Triune Kingdom. In the late eighteenth century the following medical hierarchy was established: each county had a fully trained physician and a central pharmacy, and each *kotar* — administrative subdivision — had a surgeon and a smaller pharmacy. Krapina was the medical center for the *kotar* of lower Zagorje.(105) Ivan Gaj arrived in Krapina early in 1786. He first leased the pharmacy, then purchased it from the Halters for 500 forints in October of the same year.(106) Three years later, on October 6, 1789, he married Julijana Schmidt.(107)

Julijana Schmidt was born in 1767. Her father Wilhelm Friedrich Schmidt was the surgeon for the *kotar* of lower Zagorje. He most probably came to Croatia in the 1770's, drawn by the new opportunities for medical personnel. The first local document to mention his name dates from 1782.(108) We do not know where the Schmidts came from, only that their mother tongue was German. It may have been Prussia, judging from the names of Julijana's father and one brother of whom we know — Friedrich Wilhelm Schmidt.(109) Julijana Gaj must have had some formal education for she knew some French and Latin in addition to German and Croatian (kajkavski).(110)

Ivan and Julijana Gaj had five children: Ivana Nepomučena (1792-1867); Ivan Anton (1798-1854); Franciska (1804-1855); Judith (1806-1862); and Ljudevit (1809-1872).(111) The Gaj name often appears in documents as de Gaj, od Gaj and von Gaj, indicating that they belonged to the nobility, but this was not quite the case. In 1783 Ivan Gaj, perplexed by some ambiguities in the family history, wrote to his uncle, a Captain in the Imperial Army, asking whether or not the Gajs were of noble birth. His uncle replied that the Gajs were originally Imperial Knights — the Gays of Gayerstein. They had emigrated to Hungary from Burgundy in the early seventeenth century and had later been forced into a subordinate position by a powerful Hungarian family. Captain Gaj advised Ivan to have the patent of nobility restored, and sent him a copy of the family crest.(112) Ivan Gaj never pursued the matter. It was left to his son Ljudevit to probe further into the origins of the Gaj family.

Whether or not Ivan Gaj could prove that he was a noble was of little consequence in Krapina. He was a gentleman and a good businessman. The pharmacy flourished. Ivan Gaj purchased a large house on the main street of the town, a garden in which to grow herbs and medicinal plants, and a small house which he let for income. He was a member of the town elite, elected to serve as assessor in the town government and generally recognized as an outstanding citizen and a good man.(113) By the time of Ivan Gaj's death in 1826 he had tripled the value of his original investment, leaving an estate worth 15,420 forints.(114)

Although there is a limited amount of source material available on the early life of Ljudevit Gaj,(115) historians have paid a great deal of attention to his childhood and adolescence.(116) This is not simply because Gaj became an important figure in Croatia, but because studies of his growing sense of national identity gave insight into the sources of the national awakening in Croatia. When and why did Gaj become aware he was a Croat? Was he influenced most by his family, his birthplace, his early schooling in Croatia, or his years as a university student in Austria and Hungary?(117)

Ljudevit Gaj's unfinished autobiography, "Vjekopisni moj nacrtak" is an obliging document for those who seek influences, for Gaj carefully indicates the steps he considers to have been of major importance on his way to national leadership. It was written in 1851-52, when Gaj was discredited by the Movement he led and under constant police surveillance. Although "Vjekopisni" goes only to 1830, it is the best single source for Gaj's early years, but must be used with caution.

Ivan Gaj was fifty-five and Julijana Gaj forty-two when Ljudevit was born. Ivan Gaj was a busy man, well into middle age. It was Julijana who gave the most love and attention to her young son. We know much more about Julijana as a person than about Ivan, for she was the family correspondent and many of her letters, especially those to her son Ljudevit, have been preserved.(118) She was an active and intelligent woman, deeply religious, witty, and interested in life about her. Her letters tell of the tragi-comic feuds in a small town, of political stupidities, and human frailities. She believed in hard work, spartan living and clear thinking.

Ljudevit Gaj's first six years were spent under the shadow of war, famine and disease. He writes of how his mother would sit in front of the house on a warm evening while he played by her side. Serfs would pass by them on their way home from the fields. The Zagorjan peasants worked hard for a meagre living; the soil was rocky, families were large, and there was little left after payments to the landlord and the Church, especially in the famine years of 1814 and 1816-17. Julijana told her son that such conditions were not inevitable:

> When she told me that there were peoples who were happy, who were neither barefoot, nor clothed in rags, nor hungry, and I asked her to tell me the reason for this poverty, she would say that 'for all this misery of the people the lords are to blame; they have utterly neglected and abandoned their people: because both secular and vested lords are hiding their science and learning in the Latin and German languages, and are not giving their poor brothers of the same blood even one ray of light of science in their mother tongue.'(119)

The peasants, continued Julijana, were illiterate and had no idea of how to better themselves:

> 'We need books, books in the mother tongue and they will cleanse their minds of ignorance, clothe them, and fill their granaries and barns in advance for the lean years.'(120)

This seems a somewhat sophisticated conversation to have taken place between a small boy and his mother. Julijana Gaj probably drew her son's attention to the plight of the peasant in quite simple terms when he was little, and then elaborated on this theme as he grew older. It is clear from other sources that Julijana Gaj was distressed by the poverty of the Zagorjan peasants, and had a deep belief in the importance of education as a means to progress.(121)

German, the mother tongue of both Ivan and Julijana, was the language most spoken in the Gaj home. Almost all of the family correspondence is in German, yet in "Vjekopisni" Gaj identifies Croatian *(kajkavski)* as his mother tongue:

> At that time I spoke no other language but my mother tongue, unusual indeed, because after the custom which had become prevalent in all the so-called educated families, German and Latin were spoken a great deal. Until the ninth year of my life a natural instinct guarded me against any foreign language, in fact I was loath to listen to conversations in a foreign language and often avoided them with hate.(122)

This is intentional distortion, for although we know that Gaj spoke Croatian as a child,(123) there is no evidence to support the claim that he spoke it exclusively. Could a child grow up in a German-speaking household and speak only Croatian? In adult life Ljudevit was trilingual, fluent in Croatian, German and Latin.

Ivan and Julijana Gaj were newcomers to Croatia. They identified with their country of adoption, learned the *kajkavski* dialect and participated actively in the affairs of the community, but they could not transmit to their children the cultural and historical traditions of Croatia, for these were new to them as well. Gaj cites the fine example his parents provided him as leaders of the community, in their charity to the poor, in their sense of personal responsibility for improving the conditions they saw about them, but it was the tale of the three brothers of Krapina, which first awoke in him an interest in the history of his native land:

> I strove after detailed knowledge of what had transpired in my motherland in ancient times, which to me, at that time, did not extend beyond the boundaries of my Zagorje. Whenever my father or mother gave me a coin I gave it to an old man or woman, asking of them in return to tell me something about ancient times, and especially about the brothers spoken of so often.(124)

This interest was strengthened through contacts with local priests and monks.

The Croatian clergy had played an extremely important role through the centuries as the preservers and transmitters of Croatian traditions and the Croatian language. Most of the schools were staffed by priests or monks, and priests used the Croatian dialects in their sermons and parish work. In the early nineteenth century the majority of the works in the *kajkavski* dialect, a somewhat uninspiring collection of literary calendars, church books and religious tracts, were written by clerics. (125) Therefore it is not surprising that Gaj mentions the names of several clergymen as formative influences in his first twelve years.

The first of these, Father Pavao Pobor, a priest from the Croatian Primorje who taught school in Krapina between 1812 and 1816, was a frequent visitor at the Gaj home. Fran Kurelac, who knew Gaj well from 1826 to his death, identified Pobor as the first man to awaken in Ljudevit Gaj a feeling of love for Croatia and for the Slavs.(126) Pobor wrote to Gaj in 1835:

> You know, my wonderful little friend, that Almighty God singled you out to bring fame to your people and mine, the Slavs, and to spread their power and importance; for even in your childhood when someone asked 'What are you,' you answered that you were an Illyrian . . .(127)

Ljudevit attended the local elementary school from 1818 to 1820, and then was tutored at home.(128) He mentions only one of his teachers by name — Father Eugenije Rebić, who prepared him for admission to secondary school. Father Rebić, a Paulist monk, had been exiled from the nearby Lepoglava monastery when it was closed by Imperial order in 1786.(129) He then became the Director of the Krapina Franciscan monastery. Father Rebić prepared his young pupil most thoroughly in his studies and also cautioned him that "Man must shun empty vanity and work diligently for his people (narod)."(130) Another Paulist monk, Father Augustin Vrabec, a neighbor of the Gaj family, often talked to young Ljudevit about the contributions of the Lepoglava monastery to the culture of Zagorje and Croatia.(131)

Gaj heard the *štokavski* dialect spoken for the first time by a Krapina parish priest, Father Lunjević from Dalmatia, and in his later years he still remembered the sudden, sharp pleasure the sound of *štokavski* gave him. He found *štokavski* was much lovelier than the *kajkavski* of his Zagorje.(132)

In 1821, when he was twelve years old, Ljudevit Gaj left home to begin his studies at the Varaždin *gimnazium.* The language of instruction was, of course, Latin, and the curriculum stressed Latin grammar and oratory, but there were also courses in religion, Hungarian history, geography, natural history and mathematics. The Hungarian language was offered as an elective subject.(133) There was not a single course on the history, language or literature of the Croatian people.

Ljudevit was unhappy in Varaždin. He found the school rigid and old-fashioned, and made few friends. He boarded with the Halters — the original owners of the Krapina pharmacy — and was terribly homesick.(134) Despite this, Ljudevit did very well academically. He took a placement test upon entering and was allowed to omit the first grade, or class, of this six-year school. The best students of each class were honored every semester by the designation *clasis morum: primae.* In his first year at Varaždin Gaj was fourth then tenth on this list, ranked according to grades; in the third class (1822) he reached first place and stayed among the first five on his class honor roll until he left Varaždin in 1826.(135)

After Ljudevit had sufficiently mastered Latin, he was given permission to use the library of the Krapina Franciscan monastery when home on vacation. He had first become interested in this collection while studying with Father Rebić, and hoped that there might be something in the library about the Krapina legend. There:

> . . . I chanced upon some old notes containing legends about my homeland and all the branches of our people, collected by a father Sklenski.(136)

Ljudevit then compared Sklenski's manuscripts with several Czech and Polish chronicles and decided to put all of this information into a booklet which he hoped to publish. This booklet, a brief history and description of Krapina, was written in Latin. When he presented his manuscript to the censor for approval:

> . . . the obscurantist tenor of the day placed in my path an unsurmountable obstacle. Since I was a pupil in the fifth form of the so-called Latin school, fifteen years of age, the then censor in Zagreb, Father *Klohammer* by name and an ex-Jesuit, condemned my booklet to the pyre and myself to dull studies, although I had done much better by them than they deserved. 'Brats are to study, not write books!' said he.(137)

Ljudevit's dissatisfaction with Varaždin reached a climax in the winter of 1825-1826, his last year in *gimnazium.* He asked his parents for permission to transfer to another school for his last semester, and suggested the *gimnaziums* in Triest, Rijeka or Ljubljana. This must have come as a shock to his parents. Ivan was old and seriously ill, and he wanted his son near him, so the family compromised on the *gimnazium* in Karlovac which was not so far away.(138)

The program of the Karlovac *gimnazium* was similar to that of Varaždin, but the atmosphere was much friendlier and more relaxed. Ljudevit Gaj successfully completed his secondary school studies there in the early summer of 1826.

While Gaj is silent in the *Autobiography* about the four and a half years spent in Varaždin, he speaks enthusiastically about his single semester in Karlovac. Varaždin had reached its peak of importance towards the end of the eighteenth century and was now beginning a slow and gradual decline as a center of cultural, political and economic activity. Karlovac was a young and dynamic town. Varaždin, the baroque city with its buildings of graceful proportions, its well-endowed institutions of education, its small craftsmen and bureaucrats, represented the old Croatia. Karlovac had grown from a sleepy little military outpost to a bustling commercial center in less than a century. It represented the new Croatia.

The people in Varaždin were not so different from those in Krapina, they were Zagorjans, Croats, and Catholics, while Karlovac lay on the very edge of Civil Croatia. To the immediate south stretched the Croatian Military Frontier, of which Karlovac had once been a part. To the west was the Adriatic coast, to the north Slovenia, and to the east, Civil Croatia. The years in Varaždin must have seemed unimportant to Gaj, for Karlovac awoke him to new ideas, filled his eyes and ears with new impressions:

> By then I had realized that my homeland lay also beyond the confines of Zagorje . . . At Karlovac I saw men and women of the old stock, of the core of our Croat and Serb nation. I listened to their vigorous language, and when I read Kačić's *Razgovor ugodni* the loveliness and dignity of the Illyrian language were revealed to me, but common sense suggested that I first use the dialect in use in Zagorje and in those parts of the country where nationality *(narodnost)* was a empty word.(139)

Andrija Kačić-Miošić's *Razgovor ugodni,* a popular chronicle of the history of the Southern Slavs, dates from the mid-eighteenth century. Written in the *štokavski* dialect and filled with many folk ballads and songs, it told of old knights and dukes, of wars against the Turks, of heroic deeds and fierce battles.(140) In Karlovac Gaj heard *štokavski* and *čakavski* spoken. He observed the pageantry of market days when each regional group came in different costumes and he began to understand that the people of Zagorje, of the coast, and of the Military Frontier — all belonged to one nationality.

Father Aurelie Hoermann, Director of the Karlovac *gimnazium* and adviser to the graduating class, was also the censor for Karlovac. He seems to have taken a special interest in Ljudevit and encouraged him to translate his book on Krapina from Latin to German. It was published in Karlovac early in the summer of 1826. This work, entitled *Die Schlösser bei Krapina,* would be forgotten today were it not for the later career of its author. It is a curious mélange of travelogue, history and legend. The text is liberally sprinkled with quotes from Matthison, Tiedge and Schiller, and the mood is set with a quote from Ossian:

> The chiefs of other times are departed. They have gone without their fame. Another race shall arise. The people are like the waves of ocean: like the leaves of woody Morven, they pass in the rustling blast, and other leaves lift their green heads on high.(141)

The hopeful mood of renewal and rebirth in this passage is not taken up by Gaj, whereas the brooding melancholy which mourns the passing of heroes and past glory continues throughout the text.

The ruins of the three castles of Krapina stand above the town like "question marks of the ancient world, put to the historian." Gaj endows them with personality:

> Gloomily, like Ossian's heroes, they look down from the heights upon the easily agitated race of men, the descendants of those heroes who went forth, not as so many others to destroy Empires, but with a finer purpose — to establish them.(142)

The heroes, of course, are Čeh, Leh and Meh, and the "Empires" they went forth to build: Bohemia, Poland and Russia:

> Every Slav can be proud to look upon these sacred and beloved ruins, for they were the cradle of Čeh and Leh. Here they gathered their loyal followers. From here they began their campaigns, and finally . . . we catch sight of them as founders of the mightiest kingdoms, through which they earn an immortal place in history and a devout respect for their names in the hearts of all true Slavs.(143)

The booklet ends with a pathetic description of the process of decay. The walls of the castles have split open, the mortar crumbles:

> . . . and so the strongest buildings are destroyed and lie in ruins for the wonder of connisseurs and admirers of venerable antiquity.(144)

The few chronicles and manuscripts Ljudevit had consulted in writing this booklet, seemed to prove the truth of the Krapina legend, for they told a story which seemed consistent with the oral tradition. What Gaj did not realize was that his proof was actually circular, that the chronicles were one of the sources of the folk tradition. The Krapina legend was an amalgam of several separate tales. The first, that the original home of the Slavic peoples was the Danubian basin, we find as early as the Chronicle of Nestor. The story of the three brothers was grafted on to this by the Poznan Bishop Boguhval (d. 1253), and Krapina was identified as the birthplace of Čeh and Leh in the Chronicle of Philip Kalimah (d. 1496). The Southern Slavs until about this time, the fifteenth century, had believed that they had migrated down to the Balkan peninsula from the north, but in the fifteenth century this theory began to be disputed by humanists who claimed that the Southern Slavs were descendents of the ancient Illyrians. When the legend of the three brothers from Krapina reached Croatia in the sixteenth century, it was added to the new tale of the origin of the Southern Slavs and the first example of the combined legends: that the three brothers were the sons of an Illyrian family in Krapina, dates from 1595.(145) In this form it entered Croatian oral tradition.

Ljudevit Gaj was also writing poetry in 1826. There is a collection of unpublished German poems, very much in the romantic vein of *Die Schlösser,* entitled "Weihe Meine MusseStunden,1826."(146) He had also begun to write poems in the *kajkavski* dialect, two of which were published that year in the new German literary magazine of Zagreb, *Luna.*(147) Only two other Croatian poems appeared in *Luna* in 1826, its first year of publication; one was by the noted *kajkavski* poet Tomo Mikloušić and the other by J. R. Kvaternik, professor at the Zagreb Academy.

Ivan Gaj died on April 18, 1826, only a short time after Ljudevit entered the Karlovac *gimnazium.* The Gaj family had lived simply, but had always had behind it the assurance of financial security.(148) This was now gone. Ivan Gaj's estate was divided equally among the surviving family members, each receiving 2570 forints.(149) This, however, was not cash. Much of the money was tied up in property, some of it consisted of unpaid debts. Julijana Gaj still had three children dependent upon her. Franciska and Judith would soon be ready for marriage, but the preliminaries of finding a good match required money for stylish clothing, entertainment and a respectable dowry. Ljudevit still had his professional training before him.

Janchi Gaj, the eldest son, became the new head of the family, but he was unable to fill this position well. Julijana once described him thus:

> . . . (Janchi) from his earliest years could only brag that he was the child of his moods and never master of his will and his temper, never wanted to listen to reason . . .(150)

Although Janchi had been trained well, and had inherited a thriving business, bad luck, personal difficulties and tragedy seemed to follow him throughout his life. He drank heavily, failed to succeed as a pharmacist, quarreled incessantly with others, had an unhappy marriage which produced sickly children, and was a burden to the rest of the family.(151)

Quite early, in 1822, Ivan and Julijana Gaj began to look to their youngest son, Ljudevit, as the one upon whom they could depend:

> So long as the good Lord grants us life and you continue to be good, we can look forward to being permitted a happy old age near you, then when our days have come to an end, we can gently pass away with the joyous conviction that we have given humanity a useful member.(152)

Before Ivan Gaj's death, it had been decided in family conferences that Ljudevit would receive his university training outside of Croatia.(153) Julijana was determined that Ljudevit's plans should not be altered by the loss of his father. Ljudevit's inheritance was invested and it produced an income of approximately 200 forints per year(154) Julijana would supplement this from her own income and from capital, if necessary. Ljudevit Gaj spent the summer of 1826 in Krapina and left in October to begin his university studies in Vienna.

CHAPTER IV

TOWARDS A REFORMED ORTHOGRAPHY (1826-1831)

Ljudevit Gaj was abroad from 1826 to 1831, studying philosophy then law at the Universities of Vienna, Graz and Pest. He chose Vienna first, according to "Vjekopisni," because the libraries there had a wealth of primary and secondary sources on Croatian history.(155) Julijana Gaj also favored the choice of Vienna for she was concerned about finding a suitable career for her youngest son and hoped that by attending a University in the German speaking lands he could perfect his German and prepare for a career in the Imperial Civil Service.(156) Ljudevit Gaj enrolled in the Faculty of Philosophy of the University of Vienna, in November of 1826.

Although Gaj maintains that he worked very hard in the Imperial Library, there are no notes from this period among his personal papers. From the years he spent in Graz and Pest, on the other hand, copious notes pertaining to his historical research have been preserved. It seems Gaj concentrated on tracing the origins of his family while in Vienna, and discovered that an Alois Gaj had been made Knight of the Holy Roman Empire. Ljudevit had the patent copied and verified, together with the coat of arms. He may have had some doubts about the lineage, though, for he did not mention his discovery to the family until the next summer.(157) Subsequent research has proved conclusively that Alois Gaj was not related to the Gajs of Krapina.(158)

By late December, Gaj's health had broken down, and he was advised by his physician to move to a milder climate. He decided to continue his studies at the University of Graz, where he arrived in January 1827. Graz was the capital of Styria, one of the Austrian provinces with a large Slovene population. It felt much more like home to the young man from Krapina and here he boarded with distant relatives. Gaj found other Southern Slavs among his colleagues, students from the Slovene provinces, from the Triune Kingdom, and from the Military Frontier. In "Vjekopisni" Gaj speaks of his years at Graz at length and with warmth.

Gaj was hard at work on his history of Croatia when he came to Graz:

> I took courses at the University and the Johanneum, all the while working very hard in the libraries of these institutions. I was scouring books and manuscripts to enlarge and broaden my collection of historical information and excerpts. When I compiled and prepared a chronological history of Croatia for publication, my joy knew no bounds. But when I enrolled in the University to read philosophy, the joy which sprang from my plans was dealt a bitter blow.(159)

Father Albert Muchar, Gaj's teacher of linguistics and rhetoric, heard, most probably from Gaj, that the young Croat was planning to publish a history of Croatia.(160) Gaj may have hoped that Muchar would play the same role as Father Hoermann, sponsor and protector, but Muchar was a professional historian:

> Although he (Muchar) had never seen my work he . . . told me: Burn everything you have written! The publication of works with which you want to be of service to your people, to awaken it, requires much learning, mature judgement and many years of hard work. My dear young man, you do not even know where to begin your history! Furthermore, have you a literary language in which you could publish your book and make it count? Banish these immature thoughts and get down to the work of preparing yourself and others for the task of founding a national literature which you as yet have not.(161)

Gaj was at first insulted and shocked by this criticism but soon recovered. There is no trace of the 1827 manuscript in his papers, Gaj must have taken Muchar's advice and destroyed it.

Although Professor Muchar discouraged Gaj from premature publication, the young man's interest in history was as strong as ever. Some of Ljudevit's happiest hours in Graz were spent at the Johanneum, an Institute founded in 1811 by Archduke Johann for the preservation and cultivation of the regional history and culture of Styria. The Johanneum had an extensive collection of historical documents and a large library. The Archivist, Johann Wartinger, a historian by profession,(162) took an interest in Gaj and introduced him to the basic tools of historical research.(163) There are two large folios of historical notes which date from this period (1827-1829). They are taken from the works of Engel, Jambrešić, Farlati, Lehotsky and Ritter Vitezović, and deal primarily with Croatian history.(164)

The very idea of an institute like the Johanneum, dedicated to the cultivation of regional identity, fascinated Gaj. He copied in entirety the text of an article about the goals and purposes of the Johanneum and gathered information about similar institutions: the Franzesmuseum of Moravia-Silesia, the Ferdinandeum in Innsbruck and the Bohemian Landesmuseum.(165)

While home on vacation in the summer of 1827, Gaj interviewed the old people of Krapina, asking them what they knew of the history of their town, of the origin of place names and the legend of the three brothers.(166) The conclusions he drew from this research are reflected in an unpublished fragment from the same year:

> The history of a nation is limitless and bottomless, because we do not know its beginnings. Just as the happenings of a man's first days of life are unknown to him, the first place he lived and customs of the place, a nation knows nothing of its childhood if there has been no observer to record it. A man retains only a few dreamlike impressions from his childhood, as does a nation of its childhood. The events which are in this misty realm belong to fable and must be separated from events which are recorded and true.(167)

Gaj even got his family involved in his historical research. He asked his uncle, Fredrich Wilhelm Schmidt, the surgeon of Križevci, to explore the Krizevci town archives and see whether he could find the old town charter. His uncle reported.

> . . . unfortunately the old town privileges are written in the Gothic script and no one here can read them.(168)

In a poem from 1826, "Meine Ländliche Heimat" (My Rustic Homeland), Gaj describes the simple beauty of Zagorje and laments:

> Too weak is yet the poet's hand
> To offer sacrifice to his beloved land.(169)

Less than a year later, in the spring of 1827, he wrote in a completely different mood to Johann Halter.(170) In this letter Gaj tried to prove to himself that higher education received abroad need not alienate him from his native country. He cited Halter as an example of a man of culture and education who could be happy in Croatia. The answer, said Gaj, was not to desert Croatia for a land which offered a better life, but rather to change Croatia:

> . . . in an illiterate land such as ours, it seems important, yes, most necessary, to bring all powers to bear upon awakening an effective and noble cultural patriotism. The history of our fatherland has already taught me how much (Croatia) deserves to be lifted out of the miserable Magyar darkness, at least in so far as this is compatible with the law . . .(171)

Gaj may have written to him in a similar vein earlier that year, for there is a letter from Halter to Gaj, dated March 10, 1827, in which the older man warns:

> Your last . . . letter to me was opened in Graz and stamped by both the postal authorities and the police. Perhaps the elegant calligraphy of the address . . . caught their eye . . .(172)

The need for caution was underlined in a letter from his mother later the same year. Julijana Gaj reminded her son that no matter how concerned he might be for the future of his country, he still did not know how he was going to earn his daily bread:

> So keep your thoughts to yourself. Say little and think much, and thus many will be denied an opportunity to use you for the furtherance of their own evil designs.(173)

The change in Gaj's attitude from passive concern for Croatia to active involvement in plans for a national awakening, came about primarily through contact with other students from Southern Slav lands at the University of Graz. Up to 1827 he had worked alone and without compass. Now he could carry on a dialogue with others, draw on their experiences, and gain confidence from shared interests and enthusiasms. Gaj's first friend and collaborator was Mojsije Baltić, a Serb from the Croatian Military Frontier. Baltić taught Gaj to read the Cyrillic alphabet and to speak and write the *štokavski* dialect.(174) Baltić also introduced Gaj to Vuk Karadžić's collection of Serbian folk poetry which impressed Gaj so deeply that he decided to begin to collect Croatian folk poetry himself.

In the summer of 1827 Ljudevit Gaj began to collect the folk tales, poems and proverbs of the Croatian Zagorje. He continued work on this for many years, later including materials from other parts of Croatia as well.(175) Gaj's collection was not published during his lifetime and after his death it was more or less forgotten. It has recently been rediscovered by Croatian scholars of folklore and they have found it to be of high quality.(176) Gaj was especially interested in the Zagorjan proverbs. He collected 921 manuscript pages of them, or more than 5,000 proverbs, while the other collections together total less than 100 pages. He began to look upon proverbs as the unwritten law of a nationality. In 1835, when discussing the importance of writing national history in the national language, Gaj wrote:

> . . . Who can note and discover the origin and causes of the actions and habits of a nation . . . if he does not know the most important and most commonly used words of the nation, if he does not understand the proverbs, which once supplanted law and order . . .(177)

In his polemics of the 1830's and early 1840's, Gaj frequently made skillful use of popular aphorisms. The brevity, precision and pseudo-legalistic implications of the proverb gave added weight and authority to his arguments.

Gaj's second collaborator in Graz was Dimitrije Demeter, son of a well-to-do Greek merchant in Zagreb. The friendship between Gaj and

Demeter was to last throughout their lives. Demeter came to Graz in the fall of 1827, and enrolled in the Faculty of Philosophy. He was, as Gaj, a second generation Croat. The Demeter family was closely tied to the Greek community, and the Demeter home in Zagreb was one of the meeting places of the Greek revolutionary society, the *Philike Hetairia*.(178)

There were two major bids for independence by the Christians of European Turkey in the early nineteenth century: the Serbian uprisings and the Greek revolution. Both national groups had large communities living outside of the Turkish Empire, and in both cases the political awakening had been preceded by a cultural awakening among the educated classes, often begun and carried on by the communities abroad. The Serbian revolution had already run ts course by 1827, and only three years later the small Serbian principality was granted partial autonomy by the Sultan. The Greek revolution was still in progress, and 1827 was the year of Navarino and the sudden turn of events in favor of the Greeks. Gaj and his friends must have followed the Balkan revolts with great interest. It was, however, the cultural aspect of the Greek and Serbian national awakenings which could be of most use to them at the moment.

On September 10, 1827 the Croatian Sabor passed a law making the Magyar language an obligatory subject in all the schools of the Triune Kingdom. It is impossible to reconstruct the effect of the news of this law on Gaj and his friends, for they were together and did not have to commit their thoughts to letters. But it is apparent that from 1827 on, Gaj was increasingly concerned with the problem of modernization of the Croatian language. There are many notes on language from 1827 and 1828, most of them fragmentary. In "Zverhu jezika magyarskoga" (About the Hungarian Language), Gaj describes the passage of the new law and the growing threat of magyarization, following this by a detailed compilation of the relevant parts of the laws of 1791, 1805, and 1827, which defined the official status of the Magyar language in the Triune Kingdom.(179) Gaj saw clearly that Latin was no longer suitable for modern political life. In a poem entitled "Der Zeitgeist und die Kroaten" (The Spirit of the Times and the Croats) he wrote:

> The noble daughter of Latindom must die
> Unmourned by her former heirs (180)

But what will replace it:

> You (Croats) faithful vassals of Rome —
> Do they also want to rob you of your mother
> tongue?(181)

Gaj feared that unless the Croatian language were sufficiently developed as a modern language when Latin was discarded, it would be replaced by Magyar. There is a passage from Jean Paul which must have had a special meaning for Gaj at the time, for it is quoted in two separate places in notes about the Croatian language:

> The existence of a new and bold alternative will more often topple a system than direct attack. (Jean Paul) (182)

The new and bold alternative, clearly indicated by the context of the quotation, was a modernized Croatian language.

Mojsije Baltić left Graz in the summer of 1828 to begin his career in the army. He wrote to Gaj in the fall of the same year complaining of the tedium of his present work, saying:

> Gone are the beautiful plans for sacrifice on the altar of national enlightenment. Gone is the enthusiasm for the beautiful and the good. I will carry these with the unfulfilled oath to my grave.(183)

He ends the letter with a greeting to Demeter "who thinks as we do."(184)

Gaj, Baltić and Demeter spent many hours together talking about the need for a Croatian national awakening. Each could bring a different point of view to the discussions. Baltić could draw upon his knowledge of the Serbian renaissance and the work of Vuk Karadžić; Demeter could tell his friends about the modernization of the Greek language; Gaj could contribute his knowledge of Croatian history and his research into Zagorjan folk poetry and proverbs. In 1876 Mojsije Baltić, reminiscing about his youth, said that he had belonged to an "Illyrian Club" while a student at the University of Graz. The club was supposed to have been a semi-secret society with an elaborate board of officers and a membership of students from the various Southern Slav lands. He names Gaj and Demeter as fellow members.(185) There is no mention of such a club in Gaj's correspondence, nor in "Vjekopisni." The "unfulfilled oath" of which Baltić speaks in his letter of September 29th, 1828, may have been the oath of a club, but may just as easily have been an oath taken by a group of very close friends. One suspects that Gaj would have mentioned an Illyrian Club in "Vjekopisni" if it had existed, for he emphasized everything Illyrian and devoted a good quarter of the text to his years in Graz.

In the academic year 1828-1829 Gaj and Demter became increasingly involved in the problems of the Croatian literary language. They assumed at this time that modern Croatian would be based upon the *kajkavski* dialect.(186) Although both had spoken *kajkavski* since childhood, it was their second language: the Demeter family had spoken

Greek, and the Gaj family German. Neither Gaj nor Demeter had studied *kajkavski* beyond their years in elementary school. Now they had to master the dialect in order to prove to themselves and others that it could serve as a modern literary language. They wrote poetry in *kajkavski* and translated, both individually and jointly, poems from the German:

> These linguistically poor attempts inspired in my friend (Demeter) a firm conviction that if we persevered we should gradually develop and enlarge the body of our national literature.(187)

Demeter took several of Gaj's translations to the editor of *Luna* for him, when he was home on vacation in the summer of 1828. Even though two of Gaj's original *kajkavski* poems had been published by *Luna* in 1826, the editor rejected the translations rather coldly, saying that his readers were not interested in Croatian poetry.(188)

In 1829, Ljudevit Gaj began work on his reformed Croatian orthography which in its final form, that of 1835, was adopted by the writers of the Illyrian Movement, and which, with a few minor revisions, is used by Croats and Slovenes today. Let us now try, with the help of Gaj's personal papers and a few published documents, to reconstruct how he became interested in orthography and the manner in which he arrived at his first draft of the reforms. There are no notes on language or orthography in Gaj's papers prior to his years in Graz.(189) I believe that Gaj's interest in orthographic reform had three major sources: 1) the danger of Magyarization as reflected in the language law of 1827, 2) Gaj's readings in history and language, and 3) Gaj's personal contacts with other people interested in the problems of the Latin orthography.

Although in "Vjekopisni" Gaj mentions only his reading and research in Croatian history, he had also begun to educate himself in the history and literature of the Slavic peoples. In 1827 he read P. J. Šafařik's *Geschichte der Slawischen Sprache und Literatur nach allen Mundarten* (1826).(190) In his Preface to *Geschichte* Šafařik described how difficult it was for a young Slav to gain a knowledge of the history and development of the Slavic "language" and literature, and expressed hope that his book would serve as an introduction and guide to this subject.(191) Gaj must have found much of interest in the book. The *Geschichte* was encyclopedic. It included information about Slavic history, the development of the Slavic "dialects" and their orthographies; it listed major works in each "dialect," and enumerated the libraries containing collections of books and manuscripts pertinent to Slavic literature and history, Slavic learned societies, newspapers and printing presses. Šafařík assumed that all Slavs belonged to one nationality and spoke dialects of one language. Šafařík described in detail the unsystematic use of the Latin orthography by the Catholic Slavs, which made it almost impossible for them to read each others' books, and included a table in which he compared each letter of the Cyrillic alphabet, which he considered better suited to the sounds of the Slavic language, with the traditional adaptations of the Latin alphabet in the literatures of the Dalmatians, Croats, Slovenes, Czechs and Moravians Slovaks, Poles and Sorbs.(192) This was certainly a graphic illustration of the need for a systematic and general simplification of the Latin orthography.

Gaj must also have read J. Kopitar's *Grammatik der Slawischen Sprache in Krain, Kärnten und Steyermark* (1808) during his years in Graz, for several of his manuscripts which are dated "Graz 1829" seem to be directly related to this work.(193) We know that he had read *Grammatik* by 1830 because he cites it in his *Kratka Osnova*.(194) In *Grammatik* Kopitar described the serious need for a reform of the Latin alphabet in order to adapt it to clear and simple expression of Slavic sounds. He talked of two possibilities facing the Slavic "nation:" development of separate literary languages from the major Slavic "dialects;" or the creation of an all-Slavic literary language. Kopitar seemed to believe that the second alternative was scarcely possible due to the long historic and cultural separation of the various Slavic peoples. The first alternative, on the other hand, might be acceptable if the Slavs adopted a common alphabet (Cyrillic) or alphabets (Cyrillic and reformed Latin).(195)

Gaj took up this idea in a manuscript entitled "Plan for the Establishment of a Croatian Literature."(196) In this disjointed and much revised work, Gaj proposed that the Croats replace the Latin alphabet with the Cyrillic, since Cyrillic had more letters and was better suited to Slavic sounds. He also suggested that if all the Slavs were to use the same alphabet, Cyrillic, an all-Slavic literary language might be developed.

An answer to this argument is found in a second manuscript, "Sketch for the Foundations of a Croatian Literature." It is written on the other side of the paper and much more coherent than "Plan."(197) In "Sketch" Gaj immediately dismissed the possible use of the Cyrillic alphabet by the Croats:

> For . . . The Russian (Cyrillic) alphabet is no more an original Slavic alphabet than the Latin one. This can be seen in the fact that the letters adapted from the Greek . . . are also inadequate, for not all of our sounds can be represented by the individual letters of this alphabet, although more than with the Latin alphabet.(198)

An even more important reason for keeping the Latin alphabet was that it was used by the Slovenes and the Slavonians, and it was with these Southern Slav neighbors that literary cooperation would be most fruitful.(199) The fact that some Slavs wrote in the Latin alphabet and others in Cyrillic, should not harm intellectual commerce among the different Slavic peoples, for this would be carried on by scholars in any case and they would know both alphabets. As to the possibility of an all-Slavic literary language, which seemed a desirable goal in "Plan":

> The unification of all Slavs through the medium of a common literary language remains an ideal, or rather, in the eyes of those who are familiar with the history of the Slavs — a folly, which can be as easily realized as the union of the Italians, French, Spanish, Portuguese and Vlachs in a common literary language. If such a phenomenon should occur, it would have to be the work of a colossal power or of several thousand years of coming closer to each other.(200)

The Latin alphabet should be retained but reformed:

> The so-called Church alphabet . . . can truthfully be called a Greek-Slavic alphabet. Is it not time that we make a Latin-Slavic one for ourselves? But no Methodius or Cyril has shown pity on our alphabet. Perhaps he is afraid that he will be stoned, for we do not live in the eighth century.(201)

In March of 1829, Gaj was reading J.C. Engel's *Geschichte des ungrischen Reiches und seiner Nebenländer* (4 vols., 1787-98), when he discovered several detailed passages and footnotes dealing with the life and work of Pavel Ritter Vitezović.(202)

The careful and extensive notes Gaj took on the sections of the book pertaining to Vitezović indicate his great interest in the forgotten reformer. Unfortunately, the Graz library had no Vitezović works. They were in the libraries of Vienna and Zagreb. Pavel Ritter Vitezović (1652-1713), man of letters and historian, had approached the problem of orthography twice. In *Kronika aliti szpomen vszega szvieta vikov* (Zagreb, 1696) he suggested that *sz* be replaced by *s*, *cz* by *c*, *ly* by *l'*, and the Dalmatian *x* by *sh*. Seven years later, in the Preface to *Plorantis Croatiae saecula duo* (Zagreb, 1703), he introduced the following new graphics: ç for *cs* or *ts*, ć for *ch* or *tj*, ĺ for *lj*, *lyn*, ñ for *nj*, *ny*, z for x or sh, adding that he had described his method of representing Croatian sounds by Latin graphics in his *Illyrian Orthography*. Not a single copy of this Orthography is extant.(203)

From the little Gaj could discover about Vitezović's reforms, from the information in Šafařík's *Geschichte* and from Kopitar's *Grammatik*, he now knew of some alternate solutions to the problems of Latin orthography and could begin to draft his own proposals.

In the spring of 1829 Gaj heard that Andrzej Kucharski, Professor of Slavic languages at the University of Warsaw who had been visiting Zagreb for some months, planned a trip to Krapina. Gaj hurried home. He showed the Polish scholar around the small town, took him to see the ruins of the Krapina castle, and entertained Kucharski in the Gaj home. Kucharski was the first Slavic scholar Gaj had met. They talked at length about Slavic languages and literature and about the problems of orthography.(204) Kucharski was quite impressed by the young Croat.(205)

During Gaj's Graz years the Slovenes were engaged in what the Slovene writer Matija Čop labeled the ''ABC Krieg'' (War of Alphabets).(206) Kopitar's call for a reformed Slovene orthography had been answered by P. Dajnko in 1823, and F. Metelko in 1824, but Dajnko's alphabet was designed for the Slovene dialect of Styria and Metelko's for that of Carniola. A third orthography, the traditional *bohorčica* which dated from the sixteenth century, was also in use. The Slovene students in Graz must have taken sides in this question. We know that Gaj discussed the problems of Latin orthography with at least one of his Slovene Colleagues, Georg Mathiaschitsch.(207)

Ljudevit Gaj completed the first draft of his reformed Croatian orthography by the summer of 1829. The only record we have of this first reform proposal is a letter written to Gaj by Mathiaschitsch in October of that year. Gaj had asked his Slovene friend to ask Dajnko, if possible, for his opinion of the orthography. Mathiaschitsch had not been able to see Dajnko, but had asked other interested Slovenes what they thought of the proposal and in the letter he discussed Gaj's reform letter by letter.

Gaj's Orthography of 1829(208)	*Present Day Orthography*
c	c
c,	č
đ or g	đ
l,	lj
n'	nj
z	z
x	ž
s	s
S	š

Gaj was not content to leave his orthographic proposals in manuscript. By the fall of 1829 he had already decided to publish his plan for a reformed Croatian orthography and had even discussed with his mother how the publishing costs could be met.(209)

The years in Graz were germinal ones. Ljudevit Gaj attended classes, prepared and took the requisite examinations, but his real interest lay in the work he did outside of the classroom: his historical research, his reading in works about Slavic languages and literatures, his orthographic proposal and the discussions he had about the future Croatian national awakening with his friends Baltić and Demeter. More than twenty years later, in summing up the importance of the years in Graz Gaj wrote:

> Almost every deed of note which has until now been accomplished in the business of the national awakening, was discussed and agreed upon in those days.(210)

Gaj, Baltić and Demeter talked about the importance of creating a Croatian literary language, of establishing an institute similar to the Johanneum, of the need for a national museum, and for a national theatre.

Gaj decided to end his studies in Graz at the close of the second semester of 1829, and transfer to the University of Pest. When Baltić heard of these plans he wrote:

> Continue on, spare yourself no pain, for the Motherland is your absolution and it will reward you, if tardily. Pest is the place and the opportunity now.(211)

Ljudevit Gaj enrolled in the Faculty of Law at the University of Pest in the fall of 1829. He was then twenty years old. Soon he would have to earn a living. An Austrian degree in Philosophy would be of little practical use in Croatia, but a degree in law from a Hungarian University would prepare him for a career as a lawyer or civil servant. His mother's letters continually advised him to think of his future, to train for a profession. The money she was sending to supplement the income from his inheritance was drawn from capital, a sum which was steadily diminishing.

Gaj says in "Vjekopisni" that he was drawn to Pest because of his interest in Croatian history; that he had found numerous references to books and manuscripts located in the Pest libraries. Many of these had been in the libraries of Croatian monasteries such as Lepoglava, and had been removed to Pest when the religious orders were disbanded by Joseph II in the 1780's.(212) Gaj spent many hours in the Szechenyi Memorial Library and the University Library, and took several hundred pages of detailed historical notes.(213)

The Szechenyi Library which had the most interesting collection had few other visitors. Hungarian nobles would come in from time to time to consult Parliamentary records. One of them asked the young man why he was working so diligently? Gaj explained that he was interested in Croatian history. Another day the same man said jestingly to a companion:

> My friend! It seems to me that this gentleman is preparing to conquer Hungary.
>
> *Gaj replied:* Not to conquer Hungary, but to defend Croatia.(214)

This was not simply a play of words. Ljudevit Gaj took himself very seriously. He sincerely believed that he would become an instrument through which Croatia would awaken to a sense of national identity. This theme is repeated many times in his notes and poems from the early 1830's. For example in an unfinished poem dated 1830, Gaj mused:

> From sleep beloved motherland, arise
> To a loving son do give your ear,
> His days and nights are yours, his prize
> — Your burdens — always dear.(215)

It was one thing to sit in Graz and observe the growth of Hungarian nationalism at a distance, and another to live in Pest. Pest was rapidly becoming the center of the Hungarian national movement. It was here that the Academy of Science, the National Casino and the Agricultural Society had been founded. A non-Magyar observed in 1833 that this city, which had resembled a German provincial town only six years before, had almost overnight become Magyar, the German signs over the shops had been replaced by Magyar ones, and rarely did one hear a German or Slavic word on the street.(216) New books, journals and newspapers kept appearing. The Magyars were about to embark upon their Reform Period in which they would attempt to make Hungary into a modern nation state; in 1829 and 1830 there was a mood of anticipation, restlessness and strong national pride.

Gaj recognized immediately that the goals of a Magyar nation state and a nationally conscious Croatia were incompatible. It seemed to him that the Magyars had become the enemies of the Croats, that by attempting to replace Latin by Magyar as the language of the state they were in fact trying to crush the Croatian nation.

The intensity of this feeling is clearly expressed in an unpublished poem written while in Pest:

> Brothers listen, strange things are going on
> Your neighbors, Magyars, are a strange lot.
> Ah, where are the Croats of old
> Now, when the fatherland is going to the dogs?
> Don't let yourselves be shut up in dog-houses
> Don't let our freedoms be stamped out,

We shall rather die together, united,
Than let our language be taken away from us.

Look, brothers, look, strange things are happening.
Your neighbors, Magyars are a strange lot.
Once they used to lay waste old towns
And slaughter Croats like butchers;
They want to take away from us our young tongue,
Deprive us of our rights.
Don't let the Magyars grind you into dust
We shall rather die together, united.(217)

In the spring of 1830 Ljudevit Gaj met the Slovak poet Jan Kollár (1793-1852), pastor of the Slovak Lutheran Church in Pest. Kollár was then in his late thirties, his intellectually most productive years. In 1821 he had published his first collection of poems *Básně Jana Kollára,* and in 1824 *Slávy dcera,* his most famous poetic work which predicted that the Slavs would become one of the world's great peoples. By that time Kollár was already beginning to think of the means to promote literary cooperation among the various Slavic peoples.(218) This idea was developed still further and given the Czech name *vzájemnost* in Kollár's *Rozpravy o gménach, počatkách i starožitnostech národu slawského a gého kmenu,* which appeared in 1830.(219) A fourth book, the first volume of *Nedlnj, swátečné a prjležitostné kázně a řeči,* a collection of Kollár's sermons from the years 1822-1831, was published in 1831. His ideas on Slavic reciprocity, for which he is most famous, were put into their final form in his essay "O literarnéj vzájemnosti mezi kmeny a nárečími slavskými," (1836) and the expanded German translation of this work *Über die literarische Wechselseitigkeit zwischen der verschiedenen Stämmen und Mundarten der slawischen Nation* (1837).(220)

Kollár was much influenced by Herder. He accepted Herder's idealization of the Slavs as a peaceful and industrious people, his concept of the poet as the "creator of nationality," and his ideas on the historical mission of the Slavs. Kollár conceived of his role in the Slavic world as an extension of his ministry: he was poet, preacher, teacher and guide.(221) Kollár believed that there was a Slavic nationality which existed in the language, literature and customs of the Slavs, and that there was one Slavic language with four major dialects: Russian, Czecho-Slovak, Polish and Illyrian.(222) A nationality, he insisted, did not have to have a national state in order to be strong. Since Kollár was already developing his theory of Slavic reciprocity at the time he met Gaj, it would be useful here to speak briefly of this concept so that we can later attempt to trace Kollár's influence, if any, on Gaj. Slavic reciprocity, to Kollár, meant the creation of a common Slavic literature but not a unified all-Slavic literary language. Each of the four "dialects" should develop its own literary language and literature. Educated Slavs should know all four; Slavic scholars should also know the sub-dialects (of which Croatian i.e. *kajkavski* was one); and specialists in Slavic language and literature should be familiar with living and dead Slavic dialects and the languages of the neighboring peoples. The goal was:

> . . . for all Slavs to consider each other as brothers and to create a common all-Slavic literature based upon the principle: *Slavus sum, nihil Slavici a me alienum esse puto*.(223)

In order to achieve this end the Slavs must establish Slavic bookshops in the capital cities of their states or provinces, arrange for the exchange of books and periodicals in the Slavic "dialects," found chairs of Slavic language and literature at their universities, publish Slavic dictionaries, grammars and translations of major works in non-Slavic languages, collect and publish folk poetry and proverbs, rid the Slavic language of all foreign words, and agree upon one or two (Cyrillic and or Latin) modern orthographies for use by all Slavs. They should also learn to call themselves Slavo-Poles, not Poles, Slavo-Russians, Slavo-Croats etc. (224)

Kollár believed that the cultural nationalism created by his Slavic reciprocity could be separated from political nationalism. He was loyal to the Habsburg Empire, seeing in it the best protection for his people, the Slovaks.(225)

A friendship developed quickly between the Slovak poet and the young Croatian law student. It was a relationship in which Kollár, older by sixteen years, became the teacher and mentor.(226) They had much in common: they belonged to Slavic nationalities in a magyarizing Hungary, they were interested in the development of Slavic languages and literatures, and in bringing about a national awakening among their own peoples, the Slovaks and the Croats. In 1841 Kollár reminisced about the years when Gaj was in Pest:

> It has been twelve years since we last saw each other. In Pest we took walks together, read the primer so he could learn Czech, talked about the orthography, about the newspapers and other national affairs. We planned grand things for the future . . .(227)

Although Gaj claims in "Vjekopisni" that he inspired Kollár to think about Slavic reciprocity by telling him the tale of Čeh, Leh and Meh,(228) we have already seen that Kollár had begun to develop this concept in the mid-1820's. Kollár did discuss his ideas on reciprocity with Gaj, for he wrote to him in 1836: "Appended here is a short discussion of Slavic reciprocity of which you have heard so much from me when you were here."(229)

Jan Kollár helped Gaj to see that the Croatian national awakening would be part of an even larger movement, the Slavic renaissance, and that although Gaj was a Croat he was also a "Slavo-Croat." Kollár's influence is seen quite clearly in a manuscript from 1830 or 1831 in which Gaj wrote:

> The Croatian tribe *(pleme)* is of the Slavic family. In her are its origin, its growth, its limits. Its customs are Slavic customs and it moves in the Slavic circle of learned men. Among Slavs a Croat can be a Croat. In Germany and Hungary he is the least of men, that is very much a toady.
>
> Now when the Slavic century begins in the history of the world it is a pity to linger and waste time. He, who now ominously warns the unfaithful sons of future severity, need not fear the curse of posterity.
>
> The Slavo-Croatian people has within itself a mighty potential . . . .(230)

Kollár undoubtedly encouraged Gaj to publish his orthographic proposals and may have helped him to put them in a coherent ideological framework.

Gaj's first complete draft of a reformed Croatian orthography was published in the summer of 1830 in a small booklet entitled *Kratka osnova horvatsko-slavenskoga pravopisaña* (Short Outline of a Croatian-Slavic Orthography).(231) It was published anonymously, signed L. o. G. (Ljudevit od Gaja), twenty-seven pages long, and printed in facing pages of German and *kajkavski.* The *kajkvaski* text was written with Gaj's new orthography.

The booklet began with a somewhat pathetic description of the sorrow felt by a Croat when he compared the neglected state of his language with the progress of other Slavic languages and literatures. The mother tongue must be honored and respected, for men who neglect their own language, cautioned Gaj, sin against their nation. He then proclaimed:

> Countrymen! Let us not permit Croatia, whose courage and strength once awoke wonder in men, to sink to a position of deserved inferiority in the nineteenth century. Let us now, in peacetime, become heroes of the intellect (spirit), so that our language, spoken with love and reverence by the greatest men of our nation and defended by them with their blood and property, does not, through neglect, fall into a dark grave.(232)

He was not speaking of the Croatian language as such, but of language as a symbol of the nation. The battle of 1830 was no longer a struggle of Croat against Turk on the battlefield but a war waged by students and scholars, "heroes of the intellect," who must fight to preserve the Croatian language as their forefathers fought to preserve the Croatian state.

The first step toward raising the Croatian language to a respected position in the modern world, said Gaj, should come through orthographic reform. Gaj called the Croatian orthography the very worst of all the Slavic ones. He proposed that in place of the unsystematic, foreign-influenced orthography then in use, the Croats accept a new one, based on the alphabets of the more advanced Slavs who use Latin letters: the Czechs and the Poles.

The orthography proposed in *Kratka osnova* was phonemic, i.e. each significant sound had its symbol. Instead of creating new letters, Gaj modified Latin letters by the addition of diacritical marks. The orthography of 1830 was much more systematic than that of 1829.

1829	*1830*(233)	*Present day orthography*
c,	č	č
đ	đ	đ
	ǧ	dž
l,	l̂	lj
n'	ń	nj
S	š	š
x	ž	ž

Once the new orthography was adopted, argued Gaj, the Croats would be able to communicate more easily with the other Slavs and thus become aware of "Pan-Slavism," a concept already familiar to the Poles and the Czechs, which was:

> . . . the deepest desire that all the Slavic brothers together in all ways work toward unity in the fields of linguistics and literature.(234)

The reforms in Kratka osnova were designed specifically for the *kajkavski* dialect, but Gaj hoped that they would also be adopted by the other Southern Slavs who used the Latin alphabet: the Slovenes, Slavonians and Dalmatians. A common alphabet would lead them toward cultural unity:

> Only in this manner can we await with happy certainty that the whole great Slavic language with its many variations will fuse into four main dialects, whose literature . . . will become the property of all Slavs.(235)

Here we clearly see Kollár's influence. The Slavs should work toward cultural unity, develop the four major "dialects" (Russian, Czecho-Slovak, Polish and Illyrian) into four literary languages; and the task of the Croats was now to work toward the creation of a common Southern Slav literary language which, as Gaj clearly indicated, did not yet exist. Gaj's reform proposals would make the Croatian orthography similar to that used by the Czechs and the Poles, and if the other Catholic Southern Slavs accepted this orthography the goal of a common reformed Latin orthography sought by Kopitar, Šafařík, Kollár and many other Slavic writers and scholars, would be closer to realization.

Gaj did not indicate what form the new Illyrian literary language should take, whether it would be based on the *kajkavski* dialect, the *štokavski* dialect, or an artificial blending of elements of all the Southern Slav dialects, for he had not yet begun to consider the problem seriously. Once Gaj's orthographic reforms began to win acceptance, he would turn to this even more crucial matter.

Ljudevit Gaj had been away from Croatia, except for the long school holidays, for the past four years, but he was in touch with local events through letters from his mother and from friends. In July 1830 Gaj heard from an old Varaždin schoolmate, Dragutin Rakovac, a first year law student at the Zagreb Academy. Rakovac was thinking of transferring to Pest and wondered whether Gaj and he might not room together. He also mentioned how thankful he was to Gaj for teaching him to love his mother tongue.(236) Rakovac did not come to Pest after all, but the continued correspondence is a valuable source for tracing the relationship between Gaj and the student community in Zagreb in the years 1830 and 1831.

There was not yet anything in Zagreb which could be called a national awakening, although certain individuals: Professor Stjepan Moyses, Dragutin Rakovac, Vjekoslav Babukić(237) gathered around themselves informal groups of young men concerned about the neglect of the Croatian language and nationality. The students who attended the Zagreb secondary and higher schools were, for the most part, those who were not wealthy enough to study abroad. They came from the poorer gentry, the middle class, and the peasantry (in the theological school). Most of them had some kind of fellowship, or supported themselves by ill-paid part-time work as tutors.(238) The Zagreb students lacked wealth and political power, and one of the few things they could do to try to bring about a national renaissance was to write poetry and prose in their mother tongue. Rakovac and a handful of others were writing *kajkavski* poems. The most famous of these was "Nut novo leto" (Now a New Year), a long poem by the theological student Pavel Stoos which was published early in 1831.(239) It portrayed Croatia as a black-clad old mother, alone and impoverished, who mourned the faithlessness of her sons. Ljudevit Farkaš, later known as Vukotinović, a law student, had translated two plays from German into *kajkavski.* Nikola Maraković was experimenting with orthography.(240) Rakovac kept Gaj in touch with what was being written in Zagreb. He sent Gaj manuscripts and copies of the few published works of the Zagreb students, asking him to show them to Kollár if possible.(241)

Kratka osnova was well received by the Zagreb students. Rakovac praised it highly and reported:

> You have sparked in everyone the desire to meet you. They all ask: where is he, who is he?(242)

Rakovac also reported that Professor Moyses was planning to begin the publication of a newspaper in Gaj's orthography. Moyses thought Gaj's orthography was very good, wrote Rakovac, so good in fact that he was going to give it his unqualified support.(243) Gaj answered that he was pleased to hear about the paper.(244)

Three months later Rakovac gave Gaj an interesting picture of the problems facing the young writers. The literary scene, he reported, was confused. There was growing opposition to the Gaj alphabet, although many supported the goal of national awakening. It was not yet possible to publish anything in the new orthography, since the Zagreb printing press did not have the new letters. If the Zagreb students were to wait to publish until these arrived, there would be next to nothing printed in the Croatian language. If they continued, temporarily, to publish using the old orthography, they might draw to their side some of the people who were frightened away by the idea of a new alphabet.(245)

The leader of the opposition to Gaj's new orthography was the *kajkavski* writer and priest, Thomas Mikoušić.(246) He is reported to have said upon reading *Kratka osnova:*

> . . . Nonsense, what do the Bohemians and Poles have to do with us? What does this young idiot want with the other Slavs? We Croats are enough in ourselves. We must keep ourselves separate from the other Slavs and retain the old alphabet . . .(247)

Although Mikoušić's main argument seemed to be with the Pan-Slav framework of *Kratka osnova,* he represented the old *kajkavski* literary school which would vigorously oppose Gaj's language reforms and the Illyrian Movement in the next two decades.

Kratka osnova did not revolutionize the literary scene in Zagreb, but it brought Gaj's name to the attention of the Zagreb student community, and offered a new argument for the need for orthographic reform. In 1830 and 1831, the Gaj orthography was little used and simply served as a possible alternative to the old.

Kratka osnova also aroused some interest among the Serbian students in Pest. Gaj later wrote:

> In 1830, my little book on the foundations of our phonetic orthography saw the light of day in the presses of Buda University. It made for me many sincere and devoted friends among the Serbian youth who were already burning with fires of patriotism.(248)

Pest was one of the centers of the Serbian national awakening. It was the home of *Matica Srbska,* the first Serbian national literary society which had been founded in 1826, of a press which printed Serbian books, and was the city to which many Hungarian Serbs came to receive higher education. Gaj does not mention *Matica Srbska* in "Vjekopisni." We do not know whether he ever visited the society, or met some of its members. It is quite possible that he avoided contact with *Matica Srbska;* he supported Vuk Karadžić in the battle over the literary language now being fought in the Serbian intellectual community, and *Matica Srbska,* a conservative organization, clung faithfully to *Slavenosrpski* and strongly opposed Karadžić's reforms.(249) Gaj made friends among the Serbian students and young priests, however, some of whom were active in *Matica Srbska.* He mentions only one by name in "Vjekopisni" — Paule Stamatović (1805-1860).

> *Stamatović* was the best of the lot. He was then attached to the Church of the Pest Orthodox Community, and now has the parish of Szeged. Learned debates in matters of language and history sharpened our minds and fanned in our hearts a growing love, concord, and mutual genuine respect, especially with regard to different religions.(250)

In 1830 Gaj established contact with P. J. Šafařík, probably on the suggestion of Kollár.(251) Pavel Josef Šafařík (1795-1861) was then Director of the Serbian *gimnazium* in Novi Sad. Šafařík and Kollár had been friends for many years and had collaborated on a collection of Slovak folk poetry, the first volume of which was published in 1823, and the second in 1827.(252) If Kollár was the poet of early Pan-Slavism, Šafařík was its scholar. He dedicated himself to the task of awakening patriotism and a desire for cultural unity among the Slavs by pioneer studies in literature, ethnography and history. His *Geschichte der slawischen Sprache und Literatur* was published in 1826, *Serbische Lesekörner* in 1833 and *Starožitnosti slovanské* in 1837.

In 1830, when Gaj first wrote to Šafařík, the Slovak scholar was preparing a new edition of *Geschichte.* Gaj used this as a pretext upon which to establish contact, but the real motivation seems to have been his hope to win Šafařík's support for the orthographic proposals. In his first letter, Gaj explained to Šafařík, that he had been disappointed by the section on Croatian literature in *Geschichte,* because many of the books identified as "Kroatisch" *(kajkavski)* were actually "Serbo-Kroatisch" *(stokavski).* Father Miklousić who had supplied much of the material for this section, was, unfortunately, poorly informed and completely lacking in an understanding of Pan-Slavism. Miklousić, continued Gaj, represented the forces of darkness in Croatia which opposed any change. Gaj enclosed additional information on Croatian literature which might help to remedy the errors of the first edition.(253)

He then went on to describe the sorry state of literature in Croatia, and to ask Šafařík for a letter of support for his orthographic reforms. There were influential men, he said, who were interested in the new orthography and might accept it if it were endorsed by a well-known scholar. Orthographic reform was badly needed:

> Little by little the wretched Magyarism presses into my poor blind fatherland. Its steps may be greatly hastened in the future by the almost identical orthography. On the other hand, if the Slavo-Croatian orthography were to be accepted, it would form a dam, small but better than nothing, to oppose this stream.(254)

Šafařík's answer is an intriguing document. On the one hand he praised Gaj, on the other he cautioned him not to be impatient. He thanked Gaj for the information about Croatian literature and said that he now had great hopes for a forthcoming Croatian renaissance.(255) It is true, continued Šafařík, that Croatia was in many ways backward and benighted, but was it so different in the other Slavic lands? There was dis unity and strife throughout the Slavic community, bred of old hatreds and old prejudices which must be rooted out like weeds, cautiously and slowly:

> Nature never tolerates rapid change, least of all in the life of the people. He who comes forward too quickly, will be pulled down by the current and may do more harm than good.(256)

It was not wise, cautious Šafařík, to expect the older generation to support reform. Men such as Miklousić, hinderers of enlightenment, were products of a darker age. Yet priests like Miklousić kept the national language alive through their books and ministry, and still served as spokesmen for the common people. Šafařík warned Gaj not to underestimate either their contribution or their power.

Gaj must have been disappointed by Šafařík's answer. Instead of a letter of support, he got one filled with fatherly advice. This first exchange between Šafařík and Gaj was only the beginning of a long correspondence and professional friendship.

Throughout 1831 Gaj was experimenting with alternate forms for his orthography, apparently unsatisfied with the one he proposed in *Kratka osnova.* For a while he experimented with using (ˇ) for every letter needing a diacritical mark: č, š, ž, ľ, ň.(257) The only reforms from 1830 which were not changed at all were č, š and ž. Gaj's orthography of 1831-1834 is not written down in a systematic form. His two published statements on orthography were made in 1830 and 1835. It is only from his personal papers, letters to friends, letters from people who had adopted his orthography and from the few published works of Gaj and his circle in 1832, that we are able to establish the time at which this change was made.(258)

In his second letter to Gaj in April 1831,(259) Šafařík talked in some detail about the *Kratka osnova* orthography. Šafařík was favorably impressed by Gaj's proposed reforms, but also fearful that they were too radical to be accepted:

> Languages and systems of writing are always something given, historic, positive and existing. We all know how difficult it is to introduce something better in place of what exists, just because it is new. In the case under consideration, I am afraid that people will especially resist the sounds for the soft d, l, n, and t. Without doubt they will say that the new is just as difficult as the old.(260)

Šafařík then went on to suggest that Gaj replace the letters for the soft d, l̂ and ń of *Kratka osnova* with symbols which were already familiar to the Southern Slavs, and that he find a better solution for the soft t, (expressed today as ć,) than ç. One of the reasons for this difficulty is that in the *kajkavski* dialect č and ć possess almost identical phonetic characterisitcs, and it is only in *štokavski* that the phonetic difference is articulated. It was not Gaj's task, wrote Šafařík, to create a perfect alphabet, but to make one which would work.

And that is exactly what Gaj did. From the second half of 1831, Gaj began to use dj, lj and nj in place of his 1830 forms of đ, l̂ and ń. He continued to use č for the soft t until 1835. The dj, lj and nj were forms traditional to the orthography of the Slovenes and Dalmatians.(261) This was indeed a compromise, for the orthography of 1830 had been a phonemic one, with every sound represented by one single letter which was, if necessary, modified by a diacritical mark. In no case did it include a combination of letters. The orthography as modified in 1831 could no longer be called a purely phonemic one because Gaj used combinations of letters for three sounds (the soft d, l, and n). Vatroslav Jagić, the famous Croatian philologist, wrote in 1890 that while Gaj's orthography of 1830 was clearly the most rational and consistent, and thus preferable to a philologist, the inclusion of traditional elements (dj, lj, nj) in addition to the innovations (č, š, ž) made Gaj's final orthography capable of winning immediate acceptance.(262)

In the late spring or summer of 1831 Gaj jotted down the first draft of a poem on the back of a letter from Rakovac dated April 1, 1831. It began with the words "Još horvatska nij' prepala," (No, Croatia has not perished), a paraphrase of the first line of the song of the Polish legion "Jeszcze Polska nie zginela" (1797). Gaj probably heard this song from refugees of the unsuccessful Polish uprising who began to arrive in Pest in 1831. The poem says:

No, Croatia has not perished,
Our people have not died;
Long she slept but she's not vanquished
Her sleep dreary death defied.

No, Croatia has not perished,
We are in her, still alive;
Long she slept but she's not vanquished
We shall wake her and revive.

The sweet and gentle Croat land
Shall to the Slav Achaea be;
Oh Lord, may our fatherland
Prove Eden, not Gethsemane.

Upon a night of restful sleep
Of manly vigour dawns the morn;
The strong his world in sway doth keep
In peace of reason that is born.

The length of winter nature rests
In strength to rise, in pride to stand;
This augury be to thy quests:
Thus, too, will thy motherland.(263)

This is clearly a poem of defiance and faith — defiance flung in the face of those who think that Croatia lies crushed by the apathy and ignorance of her people, and faith that she will rise again. For just as man and nature draw strength during the periods of seeming death, so does a nation. The central idea of the poem is lodged in the third stanza — a tentative assertion that Croatia will become to Slavdom what Achaea was to the Ancient Greeks: the cradle of noble virtues and undaunted will. By 1833, when Gaj wrote the second and final version of "Još horvatska," which would become a patriotic hymn, his political vision had undergone change, a broadening and strengthening of outline. The poem became a political manifesto.

Ljudevit Gaj received his law degree in July 1831. He was not yet ready to practice law or even take a position as a civil servant, for there were before him two years of work as a *jurat,* an unsalaried apprentice in the office of a lawyer or government official. In Croatia the title *jurat* signified a formal rank which was granted by the Ban's High Court upon petition to young men who had received their law degrees. When the period of apprenticeship was completed the same court would award the title *advocat* to the young lawyer.(264) Therefore, although Gaj's student days were over he still had two lean years ahead in which he would have to depend upon the income from his inheritance and occasional help from his mother. Gaj returned to Krapina in August and remained there until December, when he traveled to Samobor, a small town near Zagreb, to visit his sister and her family. In January, he moved to Zagreb.(265)

CHAPTER V

THE "GAJ CIRCLE" (1832-1834)

Ljudevit Gaj arrived in Zagreb in the first days of 1832. On January 5th, he submitted a petition to the Ban's court for admission to the rank of *jurat,* which was soon granted, and on January 22nd he began to work as a law clerk in the office of a lawyer named Valečić.(266) Gaj did his job adequately and was promoted to *advocat* in the late spring or summer of 1834.(267)

Although Gaj could have served his legal apprenticeship in any major town of the Triune Kingdom, Zagreb provided him with a fertile environment for his other, and more important, work. Dragutin Rakovac had been urging Gaj to come the Zagreb for over a year now, writing rather sharply to him in November 1831: "Although you returned home quite a while ago, you have not, to my great surprise, visited us yet. Everybody in Zagreb wants to talk to you about many things, especially literature."(268)

Fran Kurelac later described Gaj's impact on the young men in Zagreb who came to meet and talk with him. Gaj spoke to them of Kollár, of Pan-Slavism, of the Magyar danger and the need for a Croatian national language. His words poured forth "as though from a mouth of honey."(269) The Zagreb youth recognized that Gaj had a special talent. He combined the inspired rhetoric and single-mindedness of the missionary, with a gift for practical action.

The first documented meeting between Gaj and the Zagreb youth took place on January 19th, at the house of Ljudevit Farkaš-Vukotinović. Present were Gaj, Kurelac, Vukotinović, N. Maraković, and Antun Vakanović. According to Vakanović,(270) the group decided to take action to wake their nation from cultural and political apathy. Vakanović claims that it was then that they decided to use the *štokavski* dialect and the reformed Gaj orthography for the new literary language, and to call the new language "Illyrian."(271) I have not found adequate evidence to support this. The term "Illyrian" was used in 1832 when Gaj and several others met at Vukotinović's house to choose a name for a national cultural society.(272) Maraković, Vukotinović and Kurelac suggested variations of "Slavic Society of the Kingdom of Croatia, Slavonia and Dalmatia," Matija Smodek proposed "Society of Southern Slavs," but Gaj's title: *"Družtvo ilirsko — Societas culturae illyricae"* was adopted.(273) If they had already agreed on the use of the term "Illyrian," it would have been in all of the proposals, not just Gaj's. Also, while the Gaj circle were all moving toward adoption of *štokavski,* the only practical choice, there is no indication that it was decided upon yet.

The young men who met at Vukotinović's house were only part of the group which gathered around Ljudevit Gaj in 1832, and formed what I shall call the "Gaj circle." It included *jurats* (Gaj, Rakovac, A. Šuljok, Vakanović), theological students (Josip Kundek and Pavel Stoos), young instructors and students of the Zagreb academy (Matija Smodek, Maraković, Ivan Derkos, Vjekoslav Babukić), and a private tutor (Antun Mažuranić). These were indeed young men: A. Mazuranic, the oldest, was then twenty-seven. They came from all the social classes: Vukotinović, Vakanović and Šuljok belonged the the landed gentry; Derkos and Kurelac were the sons of officers in the Military Frontier; Gaj's father had been an apothecary; Rakovac was the son of an estate steward; Babukić's father was a baker, and Stoos and Mažuranić were from peasant families.(274) The Gaj circle had no political power: the nobles among them were still too young to participate in the county assemblies and *Sabors,* the others were excluded because of class origin. They lacked money as well; only Gaj and Vakanović had some private income.(275) Though powerless now, they would not remain so for long. They belonged to the small educated elite in a land in which the majority of the population were illiterate serfs. Trained to become lawyers, civil servants, teachers, priests, they would one day hold positions of influence. Now, not yet part of the "system," they could become involved in a movement to reform the life of their nation, for they were young and there was no need for them to worry about the effects of their activities upon jobs and families.

Ivan Derkos was the first to act. In 1832 he published a Latin pamphlet entitled *Genius patriae,*(276) in which he argued for the adoption of the *štokavski* dialect as the basis of a modern Croatian literary language. Derkos began by stating that a nation can only reach full intellectual development in its mother tongue, and that the Croats were greatly hampered because they did not have a literary language based on the mother tongue, possessing instead a variety of dialects. One of these should become the literary language, but which one? Derkos proposed *štokavski,* as it was spoken by the majority of the inhabitants of Civil Slavonia, Dalmatia and the Military Frontier. As to the problem of which variant of *štokavski* to choose, Derkos suggested that they could all be easily merged into one, but does not say how this would be done. While he acknowledged that *kajkavski* was the traditional dialect of the political center, Civil Croatia, and was a link to the Slovenes, Civil Croatia's historic ties were with Civil Slavonia and the former Croatian lands, he argued, not with the Slovene provinces, therefore *kajkavski* must be sacrificed for the sake of national unity.

Derkos was the only member of the Gaj circle to publish his ideas on the literary language between 1832 and 1835. Gaj dealt with the same question in two manuscripts, one quite long, the other an untitled fragment.(277) Both are undated, but on the basis of internal evidence, I would judge that they were written sometime between 1830 and 1835.

The short manuscript is similar to *Genius patriae* in its conclusion, if not in its approach. Here Gaj tried to prove that *štokavski* was a Croatian dialect, not a purely Serbian one, and he took issue with Šafařík's categorization of the Southern Slav dialects, in which the Slovak scholar identified: Slavo-Serbs of the Greek rite; Catholic Slavo-Serbs; Croats and Slovenes.(278) The Roman Catholics of Slavonia, Dalmatia and Bosnia who spoke the *štokavski* dialect were not Slavo-Serbs, argued Gaj, but "Serbo-Croats," for they were Croats who had adopted *štokavski* after many centuries of living side by side with the Serbs who had settled in those areas. The dialect of the Serbo-Croats forms the link between the *kajkavski* dialect and the *štokavski* of the Serbs. It should be chosen for the new literary language, for it would establish a common literary tradition and, through this, a national identity for all of the people of Civil Croatia and Civil Slavonia, and by drawing them together enable them to withstand the pressures of Magyarization.(279)

The second manuscript "Über die Vereinigung zu einer Büchersprache," is a difficult source to use.(280) It has two missing pages, ends in the middle of a sentence, is in rough draft form with incomplete arguments and thoughts, almost as if it were a sketch for a longer work which was never written, yet it does have a certain unity. Gaj begins by examining the Serbian minority who live in the Croatian lands, how they came there, and how large a group they really represented. (A Serb by definition being an Orthodox Southern Slav who spoke the *štokavski* dialect, whose ancestors had originally come from medieval Serbia.) The

Serbs who lived in present and former Croatian lands and the Serbo-Croats, shared the same dialect, but it was not a Serbian dialect but a Croatian one, since it was used by both Orthodox and Catholic inhabitants of Croatian territory.

Gaj then went on to disagree with Kopitar's tentative assertion in *Grammatik* that *kajkavski* was a Slovene dialect.(281) After long philological argument, Gaj concluded that *kajkavski* was a Croatian dialect, and that the Southern Slav "dialect" of the Slavic "language" had three "sub-dialects": Slovene, Croatian and Serbian.(282)

The Croatian sub-dialect had three major literary traditions: 1) the Serbo-Croatian literature of Dalmatia; 2) the *kajkavski* literature of Civil Croatia; and 3) the "tradition" of a Pan-Croatian literature as formulated by the seventeenth century Croatian writer Pavao Ritter Vitezović. The first tradition (Dalmatian literature in the *štokavski* dialect) was the richest and oldest and possessed one inestimable advantage — it contained secular works written for an urban society during the Dalmatian renaissance, thus could easily be adapted to modern use. The *kajkavski* literary tradition had developed under the protection of the Roman Catholic Church and reflected a conservative peasant society with a strong Catholic bias. The *kajkavski* dialect was more rigid and archaic in its forms than *štokavski* and little suited for a modern literary language. As to the third alternative or tradition, Gaj wrote:

> Vitezović was the first among the Croats to understand fully the idea of Pan-Slavism and incorporate with great perception in regard to his own fatherland, the best elements of all the Croatian varieties into his literary language.(283)

Gaj was referring here to a statement in the introduction to *Kronika aliti szpomen vszega szvieta vikov* (1696), in which Vitezović wrote:

> . . . do not be surprised to find (in my writing) here a Slovene, there a Pokuplje, or a Posavina, or Podravina word, or a Primorje or Carniolan expression, because I found them so written, and all these are Slovene (Szlovenzki) languages; and it is better to borrow words from them than from foreign languages, Latin, German or Hungarian. Furthermore, synonymous expressions are the pride of every language, and many learned men are endeavouring to enrich the language of their people, so it will not be dependent upon other (foreign) languages.(284)

Such a Pan-Croatian language would truly be a Croatian language.

Gaj never drew all of his arguments together, but when the manuscript ended he seemed to have proved to his satisfaction that the Croatian literary language should be based on the *štokavski* dialect, but a *štokavski* which would not be identified with a particular region or local tradition, one which contained elements of all the Croatian dialects. With the creation of such a literary language:

> . . . the existing blind narrow-mindedness would be swept away and the literary language would be the same for all the Croats in Civil, Military and Turkish Croatia, along the coast and Istria . . .(285)

thus serving as the basis for a Croatian national culture. There were even wider implications:

> . . . . Furthermore it (the new literary language) could be used throughout Hungary from the Drava river nearly to the gates of Vienna . . .(286)

Thus it would become the literary language of the Croats and Serbs of the Habsburg Empire.

"Über die Vereinigung . . ." is an important document in tracing Gaj's reasons for choosing *štokavski* and the form of *štokavski* he favored, for the new literary languxge he would introduce in 1835 and call Illyrian, was the one proposed in this manuscript with one exception, it would be designed for all the Southern Slavs.

Although the Gaj circle individually and collectively began to see *štokavski* as the dialect on which the new literary language should be based, they lived and worked in Zagreb, the center of a *kajkavski* dialect area and the capital of a Kingdom which as yet had shown little interest in cultivating its mother tongue. It was logical, then, that their first task was to make their fellow Croats aware of the need for a modern literary language, and to find some means of training them to read and write in their mother tongue, no matter what dialect they used. The introduction of the new literary language could only come after there were enough people willing and able to use it.

In May came the inauguration *(instalacija)* of the new Ban, Franjo Vlašić. The colourful ceremonies drew the important nobles, prelates and civil servants from all corners of Civil Croatia and Civil Slavonia. Gaj, Rakovac and Kundek took advantage of this ready-made public. They wrote poems in honour of the new Ban and his vice-notar, Stjepan Ožegović, published them and distributed them during the week of ceremonies for the new government. The poems express the concern of the youth for their nation, and the hope that the new Ban would lead Croatia out of her present national apathy and political weakness. They assured the Ban that he would be supported in this task by the youth. In Kundek's words:

> For the youth is arising, it is working industriously to rekindle in the older generation what has been extinguished.(287)

At about the same time Gaj arranged for the publication of *Palma,* a political satire in Latin written by Gjuro Rohony, a Slovak pastor in Hungary. Kollár had entrusted the manuscript to Gaj when he left Pest in 1831, hoping it would be published in Croatia where the censorship was less rigid. *Palma* was a sharp attack on the attempts of the Magyars to force the Magyar language on the Slavs of the Hungarian Kingdom.(288) *Palma* awoke many people to the realization that the Hungarians were serious in their goal of replacing Latin with Magyar as the language of the state, and that Croatia might soon be magyarized unless she began to defend herself. Rakovac wrote to Šafařík in 1833:

> In the past year the smaller treatises of the Croats and especially the much honored *Palma* have awakened Croatian patriotism from its deep sleep and, so to say, electrified Croatia and Slavonia . . .(289)

There was still no newspaper in the Croatian language. The importance of a newspaper to a movement of national renaissance was clearly appreciated by the members of the Gaj circle. Newspapers were cheaper and sold incomparably better than books, thus constituting a much broader platform for ideas and reforms. The language of a newspaper could exercise a powerful influence on the language of its readers, who were taught their language without becoming aware of the process. So in the first months of 1832 Gaj and his friends decided to apply for permission to publish a newspaper. Gaj was chosen to serve as editor. He alone possessed the three qualities necessary for the job: literary ability, a strong will, and a private income to underwrite the paper.(290)

A difficult and lengthy undertaking lay before Ljudevit Gaj. He would have to petition the Zagreb County Administration for permission to publish the newspaper. The Zagreb Authorities would then recommend the action to be taken and send the petition on to Hungary. The decision in such matters was taken by two Hungarian governmental bodies: the Hungarian Regent's Council in Buda, and the Hungarian Court Chancellery in Vienna. If both rejected the petition, there was one recourse left: the Emperor himself.

Gaj's first petition, dated March 31, 1832, was directed to the Palatine of Hungary and through him to the Regent's Council. Gaj who signed the petition as editor, spoke of the Palatine's interest in the cultural progress of his subjects. History proves, said Gaj, that cultural progress is directly linked with the cultivation of the national language, and one of the most effective means of developing the national language is through a newspaper or periodical. Almost all of the nationalities of the Empire: the Magyars, the Czechs, the Germans, the Italians and the Serbs, had newspapers in their mother tongues, yet there was no

Croatian newspaper. Furthermore, while foreign languages such as Arabic, Spanish, French, and English, were studied in the highest educational institutions of the Empire, Croatian was not studied at all. These facts prompted him to submit a petition asking for permission to publish a newspaper in the Croatian language. The newspaper was to be called *Danica Horvatska, Slavonska i Dalmatinska* (Morning Star of Croatia, Slavonia and Dalmatia), and would contain articles on agriculture, history, ethnography, literature, and recent political events.(291)

The petition was endorsed by the Zagreb County Estates, then in session, as a useful means of furthering the development of the national language. The petition was then sent on the Regent's Council in Buda.

The first response of the Regent's Council to Gaj's petition was dated May 1, 1832, and addressed to the Administration of Zagreb County. It asked for more detailed information about the proposed newspaper and the character and qualifications of the editor. A final decision would be made upon the receipt and consideration of the information requested. However, there was little possibility that such a newspaper would be permitted to contain political news.(292)

Now it was up to Gaj to gather as much support as possible for his petition, primarily in the form of letters of recommendation and endorsement from a broad spectrum of local institutions and officials. As for the Council's reservations concerning the inclusion of political news in the newspaper, Gaj should not have been surprised. Jan Kollár had written to him in March expressing pleasure with the newspaper plans, but also counseling that the coverage be more modest and unified, because for the time being a learned and literary journal would be of more use than a political newspaper.(293) Gaj and his friends, however, held fast to their plan. Literature and politics were not easily separated in Croatia in 1832.

Gaj left Zagreb in August and did not return until late November.

In October, Matija Smodek, then an instructor at the Zagreb Academy, asked for permission to give private and free lectures on the Croatian language — *kajkavski* dialect — in one of the Academy rooms, after hours. Permission was granted, informally at first.(294) When the lectures were announced, Magyar students at the Academy, of whom there were many, rose in vigorous protest. Fran Kurelac, then a student of law, fearful that the lectures might be cancelled, drafted twelve theses in Latin, German and *kajkavski* and posted them that night on a window of the Academy building.(295) In the morning they were discovered by a group of students, Derkos among them. Derkos read the proclamations aloud. Here are three examples:

1. Hear ye! A few people who should know well what *lingua patria* means, think that it might mean Hungarian. Won't Europe mock us?
2. Who are the Croats? Peaceful subjects in time of peace, brave warriors in time of war, conquerors of the Avars, Turks and Tartars — free men, not servants of the Hungarians.
3. Every man is born free and every nation has the right, as soon as it is unjustly oppressed by another, to make itself independent. North America separated from England, South America from Spain. We also are not bound forever to Hungary by pitiless fate. If it should come to that, then down with the Hungarians!(296)

The Croatian and Magyar students began to fight. Order was soon restored but this was, as Šišić pointed out, the first violent clash between Croats and Magyars in modern times,(297) and it was sparked by the issue of national language.

Now the Faculty Council had to take a more formal position on Smodek's lectures, and again it approved them. Smodek's first lecture was held on November 6, 1832.(298) It was delivered to a capacity audience of students from the various Zagreb institutions, professors, lawyers, writers, civil servants.(299) In his introductory remarks,(300) Smodek explained how sadly neglected the mother tongue was in Croatia, how foreign languages were still preferred by the educated people, although they had been replaced by the vernacular in other countries. Croatian was a language which tied the Croats to "almost half"(301) of Europe — the Slavs; the Croats should not be ashamed of their mother tongue, instead they should cultivate it.

Although attendance at the lectures dropped off after a while, for many had come in political protest, Smodek continued to give free lectures on the Croatian language at the Zagreb Academy until 1846.(302)

Gaj's long absence puzzled his Zagreb friends. He spent much of the fall in Krapina dealing with family problems(303) and getting local support for his newspaper petition.(304) Smodek wrote to Gaj in early November:

Forgive me. Each day we await you eagerly, but in vain. The first words of every man I meet are: Is Gaj here? When I answer, no, he asks with a flicker of anger: Where is he, then? What is he doing there? What does he find there to do? Is he only sporting with us and leading us by the nose? Every day I pass by your flat and look in, hoping that you have arrived.

Verily I wonder that now, when most important affairs concerning the advancement of our beloved Motherland are debated, you are absent; you, of all people, have failed to return at the time when every man who loves his motherland is doing everything in his power to advance her cause. When it becomes known that there is to be a

> discussion of the affairs of the Motherland, every champion and every opponent of the cause is in attendance, the former endeavoring to promote her fortunes, and the latter, spurred by ignorance or selfish wishes, wishing to bring her to ruin.(305)

November was a month of political ferment in Zagreb. It seemed as if the shadow of political apathy had suddenly lifted.

The Croatian *Sabor* was called to meet in November to choose and instruct deputies to the Joint Parliament. Shortly before the *Sabor* convened, a political pamphlet appeared which opened a new era in Croatian political life. It was entitled *Disertacija iliti razgovor . . .*, (Dissertation or discourse) addressed to the *Sabor* delegates and written by an "old patriot" *(po jednom starom domorodcu),* who was in fact Count Janko Drašković (1770-1856), a Croatian magnate then in his sixties.(306)

"Disertacija" was the first political pamphlet in modern Croatian history written in the national language. Drašković, a *kajkavac,* wrote the document in *štokavski,* or, as he said, "our language" *(naški jezik),* because it was the dialect spoken by the majority of the inhabitants of the Kingdom, and the one with the largest body of printed works. The orthography, explained Drašković, was his own improved version of the orthographies he found in old books. The unusual words, he assured the reader, were not of foreign origin; but are found in "every old dictionary."(307)

Drašković implored the deputies to represent the interests of all of the people of the Kingdom, without regard to religion, and reminded them that their allegiance should be to their fatherland and to their King. He reminded them that the Triune Kingdom had joined the Hungarian Kingdom of its own free will and could not permit an abridgement of its laws; and that the King was the real defender of their rights against the unjust aspirations of the Magyars. The Croatian deputies should make the Hungarians realize that they were not dealing with a Hungarian province, but with a sovereign nation, alive, strong and in possession of a mother tongue which could satisfy all the intellectual, cultural and political needs of a modern state. They, therefore, should not allow Magyar to be forced upon them as the official language of their Kingdom.

The deputies should lay their territorial claims before the King, not the Magyar, they should ask for the return of Dalmatia, the Military Frontier, and, when possible, Bosnia, and suggest that Slovene Illyria(308) be added to the rest. This enlarged Croatian Kingdom which Drašković calls the "Kingdom of Illyria" would then have a population of about four and a half million and would be a strong and grateful member of the Crown. The restoration of Croatian territory should be accompanied by the return to the Ban of his traditional powers and prerogatives.

The Croats themselves could do much to improve their situation. They should follow the example of other, more advanced, European nations and work to improve the social and economic conditions of their Kingdom. To eliminate the domination of foreigners in trade and industry, Croats should be trained in the modern and efficient ways of management; to loosen the hold of foreign capital on the wealth of the nation, the Croats and Hungarians should establish jointly a Hungarian National Bank, which would extend credit and stabilize the currency. "We lie in the centre of Europe, exposed to the threats of East and West," warned Drašković, "and only knowledge can save us."(309)

In this pamphlet Drašković offered the Croats a political program, one which was based on historical tradition but at the same time opened the way to creating a modern, and stronger, Croatian Kingdom, and one which suggested both old and new weapons to use in the growing conflict with the Magyars.

The *Sabor* convened on November 11. Ban Vlašić opened the session by announcing the appointment of the new Captain of the Kingdom, General Rukavina, and the *Sabor* burst into cheers when the General delivered his acceptance speech in Croatian. After several hundred years the Croatian language had returned to the Croatian *Sabor*.(310) The mood of the *Sabor* had changed. In 1830 the delegates had held firmly to the position established in 1790: solidarity with the Magyars. By 1832, the Croatian nobles had realized that they would soon have to defend the very basis of their claim to autonomy, and that this would have to be done with severely limited means, because they had surrendered most of the administrative powers of the Kingdom of Hungary in 1790-1791. Many of Drašković's proposals were debated and his program aroused some vigorous support, but the *Sabor's* final instructions differed little from those of previous years, except on one point. The deputies were to defend the Municipal Laws, they were to demand the return of the lost territories, and they were to hold fast to Latin as the language of the Triune Kingdom. If, however, the Magyars did not show themselves ready to compromise, if they again brought into question the traditional basis of Croatian autonomy, the Croatian deputies were instructed to ask that the law of 1791 (cl. LIX) be rescinded, and that Croatia once again resume the direction of her administration and finances.(311) That Drašković was regarded as a leader and spokesman for the *Sabor* can be seen in the fact that he was one of the deputies chosen to attend the Joint Parliament.

From available documents it is impossible to establish the exact date of the first meeting between Ljudevit Gaj and Count Janko Drašković. Drašković had spent most of 1832 at his country estate near Karlovac. In November when he was chosen a deputy to the Joint Parliament, he asked Ljudevit Vukotinović, the son of an old friend, to serve as his *jurat*.(312) It was customary for the deputies to the Joint Parliament to choose a *jurat* to accompany them as a kind of private secretary or law clerk. This honor was usually limited to young nobles, for it was part of their political and legal apprenticeship. It was most probably through Vukotinović that Drašković met Gaj. In the normal course of their lives these two men, an elderly and distinguished Croatian magnate, and the son of a small town apothecary who had just finished law school, would in all likelihood never have met, for they moved in different worlds. However, both had broken out of their traditional social circles in their concern for their country. The first mention of Count Drašković in Gaj's papers is in a list of errands Gaj had to complete before leaving for Vienna, dated December 1832. Item 22 reads "See Drašković about history."(313) Therefore they had met by December. This was the beginning of a long and rewarding relationship for the two men who were to play a decisive, if not always harmonious role in the formation of the ideas and institutions of the Illyrian Movement.

On November 24, 1832, Gaj submitted a second petition to the Zagreb County Government. He asked for permission to publish a political newspaper which would come out twice a week and have a weekly literary supplement. This petition was endorsed by the Zagreb County Estates, the Minister of Education for Zagreb County, the Zagreb Diocese, the Varaždin County Estates and the town of Križevci,(314) and forwarded to the Regent's Council.

In January 1833, Ljudevit Gaj left for Vienna. He hoped to find support for his petition among Court circles, and, if possible, seek the help of the Emperor. On February 5, Gaj wrote to Rakovac asking whether the new letters of support from the town of Zagreb and the Krizevci Magistrate had been sent on. He wanted all documents in hand before he applied for an audience with the Emperor. Gaj mentioned in the same letter that he had been to see some highly influential Croats, but bemoaned the slow and cumbersome methods of bureaucracy.(315)

The letters must have arrived soon afterward, for on February 14, Gaj wrote a formal letter to Ban Vlašić who was then in Vienna, asking the Ban to arrange an audience for him with the Emperor.(316) Gaj was granted a private audience on May 29. On the same day he submitted his third and final petition, addressed to the Emperor.(317) According to Gaj who recorded the details of the audience in his diary, the old

Emperor Francis received him warmly, surprised to see that the petitioner was such a young man. When Gaj explained the difficulties he had been having with the Hungarian authorities, the Emperor is supposed to have replied:

> Yes, yes, the Hungarians. They make a lot of trouble. They write too much and don't want the Croats to write anything.(318)

Gaj explained the urgency of his appeal: "the nation" had put its trust in him, and the long delay was beginning to undermine it. The Emperor assured Gaj that he would discover where the papers had "got stuck," and make sure that a decision was reached as soon as possible.(319)

The new petition was sent on to the Hungarian Court Chancellery. The Hungarians were most concerned about the political content of the proposed newspaper. It is not clear whether they were afraid of giving the Croats a political voice through the paper, or whether they were simply afraid of not being able to censor effectively. Whatever the reason, the Court Chancellery decided on September 23, 1833, that Gaj's paper could contain political news, provided this news was taken from papers already censored in Hungary and Austria.(320)

On November 12, Count Josef Sedlnitzky, President of the Police Ministry, was asked to gather information on the character and qualifications of the petitioner, and to see whether the Croats were really as strongly in favor of the newspaper as the letters of support indicated. He was to submit his recommendations to the Emperor as soon as the relevant data had been gathered.(321) Sedlnitzky held the documents on his desk for almost six months. It was not until April 1834, that he sent for information from his official correspondents in Croatia.(322) On June 15, Count Sedlnitzky submitted his findings to the Emperor. The information from Croatia, reported Sedlnitzky, described Ljudevit Gaj as a talented, well-educated, financially independent, moral and loyal young man. There appeared to be no reason to assume that he would not be trustworthy and capable of filling the post of editor of the newspaper. As to the need for the newspaper, Croatia was truly one of the less fortunate lands of the Empire. The national language and culture had been sadly neglected, and the events in Hungary were likely to cause a serious reaction in Croatia. It would not be in the Emperor's interest, argued Sedlnitzky, to allow the Croatian language to be replaced by Hungarian. Thus it would be a good moment to grant the Croats a paper in their own language, especially since the project appeared to have almost universal support among the inhabitants of the Croatian counties.(323) The Emperor signed the document granting the permit on July 9th, 1834, and the privilege was formally granted on July 16th.(324)

Ljudevit Gaj remained in Vienna from January to June 1833. Although his major preoccupation during this time was the newspaper, he was also busy gathering new supporters for the national awakening from among the Croatian and Southern Slav students in Vienna, and the *jurats* in Pressburg. The Joint Parliament opened in December 1832. The Croatian *jurats* often came to Vienna for short visits, Vukotinović and Alexander Šuljok among them, and Gaj looked them up. Vukotinović described Gaj's effect on the *jurats,* many of whom had never met Gaj before:

> We received Gaj gladly and when we heard his opinions and plans we praised him enthusiastically. Gifted with eloquence and exuberant imagination, Gaj was truly born for carrying out a mission . . . He was well educated and highly cultured, fiery and fervent. Like an apostle he knew how to inflame his listeners with his language and how, with a clear argument, to convince them of the truth of his statements.(325)

Soon afterward Gaj visited the *jurats* in Pressburg. There he was able to talk at some length with Count Drašković.

The ideas and plans which Gaj discussed with the *jurats,* with Drašković and with the students in Vienna, went far beyond the rather conservative newspaper proposal. The newspaper was meant to satisfy the immediate political and cultural needs of the Triune Kingdom. The ideal of Southern Slav unity, however, was never far from Gaj's mind, as we can see from a poem he wrote in January 1833. In this poem, the second draft of "Još Horvatska ni prepala," Gaj gave poetic form to Drašković's vision of the Kingdom of Illyria. The poem begins:

> No, Croatia has not perished,
> We are in her, still alive
> On ahigh she'll stand, unvanquished,
> When we wake her and revive;
> If in slumber deep she's languished
> When awake in strength she'll thrive,
> If asleep she lies diminished,
> Wait, she'll grow, her shackles rive.(326)

The theme of expansion, however, makes this version different from the first draft (1831).(327)

Croatia still sleeps, continues the poem, but she begins to dream joyful dreams of vigorous youth. She sees all the old counties *(županije)* reborn, the three ancient and glorious provinces *(banovine)* of the Kingdom restored. She sees Carniolans and Carinthians approaching the Croats, claiming they, too, are "old Croats" and "true brothers," deciding to join together to awaken Croatia, to rid themselves of foreign bonds and resurrect the old state and old glory. At the end of the poem there is a giant *kolo* (circle dance) in which all the "brothers" dance and sing together. There we find not only Croats, Slavonians, people from the Military Frontier, Dalmatia and Bosnia — areas which were wholly or in part within medieval Croatia, but there are Styrians, Carniolans and Istrians as well, Southern Slavs who never belonged to the old Croatian state. This version became the hymn of the Illyrian Movement.

Gaj spent many hours in the libraries of Vienna. He was still working on his history of Croatia. He also contacted Kopitar and Vuk Karadžić soon after his arrival, and visited them on several occasions; and met P.J. Šafařík for the first time when Šafařík passed through Vienna on his way to Prague.(328)

Gaj left Vienna for Krapina in June, 1833. The next thirteen months were filled with waiting. Gaj formally withdrew from his position as law clerk, refused the offer of a job as town notary in Varaždin, and his mother began to fear that nothing would ever come of him.(329) He had staked all of his hopes on the newspaper.

During the months of waiting, Gaj decided to obtain a doctorate. He was concerned about his lack of a title now that he was no longer a *jurat.* The name Ljudevit Gaj — Editor, without any symbol of rank or intellectual achievement might be too unimpressive in a land in which formal titles played an important role. The title Doctor — would fill this need. Gaj decided to get his doctorate from the University of Leipzig, for it was one of the few German universities which still conducted its work in Latin,(330) and although Gaj was fluent in German, he had done all of his secondary and university studies in Latin and felt most comfortable using it for academic matters.

Ljudevit Gaj did not take any courses in Leipzig. He went there only for his oral examination. Details of this trip are noted down in a small travel diary. Gaj arrived in Leipzig on the morning of July 8, 1834. On the 9th he paid the examination and doctoral fees, fifty-five talers and eight groschen, and on the 11th, "From 7 to 12 in the morning, from 2 to 6 in the afternoon, I took my doctorate (. . . ich doktorierte.)"(331) He left for home the following day.

Ljudevit Gaj did not write a doctoral dissertation, the University waived this usual requirement on the basis of the works he had already published, and on March 3, 1835, Ljudevit Gaj was awarded the degree of *Dr. phil. tabulis publicis.*(332)

Ljudevit Gaj returned to Zagreb in early October 1834, and rented a large apartment which would serve as his home and the editorial offices of the newspaper. All the preliminary costs of publication — printing, rent, advertising, — were to be paid out of capital, i.e. the remains of the inheritances of Ljudevit and Julijana Gaj. He hoped that the running expenses of the paper would be met by subscriptions. The newspaper was to cost six forints for subscribers in Zagreb, and eight for subscribers from outside of Zagreb. Printing costs were expected to average about 1400 forints a year. With 600 subscribers all expenses could be met with ease; 500 subscribers, at an average of seven forints per subscription, would yield 3500 forints, an adequate though somewhat tight sum. With the optimism of the inexperienced, Gaj and his friends expected that the goal of 600 subscriptions would not be hard to achieve,(333) and that all subscriptions would be paid.

Gaj's editorial assistants and the first regular contributors to the newspaper and literary supplement were drafted from the Gaj circle. In the beginning his closest associates were Dragutin Rakovac, Antun Mažuranić, Vjekoslav Babukić and Ljudevit Vukotinović, and most of the major policy decisions were made jointly. One of the first decisions the "editorial board" had to make was one of the thorniest: was the time right for the introduction of the new orthography and the new literary language? Gaj and his colleagues decided to wait. The greatest number of subscribers were expected to come from among the gentry and clergy of Civil Croatia. They had given strong support to the newspaper petition, but they were, by and large, speakers of *kajkavski* and used to the old orthography. Gaj and his associates feared the loss of their financial support if the language reforms were introduced immediately, therefore the newspaper and literary supplement would begin publication in the old orthography and using the *kajkavski* dialect.

On October 18, Babukić, Mažuranić and Vukotinović drafted separate versions of an "Announcement" *(Oglas)* which defined the purposes and goals of the newspaper and supplement, and called for subscribers. Gaj molded these into a final text, dated October 20, 1834.(334) The "Announcement" was published in 4,000 copies and distributed to interested parties and potential subscribers both within and without the Triune Kingdom.(335)

The "Announcement" was addressed to Southern Slavs of all classes and occupations. It notified them of the forthcoming publication of a newspaper *Novine Horvatzke* (Croatian News) and a literary supplement *Danicza Horvatzka, Slavonzka y Dalmatinzka* (Morning Star of Croatia, Slavonia and Dalmatia).(336) While the description of *Novine* was brief, — it would contain news from home and abroad — *Danicza* was discussed in some detail, for it was to become the mouthpiece of the Illyrian Movement. The purpose of *Danicza,* as defined in the "Announcement," was to entertain the reader and teach him about the entire Southern Slavic community through poems and articles on history, literature, ethnography, etc. *Danicza* would be printed in the *kajkavski* dialect, but it would contain poems and articles in the other Southern Slav dialects.(337)

It was hoped, continued the "Announcement," that *Novine* and *Danicza* would fill a serious gap in the national culture of the Southern Slavs:

> Almost all of the other European peoples have progressed so far in knowledge and science that books and newspapers in their national languages are read and appreciated not only in the courts of the mighty but in the homes of the common people. Is it not time that we, whose glorious ancestors were the defenders and protectors of the whole of Europe, who in the last centuries fought bravely and often for the progress of Humanity, should at last see the language of our own dear Slavic mother, a language which has an abundance of words and a sweetness of expression and which ties us to 80 million Slavic brothers, attain recognition and respect.(338)

The "Announcement" ended with details about cost of a subscription, mailing address, etc. It also invited "patriots" to send poems, articles and news items to the offices of the newspaper. The "Announcement" was signed:

Dr. Ljudevit Gaj
Publisher and Editor
The National Croatian Newspaper
Under the Royal and Imperial Franchise

CHAPTER VI

THE ILLYRIAN MOVEMENT BEGINS (1835)

There has been some disagreement among Croatian historians about which year the Illyrian Movement began. F. Fancev argued in favor of 1832, D. Šurmin and S. Ježić chose 1836, J. Šidak prefers 1835.(339) I tend to agree with Šidak. The year 1832 is too early, for there was not yet anything which could be called a Movement. While 1836 was the year in which the Illyrian platform was officially proclaimed in *Danica,* the year in which the new literary language was introduced, and the Southern Slavs were called upon to work toward cultural unity, historians tend to forget that the "Manifesto of 1836," in which Gaj first enunciated the goals of the Illyrian Movement, was actually written and published in December of 1835. It seems reasonable, therefore, to say that the Illyrian Movement began in 1835 with the publication of *Novine* and *Danica.*(340)

Novine and, more particularly, *Danica* gave Gaj and his circle a platform from which they could propagandize for the national awakening, gather supporters, and prepare their reading public for the reception of the language reform and Illyrian ideas. Throughout 1835 the readers of *Danica* were presented with a series of articles on language and history, on the development of other Slavic peoples, and descriptions of the various branches of the Southern Slavs — all of which led step by step to the Illyrian program of 1836. As the year progressed "Illyrian" was used more and more often as a synonym for Southern Slav. From the thirty-sixth issue on, the contributors to *Danica* began to be identified by the editor as "an Illyrian from Croatia," "an Illyrian from Styria," "an Illyrian from Slavonia," until by the forty-second issue, the majority of the articles and poems were signed in this manner. Gaj and his colleagues took certain liberties in assigning the title "Illyrian from . . ." for it implied that the author was sympathetic with the goals of *Danica* and, later, the Illyrian Movement, which was not always the case. For example, the author of the poem ''Sloga i nesloga,'' was identified as ''Ferić — an Illyrian from Dubrovnik.''(341) The poem was actually taken from a collection of Ferić's works published in 1794, and the author had been dead since 1820.(342) What is most important, however, is that Gaj, his friends and collaborators and some new supporters did sign themselves ''Illyrian.'' Therefore from 1835 on, it is no longer necessary to speak of the ''Gaj circle.'' We can call this group by the name they called themselves — Illyrians.

The first issue of *Novine Horvatzke* appeared on January 6, 1835, and the first issue of *Danicza Horvatzka, Slavonzka y Dalmatinzka* on January 10. Due to the restrictions placed by the newspaper franchise on the political content of *Novine,* it began its life as a rather colorless publication, almost totally devoid of news analysis, except in excerpts from approved papers. No statement of editorial policy was made. The paper contained local items, reports from Austria and Hungary, and news was gathered somewhat haphazardly at the beginning of 1835, but by the end of the year a network of local correspondents had already sprung up.(343) Local reports included announcements of the meetings of the local County Estates and of the Croatian *Sabor,* appointments and promotions, prices and markets for grain and other agricultural produce, descriptions of natural disasters, and announcements of cultural events. All other news was taken directly from newspapers already censored in Vienna and Buda. Among the most used sources were *Augsburger Allegemein Zeitung, Hirlap, Hirnök, Oesterreichischer Beobachter, Pressburger Deutsche Zeitung, Srpske Novine* and *Wiener Zeitung.* The only real freedom alloted the editor of *Novine* came in his selection or rejection of articles to be used. For example, Gaj consistently included news from the Ottoman Empire in the section devoted to news of the world, whereas coverage of events in Western Europe tended to be more spotty.

The bulk of the work on *Novine* consisted of selecting, translating and editing articles from the approved newspapers. Gaj did most of this himself the first year, but by the end of 1835 more and more of the tedious work was passed on to his editorial assistant, Dragutin Rakovac. Gaj's other assistants, Antun Mažuranić and Vjekoslav Babukić, were employed elsewhere and could devote only their free time to editorial duties.(344) Rakovac worked full time and was the only salaried assistant; the others received small sums at irregular intervals.(345)

Danica was by far the more important of the two publications. It was a literary supplement and supposedly apolitical. However, from its very first issue, *Danica* was the organ of the Illyrian Movement. Both *Novine* and *Danica* were subject to strict censorship. Each edition had to be presented to the Zagreb censor before and after publication.(346) It soon became obvious, however, that political material could pass the censor if it was cloaked in literary phrases and made sufficiently ambiguous.(347)

In 1835 Gaj was not only the editor of *Danica,* he was also one of its chief contributors. Almost every issue had an article or poem by Gaj, the articles often in two or more installments, and there were also many unsigned bits and pieces he put in fill space.(348) Although he did not do all of the editorial work himself, only his name appeared on the masthead.

Each issue of *Danica* began with a motto, such as that of the first issue in 1835:

> A nationality without nationalism
> Is like a body without bones (Croatian Proverb)

Most issues were four pages long. Very occasionally this would be stretched to six. *Danica* ordinarily began with one or two poems, generally more distinguished for their patriotism than artistic qualities.(349) These would be followed by several short articles of a mixed nature: information about other Southern Slavs, biographical notes on Russian or Serbian rulers, brief stories and anecdotes from the Slavic world, and letters from subscribers. Long articles were continued for three or four issues. *Danica* would close with literary news from the Slavic lands, wise sayings or proverbs often from the collections of Pavel Ritter Vitezović and Dositej Obradović, or a *Nětilo* (brief pointed comment) often by Gaj, emphasizing some aspect of nationalism or patriotism, as for example "Naj lěpši orszag" (The Most Beautiful Country):

> Where can it be found? I have heard a thousand people answer this question in different ways. Only one answer can stand before the judgement of a true patriot. The most beautiful country in the world . . is the beloved homeland, to which all wishes, hopes, and endeavors are bound. Here the patriot has his cradle and his grave. Here all and everything whether he be in the chill north mid snow and ice, or in the warm areas and forest streams and fragrant flowers, whether in the plains of Poland or the mountains of Switzerland. Everywhere blood is shed for her. To each true man the homeland is the most beautiful and the only country in which he wants to live and die. The homeland is like a clean conscience. Only there do you find true peace and happiness.(350)

Only there do you find true peace and happiness.(350) The articles which Gaj wrote for *Danica* in 1835 are extremely important, for through them he gradually introduced his readers to the goals and ideas of the Illyrian Movement. These 1835 articles, the few he wrote in

1836, and Gaj's *Proglas* (Manifesto) for every year of publication, are among the most important sources for the Illyrian ideology between 1835 and 1841. Therefore it will be useful to examine the more important 1835 articles in some detail.

Although *Novine* and *Danica* began publication in the old orthography of Civil Croatia, Gaj hoped to introduce his reformed alphabet as quickly as possible. There were two major problems to consider. Would the new orthography alienate the conservative Croats and endanger the life of the newspaper by reducing the number of subscribers? Would the shift to the new orthography endanger the newspaper franchise? As a concession to the first, Gaj and his colleagues decided to retain the old orthography in *Novine* throughout the first year, for it was theoretically the most important of the two, and to use *Danica* to introduce the reformed alphabet. As to the second concern, there was no specific statement in the newspaper, although the proposed title was written with the old orthography. Gaj would simply have to wait for an opportune moment and that soon came.

Emperor Francis I died on March 2, 1835. His son and heir, Emperor Ferdinand, was mentally retarded and although he was capable of signing state documents and performing the simpler ceremonial duties, the actual power usually exercised by the Emperor passed to other hands. The confusion and struggle for power among members of the Royal family and the top Court offficials would surely preoccupy the Austrian and Hungarian authorities for a while, and it was quite probable that the change from one orthography to another by a literary supplement of a small newspaper in one of the more remote areas of the Empire would escape notice. Gaj must have reasoned along these lines, for the death of the Emperor and the introduction of the Gaj orthography were too closely linked in time to be coincidental.(351) The death of the Emperor was announced in the March 7th issue of *Danica.* In the next, the March 14th issue, we find the first installment of Gaj's final statement on the question of alphabet reform ''Pravopisz'' (Orthography), and two poems printed in the new orthography.

''Pravopisz'',(352) Gaj's second treatise on orthography, differed in many ways from *Kratka osnova.* The orthography was significantly changed, and Gaj's arguments in support of the reform had a different emphasis. In *Kratka osnova* Gaj merely hinted at the possibility that all the Southern Slav dialects might merge into one modern literary language. ''Pravopisz'' began with the assumption that such a development was inevitable and desired by all true patriots, and that it was only necessary now to devise the best method for the accomplishment of the goal — the shaping of a modern Southern Slav literary language.(353)

The first step, argued Gaj, should be clear to everyone: the introduction of a reformed Latin orthography. According to Gaj, the dialects of the people living in the lands of old Illyria resembed little streams which flowed in many directions to one river. The stream beds had been dug by foreigners attempting to divert the water to their own use. They represented the various Latin orthographies used by the Southern Slavs, and the river was the Illyrian language. Once the old orthographies were discarded and a uniform orthography was adopted, all the little streams would merge into one large stream, capable of carrying large boats to the river. The river, the Illyrian language, was one of four great rivers, the four Slavic "dialects," which flowed into the common Slavic sea. This tortuous analogy is quite typical of Gaj's style.

The forms of the new orthography, continued Gaj, should not be strange and new, but based on tradition. Gaj described the contemporary orthographies of the Dalmatians, Croats and Slovenes in which old forms were mixed with foreign borrowings, and explained that there are manuscripts and books by old writers such as Vitezović in the Library of the Zagreb Bishop, written and printed in orthographies infinitely better than the ones presently in use.(354) The new orthography must get rid of distorting foreign influences, it must draw on the traditional practices of the Southern Slavs and, when these are inadequate, on the reformed orthographies of the other Slavs. Gaj proposed that the Southern Slavs who used the Latin alphabet adopt the solution used by the Dalmatians and Slovenes for the soft d, l, and n, and write these as dj, lj and nj. When there was no precedent in the old or present day Southern Slav Latin orthography for the clear and unambiguous expression of certain sounds, the Illyrians should borrow from the orthographies of the other Slavs who used the Latin alphabet. He suggested taking the č, š, and ž, used by the Czechs, Moravians and Slovaks, and the ć used by the Poles,(355) Thus he explained the č, š, and ž, the only reforms kept from *Kratka osnova.* The ć had not been discussed in *Kratka osnova* because the orthography proposed there was designed for the *kajkavski* dialect and *kajkavski* does not have the ć sound.

The new orthography would also have to find a solution for the different treatment of the "jat" sound in *ekavski, ijekavski* and *ikavski.* This had not been a problem in *Kratka osnova,* for *kajkavski* is *ekavski,* as is Slovene. The *čakavski* dialect includes both *ekavski* and *ikavski,* and *štokavski* has all three variations. Gaj proposed that the Illyrians write the "jat" sound as ě, and pronounce it in the manner to which they were accustomed: *bělo* (white) would be spoken as *bijelo* in the *ijekavski* area, *belo* by the speakers of *ekavski,* and *bilo* by those who used *ikavski.* This was a compromise measure, and the ě became one of the most controversial aspects of the new orthography.(356)

Some people might see these proposals as an attack upon tradition, concluded Gaj, unaware that the reforms were in fact drawn from Illyrian and Slavic sources, and that the bastardized, foreign-influenced orthographies still in use signified a more radical break with the past:

> To those . . . who accuse us of trying to destroy antiquity we pose a question instead of an answer. Of what does antiquity consist? Is it based upon age or upon custom? We have many customs which are not really old, and others which we view as new and strange are our legal inheritance from past ages.(357)

Therefore Gaj called upon the Southern Slavs who used the Latin alphabet to adopt his reformed orthography, by presenting it as a return to the uncorrupted past. He had obviously taken to heart Šafařík's warning about the danger of too rapid innovation.(358)

Gaj's reformed orthography was put to immediate use. More and more poems and articles were printed in it, and from the twenty-ninth issue on, *Danica* was printed exclusively in the new alphabet. Gaj could then turn his attention to the next task: proving to the Croats that the cultivation of their mother tongue was essential to their survival as a nation.

Gaj deliberately used the old orthography for the last time in his *kajkavski* article "Nima domorodztva prez lyubavi materinzkoga jezika." (There is no patriotism without love for the mother tongue), which appeared in *Danica* in May and was addressed specifically to the Croats of Civil Croatia.(359)

There are some Croats, began Gaj, who call themselves patriots and prefer to speak foreign languages. They deceive themselves. "Only those whose hearts are filled with love and respect for the Croatian language can think and feel as true Slavs and Croats."(360) Their mother tongue deserves respect, for it is part of the great "Slavic language," which is spoken by 80 million people in an area which covers half of Europe, and the Slavic language is "the key to the edifice of European languages."(361) By emphasizing the "Europeanness" and the breadth of the Slavic world, Gaj was trying to show the Croats that they belonged to a "nation" which was many times the size of Hungary, and that they spoke an Indo-European language, which the Magyars did not.(362)

What then is patriotism?

> Patriotism, in the broadest sense of the word, is the faithfulness of the nation to itself and of individuals to the nation. A nation is faithful to itself if it develops its own natural personality, cultivates its natural characteristics in its own manner, and endeavors, by the patriotic path, to reach the noble heights worthy of mankind . . .(363)

The nation, to Gaj, was a living being, a natural unit with its own personality. Humanity was divided into nations, and it was the duty of each nation to develop to its full potential. This was a concept of unity and diversity, each individual unit developing in its own way and forming together a rich and varied whole.(364)

What then of the individual patriot? Gaj explains:

> An individual is faithful to the nation if he endeavors to preserve and to improve the life of his nation within himself, if in his inner intentions as well as in his external action he does what is within his power to increase and spread the merits of his people.(365)

This reminds one a little of the Christian concept of faith and good works. Not only must the individual act publicly to advance the cause of his nation, but he must do it sincerely and constantly. Neither the task of public nor private patriotism, continues Gaj, can be carried on without love for the mother tongue.

To Gaj the mother tongue and the nation are inseparable:

> It is in language, above all things, that the life of the nation is reflected. Spirit and language are organically and inseparably united. Language is actually spirit making itself evident.(366)

Just as a child's understanding of the world finds its first, spontaneous expression in words, he argues, the spirit of the nation is reflected in the language of the nation, for they are joined as soul and body. While it is useful to know foreign languages it is dangerous, indeed fatal, if these are spoken to the exclusion of the mother tongue — the nation is thus robbed of its consciousness. Under such conditions, says Gaj, foreign languages become the gangrene of national development.

Each nation's level of enlightenment, continues Gaj, can be measured by the quality of its national language. An enlightened and free nation will have a language which reflects the inner harmony of its people. The language of an enslaved people will reflect their bondage. The spirit of the nation is expressed in its language: language is the external manifestation of the fact that the nation exists:

> A nation has nothing holier nor dearer than its natural language, for it is only through language that a nation, as a particular society, continues or vanishes.(367)

Croatia has not perished, says Gaj, nor will she as long as she has a national language. But the Croatian language has been sorely neglected. The educated and wealthy speak and think in foreign languages. A wall has come between them and the common people:

> To an egoistic renegade or turncoat the mother tongue is coarse because it is the language of the people who plough. To him the

> mother tongue is unworthy because it is spoken by the people who tend his vines . . . He does not regard his compatriots as his brothers, but as his servants whom he treats badly.(368)

For the fact that the mother tongue has become the almost exclusive property of the peasants, and that it has not developed into a mature literary language Gaj offers the following explanation: the common people, cut off from their educated brothers are ignorant, and the language they speak mirrors the condition of their lives:

> The mother tongue becomes rough and poor when it is banished from the palaces and the families of the wealthy nobles to the thatched roofs, and at last to the chimney corner where a worthy old man or perhaps a good old woman raises shaking hands to heaven praying for better times.(369)

Gaj's closing words call to the Croats to resurrect their mother tongue:

> So it is indeed time that we unite, that we return to the mother tongue its natural rights so that at least our grandsons will again be able to understand their honorable grandfathers, for it is through the medium of language that our ancestors speak to us and make known their great deeds . . . It is the one great living monument, more enduring than all the marble pillars. He who would tear down the marble pillars would indeed be considered a cruel enemy of the people. How then can a man who does not love his mother tongue . . . be considered a patriot?(370)

The warning is clear: if the Croats permit their mother tongue to die through neglect and be replaced by Magyar, their nation will disappear with it.

This, then, is a political article, although it purports to talk solely of language. Gaj's ideas are not original. They echo statements about the interrelationship of language and nationality made by Herder, Schleiermacher, Fichte, Schlegel and others.(371) Gaj was not a philosopher, nor did he pretend to be. The arguments used in "Nima domorodztva" are relatively simple, and Gaj's numerous illustrations of specific points are quite repetitive. He was trying to force into the minds of his *kajkavski* readers the realization that they did not have a modern literary language, that such a language would be a useful weapon against the Magyars, and that their new literary language could, if properly made, link them to a much larger group — the Slavs.

Although "Nima Domorodztva," "Pravopisz," the "Oglasz" of 1835, and *Kratka osnova* all mentioned that the Croats were part of the greater Slavic community, this aspect of the Illyrian ideology was not clearly stated until the second half of 1835, in a series of articles run in six consecutive issues. The first of these is a translation of Herder's description of the Slavs from his *Ideen zur Philosophie der Geschichte der Menschheit* (1784-1791).(372) This clearly indicates that Gaj was not only familiar with Herder's ideas, but that he thought them essential for an understanding of what was to follow in his own article "Naš narod" (Our People), and Šafařík's article "Značaj i izobraženosti Slavskoga naroda u obćinskom," (About the Character and Culture of the Slavs in General).(373)

Gaj's article "Naš narod" is of special interest to us because it clearly enunciates the Pan-Slav aspect of his ideology and, at the same time, defines his conception of what he was to call "Greater Illyria." The people (narod) of which he speaks are the Slavs:

> A huge giant lies across half of Europe. The top of his head is bathed in the blue Adriatic. His immense legs reach across the northern ice and snow to the walls of China. In his strong right hand, stretched through the heart of the Turkish Empire, he carries the Black Sea, and in the left, extended through the heart of the German lands, he holds the Baltic. His head is Central Illyria, wreathed with the flowers of the warm south, his chest Hungary, his breasts the Carpathian mountains. His heart lies beneath the old Tatra mountains, his stomach is the Polish plain and his belly and legs the immeasurable expanse of Russia. This giant is our nation, the Slavic nation, the largest in Europe.(374)

There is no common Slavic kingdom, but there is a Slavic nationality. The Germans, says Gaj, are in a similar position, for though they live in many separate states, they identify their nationality not as Bavarian, or Austrian, but as German. The Slavs are only now beginning to realize the immense size and potential of the Slavic nationality. They must become familiar with the major branches of the Slavs, their dialects, customs, history and literature. The only clear way to distinguish between the various Slavs, explains Gaj, is by language. They can thus be divided into four smaller or two larger categories: A — The dialect spoken by the inhabitants of 1) Greater Illyria, 2) Greater Bohemia, 3) Greater Poland, 4) Greater Russia; or B — 1) Southeastern Slavs (Russians and Illyrians), and 2) Northeastern Slavs (Czechs and Poles).(375) The first four categories are adapated from Kollár, but with a special twist: Kollár simply calls the dialects Polish, Russian, Czecho-Slovak and Illyrian, while Gaj assigns them geographical identities.(376) The secomd group of categories comes from Šafařík,(377) the major difference being that Gaj calls all of the Southern Slavs Illyrians.

Gaj identifies the inhabitants of Greater Illyria as: Croats; Slavonians; Slavs of lower Hungary; Slovenes of lower Styria, Carniola, Catinthia and Istria; Slavs of Bosnia, Montenegro, Hercegovina,

Dubrovnik, Serbia and Bulgaria.(378) Gaj's greater Illyria is thus considerably larger than the Kingdom of Illyria envisioned by Drašković, which was to include Croatia, Slavonia, Dalmatia, Bosnia, the Austrian "Kingdom of Illyria," and the Military Frontier,(379) and quite similar to Vitezović's "Croatia rediviva," made up of Croatia (Croatia, Dalmatia, Slavonia, Slovene lands and Bosnia), Serbia, Macedonia, Bulgaria, Thrace, Hungary, Sarmathia and Venedicum.(380)

In the last three months of 1835 Gaj wrote or edited a series of articles on folk poetry. It is interesting that while he could express himself clearly and without too much dependence on recognized scholars on questions such as orthography, the role of language in the preservation of national identity, and the Slavs, there is not one original article in the series on folk poetry.

The first article "Nešto verhu narodnoga pěsničtva u občinskom," (Something about Folk Poetry in General) is adapated from a longer work by J. Wenzig.(381) It tells of the recent interest in folk poetry and the realization by Herder and his followers that folk poetry can be a valuable source of literary tradition, especially for a nationality which lacks an extensive body of written literature. Folk poetry, it explains, is the record of the nationality, developed by the common people over many centuries. The Illyrian Slavs should be proud of their folk poetry for it is among the richest and most diverse in Europe. No man, no Illyrian, should consider himself a patriot unless he is familiar with the folk poetry of his nationality. The last comment is undoubtedly Gaj's own interpolation.(382)

The second article, "Slavske narodne pěsme" (Slavic Folk Poetry), adapated by Gaj from Šafařík,(383) began by saying that twenty years ago there was not one collection of original Slavic poetry. Since then various Slavic patriots had begun to collect the oral literature of their native areas, and found that Slavic folk poems compared most favorably with those of other European nationalities. For the Slavs, explained the article, such collections served as mirrors of their nationality, they taught the Slavs about themselves, their history, their customs and their Slavic brothers. Most Slavs had lived for centuries under foreign rule, their mother tongue neglected by the educated people who wrote in foreign languages. Only in the remote hills and quiet valleys was the literary tradition of the Slavs preserved — in the folk poetry of the common people. A Slavic renaissance had now begun. It was time for all true Slavs to seek out this folk poetry, to write it down before it disappeared, to make collections of it for future generations.

Both of these articles seemed to be leading to the third, "Sbirke narodnih slavenskih pěsamah," (Collections of Slavic Folk Poetry), unsigned, but apparently written by Gaj for the original text is in his handwriting. It is impossible to tell whether it is an adaptation or a compilation. The article discusses in detail various collections of Slavic folk poetry,(384) and in particular the four volumes of Karadžić's Serbian folk poetry. The only other item in this issue is the poem "Car Lazar i Carica Milica" from this collection. Gaj explained that this was the first of a series of folk poems from the same collection which would be published in *Danica.* Illyrian folk poetry, said Gaj, had been widely praised for its beauty and had already been translated into many foreign languages. The Illyrian folk poems reflected the bravery of the Illyrian people, their tribulations under foreign oppression, their freedom of spirit, their turbulent history and their love of music. The article ended with the hope that the Illyrians of upper and central Illyria (the Slovenes and the Croats) would take the example of their southern brothers to heart, and begin collections of the folk poetry of their regions.

The December 12th issue of *Danica* contained an anonymous article entitled "Něšto o dogodovščini talianskoga jezika,"(385) (Something about the History of the Italian Language), a curious mixture of fact and propaganda. The writer of the article — Gaj — begins with the statement that the Italians were once in the same predicament as the Illyrians: the Italian educated classes spoke Latin while the common people spoke a variety of dialects. Then a few patriots decided that this was wrong, that there should be a modern literary language for all of Italy, and they chose for this language the dialect of Tuscany, the sweetest and most musical of all of the dialects in which the first great authors had written, and as the name for this language they selected the neutral and ancient term "Italian." Gaj then asked:

> Brother Illyrians, when will we, inhabitants of the old, great and world famous Illyria, throw away our prejudices and self-deception and follow the glorious example of our neighbors. We thank the Almighty that we do not have fifteen dialects as the Italians, but only Serbian, Croatian and Slovene. With the other Illyrians we will rid ourselves of this selfish patriotism and then all trouble, disharmony, dismemberment . . . will cease, and the world will know that in Illyria it is clear day. Books for the common people can be written in the local dialects, but let educated and cultured Illyria have a mature and sweet language and a single literature, as her neighbor, Italy. Let us open our eyes!(386)

Gaj is clearly setting the stage for "Proglas" to follow in the next issue, in which he invokes the ancient name Illyrian for the Southern Slavs, and chooses for the modern Illyrian language the *ijekavski* form of the *štokavski* dialect, generally considered by the Southern Slavs to be the most pleasing to the ear and possessed of a rich body of literature in the works of the Dalmatian renaissance.

The first version of "Proglas" (Manifesto), a statement of editorial policy for the coming year, was published in *Danica* on December 5th, and the second on December 29th.(387) The versions are almost identical except for one important point. The December 5th "Proglas" announced that in the interest of Illyrian unity the title of *Danica* would be changed from *Danica Horvatska, Slavonska i Dalmatinska* to *Danica ilirska* (Morning Star of Illyria), and that it would henceforth be printed exclusively in the new literary language and orthography. In the December 29th "Proglas" it was announced that *Novine Horvatske* had changed its name to *Ilirske narodne novine* (Illyrian National Newspaper), and would join *Danica* in the new program. Gaj may have delayed the Illyrianization of *Novine* until he saw whether the announced change in *Danica* provoked a strong negative reaction.

"Proglas" is an important document. It is the first of a series of annual manifestos in which Gaj, as editor, explains, justifies and later reaffirms the basic ideas of the Illyrian Movement. The first few "Proglas's" would talk only about the cultural aspects of the Movement — language, literature, Pan-Slavism, etc. — but from 1839 they would also include political material of relevance to the Triune Kingdom.

"Proglas" (1835) began with an analogy. Europe, said Gaj, may be compared to a girl seated and holding a lyre in her lap. The lyre was Illyria, and the three corners of the instrument represented Skutari, Varna and Villach. The strings of the lyre were the provinces and states inhabited by Illyrians: Carinthia, Carniola, Styria, Istria, Croatia, Slavonia, Dalmatia, Dubrovnik, Bosnia, Montenegro, Serbia, Bulgaria and Southern Hungary, or as Gaj identified this group in "Naš Narod," — Greater Illyria.(388) In the past, continued Gaj, this lyre was in tune, when suddenly from the south there came a terrible hurricane (the Turks), from the north a powerful wind (the Austrians and Hungarians). The strings of the lyre were loosened and no longer rang out in harmony. Here Gaj clearly assumed that the Southern Slavs had once shared a common cultural and political past, that they were the descendents of the ancient Illyrians, and that their former unity was shattered by foreign conquest.

By shifting the focus of Croatian attention away from the weak Triune Kingdom to membership in a community of Southern Slavs — Illyria, and of "the largest nation in Europe,"(389) — the Slavs, Gaj was developing a weapon the Croats could use against Magyar pressures, reminding them that they need no longer feel fragmented and powerless, for while a minority within Hungary, they belonged to the Illyrian nation which stretched across the Balkan peninsula, and dwarfed the Magyar nation.

The Illyrians must become aware, argued Gaj, of their common past, and build a modern national culture through the medium of a common literary language, a culture which would be based on this shared heritage. The "Illyrian Press"(390) *(Novine* and *Danica)* would:

> . . . endeavour in this spirit to direct all the Illyrian intellectual forces toward one goal and to unite them in the performance of a common cultural task.(391)

All that was said about *Novine* in "Proglas" was that it would carry local and foreign news; *Danica,* on the other hand, was discussed in a long paragraph. It was to be a "Slavo-Illyrian" publication: it would contain articles about the history and literature of all the Slavs and, through discussions of the history, geography, statistics, oral and written literature of Greater Illyria, the readers of *Danica* would learn about their fellow ". . . Illyrians or Southern Slavs: Serbs, Croats and Slovenes."(392) It is interesting to note that Gaj here used "Southern Slavs" (južnih Slavjana) as a synonym for Illyrians. He later rejected this term, considering it ambiguous and inaccurate.(393)

As to the new literary language, nowhere in "Proglas" (1835) did Gaj state explicitly that the Illyrian literary language was to be based on the *štokavski* dialect, that this dialect was not the traditional dialect of Civil Croatia, and that it had been chosen because it was spoken by the majority of the inhabitants of the Triune Kingdom, the lands the Croats hoped to regain in the future, and the Serbs. The Illyrian language was presented as an all-Illyrian phenomenon:

> In Illyria there can be only one true literary language. We do not seek it in any one locality or state but in all of Greater Illyria. The Germans molded the dialects of the whole of Germany into their literary language, the Italians wove their sweet word from all the dialects of Italy. The whole of Illyria is our grammar and our dictionary. In this large garden there are always beautiful flowers; let us gather the best into a wreath, and this wreath of our nation will never wither, but grow even richer and lovelier.(394)

The reader could perceive the language Gaj was discussing only in the language of "Proglas" itself — the Illyrian version of the *štokavski* dialect.

Gaj ended "Proglas" with an attempt to anticipate the objections to his Illyrian program. Without mentioning that the new language was based upon *štokavski,* he admitted that some people might claim that this was an attempt to Serbize the Illyrians, others, apparently referring here to the *kajkavski* and *čakavski* Croats and the Slovenes, would complain because their dialect was not chosen, still others might call this new language artificial. Had the Germans and the Italians raised such questions, argued Gaj, their literary languages would never have developed. "Proglas" concluded with the plea that all patriots join together in support of the new language and Illyrian program, and that they never forget, be they Croat, Serb or Slovene, that they are also Slavs and Illyrians.(395)

The readers of *Danica* became acquainted with the vocabulary of the new literary language through a brief dictionary "Sbirka někojih rěčih koje su ili u gornjoj ili u dolnjoj Ilirii pomanje poznane," (A Collection of words less known in Upper or Lower Illyria), which was published in place of the last two issues of *Danica.*(396) In most cases the word was given its Latin and German equivalent, thus indicating the dependence of the Southern Slavs on foreign languages for unambiguous definitions, for example:

Baš, recte, accurate, just, gerade.
Bezbožan, žna, o, impius, gottlos
Hulim, iti. vitupero, beschimpfen(397)

In a few instances a *štokavski* word was also given its *kajkavski* equivalent, or a *kajkavski* word its *štokavski* equivalent, e.g.,

Ćorda, e, v. sablja
Beteg, a, m, v. bolest(398)

The first Illyrian grammar, "Osnova slovnice Slavjanske narěčja Ilirskoga" (Basic Slavic Grammar of the Illyrian Dialect), was published in consecutive issues of *Danica* for March and April of 1836.(399)

The Illyrian literary language was not identical with the Croato-Serbian of today. The Illyrian language was, first of all, conceived as a literary language for all of the Southern Slavs, not just the Croats, or the Croats and Serbs. It was based on the *ijekavski* variant of the *štokavski* dialect, as was Vuk Karadžić's new Serbian literary language, but there were important differences between the Illyrian and the new Serbian in grammar, orthography and vocabulary.

Karadžić based his Serbian language on the *štokavski* dialect of Hercegovina. In his codification of paradigms he exhibited great respect for the living, growing language, accepting certain forms which differed from the traditional written *štokavski,* such as the ending for the dative, locative and instrumental plural: (d) ženama, (l) ženama, (i) ženama, in place of the traditional, (d) ženam, (l) ženah, (i) ženama.(400) The Illyrians kept the older form because it was strongly rooted in the vernacular and literary tradition of the *kajkavski* and *čakavski* dialects, and Slovene.(401)

The Illyrian orthography (Gaj's orthography of 1835) differed from Karadžić's. Both Karadžić and Gaj, one for the Cyrillic the other for the Latin alphabet, used the phonemic orthography, i.e. each sound was represented by one symbol. However, in the question of spelling, i.e. the relationship between the spoken word and its graphic equivalent, the system of Karadžić was phonemic: he based the spelling upon the patterns and rules of the spoken language, and Gaj's was morphophomenic: in composites and derivatives the original graphics of various parts were preserved. While Karadžić told his followers "Piši kako govoriš" (Write as you speak), the Illyrians countered with "Govori za uši, a piši za oči" (Speak for the ears and write for the eyes).(402) This is perhaps best seen in the following examples:

Illyrian morphophonemic spelling	*Vuk's phonemic spelling*
iz-kidati (izkidati)	iskidati
raz-pravljati (razpravljati)	raspravljati
slad-ka (sladka)	slatka

The vocabulary of the Illyrian language was not based on the vernacular of any specific area,(403) whereas Karadžić's Serbian was. Though predominantly *štokavski,* the Illyrian vocabulary included words from *kajkavski, čakavski,* Slovene and even other Slavic languages: Russian, Czech and Polish. The Illyrian grammarians and writers were not satisfied with a vocabulary based on a peasant vernacular, even if it did have a rich oral tradition. They needed a language which could be put to immediate use in the Croatian *Sabor,* the Academy, the law courts, for the introduction of modern technology; in short, for a political, intellectual and economic life on a more complex level than that of a Hercegovinian village. Thus they borrowed from other dialects and Slavic languages when *štokavski* did not have an appropriate word, and when that vast reservoir did not suffice, they made up a new word.(404)

It is often said, that when the Croats accepted Gaj's orthography and his choice of *štokavski* for their literary language they joined their national destiny to the destiny of the Serbs, that that was the true meaning of the Croats' willingness to create a common literary language. This is only partly true. At any rate, it took the common literary language more than sixty years to assume its final form.

In the "Literary Agreement" (Književni dogovor) of 1850, drawn up in Vienna and signed by Karadžić and leading Croatian literary figures (Gaj was not among them)(405),the Croats and the Serbs decided that the *ijekavski* variant of the *štokavski* dialect would become the literary language of the two nationalities. The participants in the "Dogovor" gave the following reasons for their decision: the *ijekavski* variant of the *štokavski* was spoken by the majority of the people, it was closer to other Slavic languages than any other variant, the bulk of the folk poetry was in it, the Dubrovnik poets had used it, and it had already been accepted by the majority of Croatian and Serbian writers.(406) This did not end the controversy in Croatia between the supporters of the Illyrian language and the supporters of the Illyrian language and the supporters of Karadžić's reforms, it merely created a middle ground between them.(407) It was not until 1892 that Gaj's orthography was slightly revised and the morphophenemic spelling replaced by Karadžić's phomenic spelling. This was followed in 1899 by the Croats agreeing to use the *štokavski* dialect as spoken in Hercegovina, but, ironically, by that time the Serbs had rejected Karadžić's *ijekavski* in favor of the variant more widely used in Serbia, *ekavski,* so that even today the Serbian and Croatian languages differ, and the literary language of the Croats, *ijekavski,* is called Croato-Serbian, and that of the Serbs, *ekavski,* Serbo-Croatian.

By the end of 1835, the editorial offices of *Novine* had become the center of the national awakening. Letters poured in to Gaj from Drašković and others attending the Joint Parliament, from Šafařík and Kollár, from students in Graz, Vienna, Pest and Osijek, from sympathizers in the Triune Kingdom, Slovene Provinces, Southern Hungary and even Bosnia.(408) They spoke in glowing terms of the importance of *Novine* and *Danica,* of their hopes for Illyrian unity, of the specific problems facing Illyrians in the various areas.

If one judged from the letters alone, *Novine* and *Danica* were a success. Yet there were only 520 subscribers by the end of 1835, and not all of these subscriptions were paid.(409) The going is always difficult for a new publication in its first years of life, but the problems of any periodical or newspaper seeking more than local circulation in the Triune Kingdom in 1835 were enormous.

The overwhelming majority of the population were illiterate. Most of the townspeople were foreigners. Nobles were interested in foreign newspapers, but a "local" paper and literary supplement had less appeal. Students and young professional people, the best source of support, had little money to spend.

Communications were poor. The Triune Kingdom had no large urban settlements. Towns along the regular postal routes: Zagreb-Varaždin-Vienna, Zagreb-Ljubljana-Triest, Zagreb-Sisak-Slavonia, were relatively well served: the Zagreb-Vienna post left daily, others went from one to three times a week. Towns or villages farther away from these main lines received mail only when private parties were willing to take the mail along.(410) The weakest lines of communication were with Dalmatia, Serbia and Bosnia. Today's Yugoslavia, an area somewhat smaller than Gaj's Greater Illyria, was then a mozaic of Hungarian, Austrian, and Turkish administrative and political units. Towns which were less than a hundred miles away from each other could have been half a continent apart in terms of ease of communications. Mail service to other parts of the Habsburg Empire also ran into difficulties. For example, in a letter dated March 5th, 1835, P.J. Šafařík warned Gaj that he should not expect any paid subscriptions from Bohemia that year, because the Postal Authorities accepted money only for periodicals on the approved list, and *Novine* and *Danica* were not on that list, compiled in 1834.(411)

There were a few small public demonstrations in Zagreb in 1835. Gaj's "Još Horvatska nini propala" was set to music early in 1835 and included in a performance of a patriotic play in the German Theatre of Zagreb. It was such a success that two other such performances took place. The second performance included a new patriotic song by L. Vukotinović "Nek se hrusti šaka mala," and the third several new poems by Gaj which had been set to music. The climax came in March, when the Countess Sidonija Erdödy gave a public recital which was attended by all the important citizens of Zagreb. She included "Nek se hrusti" in her regular program and sang "Još Horvatska" as an encore, which was followed by endless and frantic applause.(412)

By the close of 1835, the Illyrians had a newspaper and literary supplement. The Gaj orthography had already been used for half a year in *Danica* and would be extended to *Novine* in January of 1836. The Illyrian literary language already had a small dictionary, would soon have a grammar, and would become the language of Gaj's publications at the beginning of the new year. The patriotic songs of the Movement were sung in the streets of Zagreb and provincial towns. The paper had 520 subscribers. Gaj and the other Illyrians had good cause to be proud of their accomplishments, for the Croatian national awakening — the Illyrian Movement — had begun.

CHAPTER VII

SUPPORT GROWS (1836-1837)

In 1836 Gaj contributed only three articles to *Danica,*(413) and there was not a single poem or article in *Danica* or *Novine* signed with his name in 1837. Now that the newspaper and supplement had survived their first year, and the editorial assistants were adequately trained, Gaj turned his attention to other matters. He still had the final say on issues of policy and kept in close touch with his staff when he was away, but the bulk of work fell to Dragutin Rakovac, Antun Mažuranić, his brother Ivan Mažuranić, and Vjekoslav Babukić. Gaj's name, however, still appeared on the masthead.

In 1836 and 1837 Gaj directed most of his energies to the task of ensuring the existence of the paper. *Novine* and *Danica* had originally been printed in 750 copies, and many of these were distributed free of charge to potential subscribers. By the end of 1835 the paper had only 520 subscribers. This number dropped to 420 by the end of 1836, and to 400 by late 1837.(414) In 1838, the trend began to reverse itself, the number of subscriptions grew steadily until it reached 800 in 1848.(415)

The introduction of the new orthography, the new literary language based upon *štokavski,* and the Illyrian name led almost inevitably to a drop in the number of subscribers from the *kajkavski* areas. The opponents of Gaj's reforms found their spokesman in the *kajkavski* poet and priest Ignjat Kristijanović in Zagreb.(416) In Varaždin county the opposition to the language reforms and Illyrian ideas was strongest among the petty gentry.(417)

Ljudevit Gaj had hoped that the anticipated loss of subscribers from the *kajkavski* counties would be offset by an increased number of subscriptions from the *štokavski* areas: the Military Frontier, Slavonia, Dalmatia, Southern Hungary. This did not happen for several years. It took some time for people living in the more isolated areas even to hear of the paper. Poor communications, inadequate postal service, and the relatively high cost of subscription contributed to the financial difficulties of the newspaper. Many letters to Gaj complained of missing copies and irregular delivery. The newspaper and supplement cost six to eight forints a year, an almost prohibitive expense for students, and a costly luxury for others. Middle rank civil servants in Croatia, for example, received an average salary of ten forints a month.(418) This problem would not be solved until student groups and reading clubs were organized, groups which took out joint subscriptions to Gaj's newspaper.

There was only one printing press in Zagreb, Franjo Suppan's, which had a *de facto* monopoly on all local work. The machinery of the press was outdated, the printers often got behind schedule, and the prices were exorbitant. There had been talk in 1831 of a second press, but the local authorities had decided that the Suppan press met the existing needs.(419) But by 1836 the situation had changed: the Croatian literary renaissance had begun, there was a serious need for adequate facilities to publish *Novine* and *Danica* and the new books which, it was hoped, would soon be forthcoming.

Gaj had considered establishing a printing press of his own as early as 1834,(420) to publish *Novine* and *Danica* at cost and subsidize the publication of books in the national language. This soon developed into plans for a Bibliographic Institute, which would combine both a printing press and a lithography shop. Although the new press would barely break even printing the newspaper, and perhaps lose money on the new books, the loss would (hopefully) be offset with the profit from regular commercial operations. Gaj originally planned to finance the Bibliographic Institute with profits from *Novine*,(421) but now that the newspaper was piling up more and more of a deficit and he was already drawing on capital to meet running expenses, Gaj began to look to the Institute as a means of saving the newspaper from financial collapse.

In the fall of 1835 Gaj began to gather letters from various local officials and institutions in support of his plan for a Bibliographic Institute. On December 30, he drew up his first petition for permission to establish a Bibliographic Institute and sent it, via the local Zagreb authorities, to the Hungarian Regent's Council. The petition was brief and businesslike. Gaj explained that there was no lithography shop in the entire Triune Kingdom or in Southern Hungary, though one was badly needed, and that a second press was needed in Zagreb to carry the increased work load. The Emperor, continued Gaj, had granted permission for the Croats to have a newspaper and literary supplement in their mother tongue, but the monopoly of the Suppan press and the resulting high printing charges had put the newspaper in financial difficulty. If Gay were granted permission to found a Bibliographic Institute the entire cultural life of Croatia would benefit, for the Institute would encourage works by new authors in the national language and insure the continued publication of *Novine* and *Danica*.(422) This petition was accompanied by letters of support from the Ban, the Bishop of Zagreb, the Zagreb County Estates, the Cathedral Clergy, the Zagreb Town Magistrate and the School Administration.(423)

In the early spring of 1836 Gaj heard unofficially(424) that the Hungarian Regent's Council had rejected his petition because he was not trained as a printer, and because the Councilors believed that a newspaper and a printing press should not be owned and run by the same individual.

Gaj then decided to go to Vienna to try to get the Imperial authorities to intervene in the matter. He left for Vienna in the last week of May, carrying with him a letter from Herman Bužan, *veliki-župan* of Zagreb County, addressed to F. von Wernekring, Imperial Court Secretary.(425) Wernekring arranged for Gaj to have an audience with Count Kolowrat, Minister of the Interior, who was one of the most powerful men in the Empire. Kolowrat had been one of the founders of the Czech National Museum, and was known as a patron of the Slavs. Count Kolowrat received Gaj on June 1 1836. Gaj presented the Count with a new petition, his second, this time addressed to the Emperor.(426)

In the second petition Gaj appealed to the Emperor for help in the name of all loyal Croats. The newspaper for which he had received an Imperial franchise in 1834, and which was supposed to further the development of the ''Croato-Illyrian language''(427) and set up a dam against subversive influences from both within and without the Empire, was now in grave danger. Due to the high printing charges imposed by the one press in Zagreb, the paper was in serious financial difficulty. At the same time certain (unspecified) factions were working busily to undermine the paper and the entire national awakening. This problem could be solved by the establishment of a Bibliographic Institute, a project supported by a wide spectrum of the inhabitants of the Triune Kingdom. If the petition did not receive a favorable reply, warned Gaj, the newspaper might be closed, the entire national renaissance might collapse, and the Croats might be forced to accept the literature and language of their orthodox (Serbian) neighbors.(428)

There is an unsigned document dated June 2, 1836, written by a court official, which analyses the political advantages which would come from a positive decision on Gaj's petition.(429) It appears to be a summary of a longer treatise written by Gaj.(430) The analysis is extremely interesting, for it reveals some of the reasons which had induced the Imperial authorities to approve Gaj's newspaper petition in 1834. First of all, support of Gaj and his national cultural activities would strengthen the Croats and Slavonians in their loyalty to the Empire and in their opposition to Magyar nationalism. Secondly, the Croatian national press would draw the Southern Slavs of the Turkish Empire towards Austria and away from the influence of Russia.(431) This explains the vague allusion in Gaj's petition of June 1, to the internal and external subversive influences the newspaper was attempting to counter. *Novine* and especially *Danica,* continued the official report, have been so successful at their assigned task in awakening Croatian patriotism and resistance to Magyar nationalism and arousing feelings of brotherhood among the Southern Slavs, that the Hungarians and Russians have begun to seek ways to have have the publications suppressed.(432)

The report then goes on to say that Gaj's petition for a Bibliographic Institute is supported by loyal Croatian officials and citizens, and that a favorable decision is expected. Refusal would not only alienate the Croats, a loyal pillar of the Empire, but would also frighten away the neighboring Slavs from closer association with Austria. Gaj's petition should be acted upon quickly and favorably.(433)

Gaj had come to Vienna at a good time, as he explained to Antun Mažuranić and his other "dear brothers" in a letter dated June 10:

> My journey here has accomplished more than we hoped it would. The application for our printing press had already been rejected *in thesi* by the Hungarian Court Chancellery, and if I had not come everything would have been lost; but now it will be given another hearing in the Imperial Cabinet. The Emperor and courtiers look upon us with great favor, and from everything one can conclude these our fathers only wait for a reasonable request to be put forth by their children . . . .(434)

The Imperial Cabinet passed Gaj's petition on to the Hungarian Court Chancellery on June 19, indicating the Emperor's special interest in the matter.(435) Gaj left for Zagreb on June 20, confident that it was only a matter of time until the petition was approved.

The favorable attitude of the Imperial Cabinet toward the Croats was a direct result of the events which occurred during the December 1832 to May 1836 session of the Joint Parliament. This session clearly indicated that a desire for economic and political reform was sweeping Hungary. Through the Royal proposals Emperor Ferdinand presented to the Parliament, he opened the way for the Magyars to adopt a program of moderate and long-awaited reform. It was soon apparent that the majority of Magyar deputies would not be content with piecemeal reform. They wanted to make their backward kingdom into a modern and prosperous Magyar nation state. Demands for closer economic ties with the Austrian provinces, gradual emancipation of the peasants, freedom of the press, coupled with blatant disregard for traditional rights of other nationalities, so alienated the King and his Ministers that in the months immediately following the dismissal of the Parliament, they imposed a series of repressive measures upon the Hungarians, and took a protective attitude toward the Croats.(436) Not only were the majority of the decisions of the Parliament vetoed by the King, but the Hungarian Court Chancellor Reviczky was replaced by Palffy, a member of the Court party, and a number of the members of the Hungarian radical patriotic organization *"Társalkodási egyesület,"* drawn from the Hungarian *jurati* who attended the Parliament, were arrested.(437) Gaj must have heard of these arrests while in Vienna for he commented in a letter to his Zagreb friends:

> The Hungarians, enemies of all goodness, mercy, and virtue, enemies of our blood, enemies of our benevolent King and Emperor, have finally been sought out in their nest. Several have already been caught, others will follow the path to jail.(438)

The Croats, continues Gaj, can expect continued protection from Vienna for:

> . . . In the future only the Croat who stands with the Hungarians will be suspect, because the Hungarian attitude is unquestionably treasonable. We thank God that it has been brought out in the open. It is our duty to follow the example of our grandfathers and stand up in the defense of the noble house of our just Emperor, yes, if need be, even to shed our blood. This House binds us to our brothers, and united strength protects us from violence both Eastern and Western. Let us therefore follow the right path . . . We can firmly hope that the joyous sun will rise for our Illyria under the auspices of Austrian sovereigns.(439)

Gaj may have been stating this case somewhat strongly, but it is true that in 1836 the goals of the Illyrian Movement and of the Imperial Government did not clash. It was in the interest of the Emperor and his Ministers to support the development of national consciousness within Croatia as a counterweight against Magyar nationalism. If this national awakening were to win the other non-Habsburg Southern Slavs to the side of Austria, then so much the better.

The Croats had played a consistently conservative role at the Joint Parliament of 1832-1836. The new *Urbarium,* which eased the economic burden of the serf without fully emancipating him, meant a serious financial loss to many marginal landowners in Croatia who depended upon the work of two or three peasants for their own livelihood.(440) Once it had been passed by the Joint Parliament and approved by the King, however, the Croatian nobles accepted the *Urbarium* despite the hardships it imposed, primarily because the King had consistently upheld the *Jura municipalia* and vetoed all decisions of the Joint Parliament which violated these traditional Croatian rights. (441)

It seemed to the Croats that their *Jura municipalia* were being attacked by the Magyars steadily and systematically, in an attempt to strip Croatia of her traditional autonomy, and make her a Hungarian province. Among the rights challenged in 1832-1836 were: exclusion of Protestants from the ownership of immovable property and public office in Croatia; the right to pay only half of the tax burden imposed upon the other parts of Hungary; freedom from the obligation to quarter and maintain troops, except in the case of national emergency; and the right to determine the language of internal administration. The Magyars had also put forth the claim that Slavonia had never been an integral part of the Triune Kingdom but had from the earliest times been Hungarian, and that the Hungarian Littoral was traditionally Hungarian, not Croatian.

It was now clear to many Croats that the *Jura municipalia* could no longer serve as the sole means of preserving the remnants of Croatian autonomy. The Croats had in effect given up the right to govern themselves, except in minor internal matters, in 1790. Now they were discovering that they could easily be outvoted by the Magyars in the Joint Parliament. As long as the King continued to veto legislation that conflicted with the traditional rights of Croatia all was not lost, but the initiative was no longer in the hands of the Croats.

The Joint Parliament of 1832-1836 jolted many Croatian nobles out of their political apathy. The Croatian nobles were, with few exceptions, afraid of any reform which would diminish their economic or political power. They began to split into two factions in 1836: one which clung stubbornly to the traditional policy of solidarity with the Hungarian nobles, even if this meant accepting moderate reform and Magyarization; the other faction came out in support of the Illyrian Movement.(442)

The Illyrian Movement seemed to offer a new line of defense. Croatia would develop her own sense of national identity through the cultivation of her mother tongue. Croatia might be small when compared with Hungary, but as a part of Gaj's Greater Illyria, she was at least Hungary's equal in size, and as part of the greater Slavic community, she belonged to a unit which dwarfed Hungary. The Illyrians were interested in creating a national identity and national literature. They stressed national not social reform. The nation of which they spoke was an ethnic nation, composed of all classes, but they did not seem to be interested in alleviating the harsh conditions of the largest class — the peasants — or of challenging the political monopoly of the nobles. Therefore it was possible to combine the conservative interests of the Croatian nobles and the national goals of the Illyrians; for they could cooperate on matters of national language and literature, defense of the *Jura municipalia* and the preservation of the nation against Magyar pressures. The nobles found a new focus for their political struggle and the young Illyrian literary men found powerful protectors and allies.

We see the first clear sign of this alliance in a speech made by the Croatian deputy Herman Bužan in March of 1836, during the language debate in the Joint Parliament. The Magyars were once again trying to have Magyar made the language of instruction in all the secondary and higher schools of Croatia, and to push through the requirement that all civil servants speak Magyar within ten years. Bužan explained that it was not the intention of the Croats to retain Latin indefinitely as the language of their state. He pointed with pride to recent developments in the modernization of the Croatian language, and said that in the near future the Croats would probably begin to use their own language as the official language of the Triune Kingdom.(443)

By the spring of 1836 the Croats had begun to speak quite freely of the ugly treatment they had received in Pressburg, of the hardships of the *Urbarium*, of the fear that the Emperor might leave them to the mercy of the Magyars. News of this growing discontent began to reach Vienna, and in July 1836 the Imperial Cabinet asked Count Sedlnitsky to require monthly reports from his police correspondents in Croatia. The Cabinet also came to the conclusion that the state of affairs in Hungary required that the Croats be handled with great care and given repeated and unambiguous assurances that the Emperor would not desert them.(444)

Ljudevit Gaj had first begun to think about a national cultural society to preserve and promote the culture of his homeland when a student in Graz, and had talked about the means for establishing such a society with Kollár during his years in Pest.(445) As already mentioned, the Gaj circle discussed the need for such a society and went so far as to give it a name — the "Illyrian Cultural Society" — in 1832.(446) It was still too early then to do anything more than talk about such an institution. An Illyrian or a Croatian cultural society would be a national, not a local or private, matter: it could not be established without the royal permission, requested and supported by the majority of the delegates to the Croatian *Sabor.* Such support was out of the question in 1832. But between 1832 and 1836 the situation had changed radically: the Croatian renaissance had begun, a very new literary language already had a brief dictionary and grammar and was used in a newspaper and literary supplement. Most importantly, the Gaj circle had now become leaders of a Movement which had by virtue of a combination of external and internal political factors suddenly won the active support of some Croatian magnates and gentry, and the passive approval of others.

Gaj and the young Illyrians were not the only Croats to be aware of the growing need for a national cultural society. In 1835, Count Drašković, who was keeping in close touch with Gaj and carefully observing and encouraging the beginnings of the Illyrian Movement from Pressburg, wrote to Gaj:

> It is an old desire of mine to found a Learned Society which would be of help to our language and orthography. When I return I will talk with you and the others about this. It would be good if you discussed this with other respected and intelligent patriots.(447)

Gaj and Drašković were effective in arousing support for the plan and in late 1835 and early 1836, when the Croatian nobles gathered in their county assemblies to elect representatives to the coming *Sabor,* they debated the need for a national cultural society. Assembly after assembly decided to propose the establishment of such a society at the *Sabor.*(448) It was not quite clear what form this society was to take. Drašković's plan for a Learned Society was somewhat premature, for there were scarcely enough scholars in the Triune Kingdom to warrant such an institution. The nobles do not seem to have made any specific recommendations, except that such a society be formed. The blueprint for the cultural society finally came from Ljudevit Gaj.

When Gaj returned from Vienna in late June 1836, he met with his closest associates and began to draw up a plan for a national cultural society dedicated to the development of the Illyrian language and literature. Since Gaj was not a noble and could not present the plan to the *Sabor* himself, he published the proposal in *Danica* and gave a Latin translation of it to one of the members of the *Sabor.*(449) Gaj prepared the way for his proposal by a series of articles in *Danica,* which stressed the need for a cultural society and discussed the various forms it might take. The first article was a translation of Jan Kollár's "O literárnéj vzájemnosti mezi kmeny a nářečimi slavskými," (1836).(450) The last installment of Kollár's essay was followed by an article of Gaj's "Někoja družtva slavjanska kao srědstva narodne izobraženosti" (Some Slavic Societies as a Means to National Enlightenment)(451) which listed the learned, national and professional societies of the Russians,

Poles, Czechs and Slovaks and their publications. As for the Southern Slavs, Gaj wrote:

> And so, while all of our Slavic brothers advance along the glorious road of national enlightenment only we, Illyrians, have not a single national society, except for our Matica at Pest. In our next issue we shall discuss what ought to be done for Greater Illyria in this respect.(452)

Gaj's proposal for a cultural society appeared in two issues of *Danica.* The first installment, containing a detailed outline of the plan, came out on August 13th, in the midst of the *Sabor* session which opened on August 5th and ended August 17th. The second installment summed up the plan and commented on the decisions of the *Sabor.* It came out on August 20th.(453) Gaj suggested that the society be called "Družtvo prijateljah narodne izobraženosti Ilirske" (Society of the Friends of Illyrian National Enlightenment), and that its primary purpose be to encourage the development of national culture, especially of the Illyrian language. Gaj emphasized that it was extremely important that scholarly work in all fields of knowledge, with the exception of politics and theology, be done in the Illyrian language. The second task of such a society would be to collect books, manuscripts, artifacts of national interest such as coins, geological specimens, and to found a national library and national museum in which to house these collections. *Novine* and *Danica* were only the first steps in the national awakening:

> *Danica* (the morning start) announces the dawn, but dawn cannot break without a national cultural society.(454)

This specific proposal was debated in the *Sabor* and passed by a majority vote on August 16th. The name of the society was changed, however, to "Družtvo za narodnu prosvjetu" (Society for National Enlightenment) as a compromise measure, for a small but vocal minority opposed the name Illyrian which they said "smelled of Russia."(455)

A delegation of distinguished magnates and prelates was chosen by the *Sabor* to present the proposal to the Emperor. Upon receipt the proposal was forwarded to the Police Ministry where it remained, in the files of Count Sedlnitsky, for many years. Sedlnitzky, disturbed by reports of political unrest in Croatia, warned the Emperor in October of 1836, that while the Croatian national awakening might stem the tide of Magyar excesses for a while, it might itself become difficult to control.(456) The plan for the cultural society was not forgotten by the Illyrians. It reappeared in 1839, in the proposal for the establishment of Matica Ilirska.

The first Illyrian organization, the "Ilirsko narodno družtvo domorodne mladeži duhovne siemeništa Zagrebskoga" (Illyrian National Society of the Patriotic Youth of the Theological Seminary of Zagreb), was formed by students of the Zagreb Theological Seminary on October 9th, 1836.(457) The formal charter of the Society stated that its goals were:

1) to cultivate the national (Illyrian) language
2) to translate the works of the Church Fathers and outstanding sermons into the national language
3) to study the history of Illyria
4) to learn about other Slavs and study their languages
5) to establish a library of books and periodicals in the national language.(458)

The faculty of the Seminary not only permitted the students to organize, but even gave them a room in which they could meet and keep their library. The students took turns giving lectures on various topics, and decided to collect folk poetry during their vacations and speak the national language whenever possible. Their Society was modeled in part on patriotic societies of seminary students in Pest and Pressburg. The Zagreb Society was in correspondence with Jan Kollár, Teodor Pavlović (editor of *Srpske Novine)* and with Slovak and Serbian students. It was, of course, in close touch with Gaj.(459)

Ljudevit Gaj was not the only man to petition the Emperor for permission to found a second printing press in Zagreb in 1835 and 1836. The inadequacy of the Zagreb press was becoming apparent to others. Two men other than Gaj submitted petitions in 1834 and a fourth in 1836. Two of the petitioners were experienced printers.(460)

In late September 1836 Gaj heard from the Zagreb Educational Authorities that his second petition for the Bibliographic Institute had been rejected by the Hungarian Court Chancellery for the same reasons as the first: the petitioner's lack of practical experience, and the undesirability of combining a newspaper with a printing press. Gaj then drafted a third petition to the Emperor, preceding it with a letter to Count Kolowrat. He explained to the Count that he was again asking for his help, because it was generally known that His Excellency was the mightiest protector and patron of the Croats.(461) This third petition, dated September 27, 1836, concentrated on refuting the reasons given by the Hungarian Court Chancellery for rejecting Gaj's first two petitions, repeated many of the arguments used earlier, and even included copies of the first two petitions. Gaj pointed out that owners of printing presses in the Austrian Empire, especially in Hungary, generally hired trained *faktors* to run their presses. He cited examples of individuals who combined the ownership of a printing press with the editorship of a newspaper. The examples were carefully chosen from Hungary. Gaj ended by repeating the warning that if the Croats were not permitted to have a second press which would encourage the development of national literature, they would be forced into closer cultural ties with the Serbs.(462)

By the spring of 1837 Gaj had not yet received an answer to his third petition. Since his personal presence in Vienna had been useful in 1833 and again in 1836, Gaj decided to travel there once more and do everything possible to ensure a favorable and rapid decision. He arrived in Vienna in early May. By this time the decision on the Bibliographic Institute was nearing completion. The Hungarian Court Chancellery finally approved Gaj's request for a printing press on May 20th. Although they continued to assert that Gaj was not trained to run such an enterprise, he was the only petitioner who was a citizen of Zagreb, and it was quite obvious by now that a second press was needed. Permission was not granted for the lithographic shop. The approved petition was then passed to the State Conference, and from there to Emperor Ferdinand, who signed it on June 7, 1837.

Gaj arrived in Vienna in the beginning of May and stayed there until August. We know a little more about this trip than about the earlier ones, for he was watched by the secret police. On May 9, Count Sedlnitzky received an anonymous report that Ljudevit Gaj was often seen in the company of Polish students and might be involved in revolutionary activity. Sedlnitzky immediately assigned an agent to watch Gaj and find out why he came to Vienna so often.(463) The report he received, dated July 13th, was quite innocuous, stating that Gaj spent most of his time in the Imperial Library, the University Library or Gerold's Bookshop, that he had come to Vienna because of his petition for a printing press, and that he was rarely seen in public places, except in coffee houses which he patronized in order to read the newspapers. Gaj did come into occasional contact with Polish students at one of the coffee houses, continued the report, but their conversation with him was not of a political nature. The report ended with the news that Gaj would soon be leaving for Prague in order to purchase equipment for his printing press.(464)

While Sedlnitzky was having Gaj followed, Gaj himself was in personal contact with the Police Minister. He talked with Count Sedlnitzky about his plans to publish *Novine* in alternate pages of Latin and Cyrillic letters beginning in 1838. Sedlnitzky seems to have given tacit but not written approval to this project. Gaj assumed that the matter was settled.(465)

Ljudevit Gaj did not spend all of his time in Vienna in the libraries and bookshops. One of the most revealing portraits we have of him comes from 1837. Ivan Kukuljević-Sakcinski, son of the Director of Education for Croatia, was a lieutenant in the Hungarian Guards. He was then twenty-one years old. He had written to Gaj in 1836 about his interest in literature.(466) Hearing that Gaj was in Vienna on business, Kukuljević paid him a call on July 9th, but Gaj was out. The young officer was quite surprised when early the next morning:

> . . . somebody knocked at the door and entered — my Gaj; the greatest patriot of our time, the most important figure of our literature; swarthy, with a high forehead, black hair and a small black moustache. His face reveals that he is an honorable, honest man preoccupied with important matters and deeply concerned with the good of our nation.(467)

Most of the descriptions of Gaj by his contemporaries were written in later years. This first-hand account, written on the day of their meeting has, to the best of my knowledge, never been cited before. It gives real insight into Gaj's technique of winning and using his followers:

> He stayed three hours and confided in me all his intentions, talked about many dark affairs, and gave me an account of all the difficulties he had had to overcome because of our newspaper . . .(468)

How flattering it must have been to the young officer to have the confidence of the man he admired so much, and to be let into many "dark affairs."

Gaj had undoubtedly been delighted to hear that Kukuljević had called, for not only was the young man interested in the national awakening, but his father was a most important man:

> Finally he began singing praises of my father, told me with disarming frankness how when Father had on a recent occasion spoken in the *Sabor,* he (Gaj) had burst into tears and at that moment had wanted nothing so much as to be his son; but he also explained to me what my father in his capacity as Director of Education could do for our cause and literature. In each of his words I saw genuine patriotism, sincerity and utter absence of guile. I promised to write to Father about many things, and also to give him (Gaj) a letter to my father which would gain him an entrance and a chance to discuss many things. He thanked me with sincere, pleasant words and a handshake. He was so glad that he found another patriot.(469)

And was it not even more rewarding when the patriot had such valuable connections?

> Finally I showed him some of my writings and poetry. He was enthusiastic. He took the poems with him and promised to print several in *Danica,* which made me very happy. Finally the sound of the

> bugle, summoning me to dinner, forced us to part. He embraced me in a friendly manner and bestowed upon me several kisses. We shook hands and he left. And I, brimming with a joyous and sweet awareness of having spoken with the greatest patriot of my fatherland, went to dinner.(470)

Gaj kept his word, and the first of Kukuljević's poems "Tuga za ljubom" appeared in *Danica* No. 50 (December 9), 1837. Kukuljević later became one of the most distinguished political figures of the Illyrian Movement and one of the most productive literary men in Croatia in the nineteenth century.(471)

Count Sedlnitzky might also have been interested to know of two other acquaintances Gaj made during this trip to Vienna: First Lieutenant Tomo Burian, Professor at the Military Academy in Wiener Neustadt; and Stefan Herkalović, an officer of a line Regiment of the Imperial Army, stationed in Raab. Burian, a Czech, taught the Czech language at the Military Academy and was the author of a Czech-German grammar.(472) Burian probably looked up Gaj in order to talk about the recent Illyrian language reforms. He was a useful contact. Quite a few youths from the Military Frontier studied at the Wiener Neustadt Academy, and since Gaj hoped that the Illyrian Movement would find supporters among the officers of the Military Frontier he was glad for this opportunity to meet the cadets. Gaj arranged to send free copies of *Danica* and *Novine* to Burian for the use of the Illyrian students.(473)

Gaj may have met Stefan Herkalović (1810-1866) through Burian. Herkalović came from the Military Frontier, and had served with the Imperial Army for thirteen years.(474) Herkalović had heard about Gaj's work in Zagreb and was an enthusiastic supporter of the Illyrian Movement. By the time he first met Gaj in 1837, Herkalović had already decided to leave the army and accept a new position as Director of the newly formed Serbian Military Academy in Belgrade. He and Gaj quickly became friends, and this friendship was to last for many years. Until now there had been no contact between the Illyrian Movement in Zagreb and the Government of the Serbian Principality, although Gaj was eager to establish such ties.(475) To this end he may have been thinking of using Cyrillic as well as Latin letters in *Novine.* Gaj knew that Herkalović, as Director of the Military Academy, would be in contact with the ruling circle of the new Serbian state. He would be able to keep Gaj informed about the more important developments in Serbia, and make propaganda for the Illyrian Movement.(476) Herkalović left for Serbia in October 1837.

Gaj kept in close touch with his editorial staff from Vienna. He must have been informed almost immediately that the Zagreb Censor had on

July 7th forbidden *Danica* to publish a translation of excerpts from Jan Kollár's *Über die literarische Wechselseitigkeit* (1837), although the entire shorter Czech version had been translated and published in *Danica* the previous year.(477) This was the first clear sign that the police were becoming apprehensive about the Pan-Slav aspect of the Illyrian Movement. The clearest example of the attention the police were paying the Movement can be found in the archives of the Zagreb Censor. There are forty documents for the entire period between 1827 and 1837, but from that time on they average one to two hundred documents per year.(478)

In a letter dated July 30th, Gaj instructed his editorial staff to refrain from publishing articles about Slavic history or ethnography, in short anything which could be considered Pan-Slav. He then went on to say, undoubtedly referring to the trouble with the Kollár article, that while the Magyar censors might be blind, the Court officials were no fools:

> Kollár, who is a great poet, a middling historian and an inferior politician, has almost managed to break our necks with his sanctimonious ostentatiousness. Judge for yourselves.(479)

Although the Illyrian Movement had developed within a Pan-Slav framework, The Pan-Slav emphasis was now beginning to take second place. In 1835 Gaj had told the Croats that they belonged to three nationalities: the Croats, the Illyrians and the Slavs.(480) Now that the Croatian elite were beginning to support the Illyrian Movement and blend its cultural program with elements of the traditional Croatian political one, the situation had changed. First loyalty would have to be to the Illyrian Movement in Zagreb, its institutions and its problems. This is symbolized in Gaj's bitter attack on the ideas of Kollár, his old mentor.

The close relationship between Gaj and Kollár was cooling off: Kollár did not write Gaj once between August 21st, 1836, and July 20th, 1842.(481) Perhaps this is because Gaj often did not answer letters. Šafařík complained to Kollár in 1837 that he had almost stopped writing Gaj, because Gaj answered so infrequently.(482) However, Gaj did make quite a few visits to Šafařík in Prague and Karlový Vary between 1837 and 1846, while he did not once travel to see Kollár in Pest, which was nearer. The two men did not meet once between 1831 and 1841, the year in which Kollár visited Zagreb. Šafařík could counsel Gaj in matters connected with his press and newspaper, he had powerful contacts with the leading figures in the Slavic world. Kollár, who had been extremely influential in the development of Gaj's ideas in the early 1830's, seems now to have outlived his usefulness.

In early August Gaj left Vienna for Karlový Vary to visit Šafařík, and then continued on to Prague. There he purchased the press machinery and type from the firm of Bogumil Haase and Sons, who manufactured the latest in printing equipment in the Habsburg Empire at that time.(483) The Haase firm cast new type, arranged for Gaj to hire a trained printer, Wilhelm Landauer, as his manager *(faktor),* and located skilled workers willing to settle in Croatia. Gaj hoped the Czech workers would train Croats in their craft. Gaj arranged with Haase and Sons to pay for the press in installments.

Gaj returned to Zagreb in late November and immediately went to see Stjepan Moyses, the Censor. He announced to Moyses that beginning in 1838, he would print *Novine* in both the Cyrillic and Latin alphabets, and that this plan had the approval of Count Sedlnitzky. Moyses wrote to Sedlnitzky asking for details.(484) Sedlnitzky replied that he had nothing against Gaj's proposal, but because of recent difficulties with the Hungarian Court Chancellery it might be better to wait for a while before making such a change.(485)

It took the equipment for the printing press several months to arrive. It was heavy and had to be transported part of the way by horsedrawn wagons over poor roads.(486) In December Gaj rented a large house on Capuchin square to accommodate the printing press, the editorial offices and to serve as living quarters for Gaj and his mother. Ljudevit Gaj, now twenty-eight, was editor of a newspaper, owner of a printing press, and leader of the fast growing Illyrian Movement.

CHAPTER VIII

LJUDEVIT GAJ — LEADER (1838-1840)

The printing press which began to operate in the first week of January, 1838, did not solve Gaj's financial problems. It created new ones. Gaj did not have the capital to finance the press. The equipment was purchased from Haase and Sons for a sum of between 7000 and 8000 forints,(487) payable in regular installments. Other expenses of the press: rent, paper, ink, salaries of the manager and workers, were met by short and long term loans. By the time the second installment to Haase and Sons was due some of the short term loans had to be paid, interest was due on the long term loans, and Gaj had to borrow again. He borrowed from his sisters, and from businessmen and supporters in Varaždin and Karlovac.(488) It is worth noting that he carefully avoided contracting debts in Zagreb.

Shortly after Gaj's press had begun to operate the editors of *Agramer Zeitung* cancelled their contract with Suppan and gave their business to the new press. This was a real triumph and the major source of income for Gaj's press in its first years.(489) The press also printed death announcements, invitations, calling cards, and occasionally did some work for the military authorities and the Church.

The Gaj printing press was the most modern press in Croatia. The manager of the press, Wilhelm Landauer, seems to have been an able man. The workers brought from Bohemia were well trained and well paid. In fact, the contract drawn up between Gaj and his workers in 1839, was the first instance of collective bargaining in the Triune Kingdom.(490)

Had the Gaj printing press been a purely private enterprise, free of any ideological involvement, it might have been a financial success. But Gaj could not play the role of an entrepreneur — he was leader of a national movement. He allowed the Illyrian authors to pay for the printing of their works over a long period, in interest-free installments. This meant that in publishing these works the press could at best break even.(491) On the other hand, certain *kajkavski* writers, such as Ignjat Kristijanović, who might have been attracted by the modern facilities of the press but who opposed the Illyrian Movement, still patronized the Suppan press. Gaj's debts continued to rise.

A national movement needs an organizational structure to coordinate its activities, attract new followers, and utilize the abilities and ideas of those who are already committed. It had been hoped in 1836 that the national cultural society would fill this need, but approval for this society had still not been granted by the King. Therefore it became necessary to develop a strictly local organization and through it a network of organizations, which could be established without petitioning Buda or Vienna. This was done in 1838, with the founding of Reading Clubs in the major towns of Civil Croatia.

A Reading Club *(Čitaonica)* was ostensibly a private club with a joint library, whose members met regularly to discuss Club business. The membership dues were used to buy subscriptions to newspapers and periodicals, books in the national language and in other Slavic and European languages. The Club rented or was given rooms in which its library was kept, and to which all members had access. It is important to remember that there were no public libraries in Croatia at the time, and that all printed matter was expensive. The Reading Clubs gave their members a place in which they could read and talk. The Reading Clubs had two annual business meetings and at one of these the officers were elected.(492) At these meetings the members also discussed other matters: the progress of the national language and literature, national problems, and concrete ways in which the Reading Club could help in the national awakening. The Clubs had other meetings during the year when the occasion arose.

The Reading Clubs were generally founded by local nobles, but the membership included teachers, merchants, civil servants, writers, men of noble and non-noble birth drawn together by their interest in the Illyrian Movement. The first Reading Club was founded in Varaždin in January 1838, on the initiative of Metel Ožegović, Chief Notary of Varaždin County and sporadic contributor to *Danica.* It was called "Prijatelji našega narodnoga slovstva" (Friends of Our National Literature). By February it had a membership of eighty among whom, as Baron Kušlan wrote proudly to Gaj, were some of the most important men of the town.(493) The second Reading Club was founded in Karlovac in March of the same year. Its first president was Karlo Klobučarić. A third Reading Club was established soon afterwards in

Križevci by Ljudevit Vukotinović, and the fourth in Zagreb in August. Count Janko Drašković was elected president of the Zagreb Club, and Vjekoslav Babukić was chosen its secretary, a post he held until 1846.

Ljudevit Gaj did not play an active role in the founding of the Reading Clubs in Varaždin, Karlovac or Križevci. He was present at the July 7th, 1838 meeting at the home of Count Drašković when plans for the Zagreb Reading Club were drawn up (the archives of the Club show him as a founding member), but his name did not appear on the formal announcement calling for members.(494) The Announcement was published in the August 4th, 1838 issue of *Danica,* signed by Zagreb town and county dignitaries: Count Janko Drašković, Josip Stajdacher (Zagreb Town Magistrate), Stjepan Pogledić (Vicar), and Valentine Vrančić (Zagreb County Treasurer). Gaj was apparently too preoccupied with other matters to play a leading role in the Zagreb Reading Club. It is, however, possible that he was also discouraged from this by Count Drašković, for Gaj and Drašković seem to have clashed over their views of the role the Reading Club should play in the national awakening. Gaj wanted the Club to be closely tied to *Novine* and *Danica.* He saw it as an "Illyrian" organization, which could serve as the organizational center of the Illyrian Movement.(495) Drašković believed that the Club should study the national language, translate useful books on trade, agriculture, politics and economics, and serve as an apolitical organization of men interested in the enlightenment of their nation.(496) The path taken by the Club was in fact a compromise between the two points of view.

The Club attracted members from a broad spectrum of Zagreb society. Credit for this should be given to Drašković who, in the beginning, carefully played down the "Illyrian" nature of the organization. As a first step towards the goal of stimulating interest in economic matters Drašković proposed at the January 1839 business meeting of the Club, that prizes be awarded for the best book in the national language on: 1) how to organize and develop the export of Croatian wine; 2) how to establish factories to process textiles and leather; 3) how to found a local paper factory; and 4) how to educate the peasants in more advanced agricultural methods.(497) The proposal was adopted by the Reading Club and Drašković personally guaranteed the prize money.(498) Not a single book was submitted.(499) The immediate need in 1838 and 1839 was for an organization to link groups interested in the Illyrian cultural reforms. By mid-1839 Ljudevit Gaj and other younger members of the Zagreb Reading Club were able to involve the Club more and more in the Illyrian Movement until the Club became its center. Its Secretary, Vjekoslav Babukić, carried on an extensive correspondence with the officers of the other Reading Clubs, thus helping to coordinate their activities. *Danica* regularly carried reports on the meetings of the Zagreb Reading Club. From the Zagreb Reading Club, which soon changed its name to "the Illyrian Reading Club of Zagreb" (Ilirska čitaonica u Zagrebu), would come plans and funds for *Matica Ilirska,* a national theatre, a national museum and library, and the National Center.(500)

Although the Reading Clubs were first founded in the major towns of Civil Croatia, one was established in Pečuh in 1839,(501) one in Bakar (Dalmatia), in the same year, one in Novi Vinodol (Dalmatia) in 1845, and there was even an abortive attempt to found a Reading Club in Bosnia in 1841.(502)

In September 1838 Gaj had his first serious quarrel with an old friend and colleague — Dragutin Rakovac. Rakovac had found the work on *Novine* boring and by 1837 had turned most of the translating over to Antun and Ivan Mažuranić. On Gaj's urging Rakovac entered the competition for a position of professor of natural law at the Zagreb Academy. Gaj granted him several months of paid leave to prepare for the "professor's exam" required of all candidates for the position.(503) Rakovac did not get the job. He began, apparently, to lose interest in the position of an anonymous paid editor of *Novine.* Gaj seems to have given his old friend more than one chance to reform(504) and finally on September 9th, 1838, shortly before leaving for Vienna, he wrote Rakovac a sharp letter in which he accused him of drinking to excess, neglecting his duties, spreading the rumor that he was co-owner of *Novine,* charging personal bills to the account of the newspaper, and, most serious of all, associating with people dedicated to the destruction of the Illyrian Movement.(505) This letter was only a warning. Rakovac apparently came to his senses and although still somewhat inefficient,(506) remained *de-facto* editor of *Novine* until 1841.

In September 1838 Ljudevit Gaj traveled to Vienna and from there to Berlin, where he was received by Count Aleksandr Benkendorf, Chief of the Russian Secret Police. Gaj presented to the Count a petition addressed to Tsar Nicholas I.

The original petition is lost, and there are no copies left in Gaj's papers, but we know its general contents from references made to this, Gaj's first, Russian petition in two other letters written by Gaj to the Tsar asking for Russian help: the first is dated November 1st, 1838, and the second July 3rd, 1840.(507) Gaj apparently asked the Tsar's financial support for his printing press, emphasizing that plans had been made for the press to begin printing *Novine* and *Danica* in both Latin and Cyrillic letters in the very near future.

Gaj was not the first Slavic cultural leader in the Habsburg Empire to ask for financial aid from Russia for his literary and publishing activities. Official Russia in the first three decades of the nineteenth century was becoming interested in Slavic history and languages. The Ministry of Public Education even invited three distinguished Western Slavs, Šafařík, Hanka and Čelakovsky, to serve as the first professors of Slavonic studies at Russian universities.(508) When this plan fell through for a variety of reasons, the Russian Academy and Government were still generous in bestowing honorary titles, gold medals and occasional gifts of money to support Western Slavic scholars and literary men in their work. V. V. Hanka and Pavel Šafařík received subsidies from Russia in the 1830's.(509) Vuk Karadžić received 300 roubles from the Russian Academy in 1820 and was granted a yearly pension for some time as well.(510) Gaj was not a scholar, but he was the "father" of the new Illyrian literary language and literature, and he may well have hoped he too would become a recipient of Russian generosity.

In November of the same year Gaj submitted a second letter to the Tsar, this time in the form of a political memorandum. It was given to Benkendorf's agent in Vienna, Colonel Ozeretskovskii, to be forwarded to the Tsar with the plea that its contents to be kept secret.(511) The letter represents a significant break with Gaj's earlier activities. Although the first letter to the Tsar somewhat contradicted the line Gaj had stressed in Vienna — that the Illyrian Movement was useful to Austria in helping to draw the Southern Slavs away from Russian influence and bringing them within the Austrian sphere — it was still within the framework of cultural Pan-Slavism. It was understandable that non-Russian Slavic literary men would turn to Russia for help, for it was the only independent Slavic state. In Gaj's second petition, however, he stepped beyond the confines of cultural Pan-Slavism toward political Pan-Slavism, seeking political, economic and military support from Russia for the Balkan Slavs. This signifies the beginning of what we will call Gaj's "secret politics,"(512) which will form a constant theme in his activities between 1838 and 1848. Gaj's secret politics would first be directed to Russia (1838-1840), then to Serbia and the right wing of the Polish emigration (1842-1848).

Gaj, in his second letter, appealed to the Tsar as the protector of all the Slavs. He warned the Tsar that the Magyars were attempting to establish a strong anti-Russian state to dominate the Balkans, and that they had found many supporters within the Triune Kingdom. Russia would now have to decide whether Illyria would become a focus of Magyar anti-Russian intrigues, or a Russian bastion.(513)

Gaj then went on to describe the sorry condition of the Southern Slavs. The soldiers of the Military Frontier, he said, were subjected to constant Germanization, their Orthodox clergymen were unfairly treated, and the standard of living was so low that over a hundred families had recently fled across the mountains to the Turkish provinces. The Illyrians of Croatia and Slavonia were victims of Magyarization, those in Dalmatia of Italianization, those living in the Turkish Empire of Turkish barbarism, while those in the Serbian principality suffered from the arbitrary and demoralizing despotism of Prince Miloš.

Russia should take advantage of this potentially revolutionary situation. She should establish a Russian focus of power in Bosnia, Turkish-Croatia, Hercegovina, Albania and Serbia. The pretext for Russian intervention, suggested Gaj, could be the freeing of Orthodox Christians from the Turkish yoke. The Military Frontier could be drawn to the Russian side if Russia were willing to subsidize a network of agents recruited from among influential men in the Frontier: officers, subalterns, priests and village elders. Gaj claimed to be in possession of exact statistical and strategic information about the Turkish provinces.

Gaj proposed that a Russian-sponsored uprising break out on the border of Montenegro and Albania. Montenegro, he assured Russia, could be counted upon as a loyal ally. The Russians should send three million gulden C.M. to aid the Illyrian inhabitants of the Turkish provinces who were in possession of small arms but lacked munitions and larger field pieces, and to pay the agents in the Military Frontier. They might also have to supply some troops. If war should break out, as threatened, between England and Russia, the uprising would be limited to the Turkish border area. If, however, Austria should enter the war on the English side, Russia could count on the troops of the Military Frontier and the support of Civil Croatia and Civil Slavonia. If war should not come the Russians should still encourage present pro-Russian sympathies among the Illyrians by supporting groups and institutions which fostered such sentiments.

Was this memorandum a wild flight of fancy, or was it based, at least in part, on fact? In 1838, it did seem possible for a while that war might break out between England and Russia over the second Mohammed Ali crisis.(514) However it was quite unthinkable that Russia would be interested in fomenting a revolution in the Balkans, which would involve the subjects of her two closest allies: Austria and Turkey. From 1833 on Russia seems to have been determined to preserve the *status quo* in the Balkans. Therefore Mosely is fully justified in saying that Gaj's memorandum "... displays a phenomenally provincial ignorance of the true currents of Russian foreign policy in that period."(515)

Was Gaj any less ignorant about the situation in the Balkans? There had been sporadic civil war in Bosnia and Hercegovina in the 1830's, but this was a struggle of the Moslem Begs against the reformist plans of Sultan Mahmud II. The Christians do not seem to have been involved. The soldiers of the Military Frontier were dissatisfied with social and economic conditions, and there were periodic flights across the mountains to the Turkish lands.(516) But although Illyrian ideas were beginning to spread in the Military Frontier awakening some of the educated groups there to an awareness of their national identity, it is highly improbable that the troops of the Military Frontier would have gone over to Russia in a war. There is no proof that Gaj knew very much about political conditions and loyalties outside of Croatia. As a newspaper editor he was more informed than the average citizen, for *Novine* and *Danica* carried articles and news items dealing with all of the Southern Slav lands, but there is no reason to assume that Gaj was, as he claimed, in possession of strategic and statistical data.(517)

It is interesting that Gaj was speaking here in behalf of all the Southern Slavs. He was beginning to think beyond the framework of Illyrian cultural unity and to hope for Southern Slav military and, perhaps, political cooperation. The liberation of the Orthodox Southern Slavs from Turkish rule by Russia with the aid of the troops of the Military Frontier — a revolutionary step at the very least — and the suggestion that Russia become the protector of the Illyrian Movement and all of "Illyria," would, had it ever materialized, have made it possible for the Southern Slavs to join together politically under Russian sponsorship. What is important here is not the inadequacy of Gaj's knowledge of the international situation and his complete lack of planning for what would happen afterwards, should Russia follow his suggestion, but the fact that he was no longer content to see the political life of the Croats limited to the role of a minority nationality in Hungary and the Habsburg Empire.

Until 1838, the Croats had had only two courses open to them in their struggle for political survival: they could try to enlist Hungarian support against Austria, as they had in 1790; or make use of Austrian fears of Hungarian nationalism. Gaj now attempted to create a third alternative. By this time he may have begun to doubt that Austrian favor for the Illyrian Movement could always be expected. If Austrian support were withdrawn, the Illyrians would be defenseless against the Magyars. This left only the other Slavs. The Western Slavs could be of little help except in an Empire-wide conflagration, the majority of Southern Slavs were still under Turkey. Russia alone had the military power to liberate the Southern Slavs so that they in turn could ''liberate'' the Croats from their historic dependency on Hungary and Austria. Gaj's bid for Russian support was naive and clumsy, but he was seeking alternatives to insure the existence of the Illyrian Movement. (518)

It was probably in connection with the political plans outlined in Gaj's second letter to the Tsar in 1838, that Stefan Herkalović set off in December of the same year on a trip to Dalmatia, Bosnia and Serbia. The trip was financed by Gaj.(519) Herkalović was arrested in Bosnia in February 1839 and accused of being a spy. Apparently he was carrying incriminating papers on his person.(520) Herkalović was released in March and returned to Zagreb in June or July of the same year. Herkalović was not the only Illyrian to travel to Bosnia in 1839. Matija Mažuranić, younger brother of Antun and Ivan Mažuranić, spent almost two years in Serbia, Bosnia and, possibly, Montenegro, returning to Zagreb in 1841.(521) He kept his brothers and Gaj informed about any important development in the lands he visited.

The last months of 1838 and the first half of 1839 passed without a word from Russia. In the meantime Gaj concentrated once again upon his work as agitator and cultural leader in the Triune Kingdom.

In 1832 it was relatively easy to trace the effect of Gaj on the small group of students and lawyers in Zagreb who began to lay plans for the Illyrian Movement: he sparked them to action. In 1835 and 1836 when Gaj's newspaper and literary supplement were the only platform of the Illyrian Movement, and when he defined the goals and means to reach them in a series of articles in *Danica,* his role was again easily identified. By 1839 although he was at the very center of the Movement he had, in some ways, become invisible. The history of the Illyrian Movement became the history of its institutions, of its writers and of the growing support it won from the Croatian *Sabor.* Gaj no longer played an active role in *Novine* or *Danica,* except in the determination of long range policy and in trying to meet the ever sharpening financial crisis. In these years he spent many months away from Zagreb, in Vienna, in Prague, in Russia, and the Movement grew and gathered strength without his presence. His press was well run by Landauer, the Reading Clubs were under the direction of Drašković and Babukić. When then did Gaj do? Antun Mažuranić, who did the bulk of the aditorial work on *Danica* and had been close to Gaj since 1835, described Gaj's role in this way:

> Gaj had talents which are given to one man in a million. An incredibly strong desire to achieve fame and greatness burned in him with an unusual flame. His mystical-poetic, even fantastic manner of speech revealed his secret belief, of which we were aware, that he was one of God's chosen. Hundreds of times I saw discouraged men come to him, even men who were his opponents. I would be working in the

> front room and they would come out of his room with shining faces, enraptured and enthusiastic supporters. Many a time was I present while he addressed such delegations, of which about ten used to come every day. On numerous occasions, to fan the fire or keep the flames bright, he revealed hopes for the national undertaking which he did not feel . . . I wondered at this, but he said: 'Do not be perplexed, I must speak like that.' . . .(522)

When Jan Kollár observed Gaj in action in Zagreb in 1841, he compared him to a magnet, drawing to himself and the Movement the most talented young men from all corners of the Kingdom and by his very strength of will neutralizing the many different individual interests and points of view.(523) Yet for all that, Gaj eludes us in this period.

Ljudevit Gaj's career, inheritance, and self-image were so tied to the success or failure of the Illyrian Movement, that it was almost impossible to separate his public life from his private life. He was, so to speak, always on stage. His home contained the editorial offices of the newspaper and the entire printing press. There was always open house at the Gajs', a fact which must have added immeasurably to the debts he was steadily incurring. Close friends such as Ljudevit Vukotinović began to complain:

> Bogović tells me that you are angry at me for something having to do with my book . . . You know that it is impossible to get you alone at your home, and for that reason I have not been able to talk to you about this.(524)

Gaj's personal charm, his ability to inflame and excite people and win them over to his cause seem to have been especially effective with the youth. He was only thirty when he made his first formal visit to the Illyrian Society of the Zagreb Theological Seminary on April 1st, 1839. Almost the entire student body of the Seminary were assembled to meet him. The officers of the Society greeted Gaj in front of the Seminary, carried him in on their shoulders, while the students gathered in a large lecture hall shouted "Zivio!" (Long may he live!) and sang "Još Horvatska nij' prepala" and other patriotic songs. After the noise had begun to subside, Gaj made his way to the podium and delivered a rousing speech about the role of the youth in the national awakening. Gaj's audience were moved to tears.(525) The Seminary Administration, shocked by the intensity of student reaction, ordered that the Illyrian Society be disbanded. The Society library was given to Vjekoslav Babukić for safekeeping. Although the Illyrian Society was permitted to reorganize in 1840, it was no longer regarded as a harmless student group and was closely watched by the Administration.

In June 1839 a disturbance broke out between several Magyar professors at the Zagreb Academy, and student supporters of the

Illyrian Movement. This seems to have come about spontaneously. It began when Professor Machik, a new teacher of the Magyar language, berated a class for its lack of interest in Magyar. He called them insulting names, and his words were answered in even sharper tones by some pro-Illyrian students in the class. Soon after this, Professor Mikusay, a professor of physics, told a class, "Guard yourselves against the Illyrians as you would against a disease. They are traitors to the Fatherland."(526) The news of these incidents spread quickly and touched off student demonstrations. Several student leaders were temporarily suspended from the Academy, and even though the tension had abated by the end of June, the students were becoming more and more militant in their support of the Illyrian Movement.

Since the permission for the Illyrian Cultural Society had not been granted, the Zagreb Reading Club decided to try once more. On March 7, 1839, the membership considered and passed a proposal to draft plans anew for a national cultural society. The major purpose of the society would be to support the publication of books in the national language. The society would be called *Matica Ilirska* and would be modeled after *Matica Česka* in Prague and *Matica Srpska* in Pest.(527) Supported by contributions from its members and gifts from interested patriots, *Matica Ilirska* would underwrite the publication of educational and literary works, old and new, in the Illyrian language. These would be printed by the Gaj press.(528)

The officers of the Reading Club drew up a petition to the Emperor asking for permission to establish *Matica Ilirska.* It was signed by distinguished patriots and given to Ljudevit Gaj to deliver to the Imperial Authorities. He submitted it when he traveled to Vienna in June of the same year.(529) It is unfortunate that the Reading Club felt it necessary to depend upon the reputation of Gaj as a man with powerful contacts at the Imperial Court to carry their petition through to success, for although there is no indication that Gaj did not apply himself to this task with the zeal that characterized his labours on behalf of the newspaper and printing press, the *Matica Ilirska* proposal lay on a desk in the Hungarian Court Chancellery for eight years. By 1846 some people in Zagreb had even begun to suspect that Gaj never submitted the petition.(530) There was absolutely no reason why Gaj should sabotage this plan, for it was in his own interest and that of the Illyrian Movement.

It was mid-1839, and Ljudevit Gaj had still not heard from Russia. He was now walking a political tightrope, proudly acclaiming that his newspaper had the support of the Austrian Emperor and his Ministers, yet afraid news of his second Russian memorandum might come into the wrong hands. The tenuousness of his position may have impelled him to seek a sign of Imperial favor. On June 24, 1839 he had an audience with Count Kolowrat. He presented the Count with bound volumes of the first four years of *Novine* and *Danica,* a gift for the Emperor, and at the same time submitted a request for some kind of formal recognition by the Emperor of his, Gaj's, services to his nation and the Empire.(531) It was not clear from Gaj's petition of June 24, exactly what kind of recognition he was seeking, but since he did not stress his financial difficulties he was probably not asking for money.

Gaj also contacted the Russian Embassy during his visit to Vienna in June. After his conversations with the Russian Ambassador, Gaj decided to send Stefan Herkalović to Russia as his personal emissary. Herkalović left for Russia in July or August of 1839. We know very little about Herkalović's journey, for Gaj destroyed almost all of his Russian correspondence in the 1850's. Herkalović's visit is mentioned in one of the few remaining Russian letters, and in a Gaj memorandum of 1840 to Tsar Nicholas I.(532) Herkalović's trip was a failure, and he returned a convinced Russophobe.(533)

While the Russians seemed quite indifferent to Gaj, the Austrians moved quickly to give him the recognition he sought. On August 27, Emperor Ferdinand signed a document awarding Ljudevit Gaj a ring valued at three hundred forints in recognition of his literary activities.(534)

The ring, a diamond, arrived in Zagreb in late September in a sealed box addressed to Ban Vlašić. The Ban, now old and sick, seems to have taken a dislike to Gaj. He presented the ring with the barest minimum of ceremony, making it clear to Gaj that he disapproved of the award. He even suggested that Gaj open the box immediately to make sure the ring was genuine.(535) The Ban's attitude could not spoil the moment for Gaj. He wore the ring proudly to the end of his life.

When Ljudevit Gaj and Dimitrije Demeter were students in Graz they decided that a national theatre which produced original plays in the national language would be an important tool in the awakening of national consciousness.(536) Demeter was not active in the preliminary planning of the Movement in Zagreb after 1832, he spent the years between 1829 and 1836 in Vienna and Padua studying medicine.(537) Upon his return to Zagreb in 1836, Demeter opened medical practice and began to write plays in the national language. In fact, his *Dramska Pokušenja* (1838) were the first plays to be written and published in the Illyrian language. These were soon followed by Ivan Kukuljević's "Juran i Sofija" in 1839.

"Juran i Sofija" was the first Illyrian play to be performed. It was staged by an amateur theatrical society in Sisak on October 2nd, 1839 and received so enthusiastically that H. Börnstein, Director of the German Theatre in Zagreb, wrote to Gaj suggesting that the Illyrians form a Theatrical Society with the goal of establishing a National Theatre. He offered practical help from his own organization: costumes, sets, a building, an orchestra, and even a director if needed.(538) Börnstein included a formal proposal in his letter which Gaj published in *Danica* and *Novine.*

The Zagreb Reading Club took up this proposal at their meeting of January 24, 1840, and decided to accept Börnstein's offer. Demeter was charged with gathering of funds for the first season. Since there were no actors proficient in the Illyrian language in Zagreb, Demeter and Börnstein, with Gaj's help, arranged to hire the Novi Sad Theatrical Company for a two month season beginning in June 1840. The first season featured "Juran i Sofija," a certain box office success. The Company performed in Zagreb, Karlovac, Varaždin, Križevci, Petrinja and Sisak.(539) Demeter was able to collect some money from various private persons and institutions for this project, but the Reading Club assumed the greatest financial responsibility.

The plan for a National Theatre soon received support from another source, the Croatian *Sabor.* The Joint Parliament which met from June 6, 1839 to May 13, 1840, had passed a resolution to establish a Hungarian National Theatre, to be financed by "voluntary" contributions of the nobles to the amount of 450,000 forints.(540) It may have been partly in reaction to this resolution that the Croatian *Sabor* voted on August 18th to support and encourage plans for the national theatre, to collect from its members the sum of 4,500 forints, and to appoint a committee headed by Count Drašković to investigate the matter and report back to the *Sabor.*(541)

This action was in harmony with earlier decisions of the *Sabor* which in its meeting of May 21st to 26th, 1839, had resolved:

> The culture of a nationality is reflected in the language of its fatherland which unavoidably engenders love for the native soil thus contributing to the strength of the nation. It is, therefore, the sense of the Croatian *Sabor* that the Illyrian language, which includes all the popular dialects and has lately developed in a most satisfactory manner, be given all attention and care.(542)

The most important institution through which a literary language can be introduced and taught to the general public is the school. The elementary schools of the Triune Kingdom had always included instruction in the national language in their curriculum, but the language taught and the orthography used was that of the local school district. By 1836 school inspectors had already begun to ask the Central School Administration whether the Illyrian language reforms might be introduced in the elementary schools.(543) Since the schools of Civil Croatia and Civil Slavonia were regulated by a Royal Educational code, all major innovations in curriculum had to be approved by the Emperor. The School Administration advised the school inspectors to be patient.

The Illyrian language, however, was already being taught in the Zagreb *Gimnazium* on an informal basis. Antun Mažuranić and Vjekoslav Babukić were professors at the Gimnazium, and in 1836 Antun Mažuranić was given permission to give free extracurricular lectures on the Illyrian language and literature to the upper classes of the Gimnazium. In 1839, these lectures were opened to all the classes, and in the same year Mažuranić published the first Illyrian language text. (544)

On January 30, 1840 Stanko Vraz wrote to Dragutin Rakovac:

> Three days ago a rescript came from the august Imperial Court, enjoining that the Illyrian orthography and language be introduced in the schools of Croatia, Slavonia and Dalmatia. Yesterday the Superintendant advised the patriots and most prominent Zagreb men-of-letters of the fact and invited them to a meeting. Since Gaj is not yet here, the question has not yet been settled.(545)

Gaj soon returned to Zagreb and final plans were made. Undoubtedly the speed with which the Illyrian language reforms of 1835 and 1836 received official sanction was in part a reflection of the political struggle between Croats and Magyars, and the desire of Vienna to protect the Croats against Magyarization. It was also a personal triumph for Dr. Ljudevit Gaj.

Therefore, from 1840 on, the Illyrian literary language with the new orthography was taught in the schools of the Triune Kingdom as the language of instruction in the elementary schools, and as an elective subject in higher schools. This decision was further endorsed by the Croatian *Sabor* at their August meeting, when they decided to petition the Emperor for permission to establish a chair of the Illyrian language in every secondary school of the Triune Kingdom, and in the Zagreb Academy.

In March 1840 Ljudevit Gaj decided to make one more attempt to win Russian support — he would go to Russia. The step was logical; his presence had in the past untangled bureaucratic snares and brought about coalescence of hitherto cautious, wavering support. But his mind before departure must have been troubled, uneasy, for he made his last will and testament.

The trip to Russia(546) remains very much in the haze of conjecture. Gaj's diary is extremely sketchy; the entries mention innocuous observations and thoughts, important meetings and events are carefully left out. The nature of his pilgrimage dictated caution. Gaj left Zagreb in April. His first stop was Brno where he visited Frantisek Zach.(547) Gaj had first met Zach in Vienna in 1838, where Zach was attempting to organize a secret society among Slavic students to work with the left wing of the Polish emigration.(548) Soon after Gaj's visit to Brno, Zach left for Paris where he joined the right wing of the Polish emigration. In 1843 he would be sent by Prince Adam Czartoryski to be his secret agent in Belgrade and would then become an important figure in the second, anti-Russian phase of Gaj's secret politics (1842-1848). Gaj's next stop was Prague where he called on P.J. Šafařík and obtained from him several letters of introduction addressed to prominent personages in Russia. From Prague Gaj went to Dresden, to collect yet another sign of high favor and recognition: he requested and was granted an audience with Friedrich Augustus of Saxony. He presented to the King the Croatian translation of Sartori's travelogue of His Majesty's journey through Montenegro and Dalmatia in 1838. The King graciously presented Gaj with a diamond stick pin in return.

On the 12th of May, Gaj was in Warsaw. He had an audience with Count Benkendorf, in the course of which the Count indicated he would much rather give Gaj a thorough hearing in St. Petersburg.(549) On July 15th, after a long journey, Gaj was received by Benkendorf again, in St. Petersburg. Gaj handed the Count his fourth and, he insisted, last petition.(550) The note was short and almost desperate in tone. It reviewed the fate of the first three petitions, then gave a blunt warning: if Gaj received no immediate support, his printing press and newspaper would either have to close down, or fall into the hands of the enemies of Slavdom. In the service of the "inimical West" and the Magyars, the press and the papers would militate against everything Russian. If Russia turned a deaf ear to Gaj's entreaties, not only would the remarkable achievements of his tireless efforts come to nothing, but every prospect of his influencing future developments would disappear. After all, continued Gaj, the fact that the Illyrian student youth and the young Catholic clergy were sympathetic to the Slav (Cyrillic) alphabet and the Slav (Orthodox) Church, was due to him.

Count Benkendorf was completely ignorant of the position of the Slavs at the time, and Gaj's demands for strong financial support coupled with his veiled indications of the benefits Russia might reap were she to strengthen her influence among the Illyrian Slavs, must have confused the bureaucrat.(551) He referred him to Count S.S. Uvarov, the

Minister of Education. Count Uvarov arranged for Gaj to attend a meeting of the Russian Academy on July 26, at which Gaj delivered an address explaining his work and his financial difficulties. The Academy, in a meeting a few days later, decided to make a gift of one thousand rubles to Gaj.(552)

Gaj then traveled on to Moscow, carrying various letters of introduction to M.P. Pogodin, Professor of History at the University of Moscow. Pogodin was a member of a Slavophile circle known as the Union of Slavs. He introduced Gaj to other members of the group. They listened with interest and sympathy to Gaj as he spoke of the meaning of Slavic brotherhood, the need for Slavic cultural unity, the problems he had encountered in his work in Croatia, of the Illyrian Movement and his plans to print more and more material in the Cyrillic alphabet so that the Illyrians would become familiar with both alphabets used in the Slavic world. The Slavophiles voted a ''sacrificial'' collection of 15,000 rubles to aid Gaj in his work. The amount collected apparently exceeded the original goal and totaled between 17,500 and 20,000 rubles.(553)

Although Gaj was warmly received in Moscow, one wonders whether the Slavophiles really understood what he was talking about. For instance, Gaj notes in his diary that on August 28th he was invited to the opening of a new theatre, and in his honor the orchestra played Russian, Polish and Hungarian (!) dances.(554)

Ljudevit Gaj returned to St. Petersburg for a few days and left for Prague on September 6th. He arrived there six days later and stayed with Šafařík until September 30th. Šafařík was especially interested in the Slavic books and manuscripts Gaj had collected on his trip. Some of these were of great value, and Šafařík encouraged Gaj to publish the most important ones as soon as possible.(555) Gaj arrived in Zagreb in the second week of October.

Although Gaj described his trip to friends as a success,(556) it was only partly so. From Count Benkendorf's attitude Gaj could conclude that his memorandum of November 1st, 1838 had been a serious mistake. The warmth of the reception accorded him by the learned societies helped bring the general position of Russia towards the Illyrian aspirations into a clearer focus: the Russians were sympathetic to the Pan-Slav cultural aspects of the Illyrian movement, but had no intention of taking a political role in the Balkans.

Gaj's trip to Russia opened his eyes. He began to realize the dangers of the policy he had been advocating. As a result of his brief foray into political Pan-Slavism he became convinced that cultural Pan-Slavism was the only kind useful to the Illyrians. This is clearly stated in two unpublished notes written in the early 1840's. In the first Gaj said that were the Pan-Slavs to begin to work toward political unification under the leadership of one of the large Slavic peoples to the end of unifying all of the Slavs in a Slavic nation state, the leading Slavic people:

> . . . will not, indeed cannot, tolerate specific, distinctive traits which might prevent the unification of small and large countries. Such unification signifies a complete transformation and the destruction of all the distinctive traits.(557)

This is then the opposite of what Gaj said would happen in the cultural unification of the Illyrians, where the local or provincial distinctions would be maintained and strengthened and would blend together into a richer and more diverse whole.(558) Cultural unification could tolerate diversity, political unification could not. In the second note he said that Pan-Slavism could be achieved in two ways, by "political power" and by "moral power."(559) If "political power" were used, Pan-Slavism would be only an illusion, for in truth it would mean the absorption of all branches of the Slavic people by the strongest — Russia. The second method, that of "moral power," was the only viable one for it was based on the ideas of cooperation and brotherhood.

As long as the contents of Gaj's November 1839 memorandum were kept secret he had little to fear. That he traveled to Russia was no secret either in Zagreb or Vienna. We do not know whether Gaj received all of the money which was collected for him in St. Petersburg and Moscow, nor do we know how and when it reached him. Ljudevit Gaj would remain sympathetic to the Russians within the framework of cultural Pan-Slavism, but now convinced that Russian political action among the Southern Slavs could only be detrimental to the Illyrian Movement, he would begin to look for other outside allies, preferably in the anti-Russian camp.

CHAPTER IX

THE ILLYRIANS ENTER POLITICS (1841-1843)

In 1841, Ljudevit Gaj was at the height of his power and influence; demonstrations and banquets were held in his honor, his advice was sought, he provided leadership and strategy in cultural and political matters, his sway over the Illyrians and his judgement appeared unchallenged. His behavior, however, was beginning to change. He was irritable, he craved praise and adulation and suspected the loyalty of his oldest friends. In April, Gaj publicly accused Vjekoslav Babukić of spreading malicious gossip and working to undermine his reputation. In a bitter and sad letter formally addressed to "Dear Sir and Friend," written in the second person plural although the two men were on intimate terms, Babukić described his numerous and futile attempts to get an explanation or apology from Gaj.(560)

His admiration and respect for Gaj were undiminished, asserted Babukić, and he had not been talking against him. He insisted however that Gaj carry out the promise made the preceding December and find a new editor for *Danica.* In the letter Babukić tried to be fair, ennumerating Gaj's many kindnesses to him as well as his own faithful service to the Movement, but he reminded Gaj that he had accepted the editorship of *Danica* on Gaj's insistence, without regular salary and with the understanding that he would do the job only so long as he had time for it.(561)

At the very end of the letter Babukić pleaded:

> I beg you in the name of all patriots — curb the accursed suspiciousness of your nature, rein in your ambition, be just to everyone, confide everything to the friends you have found tried and true, and fear nothing. Remember the folk proverb:
> 'Little things in harmony grow,
> Discord destroys everything.'(562)

Soon after this, Gaj appointed Dimitrije Demeter to serve as chief editorial assistant on *Danica. Novine* also had a new editor. In February of 1841, Gaj replaced Rakovac with Jakov Užarević as chief editorial assistant. Užarević, a physician, was not trained in newspaper work but as a native speaker of the *štokavski* dialect was at ease in the new literary language.(563) He was apparently not able to handle all of the work, for within a year Gaj hired Bogoslav Šulek to serve as technical editor of *Novine* and kept Užarević on as language editor. Šulek quickly became a key person in Gaj's editorial offices.(564)

On February 2nd, the Zagreb Reading Club decided to move to rooms in Gaj's house. The new quarters were more spacious and provided easy access to Gaj's personal library which contained a valuable collection of books and manuscripts, and, copies of many foreign newspapers.(565)

There were no public meeting rooms in Zagreb at the time. Social life was organized along class lines and gatherings were held in private homes.(566) Ljudevit Gaj held almost constant open house, using his office and mealtimes for consultations. Many key meetings were held at the home of Janko Drašković, who used dinners and evening gatherings to bring together Illyrians of various classes and to honor distinguised guests.(567) There was no hall where large public meetings could be held, no place to store the collections of artifacts intended for the national museum, no repository for the books and records of various Illyrian organizations.(568)

To meet this need, Ljudevit Gaj presented a formal proposal to the Zagreb Reading Club on March 27th, 1841, in which he suggested that the Club purchase or build a large structure which could become the center of Croatian cultural life, housing the National Theatre, the Reading Club, the National Museum, the National Cultural Society and *Matica Ilirska,* and that the Club finance this project through a lottery.

The Russian scholar I.I. Sreznevskij attended the meeting and described the events in a letter home:

> The plan for the National Center was read and approved unanimously. They then began electing members of the Committee to put the plan into action. It was done without any strife . . . It was apparent that Gaj knew how to get all those ambitious and vain wills to merge into one single patriotic will. The plan was written by Gaj, and whatever he suggests is considered sacred. One would think that Gaj is an old man. On the contrary, he is young and handsome.(569)

Among the members elected to the Committee for the National Center were Ljudevit Gaj, Count Drašković and three of the most prominent businessmen of Zagreb County: Ambroz Vranyczany, Anastas Popović, and Jovan Malin.(570)

Gaj's plan for a lottery seemed a painless way of raising money. He suggested that the Reading Club sell 20,000 tickets at 5 forints each, and award prizes amounting to 17,500 forints. Citizens who purchased more than 100 tickets would be entered in the records as "founders" of the National Center. After studying Gaj's plan, Ambroz Vranyczany advised against it. He warned that unless enough tickets were sold the Reading Club might actually lose money on a lottery, for the prize money would have to be paid. Vranyczany convinced the Committee and the Club that it would be better to collect funds for the National Center by soliciting contributions from private citizens and institutions.(571) Gaj's close work with Ambroz Vranyczany on the funding of the National Center began a friendship which would become important in the next few years.(572)

All the new national institutions to date had been established with Gaj's help and often on his initiative. On March 25th, Bishop Haulik, Janko Drašković and a handful of distinguished figures concerned with agricultural problems decided to form a new organization "Hrvatsko-Slavonsko gospodarsko društvo u Zagrebu" (Croatian-Slavonian Agricultural Society in Zagreb) for the purpose of improving the backward state of Croatian farming.(573) This was not an Illyrian organization; it drew membership from groups directly interested in agriculture: magnates, gentry, as well as a few landless intellectuals, and it represented all shadings of political opinion. By 1841 agricultural societies similar to the Croatian-Slavonian Agricultural Society had been founded in other parts of the Habsburg Empire: in the Slovene provinces, Lower Austria, Tyrol and Voralberg, Moravia-Silesia, Bohemia and Hungary. They were established by noble landowners eager to modernize agriculture, raise productivity, and increase the revenue from their lands.(574) Gaj was not present at the charter meeting, nor did he join the new society until 1842, and by then the Agricultural Society already had 630 members.(575)

Gaj's lack of interest in the Agricultural Society was not surprising. He did not own land nor did he possesss serfs. He was a man of the town, unfamiliar with agricultural problems and not especially interested in them. He never developed a program of economic and social reform for the Illyrian Movement. He was convinced that men could achieve true fulfillment in their lives only as members of their nation. While in Western Europe and even in Hungary in the 1830's and 1840's, nationalism and liberalism seemed interdependent, it must not be forgotten that they are separate ideologies. Man, to a nationalist, is first a member of a nationality, and only after that of a class and an economic system.(576) While it appears from some of Gaj's unpublished notes that he resented the dominance of the Croatian nobles in political and economic life,(577) and that he admired the freedoms guaranteed by the English constitution,(578) he did not declare himself in favor of the abolition of serfdom and class privilege and the extension of the franchise until 1848, when these had become universal demands in revolutionary Europe.

On April 6th, Ljudevit Gaj and Antun Mažuranić left Zagreb for Dalmatia. The purpose of their trip was twofold: to make personal contact with the Dalmatian intellectuals and win them over to the Illyrian Movement, and to collect manuscripts and published works of the sixteenth and seventeenth century Dubrovnik and Dalmatian writers, so that they could be published or reprinted by *Matica Illirska.*

The majority of the Dalmatian writers of the time identified with Italian culture, wrote in the Italian language and were indifferent if not at times hostile to the goals of the Illyrian Movement. Although Gaj and Mazuranic were politely and even warmly received in the major towns they visited, they found few supporters except in Dubrovnik. Though Dubrovnik had recently lost its independence and was now just another Dalmatian town, it had succeeded in staying aloof from Italianization.(579) To the Illyrians, Dubrovnik represented the Illyrian "Athens". Illyrian writers used the renaissance writers of Dubrovnik as models of style and literary language.(580) From 1837 on, excerpts from the works of Gundulić, Palmotić, Gjorgjić, Zlatarić and other Dubrovnik writers were published in *Danica,* and in 1838 with solemn ceremony, the Illyrians commemorated the two hundredth anniversary of the death of Ivan Gundulić at the Church of St. Catherine in Zagreb.(581) The affection and regard were returned. Antun Kaznačić (1784-1874), a Dubrovnik lawyer and poet, declared himself an Illyrian in 1839, and was soon joined by other Dubrovnik *literati,* for the Illyrian Movement had rekindled in them a pride in their past.

Gaj and Mažuranić were given an enthusiastic reception in Dubrovnik. Gaj was, of course, the major figure, and it was to him that odes were written, for him that serenades were sung and elaborate banquets prepared. Mažuranić, who had looked forward to this visit for many weeks, was sick and did not go out at all.(582) Gaj was received by the most distinguished Dubrovnik citizens, given access to private libraries where he found many of the manuscripts he sought, and permitted to take manuscripts with him to Zagreb so that they could be published by *Matica Ilirska.* During Gaj's visit to Dubrovnik Antun Kaznačić served as his guide and official host, yet there is a letter from Kaznačić to Gaj written in January 1843 complaining that the Dubrovnik poet had not heard one word from either Gaj or Mažuranić since they had left Dubrovnik. He hoped his letter found them in good health.(583)

Vuk Karadžić was also visiting Dalmatia in the spring of 1841. The paths of Karadžić and Gaj crossed several times and they decided to travel together to Montenegro.(584) On May 27th and 28th, Gaj, Mažuranić, Karadžić and the others of their party met with the Prince Bishop in Cetinje.(585)

Ljudevit Gaj returned to Zagreb alone; Antun Mažuranić remained in Dubrovnik to recuperate from his illness. Gaj reached Zagreb on his birthday, July 8th, 1841. He was greeted by a huge birthday celebration, replete with odes and a student serenade. On August 25th a second large party, this time a private one, was held in honor of his name-day. The host, Mirko Šandor, a man of somewhat dubious reputation,(586) invited all of the leading Illyrians and other distinguished guests to his country home, an estate near Krapina. Sreznevskij who was among the guests described the celebration in a letter. Šandor, he says, had spared no expense to make it a memorable occasion: rifles were discharged in the air to announce Gaj's arrival when he was still four kilometers away from the house. The room in which the dinner was held had in the place of honor a portrait of Gaj, wreathed with flowers. Illyrian symbols and slogans covered the walls. There was a poem in honor of Gaj under every napkin. After the soup Šandor asked the guests to fill their glasses and drink a toast:

> '. . . to him whose name today we all know.'
>
> Everybody shouted 'May God give long life to Ljudevit Gaj,' and began to sing the song which begins as follows:
>
> 'Ljudevit! You were the first to offer sacrifice for us,
> The first to give everything dear to you, to your nation . . .'
>
> We all drank. Gaj was close to tears.(587)

The Illyrian Movement was now firmly established in Zagreb. Dalmatia, as we have seen, was not very receptive to Illyrian ideas.(588) Let us now examine briefly the support the Movement found among the Serbs, Slovenes and Bosnians by 1841.

There was little interest in the Illyrian Movement among the Serbs of Hungary and those of the Principality. This was not the fault of the Illyrians, for they had worked hard to attract the Serbs. Some Serbs, in particular a small group in Novi Sad, supported the Illyrian Movement, but they were, by and large, minor literary figures who exerted little influence over the rest of the educated Serbian community.(589) The Serbs were, first of all, opposed to the use of the term Illyrian. It was to them a derivative from Latin, a dead, foreign language, and it negated the adjective derived from the beloved and ancient name of their country

— Serbian. If a neutral term was necessary to avoid particularism among the Southern Slavs, then why not use *Jugoslav,* they asked? The Serbs were little interested in adopting the Illyrian literary language. They were involved in the struggle between Vuk Karadžić's new Serbian literary language and the old *Slaveno-srpski,* and the Illyrian language had little appeal to either party for it was not specifically and traditionally a Serbian language. Lastly, the Serbs expected the Illyrians to use the Cyrillic alphabet to the exclusion of the Latin alphabet. The Illyrians, on the other hand, argued for the equality of both alphabets.(590)

Serbian opposition to the Illyrian Movement was closely tied to religion. Some Serbian writers argued that the Illyrian Movement was a tool of the Roman Catholic Church, and that it sought not only to destroy the Serbian name and language, but the Serbian Church as well. They seemed unmoved by the fact that Gaj and the other Illyrians continually called for religious tolerance and mutual respect. One of Gaj's most eloquent pleas in this behalf was made in the "Manifesto" of 1840:

> We must embrace and love each other, regardless of religious belief, though everyone must respect his own creed, because the . . . founder of the Western and Eastern Church loved us all equally . . . Let each of us be faithful to his own Church, but let us all be true to the teaching of Jesus about brotherly love. This is the only way for us to save our divided nation.(591)

However, "our nation" to the Serbs meant Serbia, not Illyria. Their preoccupation at the moment was with the development of their national language, culture and state. They were little interested in ideas of Illyrian unity or Slavic reciprocity.(592) Although the Illyrian Movement had been greeted warmly by the Serbs in 1835, attacks upon it began in 1837 and reached their height between 1839 and 1841. The Illyrian "kolo" was now, in effect, limited to the Croats, the Slovenes and the Bosnians.

The Illyrian Movement found a measure of support among the youth of eastern Styria, Carinthia and Graz,(593) but the support remained confined to small groups and individuals. Even then, it was a diffuse support of the ideological components of the Movement behind which it was possible to discern outlines of a broader Pan-Slav goal. The students, clerics and intellectuals found the idea of *vzájemnost* extremely attractive, but Gaj's Illyrian language did not attract them. Very few were willing to follow the example of Stanko Vraz (1810-1851), the leading Slovene Illyrian who began his career as a Slovene poet, then became more and more active in Illyrian cultural affairs, moved to Zagreb, and after 1839 wrote exclusively in the Illyrian language. The chances that the Slovenes might accept the Illyrian language were slim from the very beginning, and they diminished as a body of literature in the regional literary traditions began to grow. True, there was as yet no unified modern Slovene literary language, but the poetry of France Prešern (1800-1849) offered strong evidence of the viability of the Slovene language, and the idea that the Slovene and the Illyrian languages should come together, inform each other, and fuse into a new whole, began to take precedence over the demands that the Slovenes simply adopt the Illyrian language. The two points of view persist throughout the 19th century and into the 20th.(594)

A particularly impassioned defense of the Slovene language came from the distinguished Slavist Jernej Kopitar. In his opposition he was often more a Slovene and a Catholic than a scholar. He rejected the Illyrian name as unhistorical, criticised the artificial — as opposed to vernacular — nature of the Illyrian literary language, and thundered against the influence of the ''Czech Protestants'' Šafařík and Kollár in the Illyrian Movement. For Gaj he had nothing but distrust — he considered Gaj an opportunist — and Gaj's orthographic innovations, the č, š, and ž, were dismissed as ''Bohemian fly tracks.''(595)

Although the Illyrian Movement failed to attract a large following among the Slovenes, it left a mark on the patterns of Slovene cultural and political life. Gaj's orthography was accepted in the 1840's. But perhaps more important is an intangible value, brought into being by the mild debate over the language; the Slovenes' desire for a greater linguistic and literary closeness with the Croats slowly grew into a sense of cultural and political solidarity with their neighbors and the other Southern Slavs.

The Bosnian ''Illyrians'' came almost exclusviely from among the members of the Franciscan order.(596) The Bosnian friars were given their academic and religious training in Rome, Zagreb, and various parts of Hungary, and those who studied in Zagreb and Hungary came in contact with the Illyrian Movement. Several Bosnian Franciscans, among whom the most prominent were Ivan Franjo Jukić, Martin Nedić, and Grga Martić, became regular contributors to *Danica.* In 1839, a group of pro-Illyrian Franciscans attending school in Vesprim formed a secret society, and drew up plans to free Bosnia-Hercegovina from Turkish rule by means of an armed rebellion. They left for Bosnia in the spring of 1840, hoping to gather massive local support. Instead — they were dissuaded from the plot by their brother Franciscans. Although the rebellion had never gone beyond the stage of talk within monastery walls, someone reported the plot to Bishop Rafo Barišić, who immediately informed the Turkish Governor, Rome, and Vienna, that Bosnia had almost broken into armed rebellion, and that unless seditious influences within the Franciscan order were eliminated there might be real trouble.(597) The mere possibility of an uprising frightened the Turkish authorities and the Catholic hierarchy in Bosnia so thoroughly that from 1840 on the local Illyrians were kept under close surveillance. They continued to write for *Danica* and speak in favor of Southern Slav unity, but they were not free, nor were they powerful enough to establish organizations such as Reading Clubs or Drama Groups through which the Illyrian Movement might have found support among other groups of the population.

Therefore it was clear to Gaj and his colleagues by 1841, that effective support of the Illyrian Movement lay where it had begun, in the Triune Kingdom and especially in the three counties of Civil Croatia. There it had succeeded in giving the Croats a modern literary language and awakening a sense of national identity. This young nationalism was now threatened by a growing pro-Magyar faction in Croatian political life. It therefore became necessary for the Illyrians to form a political party in order to ensure the survival of the Movement.

Although Croatian political life had already begun to polarize into pro-Illyrian and anti-Illyrian factions as early as 1836, it was not until 1841 that the factions developed into political parties. The first to organize was the "horvatsko-vugerska stranjk" (Croato-Hungarian Party) in February, 1841. This Party was soon dubbed "Magyaromani" which was shortened to "Magyaroni," the name by which the Croato-Hungarian Party was best known. The Magyarones were drawn primarily from the magnates, the poorer gentry, government officials, graduates of Hungarian schools, the foreign middle class, and the peasant nobles. They included liberals who supported the reform movement in Hungary, conservatives who opposed any kind of reform, educated men and illiterate peasant nobles. The Magyarones were united in their opposition to the Illyrian Movement. They rejected the Gaj orthography and the new literary language, clinging stubbornly to the old orthography and the *kajkavski* literary tradition. They preferred absorption into a Magyar Hungary to membership in a Southern Slav cultural community. They accused the Illyrians of working against the true interests of Croatia, sometimes labeling the Illyrian Movement a tool of Viennese centralism, other times a puppet of Russian imperialism.(598)

The immediate goal of the Magyarones was to get into power in Croatia by winning the county elections, then to manipulate the county assemblies so as to make certain Magyarones were chosen as representatives to the *Sabor.* A Magyarone dominated *Sabor* would elect Magyarone deputies to the Joint Parliament and there, with Magyar help, they could crush the Illyrian Movement.(599)

All three counties of Civil Croatia were due to have elections in 1841 and 1842. Sometime in July or August of 1841, the Illyrians in response to the Magyarone threat began to organize as a political party.(600)

The Illyrians made their first appearance as a Party at the Križevci county elections on September 1st, 1841. Although the Illyrian Party entered the elections without much preparation, without even a public definition of their Party program, the Illyrian candidates won unanimously. That evening at the victory celebration, Ljudevit Gaj made the first clear statement of the goals of the Illyrian Party, one which would become the framework for the Illyrian political literature of the next few years: "Da Bog poživi konstituciju ugarsku, kraljevinu Hrvatsku i narodnost ilirsku" (May God preserve the Hungarian Constitution, the Croatian Kingdom and the Illyrian Nationality).(601)

The second country elections were held in Varaždin on November 3rd. The Magyarones were stronger here, yet the Illyrians again won a decisive victory. Ljudevit Gaj took part in the Varaždin county elections, though traditionally only prelates and nobles could participate, through a loophole in the electoral law. Widows of nobles who did not have an adult son to represent them at the county elections, and prelates, could deputize another individual, noble or non-noble, to act for them. Thus at the Varaždin county elections Ljudevit Gaj represented Baroness Ana Sermage, and at the Zagreb election, he was deputy for Abbot Krizmanić.(602)

Ljudevit Gaj was recognized immediately as a leader of the Illyrian Party. He had however two serious drawbacks as a political leader: he was a commoner, and he was inexperienced. These would not hinder his political activities in the first year of the Party's existence, but would be an important factor in his being pushed into a secondary position within the Party by 1843.

The Zagreb county elections were due to be held the following May (1842). Both parties prepared for a difficult contest, for Zagreb county was not only the center of the Illyrian Movement, it was also the home of the opposition to it.

Gaj's preoccupation with politics may have affected his behavior during the visit of Jan Kollár, who arrived in Zagreb on September 12th. The Illyrians had a busy program planned for this honored and long-awaited guest. The climax of Kollár's stay was a festive banquet sponsored by the Reading Club and attended by nearly 200 guests on September 14th. The original plan called for the banquet to be followed by a student serenade, but the serenade was cancelled on Gaj's request. Stanko Vraz, who had already begun to dislike Gaj,(603) and Sreznevskij assumed that Gaj acted out of sheer egotism.(604) I tend to agree with Horvat instead, who argues that Gaj acted for political reasons, fearing that since many of the serenaders were Catholic theological students, the Catholic hierarchy might have become angered if they had taken part in a demonstration in favor of a Protestant pastor.(605) Kollár's profession was a constant embarrassment to the Illyrians. Both Illyrians and Magyarones were seeking supporters among the Catholic clergy. The Illyrians had now openly declared themselves dedicated to the defense of Croatia's Municipal laws and one of these laws excluded Protestants from ownership of land and from public office. Although the objection to Protestant migration to Croatia was directed primarily against the Magyars who considered their Calvinist Church the "national" church, all Protestants were regarded with suspicion, even the Slovak Pan-Slav Kollár. The walls of the Zagreb Reading Club, in 1844, for example, were filled with pictures of local patriots and Slavic leaders. Šafařík was on the wall for all to see, but the portrait of Kollár with his church altar in the background, was hidden in the closet.(606)

There is no other indication that Gaj did not welcome Kollár warmly. There was a long poem about Kollár in *Danica* and an article describing the banquet for him.(607) Kollár's diary of his Zagreb visit is filled with nothing but praise and admiration for the Illyrians and for Gaj. He says:

> If we Slavs had a national Pantheon like the Romans or the French, or a Valhalla as the Germans, I would place Gaj's statue there and crown it with a wreath of linden leaves.(608)

The politicization of the Illyrian Movement had begun to attract attention abroad by the end of 1841. In October, Dr. Adam Lysczynski, an agent of Prince Adam Czartoryski the leader of the right wing of the Polish emigration, came to Zagreb to talk with Illyrian political leaders, in particular with Janko Drašković and Ljudevit Gaj.(609) He came from Belgrade, where he had stayed for several months, bringing a letter of introduction to Gaj from Stefan Herkalović (610) Prince Czartoryski was then serving as a sort of Polish government in exile. From his residence in Paris, the Hotel Lambert, with tacit French approval, he conducted a complicated foreign policy which had as its ultimate goal the liberation of Poland.(611) This policy was implemented by a network of permanent and traveling agents who gathered information and worked to win support for Czartoryski's ideas. By 1841 the Balkans had become a focal point in his foreign policy.(612) He saw Turkey as the last bulwark against Russian and Austrian expansion on the Balkans and devised a complicated policy in which he upheld Turkey on the one hand and encouraged movements for national awakening and even national independence among the Christians of the

Ottoman Empire, in particular the Southern Slavs. In 1841 he set up a permanent mission in Constantinople and then began to contact political leaders among the Southern Slavs of Turkey and Austria — hence Lyczynski's mission to Belgrade and Zagreb. Serbia was to play the key role in Czartoryski's Balkan policy as it evolved over the next three years. He hoped that Serbia would become the nucleus of a future independent Southern Slav state, one which would include Orthodox Slavs of Turkey, the Serbs of Hungary and, possibly, the Catholic Southern Slavs. Czartoryski then set out to convince the leaders of the Serbian principality to accept this new role in the Balkans and to encourage them to establish closer ties with the other Southern Slavs.(613)

1841 was a transitional year for the Illyrian Movement. The "Illyrian" aspect of the Movement during its first six years had stressed Croatian membership in the ethnic community of Greater Illyria and introduced a literary language which, it was hoped, would be acceptable to all in this community. In the meanwhile it had provided the framework for the Croatian national awakening, given the Croats a modern literary language, and institutions to foster and spread acceptance of this language. It had drawn the Croats out of provincial isolation and given them pride in belonging to a major European people, thus putting their endangered position in Hungary in wider perspective. Bogoslav Šulek perhaps best summarized this aspect of the Movement when he wrote:

> (The Illyrians) only want to demonstrate that the Croatian and Slavonian people are not as insignificant as their enemies (Magyars) constantly claim; that the Croats and the Slavonians are only one part of the great Illyrian nationality, just as the Illyrians are only one part of the great Slavic nationality; that they do not need to achieve enlightenment through the medium of a foreign language, but, rather, are capable of developing their own language and literature.(614)

Undoubtedly the Illyrians had been disappointed to find that the Illyrian language and concept of Illyrian nationality did not win support among the Serbs of Southern Hungary and the Principality and among the Slovenes, but the primary focus of their attention had been, from the first, the Kingdom of Croatia, Slavonia and Dalmatia and the former Croatian lands. By 1841 with the emergence of the anti-Illyrian faction in the Triune Kingdom as an organized political party — the Croato-Hungarian or Magyarone Party — the Illyrians were forced to subordinate their Illyrian cultural program to a political one.

The Magyarones had hopes of a victory in Zagreb county where there were several communities of peasant nobles: the large Turopolje community, and the much smaller communities of Sveti Ivan, Mosavac and Draganić. The *Comes,* elected leader of Turopolje — Daniel Josipović — was an outspoken Magyarone. Up to 1831 each community of peasant nobles had been represented by its *Comes,* who cast a single vote at the elections. In 1831 the Hungarian Court Chancellery granted the peasant nobles the right to vote as individuals and this was reaffirmed in 1835.(615) The peasant nobles had made little use of this privilege in the 1830's, when political life still continued along traditional lines, but with the emergence of political parties in 1841, the implication of their new status became clear. If one party could win the allegiance of the majority of the peasant nobles and mobilize them to come and vote, it could win the Zagreb county elections.

The months between November and May gave both parties time to prepare for the confrontation. The Magyarone *Comes* of Turopolje, Daniel Josipović, easily swung his community over to his Party. The Illyrians tried to win over the smaller communities, but only Draganić declared itself pro-Illyrian.(616)

It now became necessary for the Illyrians to explain their political goals. The Illyrian Party, or National Party as it would be called after 1843, did not adopt an official platform between 1841 and 1848.(617) It had, instead, a political program which was composed at first of broad statements of purpose, and later of proposals for specific reforms. The basic lines of this program were introduced in the Party writings of 1842.

When we speak of the "Illyrians" after September 1841, we no longer refer to the small tightly knit group of men who first called themselves by this name in 1835. The sharpening of political conflicts in Croatia, the first successes of the Illyrians organized as a Party and the personal magnetism of Ljudevit Gaj, drew into the Movement and the Party people who had been indifferent in the early years.(618) The Illyrian Movement had been just that, a movement, collecting around itself people of various classes and professions who agreed with the basic ideas of Illyrian cultural unity and Illyrian nationality. Its goals could be explained through *Danica* and *Novine* and could be taken up by hundreds of isolated individuals. This was not so with a party. In order to bid for support, it had to develop a program which was sufficiently clear and one upon which all could agree.

The Illyrian Party, the political wing of the Illyrian Movement, was composed of nobles and commoners; conservatives and democrats; magnates who could move in court circles and penniless writers. It included serf-owners, the educated sons of serfs, businessmen, ex-officers, civil servants, and professional men. Although the Party contained both nobles and commoners,(619) the Party Program had to be acceptable to the magnates and gentry within the Party for they were the only men who could lend support to the Party and the Movement from their appointive and elective positions in the Kingdom, and represent the Party at the county assemblies, *Sabor* and Joint Parliament. This heterogeneous Party could agree on the general program: defense of the Municipal laws, support of the national awakening in its Illyrian format, even gradual reform within the structure of the existing political, educational and economic institutions, but when it came to questions of radical social, political or economic reform, questions which related directly to class privilege and serfdom, the Illyrians had to remain silent.(620)

Gaj's motto of 1841 "May God Preserve the Hungarian Constitution, the Croatian Kingdom and the Illyrian nationality" set the framework for the Party program, but he left it to others to work out in detail. Three important definitions of Illyrian Party goals appeared in 1842, each somewhat different in emphasis but all agreeing on the major points: Dragutin Rakovac, *Mali katekizam za velike ljude;* Ljudevit Vukotinović, "Ilirisam i kroatisam," and Ivan Kukuljević, "Die Nationalität in Kroatien und Slawonien."(621) *Mali katekizam* is a kind of Party handbook. In a series of simple questions and answers, Rakovac set out to explain why Magyarization was a threat to national life, why the Magyarone solution was wrong and the Illyrian solution right for the immediate problems facing the Croats. He spent a great deal of time justifying use of the name Illyrian in cultural life, straying from the usual arguments in his admission that perhaps the ancient Illyrians were not Slavs, but adding that this was not important since "Illyrian" was the name used throughout history for the people inhabiting the territory of ancient Illyria.(622) His booklet ends with a good brief summary of Illyrian goals, as of 1842:

What do we want?

1. We want to have our national language, given to us by nature itself. We know that when the language of a nation dies, the nation dies with it.

2. To have our national literature, because without national literature the language must go down to ruin.

3. To educate our nation, and that can only be done in the national language. Foreign language can reeducate only the literate, never a whole nation.

4. To preserve intact our municipal rights *(iure municipalia),* for they are the foundation of our political being.

5. To remain, as we have been until now, brethren of the Magyars, under the Hungarian constitution.

> We do not want:
> 1. Any nation to consider us as simply matter to be used for the enlargement of her members.
> 2. To have others berate us, abuse us, sow doubt among us, while we are not permitted to open our mouths and say a word in answer.(623)

Rakovac's booklet was the least politically sophisticated, of the three. He mentioned support of the Municipal laws and Hungarian constitution, as articles of faith, not really explaining what they meant or how they related to the cultural program.(624)

In his article "Illirisam i kroatisam," Ljudevit Vukotinović spoke directly to Gaj's motto, explaining that "Illyrianism" was an ethnic and linguistic identification, one of intellect and feeling, valid only in literary life.(625) "Croatianism," on the other hand, did not belong in cultural life, for there it meant blind support of the provincial dialect *(kajkavski)* and its limited literature as opposed to the new Illyrian literary language and its literature. However "Croatianism" in political life, meaning here defense of the Municipal laws, loyalty to the Constitution and the King, was the very essence of the Illyrian political program.(626) The Party program, then, consisted of two major elements: cultural Illyrianism and political Croatianism.

"Die Nationalität in Kroatien und Slawonien," by Ivan Kukuljević is quite different in tone.(627) In German, directed to the nobles and educated elite, Kukuljević placed the Illyrian Movement in a broader perspective. He said that it was part of a European movement of national awakening, and that it developed in a way typical of other Slavic nationalities within the Habsburg Empire, for the idea of nationalism was first awakened through literature. A nationality, he said, regardless of its degree of political cohesion. lives or dies through its language and its literature.(628) Once this idea was accepted, he explained, and the new language and literature began to flourish, the Illyrian name was extended to the political life of the Croats and Slavonians through the new Illyrian Party. The Party adopted the name used for the reformed literature, Illyrian, for it was a general one, whereas "Croatian" would have too provincial a ring.(629) As to criticisms by ignorant opponents, of the "radical" nature of the Illyrian Program, Kukuljević stated that the Program had only two parts: 1) defense of the "Holy Constitution," the "old rights" and the "inherited nationality," and 2) enlightenment of the people, therefore it could in no way be considered radical.(630)

Thus the Illyrian Party combined traditional Croatian political goals with linguistic nationalism. These two aspects would merge at one point, only hinted at in the Party literature of 1842, when, in the next five years, the Illyrians would gradually move toward adoption of the new literary language as the language of the Triune Kingdom.

The Illyrian Party adopted a uniform: a blue or red *šurka* (a knee-length loose coat with toggle buttons worn over a waistcoat), a red cap with the Illyrian coat of arms (a crescent and a star) and a sabre. They wore these uniforms to elections, and for celebrations and demonstrations. The *šurka* was adapted from a type of coat worn by Croatian peasants,(631) the red cap was traditional to areas inhabited by Croats and Serbs,(632) and the crescent and star, the Illyrian coat of arms, were old Illyrian symbols, found on coins from Roman times, and incorporated in the coat of arms of many Croatian towns and noble families.(633)

The Illyrian Party found many supporters among the students. As the time drew near for the election, pro-Illyrian bands of students roamed the streets of Zagreb at night, singing patriotic songs and at times getting into street fights and breaking the windows of the houses of leading Magyarones. A steady stream of complaints from the Magyarone party began to reach Vienna. The authors seemed especially concerned about Ljudevit Gaj's influence on the youth. In one complaint Gaj is quoted as having said:

> The older generation can do whatever they want. The entire younger generation, even the child in his mother's womb, belongs to us.(634)

The Zagreb County elections held on May 31st 1842 were won by the Illyrians but in a manner quite different from that of the preceding two elections. The victory was a political *coup* engineered by Gaj in which the Illyrian won by a show of force. The *veliki-župan* of Zagreb County, Nikola Zdenčaj, was a member of the Illyrian party. In order to limit the size of peasant noble vote, he ordered that the elections take place in the enclosed courtyard of the Ban's palace instead of a field as the Magyarones had wanted. He also asked all participants to leave their weapons outside. The day preceding the election was filled with minor acts of violence; skirmishes between supporters of both parties, rock throwing which injured several people and a rash of broken windows.

On the morning of May 31st, the Illyrians arrived armed and forced their way into the courtyard, already packed with Magyarones who had obeyed Zdenčaj's orders and come unarmed. The Illyrians ejected their opponents by force. Zdenčaj called for military assistance to stop the fighting, the soldiers surrounded the palace, and the Illyrians, who were still inside, proceeded to hold the elections. Illyrian candidates were unanimously elected to all positions.

Ljudevit Gaj was recognized by his supporters and his enemies as the master strategist of this victory. The election was followed by fourteen days of celebration.(635) News of the *coup* spread quickly and was greeted enthusiastically by other Illyrians. In the words of one Illyrian in a letter to Gaj written five years later:

> Your deed has poured new living blood and stronger life into the dry veins of the Croat and Serb nations, and, most recently, into the veins of Carniola and Styria. You are more deserving of praise than the greatest of writers, for it is easier to rule by pen than it is to bring back to life . . . the rotten, softened multitudes. Your shield against all arrows is *your deed and the fruit of your activity — the elections of 1842,* which have accomplished more and brought more life into our people than all the fat and thin volumes of our literature.(636)

The Magyarone Party was quick to protest the illegality of the Zagreb county elections of May 31st. On June 2nd, they drew up a detailed letter to the Emperor which was signed by several hundred members of the party.(637) Similar letters went out to the Hungarian Court Chancellery, the counties of Civil Croatia and Civil Slavonia, and the Zagreb Bishop. On June 11th, the Turopolje community of peasant nobles wrote to the Emperor, asking that a Commission be appointed to investigate the legality of the Zagreb county elections.(638) Copies of this letter were sent to all Hungarian counties.

The piles of correspondence about the dangerous activities of Ljudevit Gaj, and the revolutionary nature of the Illyrian Movement on the desks of Prince Metternich and Count Sedlnitzky were growing. The first serious complaints about Gaj had come from Bosnia in 1840.

On May 31st, 1840 Mehmed Vedzihi Pasha, Governor of Bosnia wrote to Ban Vlašić complaining that "a Catholic by the name of Ljudevit Gaj in Zagreb" had been sending materials of a revolutionary nature to Bosnia.(639) Such activity, he said, endangered peaceful relations between Austria and Turkey. The letter reached Zagreb in June shortly after Ban Vlašić's death, and since the new Ban had not yet been chosen it was translated and sent on immediately to Count Sedlnitzky, who forwarded it to Prince Metternich.

Some time in June of the same year, 1840, Metternich was informed by the Russian ambassador in Vienna that the Russians had learned from an unidentified source that the Bosnian Christians were arming for revolt.(640) The Bosnians were apparently encouraged in their plans by a well-known Zagreb figure, Ljudevit Gaj. The information contained in the Russian dispatch seems to have been based on Gaj's second Russian Memorandum of 1838.

The next month, July, brought a letter from the Vatican, reporting that Ljudevit Gaj was in contact with French Revolutionaries who, with the help of Minister Thiers, had collected more than a million francs to aid Gaj in seditious actions. Gaj must be involved in subversive activities, continued this report, for he was known to be in contact with Czech Protestants and Russian "schizmatics," and should be carefully watched.(641)

Metternich was disturbed by these reports, both in regard to a possible uprising in Bosnia, and to Gaj's alleged role in a conspiracy there. Throughout the rest of 1840, 1841 and 1842, a series of letters went back and forth between the office of Count Sedlnitzky, his police agents and high Church and Government officials in Civil Croatia and Dalmatia. The unanimous opinion of all of the Croatian and Dalmatian officials and agents consulted, be they pro-Illyrian or anti-Illyrian or indifferent, was that the "Bosnian conspiracy" and the accusations against Gaj were nothing but malicious gossip. The Austrian Cabinet, however, decided to watch Gaj and the Illyrian Movement more closely than before.(642)

The Magyarone letters reporting on the illegal Zagreb county election prompted the Austrian Cabinet to action. On June 16th, 1842 a new Croatian Ban, Count Franjo Haller, was appointed to the post which had been vacant since May 1840. Ban Haller, a Hungarian magnate and Guards officer, was loyal to the dynasty and unsympathetic to the Illyrian Movement. His appointment was the first clear sign that the Austrian Court officials had changed their attitude toward the Illyrian Movement. This was followed on July 25th by the appointment of Josip Šišković as Royal Commissioner to investigate the May election.

Ban Haller and Commissioner Šišković arrived in Zagreb in October. Gaj ordered the Illyrian Party to attend the inauguration of the new Ban on October 18th in full strength, and show the Ban every respect.

Ban Haller made his first report to Metternich on October 19th. Despite the impressive showing of the Illyrian Party the day before, Ban Haller dismissed the Party as a band of foreigners and extremists, and proposed that the following steps be taken to restore order: eliminate all inflammatory articles from Croatian newspapers and periodicals, and suppress all books about Slavic unity; prohibit the use of the Illyrian name and the Illyrian coat of arms; and encourage the Zagreb Bishop to discipline unruly clerics and theological students. Although the Ban admitted that he was not yet familiar with the local political scene, he was convinced that the Illyrians wanted Croatia to separate from the Kingdom of Hungary.(643)

Ban Haller's report, which seemed to substantiate the Magyarone letters, initiated a correspondence about Ljudevit Gaj in the highest levels of Imperial Government. On December 1st, Palatine Joseph warned his brother Archduke Ludwig that Ljudevit Gaj was a dangerous liberal, "the Croatian Kossuth."(644) On December 23rd, Count Majlath complained of dangerous Illyrian influences among the students and officers of the Military Frontier.(645) Metternich tried to maintain a middle position; he pointed out that the recent trouble in Zagreb came from two sources, the Illyrian Movement and the Magyar national movement, and he argued that it would be unfair to act against only one of them, the Illyrians.(646)

In almost all of the debate about the Illyrian Movement discussed above, Gaj was cited as leader of the Movement. Yet while the Austrian authorities moved slowly toward their final decision, after the victory celebrations in May there were signs in Zagreb that Gaj no longer had the unwavering support of his old friends.

A conflict had been brewing for some time between Ljudevit Gaj and his most important Slovene convert, Stanko Vraz. Vraz had admired Gaj enormously at first, but as Gaj began to shift the focus of the Illyrian Movement to politics, Vraz declined to follow. Vraz still conceived of the Movement as one working solely for Southern Slav cultural unity within a larger framework of Slavic cultural cooperation.(647) In reaction to the politicization of the Illyrian Movement in 1841 and 1842, Vraz decided it was time to take a step he had been contemplating since 1839,(648) to found a journal of literary criticism with a truly Pan-Slav coverage. A fine poet himself, Vraz believed that the Illyrian language was now mature enough to support such a publication. Gaj opposed the plan at first, apparently fearing competition to *Danica*.(649) Vraz planned to call the new journal *Kolo.* Vukotinović and Rakovac volunteered as co-editors and two other Illyrians who had been close to Gaj from the early years of the Movement, Demeter and Antun Mažuranić, were involved in the project. Gaj was finally won over.(650) Announcements calling for subscribers to *Kolo* appeared in *Danica* and *Novine.* The first issue of *Kolo* appeared in May 1842, just at the time of the Zagreb county elections. The apparent harmony between Gaj and the editors of *Kolo* was abruptly broken when Gaj read the first issue, and specifically the brief introductory esssay by Dragutin Rakovac which discussed in some detail the role played by Obradović and other eighteenth century writers in laying the foundations for the national awakening in literature, but never once mentioned the name of Ljudevit Gaj. This may have been Rakovac's way to getting back at Gaj for problems which arose over Rakovac's editorship of *Novine*.(651)

Possibly Rakovac also felt it was not necessary to state the obvious, that the purpose of the first issue of *Kolo* was to explain why and how it had come about, not to give a history of the previous accomplishments of the Illyrian Movement. As we saw earlier in his quarrel with Babukić, Gaj seems to have become extremely sensitive to anything which could be regarded as a slight to his authorpy in the Movement, or which failed to give him credit for all he had done. Instead of blaming Rakovac for failing to mention him, he turned on Vraz, the chief editor. Gaj would find Vraz to be a most vindictive enemy in the next few years.

On September 24th, Ljudevit Gaj married Paulina Krizmanić, niece of Abbot Krizmanić of Bistrica. Paulina Kirzmanić was the orphaned daughter of an army officer, a pretty, dark, buxom woman, a head taller than her husband, neither wealthy nor especially clever.(652) Many considered her haughty. The marriage did not increase Gaj's popularity.

Gaj was badly in debt when he married, but this did not seem to matter to him any more. He kept borrowing money to pay off the interest on his loans and somehow escaped the anger of his creditors. The new couple lived simply, yet in November 1842, Gaj was forced to seek another loan. This time he turned to the Zagreb Reading Club. In February the Reading Club had decided to start collecting money for *Matica Ilirska,* even though permission for its establishment had not yet come from Vienna. Ljudevit Gaj had been elected Chairman of the Fund Raising Committee and by June, 3,000 forints had been collected.(653) In order to increase the capital while waiting for the fund to grow, the Reading Club decided to let some of the money out to reliable borrowers at a moderate interest rate. Gaj assumed that the Reading Club, of which he had been an active and distinguished member, would not even question his request. But the money was not theirs to give except when they were sure that it would be paid back promptly. In order to make this judgement the treasurer of *Matica Ilirska,* Ferdinand Zerjavić, was instructed to investigate the economic status of anyone applying for a loan.(654) The information received on Gaj forced the Club to reject his application for a loan.(655) The Reading Club was undoubtedly right in their decision, Gaj was a poor risk from an economic point of view, but it must have been a real humiliation for Gaj to be refused the loan, to have others know he had been, and to have at least some knowledge of his shaky financial situation known to people in the Movement.

From 1838 when Stefan Herkalović first went to Serbia, he kept Gaj informed of developments there.(656) Gaj's initial interest in Serbia was to find supporters for the Illyrian Movement and subscribers to his newspaper. With the abdication of Prince Miloš Obrenović in 1839, and the gradual ascent of the party known as the *Ustavobranitelji* (Defenders of the Constitution) which climaxed in the election of Prince Alexander Karadjordjević in 1842, the political situation in Serbia was much changed. The real power behind the throne was the *Ustavobranitelji* Party.(657) They stood for the gradual modernization of the political, economic and cultural institutions of the Serbian Principality and for constitutional limitations of princely power. This new regime, struggling for recognition, opposed most severely by Russia, was also being drawn slowly into Prince Czartoryski's sphere of operation and while it had not yet declared itself for the plan to use the Serbian Principality as the nucleus for a future independent Southern Slav state, it was now more aware of the other Southern Slavs and more open to contact with them.

Herkalović was a valuable link to the *Ustavobranitelji.* He had been tutor for a while to the children of two of the leading figures in the Party, Toma Vučić-Perišić and Avram Petronijević,(658) and in 1843 would be appointed to a key post in the new government, Chief of the Military Section.(659) In this position he would work closely with Ilija Garašanin, Minister of Internal Affairs.

In November 1842, Gaj opened formal contact with the *Ustavobranitelji* regime, when he sent Stjepan Car to Belgrade as his emissary. Car, a fiery and dedicated Illyrian, member of the new circle of young men which was forming around Gaj at the time, had recently lost his post at the Zagreb Academy as a result of his role in the May elections.(660) He carried with him a letter of introduction to Herkalović from Gaj which said:

> His heart is my heart, his mouth is my mouth, his life is dedicated to everlasting truth and the salvation of our brothers in blood and of our common homeland. Listen and strive so that his words may not be wasted.(661)

Herkalović introduced Car to Garašanin.(662) We do not know what they talked about. Gaj would send Car to Belgrade again in 1843 and 1844, the first time to talk about common action in Bosnia, the second time to work with Zach on a long-range plan for a Serbian Southern Slav program.(663) Car would soon be followed by other Illyrians from Gaj's most trusted circle, Albert Nugent, and Pavao Čavlović. In 1846 and 1847, Gaj would go to Belgrade himself.

By sending Car to Belgrade in 1842, Gaj opened a new phase of his secret politics. Although the ties Gaj would now build with the *Ustavobranitelji* regime would be useful to the Illyrians at times, Gaj sent Car to Belgrade as his personal representative, not as a representative of the Illyrian Party. As in his contact with Russia from

1838 to 1840, Gaj was acting on his own initiative, trying to find an outside source of help for the Movement. However his views and those of the men he sent to Belgrade to represent him were often taken by Garašanin and Zach, the resident agent of the Polish emigration, to represent those of the entire Illyrian Party.

Why did Gaj turn to Serbia for help? Here we must distinguish between immediate practical advantages and long-range political goals. Gaj now had access to the leaders of a government, through an old and trusted friend — Herkalović. While it is true that the Serbian Principality was small, young, poor, and still under Turkish suzerainty, it was a Southern Slav Principality and might be sympathetic enough to recognize Gaj's services to the Southern Slavs by helping him with money for his newspaper and Cyrillic letters for his press.(664)

But this is not the whole picture. Gaj's long range plans are more difficult to prove. Although he officially proclaimed loyalty to the Habsburg Empire and placed the Party goals firmly within the orbit of Croatia's traditional constitutional position within Hungary, Gaj seems to have come to believe that one possible alternative for the Croats in the future, would be membership in a Southern Slav state. This may always have been inherent in Gaj's ideas of Illyrian nationality, for it is only one step from ethnic and cultural unity to political unity. In his old age Gaj told Gjuro Deželić:

> Note: I was the first to tune the triangular instrument of Europe. I named the instrument a lyre, after the old Illyria. The points of the triangle are Skutari, Varna and Bjelak in Carinthia. I found these loose strings: the Carinthians, Istrians, Slovenes, Styrians, Dalmatians, Croats and Slavonians, Bosnians and Hercegovinians, Serbs and Montenegrans, Bulgars and our countrymen in lower Hungary. I endeavoured to awaken in them a yearning for union; I knew that sooner or later harmony would be achieved, so that a united homeland and a sovereign Illyria would come to life.(665)

A "sovereign Illyria" would be a Southern Slav nation state. While Zagreb was capable of supporting and initiating the idea of Illyrian nationality, it could not, under the present conditions, serve as the nucleus of an independent nation state, Belgrade could.

On this point Gaj's *Ostavština* is silent. He must have destroyed all possibly compromising Serbian material in the early 1850's along with his Russian correspondence. It is possible to reconstruct some of the lost documents with the help of Zach's summaries of his correspondence with Gaj in his reports to Czartoryski, letters from Gaj and mention of letters to Gaj which were preserved in private and government collections in Serbia, and reports on conversations with his representatives.(666) The large gaps in the Gaj correspondence begin in 1842.

There are for example no letters from Herkalović to Gaj in the correspondence between 1842 and 1848, although we know that they were in close contact during those years.(667) It is therefore from piecemeal evidence, based mostly on the testimony of others, that we will attempt to reconstruct Gaj's ideas about Serbia.

According to František Zach and Stefan Herkalović, Gaj favored the establishment of a Southern Slav state which would include the Croats and be headed by the Karadjordević dynasty.(668) Zach's report dates from the first months of 1844, and Herkalović's from the spring of 1848. Were Zach's statement to stand alone it could be discounted, for Zach based his understanding of Gaj's ideas on discussions with Car, not Gaj, and there is evidence that Zach sometimes interpreted what was told him by hearing what he wanted to hear.(669) However the testimony of Herkalović should be regarded more seriously, for he was an old and trusted friend of Gaj, and in 1848 came to Serbia as the official representative of the Croatian revolutionary government. While I agree with Šidak that it seems inconsistent with Gaj's other actions and ideas to consider leading the Croats into a Serbian-led Southern Slav state,(670) his second memorandum to Russia in 1838 was also inconsistent with his other activities at the time. In fact, as we examine the elaboration of Gaj's secret politics and public politics in the years between 1843 and 1848, we will find many inconsistencies. It seems to me that Gaj was at least considering the Serbian alternative in the 1840's, as Magyar attacks on Croatian autonomy increased and Vienna wavered in her attitude toward the Illyrians. If there was little hope for the fragmented remnants of the medieval Croatian state in modern Hungary, should the Croats not look for other alternatives?

Gaj was uneasy in the last weeks of 1842. Magyarone attacks on the Illyrians were intensifying, no one knew what action Vienna would take on the Report of Commissioner Šišković about the Zagreb county elections. This mood is reflected in Gaj's "Manifesto" for 1843, which appeared on Decmeber 7th, 1842. It differed from earlier ones in that it was more a defense than a statement of policy. The following passage is quite representative:

> Some accuse us (the Illyrians) of Western European liberalism. Others, on the contrary, of icy despotism, Russian influence, and of still other intentions which are in themselves contradictory. Every moment there is another political scarecrow, every minute another sinful aspiration, now French, now Russian, again Austrian, German or Slovenian, and all the foolish contradiction which can be cooked in the kettle of hell to blacken the Illyrian name. Who could count up all the reproaches and political wrongs with which our opponents have attempted and are still attempting to cast suspicion upon our en-

> terprises, and with which our most meritorious patriots have been constantly insulted and reproached. Every year the arrows of hatred have been sharpened and new reproaches added to the old ones. But our conscience remains clear . . . . .(671)

By the time "Proglas" appeared, Vienna had already decided on its course of action.

1842 was the last year Ljudevit Gaj and the Illyrian Movement were to be synonymous. From 1843 to 1848 the history of the Movement and life of Gaj are intertwined, but not in the same way they had been from 1835 to 1842. Gaj would remain an important figure in the Party and the Movement, but the initiative in cultural and political life would now pass to others. The one exception to this is in Gaj's secret ties with Serbia and the Polish emigration.

CHAPTER X

THE QUIET YEARS (1843-1845)

On January 11th, 1843, Emperor Ferdinand approved the decision of the State Conference which stated, that while his Imperial Majesty had no wish to hinder the development of the Croatian national language and while he considered it was his duty to protect the Municipal laws of Croatia, it was not his intention to encourage political unrest in the Triune Kingdom. For this reason he forbade use of the names Illyria, Illyrian and Illyrianism in any publications, or public meeting, or in the schools. He also forbade use of the Illyrian coat of arms.(672) The Imperial decision was proclaimed by Ban Haller on January 18th.

As a result of Commissioner Šišković's report on the Zagreb County elections of 1842, some leading Illyrians were suspended from their elective posts in Zagreb county while criminal action was initiated against them. These included Josip Bunjevac (*podžupan* of Zagreb County); Robert Zlatarović *(vice-notar);* Dragutin Kušlan (*vice-notar* of the town of Karlovac); Josip Smendrovac (Karlovac *Stadthauptman*); and Josip Stajdacher and Josip Čacković (Zagreb judges).(673) Criminal suits were also begun against several commoners who had played key roles in the disputed elections: among them Stjepan Car and Ljudevit Gaj.(674) The suit against Gaj threatened him with the loss of his newspaper and press. The pro-Illyrian Director of Education, Antun Kukuljević, was put into early retirement, replaced by the Magyarone-Bishop Josip Schrott, who promised to put an end to student disorders,(675) and Nikola Zdenčaj was forced to resign from his position as *veliki-župan* of Zagreb county.(676)

This was indeed a setback, but the Illyrian Party quickly recovered. It changed its name to the National Party *(Narodna stranka)* and continued its political activities. Although some of the Zagreb county leaders were in trouble, the National Party still held most of the elective positions in Zagreb county and all of them in the other two counties of Civil Croatia. It played an active role at the *Sabor* of 1843 and the deputies selected to go to the Joint Parliament were National Party members.(677)

At the *Sabor* of 1843 Ivan Kukuljević emerged as the new spokesman for the Party. Speaking in Croatian, Kukuljević pleaded most eloquently that the Croatian Estates cease stubborn defense of the Latin language as the language of state for the Triune Kingdom. Latin, he argued, had been useful in a more primitive age, but now it only separated the Croatian prelates and nobles from the lower classes of the Kingdom and from their ethnic brothers.(678) It was time to make plans to replace Latin with the Croatian language as the language of state. If this was not done:

> . . . we shall continue to be, as we have been until now, not a nation but the shadow of a nation, and in Europe, among nations which all use living languages, we shall be as a neglected little island in the sea, and by using a dead language sooner or later we shall die . . .(679)

With this speech Kukuljević established a reputation which would bring him a leading position in the Party. He was the youngest and least experienced of the Triumvirate (Drašković, Kulmer, Kukuljević) which now directed Party affairs. Drašković, old, ailing, and in serious financial difficulties, was now limited to directing and advising the Party from his home.(680) The "old man" of the Movement, active in Croatian politics since the 1820's, he represented the element of continuity in the Party leadership. Ivan Kukuljević had gained recognition as an Illyrian poet in the late 1830's, but he was not one of the founders of the Movement, and it was only in 1842 when he resigned his commission in the army and came to Zagreb that he began to play an active role in the Movement and the Party. Only twenty-seven years old in 1843, of noble birth, intelligent and a gifted speaker, Kukuljević represented the younger generation in the Party leadership.(681) Franjo Kulmer (1806-1853) was the most important of the three.(682) Kulmer, a Croatian magnate, had been educated at the Theresianium, trained in law and drawn immediately into administrative work, first in Hungary and then in the Hungarian Court Chancellery in Vienna. In 1836 he came to Zagreb to serve as the President of the Ban's Court, the highest court of the Triune Kingdom. Kulmer had attended the Joint Parliaments of 1832-36, 1839-1840, 1841-1842 and 1842-1844, where as a Croatian magnate he was a permanent member of the Upper House. As the Magyar attacks on

Croatian autonomy increased in intensity he found himself drawn to the Illyrians and early in 1842 joined the Party.(683) Kulmer had little sympathy for the Southern Slav aspect of the Ilyrian program. He was a political conservative, loyal to the dynasty, convinced that the only salvation for the Croats lay in close cooperation with Vienna against the Magyar nationalists.

In the second line of Party leadership were local leaders such as Ljudevit Vukotinović, Nikola Zdenčaj, Gjuro Oršić, Albert Nugent; Ambroz Vranyczany, Anton Vakanović, and Dragutin Kušlan.(684)

It is difficult to define Ljudevit Gaj's role in the Party and the Movement after 1843.(685) At first many Illyrians held him personally responsible for Vienna's change of attitude.(686) Former enemies were quick to seize upon the opportunity to attack Gaj. Stanko Vraz, for instance, wrote and circulated this epigram:

> He fell, he fell, the doctor of all art,
> Fell our Dulcamara, our great Bonaparte:
> He fell to all his fours, licked silently his fur
> Alas, he dragged us down with him, the cur.(687)

The aspects of the Movement and Party activity most under attack in 1843 were those directly associated with Ljudevit Gaj: the Illyrian name, the concept of Illyrian nationality, and the Zagreb county elections of 1842. Drašković clearly perceived Gaj as a threat to the new political leadership. First, in a fatherly way, Drašković suggested to Gaj that he leave political life, where he was in trouble, and return to literature, where he had many "protectors,"(688) he then counseled other Illyrians to ignore Gaj's political advice,(689) and in 1844 joined with Metel Ožegović in an outright campaign to depopularize Gaj.(690) Kulmer shared Drašković's distrust of Gaj.(691) Kukuljević's attitude is less easy to discern.

Some of the men in the second line of Party leadership such as Ambroz Vranyczany and Albert Nugent were close to Gaj in these years,(692) and Gaj continued to be the person to whom Illyrians and Illyrian sympathizers in the Military Frontier, Bosnia and Dalmatia would most often turn for help.(693)

As editor of *Novine,* which by 1842 had begun to replace *Danica* as the publication most important to the Movement, Gaj would normally have been able to propagandize for the Party, argue with opponents and agitate for specific reforms and policies. But from 1843 to 1845, this role was closed to him too, because of the real danger of losing his newspaper. Any potentially inflammatory material would bring him under increased suspicion, and in these years, anything Illyrian was "inflamatory." He was forced to change the name of *Novine* twice, and

Danica once. In January 1843, he cut Illyrian from the names of his publications changing them to *Narodne novine* (National news) and *Danica horvatska, slavonska i dalmatinska* (Croatian, Slavonian and Dalmatian Morning Star). In March of the next year, in reaction to Magyarone criticism of the term "Narodne" (national) in the title of the newspaper,(694) Gaj changed *Novine's* name once more, this time to *Novine horvatske, slavonske i dalmatinske* (Croatian Slavonian and Dalmatian News). *Novine* again became a colorless publication.

While Gaj could do little openly as a politician or editor, he could and did extend his contacts with the Serbs and the Polish emigration.

In October 1843, Frantisek Zach came to Belgrade to serve as Czartoryski's permanent agent in Serbia. As the result of a series of conversations with the Serbian Minister of Foreign Affairs, Ilija Garašanin, Zach began, in the first weeks of 1844, to draw up a plan outlining the role Serbia might play in the future as the gathering point for all of the Southern Slavs.(695) Zach wrote to Gaj in January 1844, explaining the major ideas he would propose in the section of the Plan dealing with the Croats, and asking Gaj, if interested, to send someone to Belgrade to represent the Illyrian point of view.(696) Zach made clear to Gaj that the long-range goal was the unification of all the Southern Slavs under the leadership of the Serbs. As a first step the Croats and Serbs should cooperate in Bosnia, where they could mediate conflicts between the Catholic and Orthodox Bosnians and help them to work together to achieve political autonomy for Bosnia. Bosnia could then become a satellite to Serbia and the gathering would have begun.

Zach's proposals were very far from the platform of the National Party, both in the goal of Southern Slav political unification under Serbia, and the immediate strategy in Bosnia. The Illyrians, as Croatian politicians before them, assumed that the sections of Bosnia which had been part of medieval Croatia (Turkish Croatia) would one day be returned to the Triune Kingdom. It would, therefore, be in their interest to discourage plans for political autonomy, especially if it brought the Bosnians into a close relationship with Serbia. Gaj did not feel himself bound by the traditional point of view, soon after receiving Zach's letter, he sent Stjepan Car to Belgrade to represent him and to work with Zach on the Croatian part of his Plan. Car reported to Zach that Gaj agreed with the ends proposed and that it was necessary now only to determine the means.(697)

Zach submitted his Plan to Garašanin in May.(698) In the course of the next few months Garasanin reworked Zach's text, changing it from a plan for Southern Slav unity to one for a Greater Serbia, and in this form it is known to history as Garašanin's "Načertanija."(699) The section of Zach's Plan which dealt with the Croats, ''Otnošenje Serbie prema Horvatskoj,''(700) was omitted from Garašanin's ''Načertanije,'' however it is of interest to us in two ways, as the fruit of Car and Zach's cooperation, and in the light it throws upon Gaj's ideas about cooperation with Serbia. It discusses the plans for Bosnia Zach had outlined in his letter to Gaj, and asserts that the Illyrians would be willing to cooperate in such a venture, for ''Gaj and the entire Illyrian Party'' favored union with Serbia in an independent Kingdom headed by the Karadjordjević dynasty.(701) Here we see that Zach, clearly, did not understand the situation in Croatia, and that he took Gaj's profession of support, relayed to him through Car, as the official declaration of support by the Party. Gaj was neither in the position to give this, nor would he have been supported in this action by the Party. Zach and the *Ustavobranitelji* leaders had no way of knowing the real situation, however, for the only Illyrians in Serbia at this time were men close to Gaj.(702)

Illyrian literature had entered a difficult period in 1843 with the appointment of a new censor. On January 11th, Stjepan Mojses, who had done what he could to aid the Illyrians, was replaced as Zagreb censor by Josip Maćhik, a Professor of the Magyar language at the Zagreb Academy. Maćhik, a Slovak, was one of the pro-Magyar professors who had sparked the student demonstrations in 1839. Hostile to the Illyrian Movement, unfamiliar with the subtleties of the new literary language, Maćhik did what he could to clamp down on Illyrian literature by arbitrary and severe censorship.(703) He forbade *Novine* to report on the meetings of the county assemblies and *Sabor* censored material critical of the Magyars which had passed the censor in other parts of the Monarchy, and refused to approve anything which could be considered the least bit controversial.(704) Under his heavy hand the books printed by Gaj's press, *Novine* and *Danica* suffered one setback after another.(705)

By 1844 censorship in Zagreb had become so severe that some Illyrian writers were forced to publish their works abroad. Dimitrije Demeter's play *Teuta,* one of the series funded by *Matica Ilirska,* was published in Vienna in 1844, as were several other literary works. Illyrian political writings could not pass the Vienna censor as easily, therefore the Illyrians turned to Belgrade for help. This was a time when they badly needed an outlet for political discussion, for Zagreb was due to have county elections soon, and a new *Sabor* would be called to act upon the decisions of the Joint Parliament. It was time to agitate, explain, and draft a program of reforms.

In December of 1843, Pavao Čavlović, an enthusiastic supporter of Gaj and the Movement since 1839, arrived in Belgrade. Čavlović (a theological student) had been Secretary of the Illyrian Club of the Zagreb Seminary. He had recently been in political trouble in Zagreb,(706) and while this may have prompted his move, his mission in Belgrade was to arrange for the publication of Illyrian writings.(707) He came with Gaj's knowledge and kept in close touch with him.(708)

With Serbian help Čavlović now arranged for the printing of Illyrian political literature. The first "illegal" publication was the anonymous pamphlet *Šta namĕravaju Iliri?* which was printed in Belgrade by the Serbian government press in March, 1844.(709) It was written by Bogoslav Šulek, and sent to Čavlović by the Illyrian Club of the Zagreb Seminary, which also funded its publication, after the pamphlet had been rejected by the Zagreb censor.(710) It was the longest and best of the Illyrian political pamphlets. Similar in form and argument to Rakovac's *Mali katekizam,* Šulek's *Šta namĕravaju Iliri?* went much more deeply into history, constitutional issues and specific political problems.

Next to appear was *Branislav,* an illegal newspaper which was published between October 1844 and February 1845.(711) Whereas the title page of Šulek's pamphlet gave the usual publishing information, *Branislav's* masthead was silent about its editor, place of publication and publisher. *Branislav* was truly an "Illyrian" publication, involving many different people in the writing, gathering of information, financing, and smuggling of copy in and out of Serbia. It was edited by Pavao Čavlović and published in Belgrade by the Serbian government press.(712) The majority of the articles were written by Bogoslav Šulek, who also forwarded much of the other material used.(713) Thus the greatest part of what was published in *Branislav* came directly from Gaj's newspaper offices. Some material was sent from Karlovac, which was the major source of funds for *Branislav.* The steamship *Sloga,* owned by a company in which Vranyczany was the largest stockholder, brought items for *Branislav* into Serbia and carried printed copies back to Croatia in its trips between Karlovac, Sisak and Zemun.(714) Albert Nugent also smuggled copies across the Zemun border under his great cloak.(715) The Illyrian writer and priest, Stjepan Marjanović, of Zemun handled the transfer of funds and arranged for the smuggling of *Branislav* past border guards through bribes or favors by travelers, when no other means were avilable.(716)

The purpose of *Branislav* was to discuss issues not permitted by the censor in Zagreb and to prepare the Croats for the coming *Sabor.* It proposed reforms to be debated at the *Sabor,*(717) reforms which became the platform of the National Party in the fall of 1845, discussed the local political scene through detailed descriptions of the meetings of county estates, and reprinted several of Kukuljević's more famous speeches. Kukuljević immediately protested publicly that the speeches were printed without his knowledge, and Čavlović had to clear him of complicity in an editorial statement.(718) *Branislav* had only a short life, but it served the Illyrians well for it was able to print materials which spoke to the immediate needs of the Croats, unhampered by the distorting hand of the censor. It is difficult to pinpoint Gaj's role in the printing of *Branislav,* but it is clear that he was one of the men behind it and it was his Serbian contacts which made the Illyrian illegal press possible.

Now that Gaj had declared himself interested in working with the right wing of the Polish emigration, Czartoryski, interpreting his assent for that of the National Party, began to include the Croats in his plans. He hoped to use Zagreb as the center around which the Slavs of Hungary could gather, then to get the Hungarian Slavs and the Magyars to cooperate against Austria, viewing them as useful future allies in the event of a Polish revolution in Galicia.(719) Czartoryski assumed that the Slavs of Hungary and the Magyars saw Austria as their primary enemy, a naive interpretation at best when one considers that the Croats viewed Austria as a protector against Magyarization. While Zagreb could serve as a center to unite the Serbs and Croats of Hungary, it would have little appeal to the Slovaks who were now beginning their national renaissance. To convince the Illyrians of the wisdom of his plan, Czartoryski sent two agents to them, the first in 1844 and the second in 1845.

First came Adam Rieth Reiner. He arrived in Zagreb in November of 1844, after long talks with the Slovaks, and stayed for almost a month.(720) His reports must be used with caution(721) for he had a vivid imagination and did not really understand the Illyrian Movement. Reiner thought, for instance, that the Illyrians wanted to create a Greater Illyria which would include the Slovaks and stretch from the Carpathians to the Adriatic sea:(722) undoubtedly his own interpretation. Some elements of his reports are more reliable and contain interesting information, especially about Gaj. Reiner wrote that Gaj had shown him a list of 570 patriotic officers from the Military Frontier and claimed he could call on them to lead 200,000 men in armed revolt if he were given the necessary funds.(723) This is almost identical to Gaj's claim in his second Russian petition of 1838. He also reported that Gaj expected money from the Polish emigration and asked why it had not yet been delivered.(724)

Reiner went on to Belgrade where he was to report to Zach. On January 26, 1845, General F. Mayerhofer reported to Metternich from Belgrade that Reiner, known to the Austrians as Rotter, was saying openly that all the troops of the Military Frontier would support a national revolution.(725) This was dangerous for Zach who was already under suspicion; he had been identified as an agent of the Polish emigration by a report from Paris in July of 1844.(726) Reiner's visit intensified Austrian interest in Zach and they began to observe his visitors.(727)

In the summer of 1845, the Austrian Police Ministry received a series of reports from the agent "Gabriel," a Pole by the name of Alois Gavrinski, which directly linked Gaj with Zach and the right wing of the Polish emigration.(728) Fortunately for Gaj, Gavrinski's reports were such a blend of fact and fantasy that Metternich dismissed them as unreliable and Gavrinski as unstable.(729)

In the fall of 1845 a second attempt was made to implement Czartoryski's new plan for the Croats when Janusz Woronicz came to Zagreb for several weeks. He accompanied the French publicist Hippolyte Desprez.(730) His assignment was to investigate the real extent of Gaj's influence in Zagreb and to try to estimate how much support the Poles could count on from Croatia in the event of a revolution.(731)

After the unsuccessful Polish uprising in February 1846, Czartoryski lost interest in Gaj and the Croats. By that time Gaj had already been drawn back into Party work, as were Stjepan Car and Dragutin Kušlan. Gaj's contact with the Polish emigration is an interesting minor theme in his activities of these years. Nothing really came of it but it is part of his secret politics, and the various reports to Czartoryski and the Austrians by agents of varying degrees of reliability, are a reflection of the mood of the pre-revolutionary years, and a valuable source of information on the extent and nature of Gaj's secret, or anti-Austrian politics.

The Joint Parliament which opened on May 14, 1843, was a stormy one, and the Croats found themselves in increasing difficulties. The Hungarian Opposition, led by Kossuth, clashed continually with the Hungarian Conservative Party over issues of social and economic reform.(732)

When the *Sabor* met on April 22nd, to elect deputies to the Joint Parliament, over 700 armed peasant nobles led by *Comes* Josipović appeared to cast their votes.(733) The Magyarones had decided to try to take over the *Sabor* by sheer weight of numbers and there was no clear defense against this unprecedented action, for the *Sabor* lacked definite rules about the size of delegations and who was eligible to vote.(734)

Ban Haller postponed the *Sabor* until the peasant nobles went home, convening it on April 24th. *Comes* Josipovic took the question of the peasant nobles' right to vote to the floor of the Joint Parliament, arguing that the Croatian deputies had been illegally elected and asking the Magyars to intervene. The National Party now tried to force Vienna to override the Hungarian decisions of 1831 and 1835, and deny the peasant nobles the right to vote as individuals. They also asked for support on the language questions. While the *Sabor* had instructed its deputies to use only Latin at the Parliament, the Croatian deputies found their speeches ignored. The King supported their right to use Latin in 1843, but this was only a temporary measure. The Crown and the Magyars finally reached a compromise in January 1844, which recognized Magyar as the language of the Hungarian State and Parliament, gave the Croats six years in which they could continue to use Latin, and declared that while the Croats could use Latin in their internal affairs, they must use Magyar in correspondence with the central and local authorities in Hungary.(735) Also, most ominously, the Magyars increasingly spoke of Slavonia and the Littoral as an integral part of Hungary, using the term "Croatia" to refer solely to the three counties of Civil Croatia.

Since 1825, when the Austrian authorities had given up plans to centralize Hungary and the Empire, they followed a wavering and unclear policy in Hungary, supporting the Constitution and bending without pattern to some of the nationalist demands.(736) By the close of the Parliament in November 1844, Metternich had decided on a new tactic. Fearful that Hungary was near revolution, he decided to counter the growing support for the liberal reforms proposed by the radical Magyar Opposition Party, by backing the Hungarian Conservative Party in a program of moderate reform.(737)

At the same time, in consultation with Baron Kulmer and other leading Croatian politicans,(738) Metternich and the State Conference reconsidered Vienna's official position toward the Illyrian Movement. They directed much attention to an anonymous memorandum sent them in 1843 by a Croat, which warned that it was a serious mistake for the Imperial government to suppress the Illyrian Movement. Only by the use of the Illyrian name, it argued, could the Croats rise above divisive provincial traditions and create a meaningful literature. Even more serious was the fact that if the Southern Slavs could not look to Zagreb as a cultural and political center, they would turn to Belgrade. The Memorandum asked specifically that the Slovak Máchik be replaced as Zagreb Censor by a Croat, that the new Censor be made subject to the Austrian, not Hungarian, censorship authorities, and that the Illyrian name be permitted again in literary life.(739) The arguments of the Memorandum were substantiated by the fact that the Illyrians were now publishing their political writings illegally in Serbia. *Branislav* especially worried the Austrians. It took them a while to discover its origin, but by December they knew it was printed in Belgrade, and were well aware that the program of reform it proposed was being widely discussed in Croatia.(740)

On January 3rd, 1845, King Ferdinand signed a decree once again allowing the Illyrian name to be used in literature. Soon thereafter Mačhik was replaced as Censor by a Croat, Pavao Muhić, and it was announced that King Ferdinand was founding a chair for the Illyrian language and literature at the Zagreb Academy.(741)

These measures signaled the beginning of a new period of cooperation between the Imperial government and the National Party against a common enemy — the Magyar Opposition. Within the next two years Kulmer would ally the National Party with the Hungarian Conservative Party in support of Metternich's new policy in Hungary. This would signify a major change in the program of the National Party, and in order to prepare the Party for this program and to make sure that the Illyrians did nothing to compromise their newly-won Austrian protection, Kulmer turned to Ljudevit Gaj for help.(742) In his letter of January 15th, 1845, Kulmer asked Gaj to use all of his influence to make certain the Illyrians accepted Vienna's recent concessions in a responsible manner. He asked Gaj to reunite the National Party, to try to reach some understanding with the Magyarones and thus calm the local political scene, to make certain the Illyrian name was used only in literature, to curb all political excesses, and to have *Branislav* stopped. He said that he had written to Drašković as well. With this letter Gaj was once again drawn into active Party work. By February *Branislav* had ceased publication.(743)

It is difficult to estimate exactly how much influence Gaj had in Croatia at this time. In 1845 *Novine* once again became the journalistic arm of the National Party. Gaj could play a political role here in shaping editorial policy, but in daily political life, as a commoner, he could only work behind the scenes.

Ljudevit Gaj still held a central position in Croatian cultural life. His press printed the major works of the Illyrian writers and the series of Dubrovnik classics funded by *Matica Ilirska*.(744) His private library was perhaps the best in Croatia at that time for Southern Slav materials, he was active in *Matica Ilirska* and the Zagreb Reading Club, *Danica* chronicled the cultural life of the Croats and *Novine* their politics, and he received in his office a steady stream of petitioners, Illyrians, and foreign visitors, etc.

There was, to be sure, criticism of Gaj from many sides, especially from the literary men. Writers had a difficult life in Croatia. Most of them were young men involved in professional careers as lawyers, civil servants, priests, doctors, teachers — who had to do their writing in their spare time.(745) They then had to pay to have their work published, unless it was short enough to appear in *Danica* or *Kolo.* Most of them were too poor to pay for the publication outright so they either got into debt with Gaj, who let them pay over a period of months or years,(746) or collected pre-paid orders for the book before it was printed.(747) Once published, there was no outlet to sell or distribute the book or even advertise it successfully. The Reading Clubs helped, but in almost all cases the author had to become a book-seller as well, an embarassing task at best, aggravated by a public which was too often indifferent.(748) The Illyrian writers were each other's best customers.

The Illyrian writers may have expected Gaj to solve this problem as he had the orthographic confusion, but Gaj had done what he could; now as a married man deeply in debt, he had other things than literature on his mind. The future of his press and paper depended upon whether Vienna dismissed the criminal proceedings against him, and whether he could raise enough money to keep his enterprises running. The first could only be solved politically, the second by petition to various sources. At the same time he could not let his financial situation be known, for credit would dry up. Gaj could no longer innovate in cultural life, his major task now was to preserve what already existed.

There is an interesting description of Gaj in the travel diary of Fedor Vassil'evich Chizhov, a Russian nobleman and Slavophile who visited Zagreb in May and June of 1845.(749) It is clear that Chizhov had difficulties balancing Gaj's evident success as a national leader with the many complaints voiced against him: that he was arrogant, that he had quarrelled with most of the important writers, that he took credit for work others did.(750) Chizhov observed:

> It is strange how Gaj has gathered all the threads in his hands, how everyone works for him and he signs their work with his name. At first I did not think it possible, but when one considers that he receives people from morning until night, that he is never free, it is more believable. His relations with everyone are bad. Yet everybody pretends that they are good. Everybody speaks well of him, gives him credit for what he has done, and finds fault with his excessive conceit.(751)

Gaj was not loath to talk of his accomplishments to others. It was as if, in a way, he was already an "old" man living in the triumphs of the past. He was then 36 years old. Chizhov described a long meeting with

Gaj in which Gaj related the story of his own development as a nationalist, at great length, as Chizhov notes ". . . exactly like a guide showing one the sights."(752) With an air of great solemnity Gaj showed Chizhov some ancient Illyrian coins, and then an old ring with three crowns a shepherd had found near Krapina, which Gaj claimed to have belonged to one of the three legendary Krapina brothers. Gaj said that he had gone on a pilgrimage with this ring in 1840:

> . . . to consecrate it in the three holy places of the Slavic nation: Prague, Warsaw and Moscow . . .(753)

The preliminaries now over, Gaj explained to Chizhov how difficult it was for him to manage expenses out of his own modest income and how he had to keep up appearances. He said that he sorely needed financial help and that he had every right to expect it from the Russians because he had awoken sympathy for Russia among the Catholic Southern Slavs. This mixture of self-adulation, pompous mystery, and unashamed request for money alienated Chizhov. He noted:

> Granted it is so (that Gaj helped awaken sympathy for Russia), yet he put it too bluntly. Well, may the Lord be with him . . .(754)

Chizhov heard rumors the next day that Gaj was also trying to get money from the French and the Magyars.(755)

Chizhov left Zagreb on June 30th, depressed by the personal antagonisms he found there, by what he considered to be empty talk about nationalism and the fact that "those who do work for the national cause worry about filling their purses."(756) But as he traveled further he began to reconsider his judgement on Gaj, writing in July from Virovitica,

> Yes here one can understand the Zagreb Movement and feel deeply grateful to Gaj. How do you awaken nationalism in this nation, where historical events are completely forgotten, if not by means of language?(757)

Gaj apparently did what he could to bring about an understanding between the National Party and the Magyarones,(758) but tensions continued to grow between the Parties as they prepared for the Zagreb county elections and the *Sabor*. The Zagreb elections which were held on July 29th, were easily won by the Magyarones who had the support of the peasant nobles. The elections proceeded peacefully, but Ban Haller, fearing trouble, had the government buildings surrounded by troops of the 13th Infantry Battalion and the troops were stationed on nearby streets as well. Shortly after the election, the troops mistakenly fired on a group of young National Party members who, embittered by the outcome of the election, were trying to force their way through the cordon. Other soldiers joined in and in the space of a few minutes thirteen men were killed, eight of these young National Party members, and thirty others were wounded, some seriously.(759)

Ban Haller, deeply shaken by this incident, sent Bishop Schrott to Gaj to ask him for assistance in preventing further bloodshed.(760) Gaj had retired from the political scene a week before the election and was not present when the shots were fired. He quickly dressed himself in his best black suit, walked with Bishop Schrott through the teaming streets protecting the Bishop from attacks by angered Illyrians, and went from there to the Ban to discuss with him the best way to calm the situation.(761) The peasant nobles were ordered to leave the town, and Gaj helped draw off public anger by an elaborately staged patriotic funeral attended by more than 4,000 people for the eight victims who were National Party members.(762)

The Magyarones were now in control of the elective positions in Zagreb county. They began their campaign against the Illyrian Movement at the County Assembly of August 5th, which the National Party boycotted because of the events of July 29th. *Comes* Josipović proposed and the Assembly passed a program which, if successful, would have undone much of what the Illyrians had accomplished since 1835. Among other measures, he proposed that the King be asked to revoke Gaj's newspaper and press privileges; that the old orthography be brought back to the schools and publications, and that *kajkavski* be made the Croatian literary language. The new censor must be removed, a *kajkavski* professor appointed to the chair at the Academy, and the King must be asked to grant the peasant nobles an individual vote both at the *Sabor* and the county elections.(763) More symbolically, the Magyarones agreed to wear Hungarian national dress to the assemblies, and the new laws passed at the Pressburg Parliament were read to them first in Magyar, then Latin. Solidarity with Hungary was their goal, the Illyrians their enemies. Luckily the Magyarones had little support in the other counties and their platform ran counter to the interests of Metternich and the State Conference.

On August 8th, two Croatian delegations left Zagreb for Vienna to make formal protests about the bloodshed at the Zagreb county elections.(764) They blamed the tragedy on the Ban who had called in troops to supervise the elections, and on the peasant nobles who had come by the hundreds to Zagreb, armed and bellicose. They were trying to force the King to make a decision on the peasant noble question before the *Sabor* convened.(765)

The State Conference responded quickly, and on September 14th, King Ferdinand signed an order regularizing attendance at the *Sabor*, which was read by Ban Haller at the opening meeting of the *Sabor* on September 23rd. The King ordered that only deputies appointed by the counties, towns, and Church, and distinguished individuals especially invited by the Ban, could participate in the *Sabor.* The announcement was greeted by shouts of "Long live the King."(766) The exact details were left to the *Sabor* to work out.

The Magyarones left the *Sabor* as a bloc, in protest against the King's decision. The *Sabor* now in National Party hands proceeded to pass the first clear legislation on the make-up of its body. Each county was to have two regular and five honorary representatives. This was to comprise half of the membership, the other half being drawn from the royal free towns, representatives of the Catholic and Orthodox clergy, magnates, administrative officials and representatives of the various corporations, such as the Zagreb Academy.(767) As to the peasant nobles, they would be represented as before 1831, solely at meetings of Zagreb county and there by one vote, that of their *Comes.*(768)

The *Sabor* then resolved to ask the King to establish a separate Court Chancellery *(Consilium regnium)* for Croatia, as had existed from 1767-1779; to raise the Zagreb Academy to the rank of a university; and to elevate the Zagreb Bishop to Archbishop and see that his Archdiocese would not be subordinate to the Hungarian Catholic hierarchy.(769) The *Sabor* closed on October 14th.

Shortly after that Ban Haller retired. He had asked in the aftermath of the July 29th bloodshed that he be permitted to leave his position as Ban and stayed on only until the *Sabor* was over.(770) Bishop Haulik, an active member of the National Party, became Acting Ban.

In early September, as preparations were being made for the *Sabor* Ljudevit Gaj left for Vienna. He needed to consult with Kulmer over the next steps to be taken toward the alliance with the Hungarian Conservatives, and to see whether his own willingness to help in this strategy might win him some concessions from the Court. Kulmer took Gaj to see Györgi Apponyi, leader of the Hungarian Conservative Party and Vice-Chancellor, but actual head(771) of the Hungarian Court Chancellery. Gaj presented a petition to Apponyi in which he asked that *Novine* be recognized as the official organ of the National Party which, as Gaj wrote, was really a "Government Party" *(Regierungspartei),*(772) and that *Novine,* for that reason, should be given royal protection and money subsidies. He did not mention the criminal suit against him which threatened his newspaper; he only alluded to the years between 1843 and 1845 as ones of trouble and misunderstanding.

While in Vienna, Gaj also looked into the matter of getting final approval from the Austrian Police authorities for his "Dogodovština

Ilirie Velike'' (History of Greater Illyria), and its accompanying bibliography ''Bibliotheca Illyrica . . .'' both completed earlier that year and already approved by the Zagreb censor.(773)

Gaj had been at work on this history for a long time and had published exerpts from it in *Danica,* but it seems that he did the bulk of the work on it in 1843 and 1844.(774) It ends abruptly with the fall of Bosnia in 1462, quite possibly because Gaj no longer had time to write. He hoped ''Dogodovština'' would become a popular book, that it would educate the Croats in a spirit of Southern Slav history and win him back undisputed leadership in the Movement.(775) ''Dogodovština'' might have enthused the youth, had it been published, but it would have been of little help to the Croats in the historiographical battle over constitutional issues then beginning with the Magyars, for it touched only superficially upon such points as the *Pacta Conventa* and the legal position of Slavonia and the Littoral.(776) ''Dogodovština'' varies between pedestrian chronological narrative and poetic exhortations to Illyrian unity, and is interesting in that it attempts to correlate the history of the various branches of the Southern Slavs. Gaj tried to prove that the Southern Slavs were the descendents of the ancient Illyrians — something he believed firmly to the end of his life(777) — but he had to try to reconcile this with newer evidence which indicated that the Southern Slavs had migrated to the Balkans from central Europe. Instead of trying to integrate the two theories, Gaj simply gave them both in different places as fact.(778) ''Dogodovština'' was scheduled for publication in 1848, other events intervened, and Gaj did not try to have it published in the post-revolutionary years. This may have been fortunate for Gaj. He had talked for many years of the history he would write, but the finished product was an amateur job. In place of a bibliography, he had Šulek compile ''Bibliotheca Illyrica . . .'' which was a general bibliography of works on the Southern Slavs. Gaj submitted the Bibliography under his own name.

Gaj returned to Zagreb, hopeful that his recent talks with Kulmer and Apponyi would finally secure the existence of the newspaper and press both politically and economically. In the next few months he would carry out the work he promised, to lead the National Party to see the value of cooperation with the Hungarian Conservatives. Subsidies and official recognition of his paper were not yet forthcoming, but ''Dogodovština''passed the Vienna censor on January 22, 1846,(779) and the criminal proceedings against Gaj were finally dropped.(780)

Now that the National Party had taken control of the *Sabor,* the Magyar Opposition moved to block its next step: alliance with the Hungarian Conservatives. In Gaj's notes there is a detailed account of an unexpected visit by a member of the Magyar Opposition.(781) He identifies him only as H. It may have been Kossuth. H. tried at first tactfully, pointing out the similar goals of the Croatian and Magyar nationalists, then by insult, citing Gaj as the man most responsible for destroying the traditional close relationship between Croats and Magyars, to convince him that it would be a serious mistake for the National Party and Gaj, himself, to become allied with the Hungarian Conservative Party. He warned Gaj that he was making a mistake in allowing his newspaper to serve as a instrument of the ever-shifting Austrian policy, that as a commoner he had no political power and might end up by losing everything. H. suggested that Gaj instead try to swing the Party over to the side of the Magyar Opposition and that Gaj, personally, would find protection in such an alliance. Gaj returned the visit that afternoon, to find that "the four Hungarian gentlemen,"(782) had already left for Rijeka.

Kossuth did stop in Zagreb on October 22nd on his way to Rijeka, where he had business relating to the projected Buda-Rijeka railroad. He spent most of his time at the Magyarone Casino, consulting the Magyarone leaders.(783) He may have seen Gaj the next day. We know that in Rijeka Kossuth met with Ambroz Vranyczany and asked him to arrange for a series of meetings with National Party leaders. The visit to Gaj would not have been inconsistent with this tactic. The discussion between Vranyczany and Kossuth was heated, and when Vranyczany reported to other National Party leaders Kossuth's desire to make contact with them, the decision was no.(784) By December, Kossuth clearly had given up hopes of deflecting the National Party from an alliance with the Hungarian Conservatives and he came out in firm support of the Magyarones and their protests over the loss of the right of individual vote of the peasant nobles.(785)

In the editorial "Proglas i pravac našega teženja," (Our Goals) of December 13, 1845. Gaj declared his newspaper in favor of an alliance between the National Party and the Hungarian Conservatives.(786) "Our Goals" redefined the focus of Illyrian political activity. Up to that time the National Party had concentrated on opposing Magyarization and the diminution of traditional Croatian rights through supporting the Illyrian cultural reforms, countering the rise of the Magyarone Party in Croatia and its effects, and defense of Croatian rights at the Joint Parliament. Now Gaj asked the Croats to move beyond this local focus, to participate actively in the conflict between forces for radical and moderate reform in the entire Hungarian Kingdom. Radical reform was the province of the aggressively nationalist Magyar Opposition, moderate reform of the nationally more conciliatory Hungarian Conservative Party. Gaj therefore proclaimed that the new goal of the National Party should be:

> . . . legal and moderate progress of our nationality and the happiness of our fatherland under the protection of our King and a free Constitution . . .(787)

This could best be accomplished, explained Gaj, by working to counter the discord sown in Croatia and in Hungary by the ''Radical Party'',(788) through joining forces with the Hungarian Conservative Party.

CHAPTER XI

YEARS OF FRUITION (1846-1847)

In January and February of 1846, *Novine* carried a series of articles which prepared the ground for the alliance between the National Party and the Hungarian Conservative Party. The most important of these was Gaj's polemic with Kossuth which took the form of two articles in January and February, the second in several installments, responding to a two-part article by Kossuth which had appeared in Hungary in December 1845 and January 1846. The readers of *Novine* who could not read Hungarian learned of the contents of the first Kossuth article only through what Gaj said of it in his first critique ''Odgovor gospodinu Kossuthu,'' (Response to Mr. Kossuth).(789) In this Gaj does not mention the title of the Kossuth work, only that it had appeared in *Budapest Hirado* on December 25, 1845.(790) Kossuth's article apparently attacked in a most bitter way some statements made against him by members of the National Party at the December meeting of the Križevci county estates. Gaj's response was a skillful piece of journnalism. He began by pointing out the contradictory and extravagant nature of Kossuth's arguments in which the Magyar called the Illyrians ''insurgents,'' ''servile tools of Vienna,'' ''Russophiles,'' ''Jacobins,'' ''Jesuits,'' etc.,(791) then described in some detail the meeting which had so angered Kossuth. The Križevci estates had been summoned to discuss a communication from the Hungarian Court Chancellery which asked for their active support in plans to build a railroad between Buda and Rijeka.(792) Kossuth had recently toured Croatia as the representative of the group backing the railroad, and the

Križevci estates declared themselves reluctant to support an enterprise in which Kossuth, a proven enemy of their nation, played such a leading role. It was not, argued Gaj, that the National Party members in Križevci, or the other Croatian counties, opposed the building of railroads, in fact they realized the many economic advantages railroads would bring, but they were suspicious of a railroad which, although it would run through Croatian territory, was not designed with Croatian interests in mind. The projected Buda-Rijeka railroad was supposed to link the capital of Hungary with the Croatian Littoral, a territory which, as Gaj pointed out, was now increasingly claimed as an integral part of Hungary by the Magyar Opposition.(793) The National Party, continued Gaj was not the rebellious band of extremists described by Kossuth, but rather a Party made up of distinguished and responsible men, a Party which enjoyed the protection of the King, and one which acted ''in complete harmony with all good-thinking Magyars,''(794) i.e. the Hungarian Conservatives.

Gaj's ''Our Goals'' which had appeared in December of 1845, and his first response to Kossuth, were highly praised by Baron Kulmer in a letter to Gaj written from Vienna on January 19th.(795) It is clear from this letter that Gaj's recent journalistic ventures were the result of talks with Kulmer the previous fall. Kulmer reported that he had already sent ''Our Goals'' to Hungary to be published there, and asked Gaj to continue his criticism of Kossuth, enclosing a copy of the second part of Kossuth's article.(796)

Gaj had Kossuth's second article translated, and it appeared as ''Odgovor na běsnilo ilirske stranke u Križevačkoj varmediji,'' (Answer to the Angry Illyrian Party of Križevci county) in two parts in January and February.(797) In this article Kossuth alternated pious protests that he and his Party, had nothing against the development of Croatian nationalism with direct attacks on the National Party. He asked, for example, why the National Party did not force the *Sabor* to adopt the Croatian national language as the language of state at their last meeting, while at the same time arguing that the recent *Sabor* had been illegal because it excluded the peasant nobles.(798) Kossuth also stated that the *Sabor* resolution to ask the King for the reestablishment of the Croatian Court Council, was tantamount to a separation from Hungary.(799)

Gaj's answer ''Odgovor gospodinu Kossuthu na drugi njegov članak,'' (Response to Mr. Kossuth's Second Article)(800) moved from the original issue, the Križevci estates meeting, to a general discussion of the reasons why the National Party distrusted Kossuth and his Party. He catalogued the many steps taken by Kossuth and the Magyar Opposition to undermine the Illyrian Movement and to discredit it in the eyes of the King and his Ministers. He explained the reasons for the platform adopted at the recent *Sabor,* and described the difficult constitutional position in which the Croats found themselves. This was not a challenge for a debate with Kossuth, but rather an attempt to use the refutation of Kossuth's arguments as a bid for support for alliance with Kossuth's Hungarian opponents, the Conservatives. Gaj's two articles in response to Kossuth are valuable guides to understanding the new platform of the National Party. Unfortunately his appearance as a political journalist ends with the second answer to Kossuth. His only other published writings between 1846 and 1848 are editorials.

On March 27, shortly after his foray into political journalism, Gaj purchased a large house in the upper town of Zagreb. It cost 12,000 forints.(801) He bought the house on credit borrowing almost all of the down-payment of 6,000 forints from the cash receipts of his newspaper and press, then mortgaging the house to return the money to his en) terprises,(802) and paying the remainder on the house in yearly installments of 2,000 forints plus 6 interest.

Ljudevit and Paulina Gaj now had two small children, Slava (born 1844) and Velimir (born 1845). In 1844 Gaj had had to ask the Reading Club to move to other quarters since the rooms they had occupied were now needed for his family.(803) The rented house Gaj had used since late 1837 for his living quarters, newspaper offices and printing press was now too cramped. The new house was modern, spacious, and centrally located. This was an enormous financial undertaking for a man already in debt.

Few people knew that Gaj had bought the house on credit. Rumors began to spread that he was now rich, and people speculated on the source of his new wealth. It was a very large house for a man of his means, and he bought it with the same blind optimism with which he had founded *Novine* and the printing press. Gaj would now be forced to seek money to pay his enormous debts from whatever source he could find it.

In April Ljudevit Gaj decided to make a trip to Belgrade, his first. He may have wanted to reestablish ties with the Polish emigration, for the last agent, Woronicz, had not returned to Zagreb as he had promised.(804) He probably hoped for gifts of money from the Serbian government or the Polish emigration, and must have believed that it was finally safe to go, now that his newspaper and press were secure, due to his cooperation with Kulmer and Metternich.

Gaj informed Kulmer of his plans to go to Serbia, explaining that the purpose of the trip was to inform himself about the political situation in

Serbia and the extent of French, Polish and Russian propaganda there.(805) The trip was to be secret and Gaj promised Kulmer that he would submit a detailed report upon his return. It is interesting that Kulmer still had doubts about Gaj's reliability, for he recommended to the Austrians that they cooperate with Gaj and make his passage over the frontier an easy one, but he also suggested that Gaj be watched.(806)

Gaj arrived in Belgrade on April 23, and left immediately for Kragujevac to see the Prince. He remained there for several days, and traveled back to Belgrade with Prince Alexander, having received promises from the Prince and Garašanin that they would give him financial support in return for his cooperation in furthering Serbian interests in the Triune Kingdom.(807) The first evidence of this support was a gift of 392 ducats from Prince Alexander.(808)

Zach was not in Belgrade when Gaj first came, but the two met on April 27th. Gaj was frank with Zach, informing him that he was working in part for the Austrians in order to convince them to support the Illyrians and the idea of Southern Slav unity.(809) Gaj told Zach about the report he had promised Kulmer, and asked him if he would draft a brief sketch which Gaj could use for the report. Zach agreed.(810) Gaj submitted his report which was in the form of a Memorandum, to Minister Gervay in May, and it reached Metternich soon thereafter.(811) Gaj's Memorandum is based party on Zach's sketch. In it Gaj pleaded with the Austrians to realizc before it was too late, that they should work to counter Russian influence in Serbia, and try to draw the Principality into their own political sphere. The Austrians were mistaken, explained Gaj, in believing that the Serbs were a semi-Asiatic people,(812) that their somewhat raw exterior indicated political backwardness. He pointed out that while many Serbs were sympathetic to Russia, the Prince and some of the men closest to him were suspicious of Russia and open to other foreign support. It was time for Austria to draw up a new Serbian policy, one which would involve both internal and foreign matters, for, argued Gaj, as long as the Slavs living outside of the Austrian Empire were convinced that their fellow Slavs in the Empire were treated unfairly by the Magyars and Austrians, they would have little reason to seek help from Austria. If the Serbs and other non-Habsburg Slavs were discouraged from alliance with Austria because of her treatment of her Slavic peoples, they would turn to Russia for outside support and one day Austria would be surrounded by a strip of Russian or Russian-influenced lands which would stretch from the Balkans to the Baltic sea.(813)

Austria should foster the development of her Slavs, she should support the Illyrian Movement which had smoothed the way for her in Serbia, and she should offer the Serbian Principality technical assistance, in the form of engineers, military experts, teachers, etc. Gaj also suggested that the Austrians make use of František Zach, a Moravian by birth who was still loyal to the Empire, a man well informed in Serbian matters and in good standing at the Court. Zach, explained Gaj, had gone through a brief period as a revolutionary in 1830, but older and wiser now, he was in no way linked to the French or the Polish revolutionary movements.(814)

Who then was Gaj working for?(815) Clearly his trip to Serbia was just another facet of his secret politics. Gaj was in a way working for Austria, the Polish emigration, the Serbian Principality, the Illyrians, and himself. His strongest loyalty seems at this time to have been to Zach, for he was frank with Zach about working for the Austrians, while he gave false information in the Memorandum to Austria about Zach.(816)

Gaj met with Metternich shortly after submitting the Memorandum in May,(817) and reported on this conference to Zach when he came to Belgrade for a second brief trip in July.(818) According to Zach, one of the reasons for Gaj's second trip was to arrange for a permanent agent to be sent by the Polish emigration to Zagreb. Another reason was to discover why the Serbian government had not come out in clear support of the Illyrian Movement, as they had promised.(819) Gaj told Zach that Metternich had been so impressed with what Gaj had reported about him, that he had asked Gaj to see whether or not he could recruit Zach as an Austrian agent.(820) Gaj did not write a formal report on his second trip to Serbia and it is not certain whether Metternich knew of it at all.(821)

Gaj spent much of the time between his two trips to Serbia in 1846,in travels to Prague and Leipzig to find a lithographer to illustrate "Dogodovština," which was now being prepared for publication.(822)

When Gaj got to Prague in June he was incensed to discover that Stanko Vraz, who had visited Prague some months earlier, had been spreading malicious rumors about him. Vraz had told Palacký and others that Gaj, who was supposed to have been collecting money for the National Center, had actually used the money for his own needs and was now living like a prince in a house he had recently purchased for 16,000 forints.(823) Gaj had been authorized by the Reading Club early in 1842 to collect money in its name for the proposed National Center. At the Reading Club meeting of January 7, 1846, Gaj had been asked to report on the money collected thus far. He replied that he had not collected any money, since his assignment by the Club had been followed by the Zagreb county elections and its unfortunate aftermath.(824) The Reading Club apparently accepted his explanation, but Vraz used this incident as a basis for rumor. He also intimated that Gaj was an alcoholic, and that he monopolized every foreign visitor so that they would not find out the real truth about him.(825)

Gaj wrote home that it was lucky he had come to Prague at this time, that he had now cleared his name and made certain that Vraz was "morally destroyed" in the eyes of the Czechs.(826) However, the incident upset Gaj greatly, and at the end of the letter to his wife and children he wrote of how he missed them:

> You, only you my three, are my soul, my heart, my life — you with the nation (narod), and in the nation is my past, present and my future.(827)

On his return to Zagreb Gaj demanded that Vraz apologize and put an end to the rumors in Prague. Vraz then wrote to Palacký and Šafařík, explaining that they must have misunderstood what he said about Gaj.(828)

The years 1846 and 1847 saw the fruition of many of the cultural reforms proposed in 1835 and 1836. With the publication in 1846 of Ivan Mažuranić's epic poem "Smrt Smail-age Čengića," the Illyrian language reached full artistic maturity.(829) In the same year Petar Preradović, perhaps the most famous Illyrian poet and one whose poems were used for the next 30 years as examples of style and language in the Croatian schools,(830) published his first collection — *Prvenci.* While these works represented some of the best of the new literature, the Illyrians were also becoming familiar with the older *štokavski* literary tradition, especially that of Dubrovnik, through *Danica* and *Kolo* and through publication of the works of Ivan Gundulić (1589-1638), in the *Matica Ilirska* series. The first Gundulić work *Osman,* with the last two cantos, which had been either lost or destroyed, rewritten in a most masterful way by Ivan Mažuranić, appeared in 1844, and the second, *Različite pjesni* (Selected Poems) in 1847.

From 1840 on, plays by Illyrian dramatists, as well as translations of foreign plays, were performed regularly in Zagreb and Karlovac, and occasionally in other Croatian towns. An Illyrian musical society had been formed in Zagreb in 1840 to sponsor the development of Croatian music. On March 28, 1846 the first Croatian opera, "Ljubav i zloba," by Vatroslav Lisinski opened in Zagreb to a large and enthusiastic audience.(831) The opera was repeated several times in the next few weeks to packed houses and it was hailed in *Danica* as a milestone in the development of Illyrian national culture.(832) Illyrian writers now had a choice of several journals and papers in which to publish their shorter works: *Danica, Kolo,* and *Zora Dalmatinska,* a new literary journal founded in Zadar in 1844.(833) The Illyrian language was now taught at the Zagreb *gimnazium* and, as of June, 1846, with the appointment of Vjekoslav Babukić to the newly created Chair of the Illyrian language and literature, it was now a regular part of the curriculum of the Zagreb Academy. Illyrian students and writers regularly gathered at a cafe in the upper town,(834) to talk about politics, literature, new cultural happenings. Only ten years before, Zagreb had been predominantly German in culture, now it was the focus of Croatian cultural life.

Plans for the National Center had been drawn up in 1842 and its formal sponsor, the Zagreb Reading Club, had been collecting money for it ever since. In 1845 they were informed that Count Dragutin Drašković was putting a large unfinished house in the upper town on the market at a reasonable price; 28,000 forints for a building of 30 rooms.(835) The Reading Club decided to buy the house, and the collections of funds intensified during 1845. The purchase was concluded on February 26, 1846.(836) The new National Center was still under construction and it was not until December that the Reading Club moved to its new quarters.(837) The other Illyrian organizations moved their headquarters there soon after, and the collection of artifacts, books, coins, pictures, etc. for the National museum to which Ljudevit Gaj had given many items from his own personal collection(838) were finally all brought together. In addition to housing the various Illyrian organizations, the National Center had several rooms for meetings, concerts, and a large assembly hall, the *dvorana.* When the *dvorana* was completed and opened to the public on February 8, 1847, over 800 people gathered there to celebrate, many of them dressed in national costume, and they danced, sang and drank toasts to Illyrian unity and success.(839)

1847 was also the year in which the King finally in July gave his approval for the formation of a national cultural society in the form proposed by the Zagreb Reading Club — *Matica Ilirska. Matica Ilirska* did not establish itself as an independent organization until after 1848-49, in the meantime it remained, as it had begun, within the organizational framework of the Zagreb Reading Club.

The tempo of political life had also begun to intensify. In November of 1846, when the Hungarian Conservative Party met in Pest to prepare its platform for the coming Parliament, the National Party sent two representatives to the meeting: Ivan Kukuljević and Stjepan Car. The Platform agreed upon by the Hungarian Party was brought back to Zagreb and published in Croatian in January 1847.(840) The next months were filled with meetings. The National Party tried to draw up a platform of its own, and prepare for the coming *Sabor* and Joint Parliament. It is not clear what role Gaj played in these deliberations, but he was invited to a meeting of National Party leaders on February 18th, to discuss the above matters and the possibility of working out the most serious differences with the Magyarones.(841)

The Program of the Hungarian Conservatives was, as they termed it, a "progressive conservative" one.(842) It had to deal with some questions of social reform, in order to offer an alternative to the program of the Magyar Opposition. This forced the National Party to consider issues they had avoided until now, and almost led to the break-off of the younger more democratic elements into a "Progressive" fraction. The split was averted, but the National Party was unable to agree on a platform. Two drafts of a Party Program remained in manuscript, one a variation on the Hungarian Conservative Platform which was drawn up by Ljudevit Vukotinović, the other written by Dragojlo Kušlan for the Progressives.(843) Both are in fact quite similar. Gaj seems to have been associated in the minds of most Illyrians with the more conservative group, and his espousal of the conservative position was much resented by the younger and more progressive members of the Party, especially those from Karlovac.(844) It would have been impossible for the National Party to adopt a really liberal program at this time had they wanted to do so, for the only Hungarian Party which could be termed liberal in its views was the Magyar Opposition, the Party which was also the proponent of magyarization and destruction of Croatian autonomy.

In 1846 and 1847 Gaj paid less attention than before to his editorial duties, reserving for himself only the decisions on editorial policy. He spent much of the time away from Zagreb and when home he was too preoccupied with politics, the move to the new house, and ways to meet his debts, to pay much attention to the newspaper. Bogoslav Šulek was now the major person in Gaj's newspaper office. In 1845, Šulek warned Gaj that *Novine's* only hope for survival was to become a "political" newspaper, and that people were beginning to lose interest in *Danica,* which should be made larger and more a literary magazine.(845) Šulek became chief editor of *Novine* in 1846, though still anonymous, and *Novine* became increasingly political, now that it was once more the journalistic arm of the National Party. Under Šulek the newspaper became more relevant and interesting, carrying an increasing number of articles on trade, economic reform, agriculture, and education, as well as detailed reports of local political activities and the meetings of the Joint Parliament. Under Šulek's direction the number of paid subscriptions rose from 500 in 1845 to 800 in 1848.(846) But Šulek, as he complained to Gaj, "had all of the responsibilities of being editor without the rights of editorship."(847) It was difficult for Šulek to work completely without Gaj, to be certain that the newspaper reflected the various shifts and inneundos in Party policy.

Gaj had not followed Šulek's advice about enlarging and reforming *Danica.* Demeter was still editorial assistant for *Danica* and he seems to have been careless about details. In a letter from Vienna in March of 1847, Stepan Pejaković, a contributor to *Danica* since 1841, and an unofficial intermediary between Vuk Karadžić and other Vienna contributors and Gaj's editorial office, complained about both Šulek and Demeter, but most of his criticism fell on Demeter.(848) Some articles, he said, were never acknowledged, nor were the authors told when and if they would be published, and if not published, why. He warned Gaj that the young Croats in Vienna were beginning to cool in their attitude toward him, and that he was making enemies among the Slavic writers there. Gaj's enemies, he reported, continued to spread rumors about Gaj's extravagance, his arrogance, his constant need to be admired, and his use of people to his own ends. Writers who had in the past contributed to Gaj's publications, were reluctant to send anything more, until they were assured their manuscripts would be given the care they deserved. The letter is startling in its frankness, which is cushioned throughout by assurances that Pejaković has nothing but the warmest feelings for Gaj, but that he believes Gaj should be informed of the situation as it exists.

When it was announced that elections would be held on July 23, for the vacant seats on the Zagreb Town Council, Gaj decided to run for the position of alderman.(849) This position was open to non-nobles and it would give Gaj an official political position. In preparation for the election, Gaj, who had lived in Zagreb since 1832, finally took out Zagreb citizenship.(850)

Gaj could not have had much time to prepare for the election, for he left Zagreb for his third brief trip to Serbia in the first week of July, arriving in Belgrade on July 7th, and leaving on the 15th.(851) He spent most of the time in Kragujevac. Gaj had come at a good time. The *Ustavobranitelji* leaders were beginning to fear that the Hungarian Serbs would soon adopt the Latin alphabet in place of the Cyrillic one.(852) Gaj may have been informed of this by Čavlović, for Čavlović came to Zagreb at this time, and returned to Belgrade with Gaj.(853) Gaj, as we know, had been hoping to make a Cyrillic edition of *Novine* since 1837, and the situation seemed quite favorable now, since he had talked with Metternich about the need for attracting the Serbs to Austria. On July 9, Gaj drew up a petition to Prince Alexander,(854) explaining that he had been unable to print books and his newspaper in the Cyrillic alphabet because he lacked Cyrillic type and it was beyond his present means to buy this type. This, he explained, had greatly hindered his effectiveness as a spokesman for Southern Slav unity. Gaj asked for the type as a gift, but said, if that was not possible, that he hoped at least to get the type at reduced cost. The Serbian Senate acted quickly and two days after Gaj's departure, it voted to give him a gift of 112 pounds of Cyrillic type.(855) Almost a year later this type, as well as a much larger amount of it granted Gaj in the first months of 1848, reached Zagreb.(856)

Gaj also asked the Prince for a gift of money but without success, getting, as he complained to Zach, ". . . promises but nothing more."(857) Gaj spent quite a bit of time with Zach at the beginning and end of this trip asked him once more to prepare a brief sketch to be used in Gaj's second report to Metternich, this time describing the internal political situation in Serbia. Zach complied, and his sketch is in Gaj's papers.(858)

Gaj submitted his second Memorandum to Metternich in early August. The Memorandum has not been located in the Vienna archives, but it is mentioned twice in the correspondence relating to Gaj's new petition for Austrian support of *Novine* in the fall of 1847.(859)

Back in Zagreb, Gaj lost in his bid for Alderman, coming last in a list of three candidates.(860) Gaj spent most of August moving his family and businesses to the new house, and dealing with new threats to his press. The Suppan press, recently taken over by Lavoslav Suppan after the death of his father in early 1847, had recently been renovated. It now had a "rapid-press" (Schnellpresse) and some other specialized equipment for fine work.(861) In order to compete effectively, Gaj found it necessary to purchase a rapid press too, something he could ill afford.(862) Then in July a certain E.J. Sassenberg of Vienna submitted a petition to the King asking for permission to establish a third printing press in Zagreb. On August 5th, Gaj and Suppan combined to avert this threat, writing a joint letter to the King in which they asked that the Sassenberg petition be denied since there was not yet enough work in Zagreb for three presses.(863)

Gaj left for Vienna once more and met with Metternich in the last week of August,(864) to ask for his help in forcing through action on Gaj's petition of 1845 in which he asked for an official subsidy for *Novine.* As a result of his talks with Metternich and conferences with other Court officials, Gaj drew up a new petition to Vice-Chancellor Apponyi, in which he asked for 12,000 forints as a subsidy for *Novine,* and an additional sum to compensate him for his "two" trips to Serbia in 1846 and 1847, which, he stressed, were made in the interest of Austria.(865)

Gaj stayed in Vienna until early November, awaiting final action on his petition. He needed money badly. He had already ordered the new press equipment in anticipation of Austrian help, was continually hounded by creditors in Zagreb, and had to meet the ever-growing demands of his wife for expensive furniture, rugs, even a piano for their new house.(866) To this end he went to see Knez Miloš Obrenović, the former Serbian ruler, who had lived in Vienna since his fall from power in 1839. Knez Miloš, a wealthy man, had expressed interest in *Novine* over the years, Gaj asked him for a gift of 2,000 forints to help his newspaper over its present financial crisis, getting instead 1,000 ducats, still a respectable sum.(867)

The Austrian authorities now moved quickly. Metternich supported Gaj's petition strongly, saying that his literary work was important both to the Croats and the Imperial Government, and that Gaj's reports from Serbia had been most interesting. Metternich made clear, however, that the Serbian trips had been made on Gaj's own initiative.(869) Metternich suggested they pay Gaj a smaller sum than he requested and that over a period of several years, adding a bit to compensate him for his trips to Serbia. By October 31, the matter had been decided by the State Conference and the Hungarian Court Chancellery. Gaj would get yearly subsidies of 1200 forints for a trial period of three years, renewable after that, and 1,000 forints at once to cover his travel expenses to Serbia.(870)

Gaj must have been bitterly disappointed to discover that instead of the anticipated 12,000 forints, he would get only 4,600 over a period of three years. On November 6, he signed a receipt for the first installment, 1200 forints for 1847, and 1,000 to cover the expenses of his trips to Serbia.(871)

The *Sabor* opened on October 18th. It was the last Croatian *Sabor* to meet in its feudal form, and it passed a clearly national program. On October 23rd, it voted unanimously to make the national language the official language of the Triune Kingdom. It also resolved to introduce the national language as the language of the schools as quickly as possible, and to this end, to establish chairs of the Illyrian language and literature in all of the secondary schools of the Triune Kingdom. It decided, as well, to ask the King to appoint a new Ban, preferably from the Imperial family, and if this were not possible, then to appoint a Ban who was familiar with the Illyrian language. It also asked that the Ban of Croatia be once again made the real, not titular, executive of the Triune Kingdom.(872)

The *Sabor* chose Herman Bužan, Metel Ožegović, and Josip Bunjik, as its deputies to the Joint Parliament, and instructed them to defend the

Municipal laws, to fight against any measures which would separate Civil Slavonia and the Littoral from Civil Croatia, and to demand once more the reincorporation of Dalmatia.(873)

The decision of the *Sabor* to make the national language the official language of the Kingdom was supported in independent action by the various towns and counties of the Kingdom in the last months of 1847 and first months of 1848. Most of the towns and counties of Civil Croatia began almost immediately to use the national language in their meetings, records and local communications. Zagreb county was the one exception: the elective positions still in Magyarone hands, it clung stubbornly to Latin.(874) The Slavonian counties and towns were a little more hesitant to act without official permission, but they were unanimous in support of the change to the national language in principle, and introduced it in some local business.(875)

Gaj left Vienna in early November and went from there to Pressburg where the Joint Parliament was now in session. He did not return to Zagreb until the second half of December. The long-awaited alliance between the National Party and the Hungarian Conservatives turned out to be a shaky one. The Croats soon came to realize that their only real protection lay with the King and his Ministers, and that they could not be relied on.(876)

Gaj played an active role behind the scenes in Pressburg, as advisor to the Croatian deputies, and go-between to the Hungarians. He decided, at this point, to petition the King to be made a noble, and his usefulness to the Croatian delegation in Pressburg is underlined by the fact that he got two letters of support for his petition which were signed by the leading Croats at the Joint Parliament and a few Hungarian Conservatives.(877) Both letters spoke of the fact that Gaj was a skilled politician, that he was hindered from playing an active political role because of his common birth, and that he was needed by his nation in the present political crisis. The letter signed by members of the lower house was effusive in its praise of Gaj.(878) The one written by members of the upper house, was much more restrained.(879) Gaj never submitted the petition, revolution intervened, and after 1848 it would no longer have been relevant.

There was a temporary lull in the conflict between the Croats and Hungarians during the time Gaj was in Pressburg, but by the second half of December, the Hungarian Opposition began vigorous action on the so-called Croatian question. Alexander Fodrocy, a delegate from Križevci, wrote to Gaj of the situation and saying that his advice was sorely needed:

> In you we lost our best friend, our wisest adviser, yes — our mentor.(880)

Here we see that Gaj's personal magnetism was once more in play, that he had not lost his ability to awaken immediate and deep personal loyalty from others.(881)

By the close of 1847, the Illyrian Movement had accomplished much of what it had set out to do. The national language, in its Illyrian form, was a recognized literary language with a fast-growing body of literature, supported by a network of cultural institutions and recognized as the language of state. The ideas about the importance of national language explained by Gaj in *Danica* in 1835, were now accepted as fact. The Croats had acted within the limit of their constitutional position, to protect their nation from cultural magyarization and political dismemberment. In many ways 1847 represents the end of the Illyrian Movement, for in the next year with the coming of revolution, the Croats would be swept into a new phase of their national history.

CHAPTER XII

REVOLUTION — AND EPILOGUE (1848-1872)

By late January of 1848, the events taking place at the Joint Parliament dominated *Novine.* The leading article in most issues was "Parliament news" which often took up half of the newspaper.(882) The Magyars had proposed the following legislation affecting the Triune Kingdom: Magyar was to be the official language of the Hungarian Kingdom and its dependencies; Croatia, refering here only to the three counties of Civil Croatia, could continue to use Latin as the language of state. A few concessions were made to the counties of Civil Slavonia and the Littoral, now considered by the Magyars as Hungarian counties: Slavonia could use Latin for six more years before changing over to Hungarian and the Littoral could use Italian in local matters. No one was to use Croatian. All correspondence between the Croatian and Hungarian administrative and judicial authorities was to be in Magyar, and Magyar was to become a required subject in all Croatian schools.(883) The decisions of the last *Sabor* were completely ignored by the Hungarians. Debate on the final details of this legislation was still in progress when revolution broke out in Paris and soon spread to Vienna and from there to Hungary.

It was not until March 3rd that news of the revolution in Paris reached Zagreb, followed soon after by reports of Kossuth's speech at the Pressburg Parliament calling for an independent and responsible Hungarian Ministry and an end to absolutism in the Habsburg Empire.(884) By the 15th, Zagreb knew that Metternich had resigned. The Pressburg Parliament was still in session and most of the Croatian politicians were still there.

Kukuljević and Vranyczany took over leadership of the revolution in Zagreb. On the 16th, they met with a few Illyrians to draw up a plan of action.(885) On the 17th, Kukuljević led a large delegation to a public meeting with the Zagreb city officials at which, on Kukuljević's suggestion, a committee was chosen to draw up a national petition to be presented to the King, and a delegation of six men headed by Vranyczany was chosen to take it to Vienna.(886) Plans were also made for the establishment of a National Guard.

Gaj was not present at these meetings. He had left Zagreb several days earlier for Graz to try to win the support of General Laval Nugent and Archduke Johann for the immediate appointment of Colonel Josip Jelačić as Ban of Croatia, a position unfilled since 1845. Gaj explained to them that the Croats needed more than anything else a Ban with wide popular appeal, loyal to the dynasty, who could direct the revolution in a course favorable both to the Croats and the King.

Why should Gaj have taken this action? Were the concerns expressed to the Archduke the most important? Is it not possible Gaj hoped that Jelačić, a professional military man without real political experience, a loyal Illyrian and enthusiastic follower of Gaj, might not be able to be controlled by him? Jelačić and Gaj had been in contact since 1840, and Jelačić had cherished a secret desire to be Ban for a long time, one he may have expressed to Gaj.(887)

Gaj found both Nugent and Archduke Johann amenable to his proposal, and the Archduke and Gaj traveled on to Vienna where Archduke Johann consulted with his brothers and court officials. The appointment of Jelačić was, ironically, already settled by that time. From the 13th to the 15th, unbeknownst to Gaj, Franjo Kulmer, Ljudevit Bedeković and Metel Ožegović had met, decided on the need to choose Jelačić, and consulted with the Regents Council.(888) When Gaj talked to Kulmer about joint action to force through the appointment of Jelačić as Ban, Kulmer kept silent about his own negotiations, suspicious of Gaj's intentions.(889)

On May 20 and 21, Gaj met with Slavic students at the University of Vienna in one of the large emotional meetings held in the *Aula* in those days. The University had become one of the focal points in the Viennese revolution. Vranyczany was present as well. At the meetings, a group of Slavic students with Croats among them drew up two proclamations. In the first one they called upon the Croats to join in the universal liberation of the Slavs.(890) The second spoke of the need for the Croats to join the Slavic revolution which had now begun, and advised them to do so under the guidance of the one man in their midst who had awoken respect for the Croatian cause among Slavs and throughout Europe —

Dr. Ljudevit Gaj.(891) It proposed specifically that Vranyczany, and Kukuljević join together with Gaj and serve as a provisional revolutionary committee. Vranyczany reported on this meeting to Kukuljević, advising him to make peace with Gaj.(892) Thus, as Šišić wrote, . . . "the youth once more brought Gaj into political life."(893)

The documents naming Josip Jelačić Ban of Croatia, promoting him to Lieutenant Field Marshall, and putting the two Banal regiments under his command, were being prepared as Gaj left Vienna by train on March 22nd.

In Zagreb Kukuljević, Drašković and others were busy preparing for the National Assembly which was to meet on March 25th, to decide on the petition of National Demands. Representatives poured into Zagreb from all parts of the Triune Kingdom and meetings were held continuously to discuss the various points to be included in the petition. One March 22nd, in large letters *Novine* announced that the press was free, followed by an article by Šulek whose opening words express the mood of the moment:

> Finally justice has triumphed. The chains which bound the soul of man are broken, the yoke which stifled freedom is lifted, the ugly shadow of selfish absolutism flees before the bright face of the sunrise . . .(894)

A meeting was held that night to discuss the best choice for a new Ban, and the majority voted for Jelačić.

Gaj reached Zagreb on March 24th in the late afternoon. The streets were already filled with delegates to the Assembly, colorful in their national costumes. Baron Neustaeder, described Gaj's trip from the station:

> . . . in a coach drawn by four horses, he (Gaj) was quickly taken up the long Ilica to the upper town. The crowds recognized him and ran after him to find out the latest news from Vienna. But his coach was traveling too fast for him to talk and he simply shouted from left to right "Revolution, revolution, revolution!"(895)

Gaj scarcely had time to greet his family before he was drawn into the dining room to talk with people assembling there. He went on with them to the National Center where a large group had already gathered in the *dvorana* for a night meeting. Mijo Krešić, a young businessman from Karlovac, described the meeting vividly in his diary.(896) When Gaj entered, he was greeted with shouts of "Živio!" After the noise died down Gaj began to speak. What was at stake now, he said, was not just a matter of national language and piecemeal reform, but of revolutionary action in concert with the entire Slavic population of the Empire. The Croats should chose a new Ban, demand independence from Hungary, and these with the other demands should be taken by a large delegation to the King. Kušlan then read the proclamations of the Slavic students at the University of Vienna and the assembly again shouted "Živio." Their suggestion about the provisional revolutionary triumvirate — Gaj, Kukuljević and Vranyczany, was accepted without debate.

Someone reported that the Magyarones were gathering weapons in the Kasino in preparation for armed confrontation. Tempers ran high, but Gaj won the assembly over to a plan of pacification and headed a group which went to the Kasino and asked the Magyarones to join the meeting. Some of the most important leaders came back with them, and Gaj spoke once more, explaining the goals of the revolution. A few of the liberal Magyarones decided to join the revolution, now that it espoused a liberal as well as national platform, but the more conservative ones held back.(897)

As soon as Gaj arrived in Zagreb he seems to have taken over from the leaders there. It is not difficult to imagine how some of the others — Kukuljević, Drašković — must have felt when this happened. Kukuljević was a fine orator with an impressive voice tightly reasoned arguments and measured phrases.(898) This was fine for the *Sabor* but not for a crowd. Gaj was a gifted agitator, his grasp of the spoken language stirred his contemporaries to wonder,(899) he knew how to play on the emotions of an audience; his arguments were not always logical, but he knew how to convince the listeners of the rightness of his cause.(900) In these emotional days, he remained center stage.

The next day was packed with activity. Gaj worked with Kukuljević, Zerjavić and Nikola Vakanović on the final draft of the National Demands.(901) He then went on to agitate at the Zagreb Academy and Seminary, making sure of student support for the revolution and urging them to come to the National Assembly. His next task was to collect funds to meet the expenses of the delegation which was to go to Vienna. He forced the Zagreb *kaptol* (Cathedral Chapter) to contribute 10,000 forints as a sign that they did not oppose the revolution, and got a contribution of 1,200 forints from the small Zagreb Jewish community, which was frightened by the rumors of pogroms elsewhere in the Empire.(902) Voluntary contributions poured in as well, most of them from one to ten forints, and Gaj noted them all down carefully in a notebook.(903)

The National Assembly opened at 3:00 P.M. in the *dvorana,* which was packed. First the proclamations from the Slavic students in Vienna were read, to give legitimacy to the new leadership. Then Gaj read the first article of the petition: that the Assembly acting for the nation choose Josip Jelačić to be the new Ban of Croatia and that the King be asked to approve this appointment. Then:

> . . . Not taking into consideration the pride of those of his colleagues who would have liked to express their personal support of this act, he cried out "Long live our Ban Josip Jelačić."(904)

According to the report in *Novine* the cheers and shouting which greeted Gaj's words lasted for fifteen minutes.(905) Thus the election of Jelačić as Ban was done unanimously and without debate, and it was so with the other points as well. These were read so quickly by Dragutin Galac that, as Neustaedter notes, people present could scarcely hear, much less follow them, and again, after every point, Gaj led the crowd to accept them without discussion by leading deafening shouts of "Živio!"(906)

This does not mean that Gaj sneaked something through, for most of the demands had been debated at length in the preceding week. The 30 articles of the National Demands (Zahtevanja naroda) were an interesting blend of old and new. Among the familiar points were: reincorporation of Dalmatia, the Military Frontier and the Littoral (No. 3), introduction of the Croatian language as the language of administration and the language of instruction in the schools (No. 6); and creation of a national university (No. 7). New ones included: independence from Hungary (No. 4), creation of a national bank (No. 15), a responsible ministry (No. 5); convocation of the *Sabor* by April 1st (No. 2); election of Ban Jelačić (No. 1), representation to the *Sabor* from all classes (No. 11); equality of citizens before the law (No. 12) and in the sharing of the tax burden (No. 13). A tentative step was taken toward emancipation of the serfs by demanding that they no longer pay the *robot* (No. 14). All foreigners should be removed from government, church and military positions (Nos. 18 and 19), the troops of the Military Frontier should become anational army and be called back from Italy (No. 18), and all reforms should apply to the Military Frontier as well as to the Civil parts of the Kingdom (No. 16).(907) This was indeed an announcement of the end of the old order.

Dragutin Kušlan was delegated by the Assembly to go to Glina and informa Colonel Jelačić of his election. Jelačić had mixed reactions to the news, while pleased to hear of his election, as a professional military man trained to obedience to his King and government, he realized that such an election was not "legal."(908) He gave an inconclusive response to Kušlan's question of whether he accepted the Banship, giving as an excuse that he needed to complete military preparations for a rumored Turkish attack. That this was not the real reason can be seen in the fact that he also promised to come to Zagreb the next day to talk with the political leaders there.(909) Fortunately for Jelačić, the documents bestowing his new authority reached him while on his way to Zagreb, thus he was Ban now by appointment of the King as well as by election of the National Assembly. He called Gaj to him soon after he arrived in Zagreb and showed him a declaration in which he said, "From now on I belong in soul and body to the nation, the homeland and the King."(910)

It could well be asked whether a revolution should have such a leader, one who links loyalty of the nation with loyalty to the King, for in the end, Jelačić sacrificed the Croatian revolution to military intervention in order to save the dynasty. It could therefore be said that the choice of Jelačić as Ban, one favorable to conservative elements in Vienna, was a mistake. At the moment, however it seemed immensely popular and right. Jelačić left for Glina the next day and it was not until mid-April that he returned to Zagreb to serve as Ban. He appointed Mirko Lentulay to rule in his absence carefully avoiding giving power to the triumvirate.

Gaj and the other two leaders left for Vienna with a delegation of 400 on March 27th, arriving there on the 30th. They were greeted by an enthusiastic crowd. The Slavic legion carried the Croatian flag, bands played Croatian marches. The delegation must have been an impressive sight. Krešić writes:

> All members of our deputation, four hundred people, were dressed in national costumes, the *šurka* and white or blue trousers, with *kolpaks* or red caps and swords. A few national guardsmen wore their uniforms and the clergy were dressed in their habits.(911)

After speeches of welcome, answered by Gaj, the deputation marched slowly through town to the hotel where their leaders would stay, while students shouted "Vivat," women waved white handkerchiefs to them from the windows, and the National Guard cleared the way.(912)

Gaj and the other leaders consulted with Kulmer about the best way to get to the King. Kulmer did not approve of the National Demands, but thought them a useful tool against the Magyars.(913) He took Gaj and the others to Minister Fiquelmont, who told the Croats that their petition was too long and that its tone must be made more moderate, otherwise the King would not listen to them. They then compressed the 30 points into 11, Gaj doing most of the work, introduced them with references to the storm now sweeping Europe and Croatia's need to defend herself, and eliminated the articles dealing with the election of Ban Jelačić, independence from Hungary, and reform in the Church.(914) On March 31st, the revised Demands were presented to the King by a delegation of 14. It was clear from their brief session with the

King that the pro-Magyar ministers now held sway.(915) The delegation then went back to their hotels and waited, expecting immediate action.

In the meantime the Croatian delegation paid formal visits to the Slavic students at the University, and received visits from the Lower Austrian Estates and from national delegations of Poles and Czechs.(916)

Gaj, Vranyczany and Kukuljević did not always agree on policy. This is most clearly demonstrated in the incident involving Bishop Haulik, the former Acting Ban. Haulik had come directly to Vienna from the Pressburg Diet as the revolution began. He kept in close touch with Zagreb but though he had played an active role in the National Party in the last few years, he was essentially a man of the court and a conservative.(917) The liberal Bishop Schrott(918) and Gaj had already led some demonstrations against Bishop Haulik in Zagreb, accusing him of opposing the revolution.(919) Kukuljević and Vranyczany decided to visit the Bishop and assure him of their loyalty. When Gaj heard of this he gathered a large group of delegates together and led them to tell Bishop Haulik, "the true sentiments of the Croatian patriots,"(920) meeting the other two leaders on the way and forcing them to come with him. Gaj informed the Bishop that the Croats no longer saw him as their spiritual leader and should he return to Zagreb his personal safety could not be guaranteed. After the Croats left, the Bishop sat down to write his resignation, when Kulmer came in and dismissed Gaj's statements as extreme and guaranteed that Ban Jelačić would protect the Bishop should he return.(921) Bishop Haulik did not come to Zagreb until June 14, 1848.

There was still no answer from the King. Krešić wrote:

> Well this is the fifth day that 400 of us sit here spending our Croatian pence and waiting for the new laws.(922)

and as they waited, the political climate in Vienna began to change. The idea of German national unity began to sweep the city, the Slavic legions were replaced on the streets by German *Burschen* and thousands of Viennese gathered at St.Stephen's square to sing "Where is the German Fatherland."(923) The Croatian delegates began to leave Vienna, disappointed with the outcome of their mission. Gaj stayed on to wait for Jelačić who arrived April 4th. The new Ban consulted with Court and military officials, met with Polish and Slovak leaders then in Vienna to discuss possible joint action against the Magyars, and received advice from both Kulmer and Gaj.(924) On April 8th, Jelačić was formally promoted to Lieutenant Field Marshall and commander of the Croatian Military Frontier. In gratitude to Gaj, who Jelačić believed most responsible for his new positions,(925) the Ban arranged that he be honored too. Jelacic hoped to get Gaj the title K.K. *Hofrath,* but succeeded only in getting him the title K.K. *Rath,* one with little meaning.(926)

Ban Jelačić and Gaj returned to Zagreb together, arriving on April 18th. In the next few weeks Gaj was the Ban's closest advisor. There was much to be done and no clear guidelines to follow: the peasants were revolting, there was unrest in the towns, and the Magyarones had begun to emigrate and seek support for their cause in Hungary. On April 25th, Ban Jelačić proclaimed it was time for a national renaissance; that the traditional social and political order had fallen and the nation needed new laws. To this end, he announced the convening of a popularly elected national *Sabor* as soon as the electoral procedures could be worked out and elections held.(927) On the same day he decreed the end of serfdom, and on April 27th, the establishment of martial law. To implement these decisions and avoid the appearance of arbitrary rule, Jelačić established the Ban's Council which was staffed with some of the most important political figures in Croatia and had six sections: political, internal affairs, judicial, educational, financial and military, each headed by a Counselor. The Council met daily, decided matters by majority vote, dealt with immediate crises and set up election procedure for the *Sabor.*(928) Gaj headed the Political section, a key post, for he worked with Jelačić on both domestic and foreign affairs. In the foreign field Gaj concentrated on building ties with the Hungarian Serbs and the government of the Serbian Principality, in domestic matters he dealt with countless delegations from counties, towns, villages. Ban Jelačić was relatively young, only 47 years old, and inexperienced as a politician. He ran his affairs informally, as was noted by surprise by Brigadier Johann von Kempen of the Military Frontier who came to Zagreb to consult with the Ban on military matters in early May:

> He (the Ban) conducted almost everything publicly, something which should not be allowed. He read letters from Vienna to others, consulted freely with members of a delegation which had just returned from Vienna, received reports from Counselor Gaj and gave him orders. This man (Gaj) seems to have much influence over Jelačić and to watch his actions carefully.(929)

The new Croatian government faced serious financial problems. Jelačić liked to joke about how he had been appointed Ban with only 5 forints of his last salary in his pocket, and how he had had to ask for a large advance on his salary as Ban before he could come to Zagreb to take up his new post.(930) It would have been impossible to expect him to finance the revolution out of his own pocket, but a little money would have helped. On May 16, Jelačić proclaimed that Croats should continue to pay taxes as usual, and called on them to donate money for domestic and military needs.(931)

It looked as if the Croats might have to go to war with the Magyars. Gaj returned from Vienna convinced this was so. In an unpublished note he wrote that the King was now a captive of the Hungarians, predicting "Vienna last saw us as petitioners — Vienna shall see us as her saviors."(932) Ban Jelačić tried to steer an independent course between contradictory action on the part of the Austrians, and orders from the new Hungarian government which the Croats did not recognize. One of the key points of controversy was over the actual control of the Military Frontier. The new Hungarian government claimed all troops of the Military Frontier and all troops stationed in Croatia to be under its command. They were supported in this on May 7th, by a decree of King Ferdinand, while the Imperial War Ministry kept issuing orders as before.(933) Jelačić refused to recognize orders from the Hungarian War Ministry, and began to shift troops from the Turkish to the Hungarian border.(934) The situtation was complicated by the spread of revolution into the Military Frontier; the Croats there looked to Zagreb for leadership, and the Serbs to the newly formed autonomous government of the Voivodina in Novi Sad.

The Hungarians appointed Lieutenant Field Marshall Johann Hrabowski, Commander of the Slavonian-Syrmian troops, to establish Hungarian control of the Frontier and replace Jelačić as commander of the Croatian Military Frontier.(935) Hrabrowski was unable to carry out his task, but his appointment complicated matters still further. It was most probably due to financial and military pressures that Jelačić turned to the Serbian Principality for help.

The Serbs had taken the initiative. In early April Matija Ban arrived in Zagreb to talk with Jelačić and Gaj. He had been sent by Prince Alexander to find out what was happening there and assure Gaj and Jelačić of his concern. Ban said that the Prince considered the revolution itself of little direct concern to the Principality, but should it erupt into war with the Magyars, it would pose a threat to the Principality. Ban asserted that in that case the Prince would use all of his influence to raise military support for the Croats among the Hungarian Serbs, leaving unclear whether or not he himself would intervene militarily.(936)

As a result of these conversations which took place in mid-April, Gaj sent Stefan Herkalović and Dragutin Galac to Serbia to serve as official representatives of the new Croatian government there. The Croats also sent representatives to the Slavic Congress in Prague.(937)

By mid May the financial and military situation had worsened. On May 16th, Ban Jelačić wrote to Prince Alexander Karadjordjević, asking the Serbian government for help of three kinds: moral, military and financial, more specifically he asked for a loan of 30,000 dukats to be co-signed by himself and Gaj, and for military help should the Magyars invade. He left the details for the Serbs and the Croatian representatives there to work out.(938)

He also sent formal representatives to the new revolutionary government of the Voivodina, which on May 13th at a national congress, had drawn up a list of national demands, one of which expressed the desire for close ties with the Croats.(939) On May 13th they chose Colonel Stefan Suplikac as *vojvoda* and elevated Metropolitan Josif Rajačić to the position of Serbian Patriarch.(940) Ban Jelačić invited the Patriarch to come to Zagreb for the ceremonies marking his formal inauguration as Ban on June 5th, and asked the new government to send a delegation to the Croatian *Sabor.*

On May 21st Miloš Obrenović arrived in Zagreb, and his visit entangled Gaj in a scandal which would soon remove him from politics forever, in what is known as the ''Miloš affair''(941) The former Serbian Prince claimed to have been invited by Gaj to attend the installation of the Ban. He was rumored, on the other hand, to have stopped there on his way to Serbia where he hoped, with Magyar and Turkish help, to lead a revolt and get back into power. The Serbs of the Principality had been watching him carefully for some time and warned Gaj Miloš might appear in Zagreb. Gaj urged Jelačić to put Knez Miloš immediately under house arrest, which was done, and suggested that he be divested of all papers and money, for he might try to bribe his way out.(942) This was not done. During these first days Gaj met and talked with Miloš several times. Herkalović wrote to Gaj from Serbia expressing Garašanin's concern about Prince Miloš's arrival in Zagreb, suggesting ''Miloš does not need to leave Zagreb alive.''(943) Herkalović played on the Miloš arrest to get money from the Serbs.

It is here that we see that Gaj and Jelačić, despite the look of unanimity, had quite different ideas about alliance with Serbia, and that the informal ambassadors there represented Gaj's policy more than that of the Ban. Jelačić wanted Serbian cooperation in order to save Croatia and the dynasty; Gaj wanted to create a Southern Slav Kingdom with Serbia at the center, a plan he had been cultivating since 1842. This divergence was clearly expressed in a letter from Ilija Garašanin to Stojan Šimić in which he reported on a conversation with the Croatian representatives to the Prince: Stefan Herkalović and Dragutin Galac.(944) Herkalović asked for 20,000 dukats for the Croats, 5,000 immediately and the rest later. These would be used by Gaj to implement his plan for Southern Slav unity, one which was not espoused by Jelačić.(945) The Serbs promised to help and finally gave Herkalović 1,000 dukats in June. (946)

Preparations for the inauguration of the Ban, elections to the *Sabor,* and plans for its convocation now preoccupied Gaj and the Ban. Gaj was chosen by the Zagreb Academy as their representative to the *Sabor.* The Austrians ordered Jelačić on May 29th to delay the opening of the *Sabor,* now scheduled for June 7th; he refused. There was also the problem of who was to formally preside at the inauguration ceremonies, as this was traditionally done by the Zagreb Bishop and Haulik was still in Vienna.(947) The role would most logically have fallen to the second in command, Bishop Schrott, but Gaj persuaded Jelačić to ask Patriarch Rajačić to take Haulik's place, as a symbol of Southern Slav unity. Jelačić agreed reluctantly and the Patriarch accepted, also with hesitation.(948) This was a personal triumph for Gaj but it won him many enemies among the Zagreb Catholic clergy. Brigadier Kempen noted in his diary on June 6th, that feeling was growing against Gaj in Croatia, that perhaps he should be "sacrificed."(949) Kulmer wrote to Metel Ožegović from Vienna in much the same vein, saying that he had heard rumors that Gaj was trying to create an independent Southern Slav state and that he should perhaps be removed.(950)

The Ban's inauguration took place on June 5th, with great ceremony and jubilation.(951) The *Sabor* opened on June 7th. Gaj played a leading role in the first sessions, speaking often and urging the Croats to work immediately for separation from Hungary and close alliance with the Hungarian Serbs.(952) On the same day Gaj asked the Ban for permission to visit Prince Miloš, who had recently been removed to more secure quarters. His request was granted. The next day Prince Mihail Obrenović arrived in Zagreb to arrange for his father's release. Ban Jelačić sent for Prince Miloš and in the course of their talk, the Prince complained that Gaj had taken 2,000 forints from him in gold and 3,000 in banknotes for the Ban's use.(953) Jelačić gave the Prince permission to leave Zagreb immediately. Furious at Gaj, the Ban then went in to dinner where he had guests waiting and told them of what had happened.(954) Gaj, hearing of Miloš's departure, came to the Ban's residence that evening with a group of his followers and demanded to see Jelačić. He was refused entrance.(955) News of the Miloš Affair quickly spread through Zagreb and on June 10th, a large public demonstration was held against Gaj.(956) On the same day, Ban Jelačić turned the investigation of the Affair over to a special Commission made up of distinguished members of the *Sabor,* which included Vjekoslav Babukić and several other personal friends of Gaj.(957) It was also on June 10th, that the Emperor, who had fled to Innsbruck with his Court, gave in to Magyar pressure and signed an order stripping Jelačić of his new office, an edict which was soon remanded, but one which presented Jelačić with problems more pressing than those of the accusations against his former assistant — Ljudevit Gaj. Gaj wrote a long letter to the Ban, protesting the formation of the Commission, explaining that the accusations against him were contrived by Prince Miloš, and that the arrest and departure of Miloš were intimately connected with foreign policy and should not be made public.(958) The investigation continued. After Miloš had lodged his first accusations, Gaj lost his position on the Ban's Council, but he still participated in the *Sabor* for several weeks and was even appointed to two standing committees, the most important being the Commitee to draw up the new constitution.(959) After the third week of June Gaj's name was no longer mentioned in *Novine's* detailed reports of the *Sabor* debates. His political career was now ended.

Nothing definite could be proven against Gaj. There was evidence that he had cashed several banknotes for 1,000 forints during the period in question.(960) No one had actually seen him take any money from Prince Miloš. Prince Mihail Obrenović testified that he thought Gaj was blameless and that his father, Prince Miloš, was lying.(961) The amount Prince Miloš accused Gaj of taking grew the further he got from Zagreb. It was 5,000 forints in Zagreb, more in Ljubljana and 28,000 by the time he made his formal deposition in Innsbruck on June 20, 1848.(962) The Commission turned the matter over to the Zagreb Town Court after two months of investigation, and on March 24, 1849, the Town Court closed the case, concluding that the evidence against Gaj was not sufficient.(963) Therefore Gaj was never found guilty of extorting money from Miloš, although the suspicion that he had done it was still strong in many minds.

It is quite possible that Gaj did accept money from Miloš. We know that he was not careful about accepting money from contradictory sources. He needed funds badly at the time for he had to draw time and again on his personal income to finance his political work as Jelačić's right-hand man. I doubt that he asked the Prince for money in the Ban's name, for this accusation was made only in Zagreb; the Innsbruck formal complaint says that Gaj needed it for his own work.(964) It is unlikely that he took 28,000 forints, it was more likely close to 7,000 forints, for in 1853 Gaj arranged with Miloš for the Prince to clear him of all guilt in a public letter which was published in the *Wiener Zeitung* on October 3, 1853,(965) in return for secret repayment to the Prince of a "debt" of 7,500 forints.(966) This was a final desperate attempt by Gaj to clear his name.

Ljudevit Gaj never regained his lost popularity and lived out the rest of his life in relative obscurity.(967) He was bitter to the end of his life about what he considered to be the treachery of Jelačić:

> ... whom I carried on my back and raised up high so that the nation would see him and respect him ...(968)

In his old age he still spoke of the Miloš affair as the product of an intrigue by his enemies.(969) Perhaps it was.

In December of 1849, Gaj formally entered the service of the Bach regime, signing a contract which made *Novine* an official government newspaper. For this he received a yearly subsidy of 1,000 forints.(970) Almost symbolically, *Danica* ceased publication at the end of 1849. In 1850 and 1851 Gaj's financial position was relatively good; not only was his newspaper subsidized but his press got the largest part of the government business, and in these years there were hundreds of edicts, laws, proclamations.(971) In 1850 he purchased a county estate on a hill near Zagreb which he named *Mirogoj*(972) (Place of Rest) for 7,000 forints,(973) and then proceeded to build an elegant house and buy what land he could around the original property.

Although Gaj was dead as a political figure, the police continued to watch him carefully. It was at this time that he destroyed all compromising papers. In October of 1853, on the way back from a trip to Prague, Ljudevit Gaj was arrested in Vienna on suspicion of treason. The charges were quite ridiculous. They stemmed from some irresponsible talk by Pavel Čavlović and suspicions arising from Gaj's recent reconcilation with Prince Miloš and his former contact with Serbia.(974) Gaj was released on December 23, 1853.(975)

The expenses incurred in his release from jail, the repayment of the debt to Prince Miloš, the cost of his new country home, led Gaj to seek expensive short-term loans to pay the interest on other debts, and in 1858 Ljudevit Gaj and his wife were drawn into lengthly and humiliating bankruptcy proceedings. From that time on Gaj and his family lived in straitened circumstances.(976) The Gajs now had four children, a fifth died in childhood. The eldest daughter Slava was married, and the three boys Velimir, Svetoslav and Milivoj were still at home. The Gajs were permitted to live at Mirogoj, and Ljudevit Gaj continued to run his newspaper and press, but they really did not belong to him any more but to his creditors through the court.(977)

Ljudevit Gaj made a brief attempt to re-enter politics in 1868 but failed. In his last decades of life he became a perpetual petitioner: to Vienna, to the Ban, to the *Sabor.* Paulina Gaj died in April, 1869.

Ljudevit Gaj died on April 20, 1872 in the editorial offices of *Novine*. He was buried two days later. The funeral oration was given by his old friend Fran Kurelac. In the oration, Kurelac reminded people once more the role Gaj had played in the first years of the national awakening, and asked them to forgive him his human mistakes, and value him for what he had contributed to the nation.(978) Another less charitable comment was made by an anonymous writer at the time:

> Gaj's body died on April 20, 1872. His spirit died many years ago. For his family he died this year, but for the nation he had long been dead.(979)

The interaction between Ljudevit Gaj and the Illyrian Movement falls into two distinct phases: 1835-1842; 1843-1848. In the first phase Gaj was at the center of the Movement and his ideas shaped its development. In the second he found himself forced from the leading position by a combination of circumstances, some of his own making, some not, and he played a secondary role in the Movement until 1848, when he rose to leadership once more for several months. There is much more material from which to reconstruct Gaj's ideas, concerns and motives in the first phase and the years preceding it, than in the second. In the formative period of Gaj's ideological development, 1826-1836, he worked out many of his ideas on paper, and his unpublished notes, fragments and poems, as well as his published works, are invaluable sources. In *Danica* in 1835 and 1836, he published definitive statements on the interrelationship between language and nationality, orthographic reform, the nature of the new literary language, the Illyrian nationality, Panslavism, and the need for cultural institutions to support the new national awakening. After 1836 he concentrated more on organizational work, on agitation, and on trying to secure the precarious financies of his newspaper and, leter, press.

It is impossible to reconstruct the impact of Gaj as he moved from the written word to the spoken word. We have only the testimony of his contemporaries to his almost hypnotic quality, his pleasing voice, his masterful grasp of the new literary language, and his ability to move an audience to emotional heights. While we know that he met constantly with individuals and groups in his office, at meals, and in formal gatherings, there are only occasional glimpses of what was discussed. By 1838, though Gaj was firmly at the center of things he begins to elude us. This is underlined by the emergence of Gaj's secret politics in 1838, where he began on his own initiative to seek political support for the Movement from outside powers. It is possible that he also had many unpublished papers relating to this move, and that these were destroyed in the early 1850's when he destroyed his Russian and Serbian correspondence. All of Gaj's official Illyrian pronouncements in these years profess loyalty to the King, the Hungarian Constitution, the Triune Kingdom, while his secret politics have an anti-Austrian, revolutionary Southern Slav focus. Gaj's first attempt at secret politics (1838-1840) met with failure and he turned back to work once more within the given situation, in 1841 leading the Movement from its first emphasis on a Croatian cultural renaissance within a Southern Slav and Pan-Slav framework to organized political action by the Illyrian, later National, Party.

The duality of motive which emerged in 1838 became a major theme in Gaj's activities between 1843 and 1848. Gaj was still a central figure in Croatian cultural life, as editor and publisher, and a minor but not insignificant one in political life. Barred from active participation in the political institutions of the Kingdom by the fact of common birth, distrusted for a while by Austria, aware that the success of the Movement now depended on the ability of the National Party to establish clear goals, harness local support, win the protection of the King and his Ministers, Gaj could only work behind the scenes, advise if asked, editorialize if permitted. He must have felt a great frustration seeing others take over the leadership of the Party, no longer able to direct and control developments, his future dependent on forces beyond his control. Perhaps this is why he returned to his secret politics in these years. What were his real loyalties? On this question his papers are mute.

The years between 1843 and 1848 in the Triune Kingdom are dominated by the actions of the National Party, the shifting policy of Austria, the intensification of Magyar pressure on the Croats and the responding intensification and spread of political support for the Illyrians. It is also the period in which the cultural reforms of the first eight years reach maturity. Gaj moves in and out of this picture somewhat indistinctly, except for moments of crisis such as July 1845 and 1848. He traveled to Vienna, to Prague, to Belgrade, pledging cooperation to Austria, the Polish emigration, the *Ustavobranitelji,* the National Party. The almost frenetic pace of his travels in 1846 and 1847 is in itself a witness to the complexity of his secret and public politics and his constant need for money. In the Miloš Affair in June 1848, these separate threads intertwine for a moment, and lead to Gaj's fall from power.

Throughout his career as an Illyrian leader Ljudevit Gaj was able to awaken a deep response from the educated youth. By the late 1830's most of the members of the original Gaj circle became themselves leading figures in specific aspects of the Movement, no longer willing nor needing to be led. Gaj drew his new circle from the new generation of academic youth, the group which clustered around him in the early 1840's. The original Gaj circle were partners in the birth of the national awakening, the second group participants in his secret politics. It was the student group participants in his secret politics. It was the student youth in Vienna and Zagreb who once again in 1848, gave him a mandate for political leadership, through the manifesto of the Vienna students, and election by the Zagreb Academy to the 1848 *Sabor.* But young people expect much of their leaders, vision, dedication, a certain charismatic quality and morality.

Gaj could not completely measure up to the last, for neither in money matters nor in politics were his morals impeccable. Perhaps the most bitter published attack on Gaj after his fall was B. Šulek's "Krive Mesije," (False Messiahs) in 1849. In it Šulek castigated Gaj for misleading the youth, charming them by his rhetoric, air of mystery, praiseworthy goals, and deceiving and using them to his own ends.(980) If Gaj had not fallen so deeply into debt, if he had not pursued both public and secret politics, there would not have been that backlog of mistrust which was put aside for a few months in early 1848, only to reappear in full force in June.

Gaj's money problems which were most significant in leading to his fall had a long history. He was the first "professional" nationalist. The others in the Gaj circle continued at their studies or professional careers as teachers, lawyers, priests, civil servants, while Gaj spent a minimum of time in 1832 and 1833 at the profession for which he had been trained — law — and left it for good in 1834 for an uncertain life as a journalist, agitator and, later, publisher. He invested his own inheritance, and that of his mother and sisters in the newspaper and printing press, thus making his financial future and that of his family success dependent on the success of the national awakening. Until his marriage his public life was in many ways his private life, and even after 1842 he continued to identify his future and that of his wife and children with the Movement and the mission he had felt so strongly since 1827. Gaj lived far beyond his means. He had little money sense. By the late 1840's he took money from whomever would give it. He helped finance the national awakening and paid some of the costs of the first months of revolution from his own pocket. His feeling that he had to keep up appearances was probably a direct result of being a commoner in a society dominated by nobles. He tried to win their respect by living nobly.

Ljudevit Gaj contributed a good deal to the history of the Croats in the early nineteenth century and to the later development of Southern Slav nationalism. He awoke the Croats from provincial obscurity, division, and weakness, to an awareness of their ethnic nationality, helped in the development of a modern literary language which could be counterposed to the Magyar language and which could serve as the basis of a rich national cultural life. He put the national awakening within the framework of Southern Slav cultural unity and Pan-Slavism, thus making the Croats aware that although they were a minority nationality in Hungary and Austria, they belonged to a nationality which covered the Balkan peninsula and that the Southern Slavs were part of the huge Slavic "nationality." As a young man Gaj had become convinced that his mission was to bring the Croats to a recognition of their national identity so that they could set up a dam against Magyarization. By the last months of 1847, at least within the Triune Kingdom itself, this was accomplished. In 1848 fully developed Croatian and Magyar nationalism met head-on in the Revolution, and the Croats took up arms against the Magyars.

The Triune Kingdom emerged from the Revolution with its territory intact, in fact slightly expanded. The nationalist program which was being passed by the Magyars just as the Revolution began, one which would have stripped the Kingdom of most of its territory and rendered it incapable of defending itself further against Magyarization, was never put into practice. The Military Frontier was returned to the Kingdom in the 1870's. Dalmatia remained under Austria until the Empire collapsed, but Croatian nationalism spread to Dalmatia in the last decades of the nineteenth century, setting down firm roots. By World War I, the former territories of medieval Croatia with the exception of Bosnia-Hercegovina, a special and extremely complicated case, were strongly infused with a sense of Croatian national identity. The second aspect of the Illyrian Movement, the awareness of membership in the Southern Slav ethnic and cultural community, helped lay the foundations for Southern Slav political unity.

The Illyrian Movement was in essence the Croatian national awakening. That this awakening occurred in a Southern Slav context was in part a function of the need for the Croats to identify with a cultural community much larger than Hungary, and in part a need to find an identity which would link the Serbs and Croats who lived within the Triune Kingdom and in its former lands. Gaj begged the question of what a Croat was, what a Serb was. He simply called them all Illyrians, and for the moment it was enough. Civil Croatia, Civil Slavonia, and the Military Frontier, joined together in 1848 to fight the Magyars. After 1848, when the name Illyrian was replaced by Croatian, it began to be evident that the Illyrian Movement had left the Croats with a somewhat ambiguous national identity.

The Illyrian Movement does not represent the final stage in the development of Croatian nationalism, only its beginning. The unsolved problems of the Illyrian period would be taken up by later reformers; the language would be pruned of its Southern Slavisms, the definition of national identity would be made more precise, the nationalism which was limited to the social and political elite in the Illyrian period, would be transmitted to the peasantry. The Southern Slav character of the Croatian national awakening would ease Croatia's transition from the Habsburg Empire to membership in a Yugoslav nation state, and the continuance of Croatian nationalism would serve to complicate its existence there.

NOTES

CHAPTER I

1. Among the many books on nationalism I have found most useful: Hans Kohn, *The Idea of Nationalism* (New York: Macmillan Co., 1944); Elie Kedourie, *Nationalism* (2nd ed.; New York: Frederick A. Praeger, 1961); H. Munroe Chadwick, *The Nationalities of Europe and the Growth of National Ideologies* (Cambridge: University Press, 1945). For the problem of nationalism within the Habsburg Empire: Robert A. Kann, *The Multinational Empire,* 2 vols. (New York: Columbia University Press, 1950). The variety of approaches to nationalism is well illustrated in: Karl Wolfgang Deutsch, *Interdisciplinary Bibliography on Nationalism* (Boston: Technology Press of M.I.T., 1956).

2. Two basic studies which treat this early period of Pan-Slavism are: Alfred Fischel, *Der Panslawismus bis zum Weltkrieg* (Stuttgart und Berlin: J.G. Cotta, 1919), and Hans Kohn, *Pan-Slavism, Its History and Ideology* (Notre Dame, Ind.: University of Notre Dame Press, 1953). For a brief and clear definition of the difference between this early Pan-Slavism and Russian Pan-Slavism see: Michael Boro Petrovic, *The Emergence of Russian Panslavism, 1856-1870* (New York: Columbia University Press, 1956), ch. I.

3. Duje Rendić-Miočević, "Iliri," *Enciklopedija Jugoslavije,* IV, 328-34.

4. Mate Suić, "Ilirik," *Ibid.,* pp. 334-36.

5. Francis Dvornik, *The Slavs, Their Early History and Civilization* (Boston: American Academy of Arts and Sciences, 1956), ch. vi.

6. Students from Croatia, Slavonia, Bosnia and Dalmatia who attended the University of Graz in the early sixteenth century identified themselves alternately as "Croat," "Slav" or "Illyrian." Franjo Fancev, "Ilirstvo u hrvatskom preporodu," *Ljetopis Jugoslovenske akademije znanosti i umjetnosti,* (henceforth cited as *Ljetopis),* XLIX (1937-38), 148-49. See also Jaroslav Sidak, "Prilog razvoju jugoslavenske idejedo g. 1914," *Naše teme,* IX (1965), 1291-93.

7. B. (Jernej) Kopitar, *Grammatik der Slavischen Sprache in Krain, Kärnten und Steyermark* (Laibach: Wilhelm Heinrich Korn, 1808), p. XX. Kopitar was well aware of the ambiguities of the word "Illyrian." By 1822 he had discarded its use for any other than geographical description, stating that the ancient Illyrians had probably not been Slavs at all. See K. (Jernej Kopitar), *"Institutiones linguae slavicae,"* (1822) in *Spisov,* ed. by R. Nahtigal, II Del, 1 Knjiga (Ljubljana: Slovenska akademija znanosti in umetnosti, 1944), p. 201.

8. Some important questions about the authenticity of the *Pacta Conventa* have been raised in the new work by Nada Klaić, *Povijest Hrvata u ranom srednjem vijeku* (Zageb: Skolska knjiga, 1971), pp. 513-17.

9. For the traditional Croatian interpretation see: Ferdinand (Ferdo) v. Šišić, *Geschichte der Kroaten* (Zagreb: L. Hartmann, 1917), vol. I, 367-79. For the Hungarian interpretation: Balint Homan, *Geschichte des Ungarischen Mittelalters* (Berlin: Walter de Gruyter and Co., 1940), vol. I, 368-76. For the most recent analysis see: N. Klaic, *Povijest Hrvata,* pp. 513-37.

10. As cited in Šišić, *Geschichte,* I, 380.

11. On the early history of the Military Frontier see: Gunther Eric Rothenberg, *The Austrian Military Border in Croatia, 1552-1747,* Illinois Studies in the Social Sciences, No. 8 (Urbana, Illinois: University of Illinois Press, 1960).

12. For an analysis of the ethnic changes caused by the Turkish invasions see: "Seobe i etničke promjene u jugoslavenskim pokrajina od XV. do početka XIX. stoljeća," in Bogo Grafenauer, *et al.* eds., *Historija naroda Jugoslavije* (Zagreb: Skolska Knjiga, 1953-59) II, ch. xxxviii.

13. The Regiments included within the Croatian and Slavonian Military Frontier in the early nineteenth century were:

A. *Croatian Military Frontier:* 1) The Karlovac Generalate — a) Lika Regiment, b) Otočac Regiment, c) Ogulin Regiment, d) Slunj Regiment. 2) *The Ban's Frontier* —a) Ban's First Regiment, b) Ban's Second Regiment. 3) The Varaždin Generalate — a) Durdevac Regiment, b) Križevac Regiment.

B. *Slavonian Military Frontier:* a) Gradiška Regiment, b) Brod Regiment, c) Petrovaradin Regiment, d) Regiment of Čajkovci.

14. For the somewhat complicated history of Rijeka and the Hungarian Littoral in the first half of the nineteenth century see: Ferdo Hauptmann, "Pregled povijesti Rijeke do Bachova apsolutizma," *Rijeka - Zbornik,* ed. by Jakša Rvalić (Zagreb: Matica Hrvatska, 1953), pp. 209-210, and Ferdo Šišić, *Pregled povijesti Hrvatskoga naroda,* ed. by Jaroslav Sidak (Zagreb: Matica Hrvatska, 1962), pp. 331-332, 339.

15. Fran Vrbanić, "Jedno stoljeće u razvoju žiteljstva Hrvatske i Slavonije," *Rad Jugoslavenske akademije znanosti i umjetnosti,* (henceforth cited as *Rad),* CXL (1899), p. 29.

16. There are no census figures for 1825; in fact no full census was taken in the Triune Kingdom between 1787 and 1851, but there are fairly reliable estimates of population based upon partial counts and parish records. On the problem of historical statistics see: *Ibid.*, pp. 17-58; Dorothy Good, "Some Aspects of Fertility Change in Hungary," *Population Index,* 30 (1964), pp. 137-171; Joszef Kovacsics (ed.), *A törteněti statisztika forrásai* (Budapest: Központi Statisztikai Hivatal, 1957); and Mladen Lorković, *Narod i zemlja Hrvata* (Zagreb: Matica Hrvatska, 1939), pp. 73-99.

17. Computations based on the figures given in Table 2.

18. These figures are for 1845. Austria, Direction der administrativen Statistik in K.K. Ministerium für Handel, Gewerbe und öffentliche Bauten, *Tafeln zur Statistik der oesterreichischen Monarchie,* 1846, I, Table 2.

19. See: Rudolf Bićanić, "Oslobodenje kmetova u Hrvatskoj godine 1848," in his *Počeci kapitalizma u Hrvatskoj ekonomici i politici.* (Zagreb: Školska knjiga, 1952), pp. 66-113; and Igor Karaman, "Ekonomske prilike u vrijeme hrvatskog narodnog preporoda," in his *Privreda i društvo Hrvatske u 19. stoljecu,* Institute of Croatian history, University of Zagreb, Rasprave i članci, I (Zagreb: Školska knija, 1972), pp. 9-22.

20. In Civil Croatia the payments were primarily in kind. The Croatian serfs had a *robot* of 52-104 days a year. In Civil Slavonia money payments had begun to replace the others, for the land was more fertile and the serfs could sell their surplus produce and livestock. The Slavonia *robot* was also lighter, 24-48 days a year. Bićanić, "Oslobodenje Kmetova," 81-88; and Jozo Tomasevich, *Peasants, Politics and Economic Change in Yugoslavia* (Stanford: Stanford University Press, 1955), 60-63, 69-74.

21. Bićanić, "Oslobodenje kmetova," p. 78.
22. Jaroslav Šidak, "Hrvatsko pitanje u Habsburskoj monarhiji," Pt. I, *Historijski pregled,* IX (1963), 104.
23. Bićanić, "Oslobodenje kmetova," p. 77, Table I.
24. Grafenauer, ed., *Historija naroda Jugoslavije,* I, pp. 433-38.
25. This would be true until 1831 when the Hungarian Court Chancellery granted the peasant nobles the right to vote as individuals, a right which lasted only until 1845. *Infra.*
26. Vrbanić, "Jedno stoljeće u razvoju žiteljstva," p. 31.
27. Bićanić, "Oslobodenje kmetova, p. 70-75; and Karaman, "Ekonomske prilike," pp. 15-18.
28. There is a good analysis of this problem and a useful bibliography in Rudolf Bićanić, *Doba manufakture u Hrvatskoj i Slavoniji* (Zagreb: Jugoslavenska akademija znanosti i umjetnosti, 1951, 325-30.
29. *Ibid.,* Ch. III.
30. Lorković, *Narod i zemlja Hrvata,* p. 74.
31. Johann v. Csaplovics, *Gemälde von Ungern* (Pest: C.A. Hartleben, 1829), I, 165-66.
32. *Ibid.* On Karlovac see: Igor Karaman, "Ekonomsko-socijalne determinante razvitka grada Karlovca u predindustrijsko i industrijsko doba," in his *Privreda i drustvo,* pp. 38-50.
33. As cited in Šišić, *Geschichte,* pp. 380-81.
34. Šišić, *Pregled,* p. 329.
(Zagreb: Matica Hrvatska, 1962), p. 329.
35. On the Hungarian Court Chancellery see. Béla K. Király, *Hungary in the Late Eighteenth Century,* East Central European Studies of Columbia University, (New York: Columbia University Press, 1969), pp. 90-93.
36. Šišić, *Pregled,* p. 329.
37. *Ibid.,* pp. 346-47.
38. *Ibid.,* p. 348.
39. *Ibid.,* p. 349. Cf. C.A. Macartney, *The Habsburg Empire, 1790-1918* (New York: The Macmillan Cmpany, 1969), pp. 24-25.
40. Šišić, *Pregled,* p. 350.
41. "Hrvatska municipalna prava," *Historijska čitanka za hrvatsku povijest,* ed., Jaroslav Šidak (Zagreb: Školska knjiga, 1952), I, 177-78.
42. See the list of Croats attending the Hungarian Parliament of 1832-1836 in Ferdo Šišić, *Hrvatska povijest* (3 vols.; Zagreb: Dionička tiskara, 1906-1913), Vol. III, 178-79.
43. Šišić, *Pregled,* p. 351. See also Kiraly, *Hungary,* pp. 110-11.
44. Macartney, *Habsburg Empire,* p. 10, note 1.
45. "Instrukcija gg. poslanicima za državni sabor slavnoga kraljevstva ugarskoga i pridruženih mu strana, što je bio sazvan za 6. lipnja 1790," *Historijska Čitanka,* I, 169, art. IX.

CHAPTER II

46. Tade Smičiklas, *Povijest Hrvatska* (2 vols., Matica Hrvatska, 1879-1882), Vol. II, 389.

47. See Király, *Hungary,* pp. 153-70.

48. G.F. Cushing, "The Birth of National Literature in Hungary," *The Slavonic and East European Review,* XXXVIII (June, 1960), 459-75; Johann Heinrich Schwicker, *Geschichte der ungarischen Literatur* (Leipzig: Wilhelm Friedrich, 1889), pp. 226-336; and Louis J. Lekai, "Historiography in Hungary, 1790-1848," *Journal of Central European Affairs,* XIV (April, 1954), 3-18.

49. This is well treated in Harold Steinacker, "Das Wesen des madjarischen Nationalismus," *Die Nationalitätenfrage im alten Ungarn und die Südostpolitik Wiens,* ed. by F. Walter and H. Steinacker (München: R. Oldenbourg, 1959), pp. 29-67.

50. Johann Gottfried Herder, *Ideen zur Philosophie der Geschichte der Menschheit,* Vol. XIV of *Sämmtliche Werke,* ed. B. Suphan (Berlin: Weidmannische Buchhandlung, 1909), 268-69 (Magyars), 227-80 (Slavs).

51. Fenyés, *op. cit.,* p. 37. On the reliability of Fenyés' figures, *Supra.*

52. Even the Croatian nobles were considered to be "Magyar" since they shared in the rights of the Sacred Crown *(Corpus Sacrae Coronae).* Henry Marczali, *Hungary in the Eighteenth Century* (Cambridge: University Press, 1910), pp. 33, 103.

53. Johann Gottfried Herder, *Briefe zur Beförderung der Humanität,* Vol. VII of *Sämmtliche Werke,* ed. B. Suphan (Berlin: Weidmannische Buchhandlung, 1881), p. 58.

54. *Ibid.,* pp. 58-59.

55. See Kedourie, *op. cit.,* ch. v.

56. Jules Szekfü, *État et Nation* (Paris: Les Presses Universitaires 1945), pp. 20-30.

57. Šišić, *Hrvatska povijest,* III, 1-59; and Julius Miskolczy, *Ungarn in der Habsburger Monarchie* (Wien: Verlag Herold, 1959), pp. 37-42.

58. "Izjava nuncija kralj. Hrvatske o uvodjenju madjarskoga jezika g. 1790," trans. by J. Šidak, *Historijska čitanka,* I, 171-75.

59. An excellent introduction to the complex problems of creating a Croatian literary language can be found in Ljudevit Jonke, "Osnovni problemi jezika hrvatske knjizevnosti u 19. stoljecu," *Radovi slavenskoga instituta* (University of Zagreb) (1958), pp. 75-90. See also Dalibor Brozović, *Standardni jezik* (Zagreb: Matica Hrvatska, 1970), pp. 119-23.

60. Alexander Belić, "Jezik Srpskohrvatski (Hrvatskosrpski)," *Enciklopedija Jugoslavije,* IV, 500-01.

61. "What is, is and it has always been so,
What will be, will be, and somehow it will always be!"
Miroslav Krleža, "Khevenhiller," *Balade Petrice Kerempuha* (Zagreb: Nakladni zavod Hrvatske, 1946), p. 64.

62. Mate Hraste, "Kajkavski dijalekt," *Enciklopedija Jugoslavije,* IV, 508-509.

63. Mate Hraste, "Čakavski dijalekt," *Ibid.,* 506-508.

64. Mihajlo Stevanović, "Štokavski dijalekt," *Ibid.,* pp. 501-06.

65. "I told the child to give me milk."

66. For examples of the variations in Croatian orthography at the time see Ljudevit Gaj, "Kratka osnova hrvatsko-slavenskoga pravopisána, (1830)" reprinted in *Gradja za povijest knjizevnosti Hrvatske,* (henceforth cited as GPKH) XII (1933), ed. F. Fancev, pp. 221-36.

67. With the exception of the *gimnazija* in Rijeka where Italian was the language of instruction. Anton Cuvaj, ed. *Gradja za povijest školstva kraljevina Hrvatske i Slavonije* 8 vols., (Zagreb: kr. zemaljske tiskare, 1910-13), II, 337.
68. *Ibid.*, pp. 82-90, 335-39.
69. *Ibid.*, Vol. III, 171.
70. Anton Nagy, "Novi i stari kalendar horvatski," *GPKH*, 125.
71. *Ibid.*
72. Josip Horvat, *Povijest novinstva Hrvatske* (Zagreb: Stvarnost, 1962), pp. 59-62, 68-74. Cf. Ferdo Šišić, "O stogodišnjici ilirskoga pokreta," *Ljetopis*, XLVIII (1937-38), 105, 118-30. It is interesting to note that all three editors planned to use the *štokavski* dialect.
73. Ferdo Šišić, "Une tentative pre-illyrienne: le journal de Sporer," *Le Monde Slave*, XII (June, 1935), 382.
74. Bishop Vrhovac was aware of the progress being made by the other Slavs of the Habsburg Empire in the development of their national languages and cultures, for he was in correspondence with two of the leading Slavic scholars of the day, Josef Dobrovský and Jernej Kopitar. Djuro Šurmin discusses the plans and cultural work of Bishop Vrhovac in *Hrvatski preporod*, (2 vols., Zagreb: Dionička tiskara, 1903-04), I, 39-49.
75. Mihovil Kombol, *Povijest hrvatske književnosti do preporoda* (2d ed.; Zagreb: Matica Hrvatska, 1961), pp. 401-03; and Šurmin, *op. cit.*, pp. 44, 49.
76. Antun Mihanović, "Reč domovini od hasnovitosti pisanju vu domorodnem jeziku, "reprinted in *GPKH* XII,118-23. Much of this pamphlet is derived, and in some parts a direct translation of a contemporary Italian work. See Tomo Matić, "Mihanovićeva "Reč domovini od hasnovitosti pisanju vu domorodnem jeziku," *Historijski zbornik* II (1949), pp. 177-83.
77. Šišić, *Hrvatska povijest*, III, 55.
78. There were several such attempts to raise the Academy to full university status in the following eighty years. This goal was not achieved until 1874.
79. "Pretstavka zagrebačke kralj, akademije zbog svoga podignuća na stepen sveučilišta . . . ," *GPKH*, XII, 31-32.
80. *Ibid.*, pp. 98-9.
81. France Kidrič, *Zgodovina Slovenskega slovstva od zacetkov do Zoisove smrtil* (Ljubljana: Matica Slovenska, 1929-39), pp. 505-09.
82. See the able discussion of this question in George Prpic, "French Rule in Croatia; 1806-1813," *Balkan Studies*, V (1964), 264-276.
83. See Jaroslav Šidak, "Odjeci Francuske revolucije i Napoleonova vladavina u hrvatskim zemljama," *Napoleonove Ilirske province* (Ljubljana; Narodni muzei, 1964), 43.
84. On the political and economic impact of French rule from 1809-1816, see: Šidak, "Odjeci Francuske revolucije," 37-44; and Prpic, "French rule in Croatia."
85. A classic treatment of this problem can be found in Kann, *The Multinational Empire*, I, chs. vii, x and xi.
86. Statistics for 1851 can be found in Hugo Franz Brachelli, *Deutsche Staatenkunde* (2 vols.; Wien: Wilhelm Braumüller, 1856), II, 203-08.
87. J. Gardner Wilkinson, *Dalmatia and Montenegro* (2 vols. London: John Murray, 1848), I, 89.
88. Grga Novak, *Prošlost Dalmacije* (2 vols. Zagreb: Bibliografski Zavod, 1944), II, 322-27.

89. In 1851, out of a total population of 1,426,221, there were 333,189 people who identified their mother tongue as Serbian in the area traditionally known as the Voivodina. Austria. Direction der administrativen Statistik im k.k. Handels-Ministerium, *Mittheilungen aus dem Gebiete der Statistik,* (1851), p. 4.

90. It is impossible to give population figures for this large group. The first Turkish census appears to have been made in 1844, however the figures were not published. Turkish census material according to modern demographers, is at best, incomplete. See discussion of this question in Nikola Mihov, *La Population de la Turquie et de la Bulgarie au XVIII et XIX s.*, 4 vols. (Sofia: Academie Bulgare de Sciences, 1915-1935), Vol. I, pp. xvi-xvii.

91. Robert Auty, "The Formation of the Slovene Literary Language against the Background of the Slavonic National Revival," *The Slavonic and East European Review,* XLI (June, 1963), p. 392.

92. Kopitar, *Grammatik,* p. III.

93. The problems of the Slovene language are clearly explained in Auty, "The Formation of the Slovene Literary Language," pp. 391-402. See also Joze Toporišić, "Jezik Slovenski," *Enciklopedija Jugoslavije,* IV, 495-500; and Anton Slodnjak, *Geschichte der Slovenischen Literatur* (Berlin: Walter de Gruyter & Co., 1958), pp. 49-114.

94. France Jakopin, "Kopitar, Jernej," *Enciklopedija Jugoslavije,* V, 307-08.

95. The traditional literary language of the Serbian clergy and intelligentsia, who to the second half of the eighteenth century in the Vojvodina were one and the same, was *Slavenosrpski:* in the early eighteenth century the Serbian variant of Church Slavic. By the late eighteenth century *Slavenosrpski,* although still based upon Russian Church Slavic, included elements of the Serbian vernacular as well. Mihajlo Stevanović, "Književni jezik kod Srba of Dositeja i Vuka," *Enciklopedija Jugoslavije.* IV, 521.

96. A useful bibliography of works on Vuk Karadžić can be found in Aleksander Belić, "Karadžić, Vuk Stefanović," *Enciklopedija Jugoslavije,* V, 195-96.

CHAPTER III

97. Ivan Crkvenčić, "Hrvatsko Zagorje," *Enciklopedija Jugoslavije,* IV, p. 283.

98. In 1846, according to Fenyés, there was not a single person of Orthodox faith resident in the county of Varaždin. Fenyés, *op. cit.*, pp. 38-41.

99. Ivan Srebrnić, "Krapina," *Enciklopedija Jugoslavija,* V, p. 384. A more detailed but rambling account can be found in Antun Kozina, *Krapina i okolice kroz stoljeća* (Varaždin: Narodna tiskara, 1960).

100. Josip Horvat, "Ljudevit Gaj, njegov život njegovo doba" (unpublished manuscript, completed in 1959), p. 9. (This work will henceforth be cited as Horvat, "Gaj.")

101. Ljudevit Gaj, "Vjekopisni moj nacrtak," in Velimir Gaj, ed., *Knjižnica Gajeva* (Zagreb: Narodne tiskara Gajeve, 1875), pp. XVIII-XIX.

102. Ferdo Šišić, "Podrijetlo Gajeva roda," *Jugoslovenski istoriski časopis* (Belgrade), V (1939), p. 160.

103. Purchase of a pharmacy in the Kingdom of Hungary at that time was a large capital investment. This is discussed in some detail in: Csaplovics, *Gemälde von Ungern,* II, p. 205. For a description of the education of pharmacists see: Šišić, "Podrijetlo," p. 160.

104. Horvat, "Gaj," pp. 9, 40, n. 12.

105. Kozina, *Krapina,* p. 168.

106. Šišić, "Podrijetlo," p. 163.

107. *Ibid.*

108. Josip Horvat and Jakša Ravlić, eds., "Pisma Ljudevita Gaju," *GPKH,* XXVI (1956), p. 453, n. 1.

109. Friedrich Wilhelm Schmidt was born *ca.* 1780 and later became a surgeon in the royal free town of Križevci. *Ibid.*

110. The vast majority of Julijana Gaj's letters are in German although she began to attempt to write in Croatian in the mid-1830's. They occasionally contain a Latin or French phrase. The Julijana Gaj Correspondance is located in the Sveučilišna Knjižnica in Zagreb, R 3989. (The Julijana Gaj Letters will henceforth be cited as *PJG,* the Zagreb University Library as SKZ.)

111. Šišić, "Podrijetlo," p. 163. Ivana married Anton Cantilly, pharmacist of Samobor; Ivan became a pharmacist; Franciska married Dr. Josip Kincl, an army doctor; and Judith married Lieutenant, later General, Gideon Laaba. Death dates for Judith Laaba and Franciscka Kincl are from *GPKH,* XXVI, p. 91, n. 1 and p. 248.

112. Šišić, "Podrijetlo," pp. 155-61.

113. During the Napoleonic wars, armies passed back and forth through Krapina. There was no local hospital, only some private facilities to care for the indigent poor. In 1809 Ivan Gaj set up a temporary hospital with his own funds to care for the wounded and sick soldiers. Famine and epidemic struck Zagorje in 1814, 1816 and 1817. The hospital was again filled, now with civilians. In 1813 and 1815, Ivan Gaj received citations for his humanitarian service from the local governments of Varaždin and Krapina. SKZ, *Ostavština Ljudevita Gaja* (Collected Papers of Ljudevit Gaj), R 4700 a a 2 3. (This collection will henceforth be cited as SKZ, *LG).* See also Kozina, *op. cit.,* p. 171.

114. Estate of Johann Gaj, "Theilungs Briefe," June 27, 1826. SKZ, *LG,* R 4700 b.

115. There are two autobiographical fragments in Latin which date from the early 1830's in SKZ, *LG,* R 4701 b I 1; the unfinished Croatian autobiography "Vjekopisni moj nacrtak," in V. Gaj, ed., *Knjižnica Gajeva,* pp. XVIII-XXIX; records of conversations with Gaj as an old man in Gjuro Stj. Deželić, ed., "Gaj o sebi," *Dragoljub ili upisnik kalendar za javne urede,* (1893), 53-57; (1894), 44-45; references to unpublished material from these conversations in the Gaj biography written by G.S. Deželić's son — Velimir Deželić, *Dr. Ljudevit Gaj* (Zagreb: Anton Scholz, 1910). The bulk of the family papers are found in SKZ, *LG,* R 4700-4710, R 3989 and in the Državni Archiv of Zagreb in *Acta Gajana.* (Henceforth cited as DAZ, *AG.)*

116. The most important of these works are Velimir Deželić, *op. cit.,* and the author's introduction to his edition of "Pisma pisana dru. Ljudevitu Gaju i

njeki njegovi sastavci,'' *GPKH,* VI (1909); Franjo Fancev, ''Hrvatski ilirski preporod jest nas autohton pokret,'' *Hrvatsko kolo,* XVI (1935), 3-58, and Fancev's introduction to his ed., ''Dokumenti za naše podrijetlo hrvatskoga preporoda 1789-1832,'' *GPKH,* XII (1933); Gyula Miskolczy's introduction to his ed., *A horvat kérdes törtenete es iromanyai a rendi allam korabąn* (2 vols.; Budapest: Kiadja a Magyar tortęnelmi tarsulat, 1927-28), I; Ferdo Šišić, ''Podrijetlo Gajeva roda,'' and his ''Školovanje Ljudevita Gaja u domovini,'' *Hrvatsko kolo,* XIX (1938), 58-81; and Horvat, ''Gaj.''

117. Fancev attempts to prove that the years before 1826 were the decisive ones, that the Illyrian Movement rose out of forces and ideas already at work in Croatian society which Gaj merely absorbed and articulated. Deželić, Šišić and Horvat take a more balanced position, while Miskolczy emphasizes the Austrian and Hungarian influences. The works of Deželić, Fancev and Miskolczy are based on the autobiographical fragments and letters. Šišić introduces some new background material. Horvat has taken a new approach, based on extensive reading of the family papers.

118. SKZ, PJG.

119. Gaj, ''Vjekopisni,'' p. XXI.

120. *Ibid.*

121. Šišić, ''Podrijetlo,'' pp. 165-66, and Horvat, ''Gaj,'' pp. 17-18.

122. Gaj, ''Vjekopisni,'' p. XXII.

123. He is quoted in a letter from Julijana Gaj to her son Janchi. ''Der Ludwig sagte ja bi sze pak plakal dabi mi Bratecz umerl.'' Letter of Julijana Gaj to Janchi Gaj, March 28, 1813, SKZ, *PJG.*

124. Gaj,'' Vjekopisni,'' p. XX.

125. Imbro Tkalac, *Uspomene iz Hrvatske,* trans. by Josip Ritig, ed. by Stanko Dvoršak (Zagreb: Matica Hrvatska, 1945), pp. 257-58. See also Slavko Ježić, *Hrvatska književnost od početka do danas, 1100-1941* (Zagreb: A. Velzek, 1944), pp. 180-85.

126. Fran Kurelac, ''Slova nad grobom Ljudevita Gaja izgovorena Franom Kurelcem,'' in Slavko Ježić, ed., *Ilirska antologija* (Zagreb: Minerva, 1934), p. 157. See also Šišić, ''Skolovanje,'' pp. 59-61.

127. Letter of P. Pobor to L. Gaj, August 3, 1835. *GPKH,* XXVI, p. 391.

128. Šišić, ''Školovanje,'' p. 58.

129. The Lepoglava monastery, founded ca. 1400, had been one of the most important centers of learning in Croatia. The monastery opened the first public secondary school in Croatia, public in that it did not limit its student body to future priests. It became an Institution of Higher Education in the seventeenth century, offering advanced training in philosophy (from 1656) and theology (from 1687). The Paulist order was disbanded by order of Emperor Joseph II in 1786, and the monastery buildings were later converted to a prison. Andjela Horvat, ''Lepoglava,'' *Enciklopedija Jugoslavije,* V, 514-515.

130. Gaj, ''Vjekopisni,'' p. XXII.

131. Deželić, *Dr. Ljudevit Gaj,* p. 64.

132. G. Deželić, ed., ''Gaj o sebi,'' (1893), 53.

133. Ljudevit Gaj took Hungarian for one semester in the fifth class. Šišić, ''Školovanje,'' p. 62.

134. This is clearly reflected in the letters Julijana Gaj wrote to her son in these years, 1821-1826. See for example: Letters, Julijana Gaj to Ljudevit Gaj, April 25, 1822; January 19, 1823; February 26, 1826; SKZ, *PJG.*

135. Šišić, ''Školovanje,'' pp. 64-65.

136. Gaj, "Vjekopisni," p. XXII. These "notes" were in fact two manuscripts "Compendium historicum" and "Brevis descriptio antiquissimi i famosi loci Krapinae" by Father Vjenceslav Sklenski, a Czech monk who had lived in the monastery in the late 18th century. Horvat, "Gaj," p. 27 and Šišić, "Školovanje," p. 79, n. 31.

137. Gaj, "Vjekopisni," p. XXII.

138. Letter, Julijana Gaj to Ljudevit Gaj, February 26, 1826, SKZ, *PJG.*

139. Gaj, "Vjekopisni," p. XXIII.

140. Fra Andrija Kačić-Miošić (1704-1760), *Razgovor ugodni naroda slovinskoga.* First published in Venice in 1756, this book was so popular that it was reprinted in 1759 and again in 1825. It was a kind of national primer, weak as a piece of history, but accepted uncritically by the common people as a mirror of their past. See Mihovil Kombol, *op. cit.*, pp. 362-66.

141. Ljudevit Gaj, "Die Schlösser bei Krapina," *GPKH* XII, 182. English text from James Macpherson, *The Poems of Ossian* (London: T. Bensley, 1807), II, 385-386.

142. Gaj, "Schlösser," p. 184.

143. *Ibid.*

144. *Ibid.*, p. 189.

145. Ferdo Šišić, "Ime Hrvat i Srbin i teorije o doseljenju Hrvata i Srba," *Godišnjica Nikole Čupića* (Belgrade) XXXV (1923), pp. 35-51. See also Fischel, *Panslavismus*, pp. 16-17.

146. DAZ, *AG*, Personalia, Folio II 1. These poems are discussed in Velimir Deželić, "Gaj kao njemački pjesnik," *Illustrovani obzor*, II (1909), 432-40. Deželić concludes that Gaj showed promise as a German poet and he includes the text of several of Gaj's 1826 poems.

147. Ljudevit Gaj, "Razvezanje vu listu Nro. 6 Novin Zagrebečkeh," and "Pesma od Zagorja." These were originally published in Numbers 11 (5.VIII. 1826), and 35 (28.X. 1826) of *Luna.* They are reprinted in *GPKH* XII, pp. 198-99.

148. The Gajs had followed an almost spartan style of life. They bought little in imported goods, were very sparing on clothing and entertainment. Their only luxuries were books and education, and that only for the sons. Horvat, "Gaj," pp. 13-14.

149. "Theilungs Briefe," June 27, 1826. SKZ *LG*, R 4700 b.

150. Letter of Julijana Gaj to Ljudevit Gaj, December 10, 1834, SKZ, *PJG.*

151. Janchi and his problems form a constant theme in the letters of Julijana Gaj to her son Ljudevit. The family situation finally became so strained that Julijana moved away from the family home in Krapina in 1835 to live with her daughter Ivana in Samobor and, finally, in 1837 she came to Zagreb where she spent her last years with Ljudevit.

152. Letter, Julijana Gaj to Ljudevit Gaj, January 16, 1822, SKZ *PJG.*

152. Letter, Julijana Gaj to Ljudevit Gaj, Februrary 26, 1826, *PJG.*

154. Horvat, "Gaj," p. 34.

CHAPTER IV

155. Gaj, "Vjekopisni," pp. XXIII-XXIV.

156. Letter, Julijana Gaj to Ljudevit Gaj, July 16, 1826, SKZ *PJG.*
157. Horvat, "Gaj," pp. 44-45.
158. Šišić, "Podrijetlo Gajeva roda," pp. 152-53.
159. Gaj, "Vjekopisni," p. XXV.
160. Albert von Muchar (1786-1849), was a Benedictine monk and Professor of Classicial Philology and Aesthetics at the University of Graz. In 1826-1827 he had just begun to publish articles on the history of Styria and had commenced the research which would finally result in his *Geschichte des Herzogthums Steiermark* (8 vols., Graz, 1845-1867). Constantin von Wurzback, *Biographisches Lexicon des Kaiserthums Osterreich,* XIX (1868), 306-11. See Gaj's version of their contact in Gaj, "Vjekopisni," p. XXV.
161. Gaj, "Vjekopisni," p. XXV.
162. Johann Wartinger (1773-1861). He began his career as a secondary school teacher of history. Ill health forced him to find a queter post and he worked as an archivist and historian until his death. Wartinger played an extremely important role in the organization of historical studies in Styria during his lifetime. Wurzbach, *Biographisches Lexicon,* Vol. 55 (1886), 116-25.
163. Gaj, "Vjekopisni," p. XXVI. Kurelac, "Slova," p. 157.
164. SKZ, *LG,* R 4701 B II.
165. SKZ, *LG,* R 4701 B IV.
166. Ljudevit Gaj, "Vszakojachka pripovedanya od Krapina iz vuzt ztareh lyudih pobrana," SKZ, *LG,* R 4701 C 4.
167. SKZ, *LG,* R 4701 A II 22.
168. Letter, F.W. Schmidt to Ljudevit Gaj, May 16, 1828, SKZ, R 3989.
169. Ljudevit Gaj, "Meine Ländliche Heimat," DAZ, *AG,* Folio II 1.
170. Johann Halter (1793-1857), owner of the Varaždin pharmacy, with whom Gaj had lived during his years in Varaždin, was an old family friend and, after the death of Ivan Gaj, seems to have become the financial adviser to Julijana Gaj and her children. See letters of Johann Halter to Ljudevit Gaj in *GPKH,* XXVI, pp. 193-97.
171. Draft of letter from Ljudevit Gaj to Johann Halter dated "Frühlng, 1827," SKZ, *LG,* R 4702 A. Cf. Horvat, "Gaj," p. 57, who believes that it was written in 1828.
172. Letter, Johann Halter to Ljudevit Gaj, March 10, 1827. *GPKH,* XXVI, p. 195.
173. Letter, Julijana Gaj to Ljudevit Gaj, December 23, 1827. *PJG.* See also Horvat, "Gaj" pp. 51-52.
174. Gaj, "Vjekopisni," p. XXIV.
175. Ljudevit Gaj, Narodno blago: a) Skup provincialskih horvatskih poslovicah starom ortografijom, 1827-1828; b) Poslovice; c) Provincijalske narodne horvatske popoevske i druge neke bilješke; d) Vszakojachka iz vust puka horvatskoga. SKZ, *LG,* R 4701 C 1 2 3 4.
176. This is discussed by Nikola Bonifačić Rožin in his "Odnos Ljudevita Gaja prema narodnom stvaralaštvu," a paper delivered on November 9, 1973, in Zagreb at the *Naučni skup o Gaju,* sponsored by the Institute of Croatian History of the University of Zagreb. Dr. Bonifacic Rožin kindly let me have a copy of his paper.
177. (Ljudevit Gaj), "Netilo," *Danicza Horvatzka, Slavonzka; Dalmatinzka,* I (29. Szechna, 1835), 32.
178. Vladimir Mažuranić, "Životpisna crta," in D. Demeter, *Teuta*

(Zagreb: Matica Hrvatska, 1891), p. III. See also Slavko Ježić, "Dimitrije Demeter," *Enciklopeija Jugoslavije* II, 687.

179. Ljudevit Gaj, "Zverhu jezika magyarskoga," SKZ, *LG,* R 4701 A III 3.

180. Ljudevit Gaj, "Der Zeitgeist und die Kroaten," DAZ, *AG,* Folio II.

181. *Ibid.*

182. SKZ, *LG,* R 4701 A II 22.

183. Letter, Mojsije Baltić to Ljudevit Gaj, September 29, 1828, *GPKH,* XXVI, 30.

184. *Ibid.*

185. Tade Smičiklas, *Život i djela Vjekoslava Babukića* (Zagreb: Narodne Novine, 1876), p. 5. This story is accepted by V. Deželić in *Dr. Ljudevit Gaj,* p. 33 and by F. Šišić, in *Hrvatska povijest,* pp. 159-60. F. Fancev, in "Mojsije Baltić," *Hrvatska Enciklopedija* V. II, p. 170, attempts to disprove this statement on rather shaky evidence. Horvat, *"Gaj,"* p. 70 n. 3, presents the most balanced picture. It seems that there was a Serbian club in Graz in 1829, which had many of the characteristics mentioned by Baltić, but Horvat believes that the "Illyrian Club" was a figment of Baltić's imagination.

186. Although Gaj studied *štokavski* with Baltić and claims in "Vjekopisni" to have decided upon the use of *štokavski* as the dialect for the new literary language as early as 1826, there is nothing in his personal papers to indicate that he thought seriously about the use of *štokavski* before 1831 or 1832, Gaj, "Vjekopisni," pp. XXIII-XXIV. All of Gaj's published works, manuscripts, letters and notes which predate 1835 are written in *kajkavski,* German or Latin.

187. Gaj, "Vjekopisni," p. XXVI. Gaj kept some of these Graz translations in his personal papers: a joint translation he had made with Demeter of Schiller's "Ode to Joy" and several of his own translations of German poems. SKZ, *LG,* R 4701 A I c.

188. Letter, Dimitrije Demeter to Ljudevit Gaj, September 26, 1828. *GPKH,* VI, 48.

189. Cf. Fancev, "Hrvatski Ilirski preporod jest naš autohton pokret," pp. 3-24. This article is based upon what seems to me a highly superficial reading of Gaj's personal papers on language and his autobiographical fragments. Fancev assigns dates to undated manuscripts, states incorrectly that Gaj studied at the Zagreb *gimnazium* in the first semester of 1825-26, and in a jumbled and dangerously uncritical manner tries to prove that Gaj, before leaving Croatia for his university studies, was familiar with most of the books on Croatian history, language and literature which had been published in the eighteenth and early nineteenth centuries.

190. Gaj mentions the year he first read this work in his draft of a letter to P.J. Šafařík in 1830, no specific day or month given, *GPKH,* VI, 337.

191. Paul (Pavel) Joseph Šafařík, *Geschichte der Slawischen Sprache und Literatur nach allen Mundarten* (2d ed.; Prague: Friedrich Tempsky, 1869), pp. IV-VIII. Although a second edition, the text is unchanged from the 1826 printing.

192. *Ibid.,* pp. 67-68.

193. These manuscripts will be discussed below. Ljudevit Gaj, "Plan zur Begrundung einer kroatischen Literatur," and "Entwurf zur Grundlage einer kroatischen Literatur," SKZ, *LG,* R 4701 A III 15.

194. L. o. G. (Ljudevit Gaj), "Kratka osnova horvatsko-slavenskoga

pravopisańa poleg mudrolubneh narodneh i prigospodarneh temelov i zrokov,'' (1830) in *GPKH,* XII, 222-23.

195. Kopitar, *Grammatik,* pp. XIX-XXI.

196. Ljudevit Gaj, ''Plan zur Begründung einer kroatischen Literatur,'' Graz 1829, SKZ, *LG,* R 4701 A III 15.

197. Ljudevit Gaj, ''Entwurf zur Grundlage einer kroatischen Literatur,'' SKZ, *LG,* R 4701 A III 15.

198. *Ibid.*

199. *Ibid.,* Gaj became increasingly aware of the similarities between the Slovene dialects and *kajkavski* during his years in Graz. Although he had not yet begun to think of uniting all of the Southern Slavs in one cultural community with one literary language, he had considered the possibility of Slovene-Croatian cooperation. In the midst of a page of notes on orthography we find: ''If the Styrian Slovenes unite with the Croats, a star hitherto unseen upon the horizon of Slavdom will rise from our people.'' SKZ, *LG,* R 4701 B II 7.

200. Gaj, ''Entwurf.''

201. *Ibid.*

202. Ljudevit Gaj, ''Materialen zur Literatur der Geschichte von Croatien,'' SKZ, *LG* R 4701 B II a. The Engels excerpts are dated: Graz, March 19, 1829.

203. Vjekoslav Klaić, *Život i djela Pavla Rittera Vitezovića 1652-1713,* (Zagreb, Martica Hrvatska, 1914), pp. 106-107, 185.

204. Zlatko Vince, ''M. Bobrowski: A. Kucharski - svjedoci; suradnici reforme hrwatske (sic) latiničke grafije u 19. stoljeću,'' *Rocznik Slawistyczny* (Crakow) XXXIII (1972), pp. 54-57.

205. R. Kvaternik accompanied Kucharski on the trip to Krapina. His account of the meeting between Gaj and Kucharski is in *Ibid.,* pp. 55-56.

206. See Auty, ''Formation of the Slovene Literary Language against the Background of the Slavonic National Revival,'' 395-98.

207. Letter, George Mathiaschitsch to Ljudevit Gaj, October 23, 1829, *GPKH,* CI, 134-35.

208. *Ibid.*

209. Horvat, ''Gaj,'' p. 69.

210. Gaj, ''Vjekopisni,'' p. XXVI.

211. Letter, Mojsije Baltić to Ljudevit Gaj, September 23, 1830, *GPKH,* XXVI, 30.

212. Gaj, ''Vjekopisni,'' p. XXVI; and Duro Šurmin, *Hrvatski preporod,* I, 127.

213. SKZ, *LG,* R 4701 B II.

214. Gaj, ''Vjekopisni,'' p. XXVIII.

215. SKZ, *LG,* R 4701 A II 22.

216. (S. Hoić), *Sollen Wir Magyaren werden? Fünf Briefe geschrieben aus Pesth an einen Freund an der Theis* (Karlstadt: Joh. Nep. Prettner, 1833), pp. 204-05.

217. SKZ, *LG,* R 4701 A II a.

218. Robert Auty, ''Jan Kollár, 1793-1852,'' *Slavonic and East European Review,* XXXI (1952-53), p. 89. I have had to limit my research on Kollár's writing and ideology to those of his works which are either written in German or translated into Western European languages or Croatian. As Robert Auty points out in his article on Kollár, very few of Kollár's works and even fewer of the

major critical studies on him are available to scholars who do not know Czech. *Ibid.*, pp. 74-75.

219. The section from this work which deals with Slavic reciprocity is included in Jan Kollár, *Rozpravy o slovanské vzájemnosti,* ed. by Miloš Weingart, Knihovna Slovanskehó ústavu, svzaek 1 (Prague: Slovanské ústav, 1929), pp. 29-30.

220. Jan Kollár, "O literarnéj vzájemnosti mezi kmeny nárečími slavskymí," *Hronka* II (1836), 39-55; and *Über die literarische Wechselseitigkeit zwischen den verschiedenen Stämmen und Mundarten der slawischen Nation* (Pest: von Trattner, 1837). Both of these works are reprinted in facing pages in Kollár, *Rozprávy,* pp. 31-166.

221. Herder's influence on Kollár is discussed in Milada Součkova, *The Czech Romantics* (S' Gravenhage: Mouton & Co., 1958), pp. 24-27. On Herder see A. Gillies, *Herder*(Oxford: Blackwell, 1945), pp. 129-30.

222. Kollár, "Über die literarische Wechselseitigkeit," *Rozprávy,* p. 45.

223. *Ibid.*, p. 47.

224. *Ibid.*, pp. 153-163.

225. Frank Wollman, "Tchéqueoslovaques et Illyrisme," *Le Monde Slave,* XII (Juillet, 1935), p. 6.

226. This is especially true before 1837. See Jan Kollár's letters to Ljudevit Gaj, *GPKH,* VI, 96-101; and XXVI, pp. 259-62.

227. Milivoj Šrepel, ed. and trans., "Slika Zagrebačkoga života g. 1841. i slavni pjesnik Jan Kollár, "*Stari i novi Zagreb,* ed. by E. Laszowski (Zagreb: Hrv. štamparskog zavoda D.D., 1925), p. 228.

228. Gaj, "Vjekopisni," p. XXIX.

229. Letter, Jan Kollár to Ljudevit Gaj, (July) 19, 1836, *GPKH,* VI, 100.

230. SKZ, *LG*R 4701 A II 22. Gaj must have taken this term from Kollár for Šafařík uses the term "Slawoserben" for all of the Southern Slavs but the Croats and Slovenes: "Slawoserben griechischen Ritus" (Serbs and Bulgarians), "katolischen Slawoserben" (Dalmatisn, Bosnians, Slavonians), but: "die Kroaten" (*kajkavski* Croats) and "die windische Sprache" (Slovenes). Šafařík, *Geshichte,* pp. 191-270.

231. Not "Short Outline of a Croat-Slovene Orthography," as translated by Hans Kohn in his *Pan-Slavism,* p. 60. L. o. G. Ljudevit Gaj, *Kratka osnova horvatsko-slavenskoga pravopisańa poleg mudrol̂ubneh narodneh i prigospodarneh temelov i zrokov,* (Buda: Kralevskoga vseucilisca, 1830), reprinted in *GPKH,* XII, 221-35.

232. Gaj, "Kratka osnova," *GPKH,* XII, p. 223.

233. *Ibid.*, pp. 224-33. For an analysis of the probable sources of this reform proposal, which includes a table in which the author compares Gaj's orthography of 1830 with the Latin orthographies of Vitezović and Dobrovský, see: Krešimir Georgijević, "Gajevo školovanje u tudjini," *Pitanja književnost i jezika* (Sarajevo), II (1-2, 1956), 23-44.

234. Gaj, "Kratka osnova," pp. 232-33.

235. *Ibid.*

236. Letter, Dragutin Rakovac to Ljudevit Gaj, June 28, 1830. *GPKH,* VI, 161-162.

237. Stjepan Moyses (1797-1869), a Slovak priest, was then Professor of Philology at the Zagreb Academy. Vjekoslav Babukić (1812-1875), a student from Slavonia, was then studying in the Faculty of Philosophy of the Academy.

Moyses' role comes through clearly in Rakovac's letters. On Babukić in 1830-1831 see Smičiklas, *Život i djela Vjekoslava Babukića*, p. 8.

238. Krešimir Nemeth, "Zagrebačka akademija uoči narodnog preporoda," *Iz starog i novog Zagreba*, I (1957), 174-79.
239. Pavel Stoos, "Nut novo leto," (Zagreb: Fran Suppan, 1831), reprinted in *GPKH*, XII, pp. 255-60.
240. Letter, Dragutin Rakovac to Ljudevit Gaj, January 20, 1831, *GPKH*, VI, 166-68.
241. Letter, Dragutin Rakovac to Ljudevit Gaj, April 1, 1831, *Ibid.*, 168-70.
242. Letter, Dragutin Rakovac to Ljudevit Gaj, January 20, 1831, *GPKH*, VI, 166.
243. *Ibid.*, Moyses' venture failed.
244. Letter, Ljudevit Gaj to Dragutin Rakovac, March 20, 1831, in M. Šrepel, ed. "Iz ostavštine D. Rakovca," *GPKH*, III (1901), 249-52.
245. Letter, Dragutin Rakovac to Ljudevit Gaj, May 1, 1831, *GPKH*, VI, 168-70.
246. Tomas Mikloušić (1767-1833) was a typical representative of the older generation of *kajkavski* writers. He had received his education at a time when the schools were narrowly clerical. He wrote school books and religious tracts, collected folk poetry and proverbs, dabbled in history and literary history, and contributed to various Latin and *kajkavski* yearbooks. He wrote for the common people in their own language and was more a popularizer than a creative writer. See M. Franičević, "Mikloušić, Thomas," *Enciklopedija Jugoslavije* VI, 105 and Ivan Kukuljević-Sakcinski, "Prinesci za povijest književnosti hrvatske," *Arkiv za povjestnicu Jugoslavensku*, XII (1875), 53-55.
247. Quoted in the draft of a letter from Ljudevit Gaj to P.J. Šafařík, the only date given is 1830, *GPHK*, VI, 337-38.
248. Gaj, "Vjekopisni," p. XXIX.
249. Jovan Skerlić, *Istorija nove srpske književnosti* (3d ed.; Beograd: Rad, 1953), p. 119.
250. Gaj, "Vjekopisni," p. XXIX.
251. That Gaj took the initiative in this is clear in the draft of his first letter to Šafařík, undated except for the year — 1830, *GPKH*, VI, 337-38. Cf. Gaj "Vjekopisni," p. XXXIX.
252. This was one of the first collections of folk poetry in the Slavic world. See Jiri Horak, "Pavel Josef Šafařík, *Historica* (Prague), IV (1962), 291.
253. Draft of letter from Gaj to Šafařík, 1830, pp. 337-38.
254. *Ibid.*, p. 339.
255. Letter, P.J. Šafařík to Gaj, February 12, 1831, *GPKH*, VI, pp. 175-76.
256. *Ibid.*, p. 176.
257. These forms are used in a letter from Ljudevit Gaj to Dragutin Rakovac, March 3, 1831, *GPKH*, III, 249-52.
258. These changes may be traced by a close examination of Gaj's notes on language and his unpublished poems from 1831. The notes on language are in fragmentary form, jottings, translations of phrases, experiments with different orthographic forms. These are located in SKZ, *LG*, R 4701 A II 14. The first draft of "Još Horvatska mij' prepala," which was written in mid-1831, already used the new forms. Rakovac used these forms in a letter to Gaj dated October 6, 1831, *GPKH*, VI, 170. For published use of the 1831 orthography see Josip

Kundek "Reč jezika narodnoga" (1832) and Ljudevit Gaj, "Slavoglasje iz Zagorja" (1832) reprinted in *GPKH,* XII, 261-67.

259. Letter, P.J. Šafařik to Ljudevit Gaj, April 7, 1831, *GPKH,* VI, 178-80. See discussion of this letter in Duro Šurmin, "Bilješke za hrvatski preporod," *Vijenac,* XXXVII (1902), 441-42.

260. Letter, Šafařik to Gaj, April 7, 1831, p. 179.

261. Ljudevit Gaj, "Pravopisz," *Danicza Horvatzka, Slavonzka y Dalmatinzka,* I (March 14, 1835), 39.

262. Vatroslav Jagić, "Istorija Hrvatskoga pravopisa Latinskim slovima . . . ," (1890), in V. Jagić, *Izabrani krači spisi,* ed. M. Kombol, (Zagreb: Matica Hrvatska, 1948), p. 487.

263. SKZ, *LG,* R 4701 A I a. See also F. Fancev, "Postanak i historijska pozadina Gajeve pjesme: "Još Horvatska nij' prepala," *Hrvatska revija,* VIII (1935), 617-633.

264. Matija Murko, "Početak Gajevih 'Novin' i 'Danice,' *Spomen-Cvieće Matice Hravatske* (Zagreb: Matica Hrvatska, 1900), p. 570; and Horvat, "Gaj," p. 99.

265. Horvat, "Gaj," pp. 99-100.

CHAPTER V

266. *Ibid.,* pp. 105-106.

267. Report of Marcus Delivuk, Zagreb lawyer and police informant, to K.K. Minister of Police Graf Sedlnitsky, May 28, 1834, Jugoslavenska Akademije Znanosti i Umjetnosti, Ostavstine Ferde Šišića, 172 6 11. (Henceforth cited as JAZU, *OFS)* See also Aleksandar Čupović, "Dr. Ljudevit Gaj i odvjetnistvo," *Odvjetnik* XVIII (rujan, 1968), 309-15.

268. Letter, Dragutin Rakovac to Ljudevit Gaj, November 6, 1831, *GPKH,* VI, p. 170.

269. Kurelac, "Slova," p. 158.

270. Anton Vakanović, "Kako je postao ilirizam," SKZ R 3801 A 2. Although this manuscript was written when Vakanović was an old man, it seems to have been based on extensive notes, perhaps a section of Vakanović's diary, for it includes names, dates and detailed descriptions of people and conversations. I was able to consult certain parts of Vakanović's diary, those written in German and Croatian *(kajkavski,* later *stokavski),* but I could not make any sense of the parts in which he wrote in a mixture of Latin and other languages, with many abbreviations. This, unfortunately, is typical of the entires in the early 1830's. The Vakanović diary is located in SKZ, *Ostavstina Anton Vakanovića,* R 3801 B.

271. Vakanović, "Kako je postao ilirizam."

272. The meeting was held at an undisclosed date, the only notation being that it was held at Vukotinović's house in 1832. SKZ, "Societas culturae illyricae," R 3998 I.

273. The other suggestions were: *Drushtvo Slavesko vu Kraljestvih H S & D* (Maraković); *Društvo Slavenčka v. kr. H S & D* (Vukotinović); *Družtvo Slavensko z kr. H S & D* (Kurelac); and *Družtvo Slavonsko: Slavoncev južnih* (Smodek). *Ibid.*

274. For more detailed biographical information on the better-known members of the Gaj circle (the ones mentioned above), see the relevant sections of S. Ježić, *Ilirska antologija;* Anton Barac, *Hrvatska književnost,* Vol. I: *Književnost ilirizma* (Zagreb: Jugoslavenska akademija znanosti i umjetnosti, 1954); *Enciklopedija Jugoslavije;* and *Narodna Enciklopedija srpsko-hrvatsko-slovenačka.*

275. Horvat, "Gaj," p. 108.

276. Joanne Derkosz (Ivan Derkos), *Genius patriae super dormientibus suis filis, seu folium patrioticum . . .* (Zagreb: Fran Suppan, 1832), reprinted in *GPKH,* XII, 273-96. A skillful but heavily edited Croatian translation can be found in Ježić, ed., *Ilirska antologija,* pp. 97-98. Derkos (1808-1834) was one of the most promising members of the Gaj circle. He was trained as a lawyer, widely read in history and linguistics and would, most probably, have become one of the leading figures in the Illyrian Movement had it not been for his premature death from tuberculosis in 1834.

277. Ljudevit Gaj, "Über die Vereinigung zu einer Büchersprache," SKZ, *LG,* R 4701 B II 22. 10 manuscript pages; and an untitled fragment R 4701 B IV. "Über die Vereinigung . . ." is discussed briefly by Fancev in "Hrvatski ilirski preporod jest naš autohton pokret," pp. 21-22; and by Stjepan Ivšić in "Jezik Hrvata kajkavaca," *Ljetopis JAZU,* 48 (1934-35), 52. Fancev dates this manuscript around 1830, Ivšić as pre-1835.

278. Šafařík, *Geschichte,* pp. 23-25.

279. Ljudevit Gaj, SKZ, *LG,* R 4701 B IV.

280. Ljudevit Gaj, "Über die Vereinigung zu einer Büchersprache," SKZ, *LG, R 4701 B.II.22.*

281. Kopitar himself wrote in the footnote to his classification which he based on Dobrovský, "Wird vielleicht bey näherer Untersuchung anders befunden werden." Kopitar, *Grammatik,* p. xx, n.

282. Gaj, "Über die Vereinigung . . ."

283. *Ibid.*

284. As cited in Klaić, *Vitezović,* p. 106. Pokuplje, the area between the rivers Sava and Kupa, around Jastrebarsko; Posavina, the area north of the river Sava; and Podravina, the area south of the river Drava, were parts of Civil Croatia and the Military Frontier. Gaj mentions *Kronika* in this section of his manuscript.

285. Gaj, "Über die Vereinigung . . ."

286. *Ibid.*

287. Josip Kundek, "Reč jezika narodnoga" *GPKH,* XII, 263. Rakovac wrote a verse play entitled "Duh." Gaj's poem "Slavoglasje iz Zagorja" is also reprinted in *Ibid.,* pp. 265-267.

288. It is interesting that Gaj waited almost a year to publish this tract. He may have been short of money, for he paid for the publishing costs himself; he may have feared that *Palma* would get the author, or perhaps Gaj himself, into trouble. Kollár informed Gaj in March 1832 that Rohony had just died of cholera and asked rather pointedly whether Gaj was planning to have the manuscript published. Letter, Jan Kollár to Ljudevit Gaj, March 9, 1832. *GPKH,* VI, 97.

289. Letter, Dragutin Rakovac to P.J. Šafařík, March 3, 1833. *GPKH,* III, 255.

290. Ljudevit Vukotinović, "Uspomena na godine 1833-1835," in Ježić,

ed., *Ilirska antologija,* pp. 161-62.

291. Gyula Miskolczy, *A horvát kérdes* (Budapest: Kiadja a Magyar Történélmi Tarsulat, 1927), Vol. I, No. 23, 525-27.

292. *Ibid.,* No. 23, p. 527.

293. Letter, Jan Kollár to Ljudevit Gaj, March 9, 1832. *GPKH,* VI, 98.

294. Jaroslav Šidak, "Regia Scientiarum Academia," in Jaroslav Šidak *et al,* eds. *Spomenica u povodu proslave 300-godišnjice Sveučilišta u Zagrebu,* (2 vols., Zagreb: Jugoslavenska Akademija, 1969), Vol. I, 69.

295. Jaroslav Šidak, "Studentski pokret do otvaranja Sveucilista," *Ibid.,* p. 438.

296. Fran Kurelac, as quoted in Mirko Breyer, *Fran Kurelac* (Zagreb: Tipografija, 1939), pp. 23-24.

297. Šišić, *Hrvatska povijest,* III, p. 165.

298. On the controversy surrounding the date of this lecture see Šidak, "Regia Scientiarum Academia," p. 70, n. 37.

299. Šurmin, *Hrvatski preporod,* I, pp. 156-57.

300. Matho (Matija) Smodek, "Blagorečje pri početku navučanj iz materinskoga Jezika U Zagrebu," in J. Šidak *et al,* eds. *Spomenica,* Vol. I, pp. 334-35.

301. *Ibid.,* p. 335.

302. Šidak, "Regia Scientiarum Academia," p. 70.

303. Janchi Gaj and his wife were getting along badly and she finally left him in August. Letters of Julijana Gaj to Ljudevit Gaj, July 23, 1832 and August (no day given), 1832, SKZ, *PJG.*

304. Duro Šurmin, "Početak Gajevih novina," *Rad JAZU* 162 (1905), 113, 117-120.

305. Letter, Matija Smodek to Ljudevit Gaj, November 13, 1832. *GPKH,* VI, 173.

306. (grof Janko Drašković), *Disertacija iliti razgovor, darovan gospodi poklisarom i budućem zakonotvorcem kraljevinah naših, za buduću Dietu ungarsku odaslanem,* (držan po jednom starom domorodcu Kraljevinah ovih), (Karlovac: J. Prettner, 1832), republished in *GPKH,* XII, pp. 297-315. On Drašković see: Jaroslav Šidak, "Hrvatski preporodni pokret i grof Janko Drašković, in his *Studije iz hrvatske povijesti XIX stoljece,* Rasprave i članci of the Institute of Croatian History of the University of Zagreb, Vol. II (Zagreb: Graficki zavod, 1973), pp. 184-90.

307. (Drašković), "Disertacija," p. 297. Drašković's solution of the confused language question resembles Vitezović's.

308. The Austrian Kingdom of Illyria.

309. (Drašković), "Disertacija," p. 309.

310. Šišić, *Hrvatska povijest,* III, p. 170.

311. *Ibid.,* p. 173.

312. Horvat, "Gaj," p. 107.

313. Ljudevit Gaj, "Poszli vszakojachki," December 1832, SKZ, *LG,* 4701 B I 3.

314. Šurmin, "Početak Gajevih Novina," pp. 114-120.

315. Letter, Ljudevit Gaj to Dragutin Rakovac, February 5, 1833, *GPKH,* VI, 333-34.

316. Letter, Ljudevit Gaj to Ban Franjo Vlašić, February 14, 1833, *Ibid.,* p. 335.

317. Miskolczy, *Horvat Kerdes,* I, No. 26 a, pp. 529-31.

318. Ljudevit Gaj, ''Gajeva audijencija kod krala g. 1833,'' *GPKH,* VI, 352. The Emperor may have been referring to the fact that certain of the Hungarian deputies at the Parliament (Joint Parliament) then in session had begun to call for freedom of the press. See Anton Springer, *Geschichte Oesterreichs seit dem Wiener Frieden 1809* (2 vols., Leipzig: S. Hirzel, 1863), vol. I, 490.

319. Gaj, ''Gajeva audijencija kod kralja g. 1833.''

320. Miskolczy, *A horvát kérdes,* I, No. 26 b c pp. 531-535.

321. *Ibid.,* No. 26 e, p. 536.

322. These were: Mirko Delivuk, a Zagreb lawyer; George Zlatarović, a civil servant in Samobor, and Stjepan Moyses, Professor at the Zagreb Academy. Their reports are discussed in detail in: Matija Murko, ''Početak Gajevih 'Novin' i 'Danice,' '' pp. 574-77.

323. Miskolczy, *op. cit.,* No. 26 e, pp. 536-39.

324. *Ibid.,* No. 26 f g, pp. 539-60.

325. Vukotinović, ''Uspomena na godine 6833-1835,'' Ježić, ed., *Ilirska antologija,* p. 161.

326. Ljudevit Gaj, ''Još Horvatska ni prepala,'' SKZ, *LG, R 4701 A I a.*

327. For the text of the 1831 version *Supra.*

328. Gaj, ''Gajevih audiejencija kod kralja g. 1833,'' *GPKH,* VI, 350-53.

329. ''. . . ich hätte Ursach recht traurig zu sein, da Ludwig so lange zu nichts kommt.'' Letter, Julijana Gaj to Ivana Gaj Cantilly, August, 1834. *SK-Z,* PJG.

330. Horvat, ''Gaj,'' p. 143.

331. Ljudevit Gaj, ''Bilješke s puta u Njemačku, *SKZ, LG,* R 4701 B I 5.

332. Letter to Elinor M. Despalatović from D. Munz, Universitätsbibliothek, Karl-Marx-Universität, Leipzig, D.D.R., December 12, 1968.

333. Josip Horvat, *Povijest novinstva Hrvatske* (Zagreb: Stvarnost, 1962), pp. 100-1.

334. The texts of the Babukić, Mažuranić, Vukotinović and Gaj *Oglas*'s are in: SKZ, *LG,* R 4706 15 1,2,3,4.

335. Horvat, *Povijest novinstva,* p. 104.

336. Not ''Croatian, Slovenian and Dalmatian Newspaper'' and not ''The Dawn'' as translated by Hans Kohn. The newspaper did not begin publication until January 1835, although Kohn says it began in 1834. Kohn, *Pan-Slavism,* p. 61. This third mistake may be due to the fact that the *kajkavski* word for January *(prosinec)* is the same as the *štokavski* word for December *(prosinac),* and the first issues used the kajkavski names for months.

337. The text of the *Oglas* is reprinted in S. Ježić, *Ilirska antologija,* pp. 104-5.

338. *Ibid.*

CHAPTER VI

339. F. Fancev, ''Uvod,'' *GPKH,* XII, pp. XI-XLVI; Đ. Šurmin, *Hrvatski preporod,* Vol. I, pp. 221-223; S. Ježić, *Ilirska antologija,* pp. 57-58; J. Šidak, ''Ilirski pokret,'' *Enciklopedija Jugoslavije,* IV, 338-39. The article by Šidak discusses this question in some detail.

340. The term *Novine* will be used throughout this text and the footnotes as a shortened form for *Novine Horvatzke* (1835), *Ilirske narodne novine* (1836-1843), *Narodne novine* (1843-1844), *Novine horvatsko slavonsko i dalmatinsko* (1844-49). In the same way we shall use *Danica* as a shortened version of *Danicza Horvatzka, Slavonzka i Dalmatinzka* (January to July 18th, 1835), *Danica Horvatska, Slavonska i Dalmatinska* (July 18th to December, 1835), *Danica ilirska* (1836-1843), *Danica horvatska, slavonska i Dalmatinska* (1843-1849). From this point on all months will be given in English so that they are consistent with the text. This is especially important for the first year, when the names of the months differ from those in later years, as they are taken from the *kajkavski* dialect.

341. Ferić (Georgii) -Ilir iz Dubrovnika. ''Sloga i nesloga,'' *Danica,* II (April 30, 1836), 69.

342. F. Petré, *Poizkus ilirizma pri Slovencih (1835-1839)* (Ljubljana: Matica Slovenska, 1939), p. 106.

343. J. Horvat, *Povijest novinstva,* p. 110.

344. Antun Mažuranić was then an instructor *(suplent)* at the Zagreb Smiciklas, ''Antun Mažuranić,'' in T. Smičikas and F. Marković, *Matica Hrvatska od godine 1842. do godine 1892- Spomen-knjiga* (Zagreb: Matica Hrvatska, 1892), p. 291. Vjekoslav Babukić was then working as a notary. *Ibid.,* ''Vjekoslav Babukić,'' p. 247.

345. In 1835, Rakovac received fifteen forints per month, plus lodging, heat and light. Horvat, *Povijest novinstva,* p. 110.

346. SKZ, Spisi Zagrebačke censure R 3991 2.

347. For example, ''Još Horvatska nij' prepala'' and the more vigorously anti-Hungarian ''Nek se hrusti šaka mala'' by Vukotinović which were published in *Danica* in 1835, were identified as folk songs which had been composed by the loyal troops of the Croatian Military Frontier in the battles against the French armies during the Napoleonic Wars. The Zagreb and Austrian censors seem to have accepted this story, but the Hungarians were highly skeptical. Miskolczy, *Horvát Kérdes,* I, 553-555.

348. For instance, ''Dr. Jakov Supan,'' *Danica* I (April 18, 1835), 60. Original draft in SKZ, *LG,* R 4701 A II 6.

349. A few sample titles might better illustrate this point: ''The Homeland and its Daughters'' (J. Horvatica), ''The Croatian fairy *(Vila)* weeps at the death of His Majesty the Emperor Francis I'' (Pavel Stoos), ''Slavonian Soldier'' (M.D.), ''Sad Bosnia,'' (M. Topalovic) etc. All 1835.

350. (Ljudevit Gaj), ''Naj lěpši orszag,'' *Danica,* I (February 7, 1835), 20. Original is in SKZ, *LG,* R 4701 A II 6.

351. See Horvat, ''Gaj'', p. 169.

352. Ljudevit Gaj, ''Pravopisz'', *Danica,* I (March 14-28, 1835), pp. 39-40, 41-43, 46-48.

353. *Ibid.,* pp. 38-9.

354. *Ibid.,* p. 39.

355. *Ibid.,* p. 48. See Šafařik, *Geschichete,* pp. 67-68, which indicates that the ''Bohemians-Moravians-Czechs'' used č, š and ž, and the Poles ć.

356. For a detailed discussion of this controversy see: Ljudevit Jonke, ''Sporovi pri odabiranju govora za zajednicki književni jezik u Hrvata u 19. stoljeću,'' *Radovi Slavenskoga instituta* (Zagreb), III (1959), 5-33.

357. Gaj, ''Pravopisz,'' p. 48.

358. *Supra.*
359. Ljudevit Gaj, "Nima domorodztva prez lyubavi materinzkoga jezika," *Danica,* I (May 2-30, 1835), pp. 65-67, 70-71, 73-74, 77-78, 81-83.
360. *Ibid.,* pp. 65-66.
361. *Ibid.,* p. 67.
362. In an unpublished note from 1835, Gaj wrote: The Magyars seem to want to Magyarize us. Is it not time that we Europeanize them? SKZ *LG* A II 22.
363. Gaj, "Nima domorodztva," p. 66.
364. This argument is typical of early nineteenth century nationalism. See discussion of the role of diversity in Kedourie, *Nationalism,* ch. 4.
365. Gaj, "Nima domorodztva," p. 66.
366. *Ibid.,* p. 66.
367. *Ibid.,* p. 70.
368. *Ibid.,* pp. 77-78.
369. *Ibid.,* p. 81.
370. *Ibid.,* p. 83.
371. For a cogent discussion of the philosophical theories behind the early nineteenth century belief especially among the Germans, Italians and East Europeans, that a nation exists through its language regardless of whether it has a state, see Kedourie, *Nationalism,* ch. 5.

372. (J. G.) Herder, "Slavenski puki," *Danica,* I (August 22, 1835), 231-32.
373. Ljudevit Gaj, "Naš narod," *Ibid.,* (August 29, 1835), 234-36; and (P. J.) Šafařík, "Značaj i izobraženost Slavskoga naroda u obćinskom," *Ibid.,* (September 5-26, 1835), pp. 238-40, 242-44, 247-48, 250-52. Gaj was careless, especially in 1835, about identifying whether or not an item in *Danica* was original, or translated and adapted from a published article or book. Since there is nothing in Šafařík's letters to Gaj to indicate that he was writing anything specifically for *Danica* except for a few brief notes on newly published Slavic books, we can assume that this was not an original article. See letters of P. J. Šafařík to Ljudevit Gaj, March 5, 1835; March 15, 1835; May 5, 1835; August 12, 1835; *GPKH,* VI, 185-90.
374. Ljudevit Gaj, "Naš narod," p. 234. There is an unpublished fragment from approximately the same time. Although it does not fit the image anatomically, it does express a feeling that was not safe for Gaj to print: "The Hungarians are a splinter in the finger of the Slavic giant. They must take care that the wound does not fester, or the splinter shall have to be removed." SKZ, *LG,* R 4701 A II 22.
375. Gaj, "Naš narod," p. 235.
376. Kollár, "Uber die literarische Wechselseitigkeit," p. 45.
377. Šafařík, *Geschichte,* pp. xiii-xvi.
378. Gaj, "Naš narod," pp. 235-36.
379. *Supra,* p. 145.
380. Pavao Ritter Vitezović, *Croatia rediviva; regnante Leopoldo Magno Caesare, deducta ab Eq. Paulo Ritter* (Zagreb, 1700) as quoted in Klaić: *Vitezovic,* p. 144.
381. G. polag J. Wenziga (Gaj adapted from J. Wenzig), "Nešto verhu narodnoga pěsničtva u obćinskom," *Danica,* I (October 31, 1835), 270-72.
382. When Gaj adapated he cut, shaped and translated texts, interspersing

them with comments of his own which are not in any way separated from the body of the article.

383. G. (Gaj) polag Dra. Šafařika, "Slavske narodne pěsme," *Danica,* I, (November 7, 1835), 275-76.

384. (Ljudevit Gaj), "Sbirke narodnih slavenskih pěsamah," *Ibid.,* (November 14, 1835), 288-81. The original manuscript is in SKZ, *LG* R 4701 A III 8.

385. (Ljudevit Gaj), "Něšto o dogodovščini talianskoga jezika," *Danica* I (December 12, 1835), 286-88. The original manuscript is in SKZ *LG* R 4701 A III 11.

386. *Ibid.,* p. 288.

387. Ljudevit Gaj, "Proglas," *Danica,* I (December 5, 1835), 292-93, and as a flyer to the issue of December 29, 1835.

388. *Ibid.,* p. 292.

389. *Ibid.*

390. *Ibid.*

391. *Ibid.*

392. *Ibid.,* p. 293.

393. See Ljudevit Gaj, "Proglas," *Danica,* V (November 23, 1839), 187.

394. Gaj, "Proglas," (1835), 293.

395. *Ibid.*

396. Ljudevit Gaj, "Sbirke někojih řečih, koje su ili u gornjoj ili u dolnjoj Ilirii pomanje poznane," *Danica,* I (1835), special supplement, 22 pp.

397. *Ibid.,* p. 1.

398. *Ibid.*

399. Vjekoslav Babukić, "Osnova slovnice Slavjanske nařečja Ilirskoga," *Danica,* II (March 5-April 9, 1836), 37-60.

400. Ljudevit Jonke, "Osnovni problemi jezika hrvatske književnosti u 19. stoljeću," *Radovi slavenskoga instituta* (Zagreb University), II (1958), 83.

401. *Ibid.,* 83-85.

402. *Ibid.,* p. 83.

403. Gaj, "Proglas," *Danica,* I (December 5, 1835), p. 293.

404. For an analysis of the kinds of words the Illyrians borrowed from Slovene, Russian, Czech and Polish, see: Jonke, "Osnovi problemi," pp. 85-88.

405. Among the Croatian signers of the *Književni dogovor* of 1850 were: Ivan Kukuljević, Ivan Mažuranić, Dimitrije Demeter, Duro Danicic and Fran Miklošić. Ljudevit Jonke, "Kniževi jezik u Hrvata od Gaja dalje," *Enciklopedija Jugoslavije,* IV, 523-24.

406. *Ibid.*

407. This conflict is ably discussed in Ljudevit Jonke, "Ideološki osnovi Zagrebačke filološke škole 19. stoljeća," *Filologija,* I (1956), 77-86.

408. See letters dated 1835 in *GPKH* VI and XXVI. The second collection, edited by J. Horvat and J. Ravlić, is to my mind the more valuable one for getting a feel of the various types of people who sympathized with and joined the Illyrian Movement. The first volume, *GPKH* VI, includes letters from the better known figures of the day and from foreigners. The letters of the "little people" which fill *GPKH* XXVI, although there are some from important people as well, are accompanied by detailed biographical and historical notes and form an extremely important source for anyone studying this period.

409. Horvat, *Povijest novinstva,* p. 123.

410. *Ibid.*, pp. 108-110.
411. Letter, P.J. Šafařík to Ljudevit Gaj, March 5, 1835, *GPKH*, VI, 185.
412. Šurmin, *Hrvatski preporod*, I, 194-95.

CHAPTER VII

413. Ljudevit Gaj, "Kratki uvod u dogodovščinu velike Ilirie," May 30, pp. 69-72; "Nekoja družtva slavjanska," July 30, pp. 123-34; and "Družtvo prijateljah narodne izobraženosti Ilirske," August 13, pp. 130-31, and August 20, p. 136. All from *Danica* 1836.

414. Horvat, *Povijest novinstva*, p. 123.

415. *Ibid.*, p. 133. Yet the *Agramer Zeitung* had 1350 subscribers in 1848.

416. Ignjat Kristijanović (1796-1884) was the nephew of T. Mikloušić. He was a staunch defender of the *kajkavski* dialect and believed it to be the only true Croatian dialect. He opposed the Illyrian reforms step by step, publishing his own calendar, *Danicza zagrebačka* (1834-1850), a *kajkavski* grammar in 1837 and 1840, and continually agitating against the Illyrian language and the new literature. See Ivan Kukuljević-Sakcinski, "Prinesci za povijest knjizevnosti hrvatske," *Arkiv za povjestnicu Jugoslavensku* XII (1875), pp. 56-60.

417. In a letter dated January 12, 1836, Julijana warned her son Ljudevit that certain of these "paper nobles" were rumored to have lodged a formal complaint with the Palatine about the actions of Gaj. *PJG.* See also Horvat, "Gaj," pp. 200-01.

418. Jakša Ravlić, "Povijest Matice Hrvatske," in Jakša Ravlić and Martin Somborac, *Matica Hrvatska, 1842-1962* (Zagreb: Matica Hrvatska, 1963), p. 26.

419. Miskolczy, *Horvát Kérdes*, I, No. 29, p. 549.

420. Gaj talked this plan over with Šafařík when he visited him in Karlový Vary in the summer of 1834 on the way to Leipzig. Letter, P.J. Šafařík to L. Gaj, March 5, 1835, *GPKH*, VI, 187.

421. Horvat, *Povijest novinstva*, p. 101.

422. The text of this petition can be found in: *GPKH* VI, 339-341.

423. For the texts of Gaj's letters to various officials asking for support and copies of some of the supporting letters see: SKZ, *LG*, R 4704 1-11. One of the most interesting is a letter from the High Command of the Croatian Military Frontier dated December 5, 1835, in which the High Command not only refuses to send such a letter but expresses complete indifference to the whole national awakening. *Ibid.*, No. 10.

424. Letter, A. Vakanović to L. Gaj, March 29, 1836, *GPKH*, XXVI, 474-75.

425. Letter, Bužan to F. von Wernekring, May 22, 1836, Miskolczy, *Horvát Kérdes*, I, No. 28 1, pp. 543-45.

426. Gaj mentions this fact in a letter to Count Kolowrat dated November 26, 1836, SKZ, *LG*, R 4704 16. For text of Gaj's second petition see *GPKH*, VI, 343-45.

427. L. Gaj, "Petition of June 1, 1836," *GPKH*, VI, 343.

428. *Ibid.*, p. 345.

429. "Darstellung der politischen Verhältnisse hinsichtlich der Agramer Zeitung in der kroatischen Sprache und hinsichtlich der zweiten zu Agram einzuführenden Buchdruckerei," Wien, June 2, 1836. Miskolczy, *Horvát Kérdes,* I, No. 28 b, pp. 545-548.

430. Ljudevit Gaj, "Darstellung der auf ein Seiner Majestät aller unterthanigst unterbreitetes Gesuch des Dor. Ludwig Gaj . . . Bezug habenden politischen Verhältnisse in Croatien." SKZ, *LG* R 4704 15. Cf. Šišić, *Hrvatska povijest,* III, p. 206 who claims Gaj knew nothing about the June 2nd document (!).

431. Miskolczy, *Horvát Kérdes,* I, No. 28 b, p. 545.

432. "Darstellung der politischen Verhältnisse," Miskolczy, I, p. 546.

433. *Ibid.,* pp. 546-548.

434. Ljudevit Gaj to Antun Mažuranić *et al,* June 10, 1836. As cited in Šišić, *Hrvatska povijest,* III, pp. 206-207.

435. Miskolczy, *Horvát Kérdes,* I, No. 29, p. 548.

436. For detailed analysis of the Parliament of 1832-1836 see the following: Šišić, *Hrvatska povijest,* III, pp. 175-188 (Croatian view); Michael Horvath, *Fünfundzwanzig Jahre aus der Geschichte Ungarns* (2 vols., Leipzig: F. A. Brockhaus, 1867), I 250-443 (Hungarian view); and Springer, *Geschichte Oesterreichs seit dem Wiener Frieden* I, 466-508 (Austrian view, best balanced narrative).

437. M. Horvat, *Fünfundzwanzig Jahre,* I, 431.

438. Letter, Gaj to A. Mažuranić *et al.,* June 10, 1836. As cited in Šišić, *Hrvatska poviject,* III, p. 207.

439. *Ibid.*

440. Report of Stjepan Moyses to Count Sedlnitsky, August 18, 1836, JAZU, *OFS,* XIII B 84 7.

441. *Ibid.*

442. There has been some controversy over whether or not a third political faction existed in Croatia in 1836. This matter is very well discussed and the existence of the third faction proven false in the article by Jaroslav Šidak, "Prilozi historiji stranački odnosa u Hrvatskoj uoči 1848," *Historijski zbornik,* XIII (1960), 167-75.

443. Šišić, *Hrvatska Povijest,* III, pp. 186-187. Moyses reported to Sedlnitsky on December 15, that had the Magyars not attacked the Croatian Municipal Rights and forced through the new *Urbarium* in the Joint Parliament, the majority of the Croatian nobles would probably have accepted the Magyar language, as the language of the state quite docilely. Miskolczy, *Horvát Kérdes,* I, No. 35, pp. 561-562.

444. Miskolczy, *Horvát Kérdes,* I, No. 30, pp. 553-55.

445. Ljudevit Gaj, "Družtvo prijateljah narodne izobraženosti Ilirske," *Danica,* August 20, 1836, p. 131.

446. *Supra.*

447. Letter, Count Janko Drašković to Ljudevit Gaj, February 15, 1835. *GPKH,* VI, 51.

448. Miskolczy, *Horvát Kérdes,* I, No. 32, pp. 558-59.

449. Possibly Drašković. Latin copy written in Gaj's hand with a notation that it was submitted to the Sabor: SKZ, *Societas culturae illyricae* R 3998 2.

450. Ivan Kolar, "O slovstvenoj uzajemnosti medju koljeni i narečji Slavskimi," *Danica,* II (July 9-July 30, 1836), pp. 114-16, 117-20, 122. This is

an exact translation of the complete Slovak text. For the original see Kollár, "O literárnéj vzájemnosti . ." in Weingart, ed. *Rozprovy,* pp. 31-160. This was apparently the second foreign translation of Kollár's essay; the first was published in *Serbski narodni list.* For a discussion of the various translations see: Auty, "Jan Kollár," p. 88, no. 79.

451. Ljudevit Gaj, "Někoja družtva slavjanska kao srědstva narodne izobraženosti," *Danica,* II (July 30, 1836), pp. 123-24.

452. *Ibid.,* p. 124.

453. Ljudevit Gaj, "Druztvo prijateljah narodne izobrazenosti Ilirske," *Ibid.,* (August 13-August 20, 1836), pp. 131-32, 136.

454. *Ibid.,* p. 131.

455. Šišić, *Hrvatska povijest,* III, pp. 209-10. Here we begin to see the factional divisions among the Croatian nobles. The men who protested against the Illyrian name: Count Alexander Drašković, Baron Levin Rauch, Pavao Keresztury and Antun Josipović, were among the founders of the *Horvatsko-Ugarska,* or, as it was better known, the "Magyarone" party in 1840, which sought to destroy the Illyrian Movement.

456. Miskolczy, *Horvát Kérdes,* I, No. 33, pp. 560-61.

457. Josip Buturac, *Povijest zbora duhovne mladeži Zagrebačke* (Zagreb: Dionička tiskara, 1937), p. 17.

458. *Ibid.,* pp. 18-19.

459. *Ibid.,* p. 16.

460. Johann Prettner submitted a petition in 1834, Anton Stadler in July 1835, Ljudevit Gaj in December 1835, and J. Goriček sometime in 1836. The qualifications of each of these men are discussed in Miskolczy, *Horvát Kérdes,* I, No. 29, pp. 548-53.

461. Letter of Ljudevit Gaj to Count Kolowrat, September 26, 1836. SKZ, *LG,* R 4704 16.

462. Ljudevit Gaj, "Utok na cara," September 27, 1836. *Ibid.,* R 4704 17.

463. JAZU, *OFS,* XVIII B 172 5.

464. *Ibid.,* 172 6.

465. Šišić, *Hrvatska povijest* III, p. 211.

466. Kukuljević to Gaj, January 25, 1836. *GPKH,* VI, 117.

467. Diary of Ivan Kukuljević-Sakcinski, in the private library of his great grandson, Dr. Ladislav Šaban. I would like to thank Dr. Šaban for permission to make use of this material and for his transcript of this excerpt.

468. *Ibid.*

469. *Ibid.*

470. *Ibid.*

471. Ivan Kukuljević-Sakcinski (1816-1889). See S. Ježić, *Ilirska antologija,* p. 193; and detailed biographical sketch by J. Šidak, "Kukuljević-Sakcinski, Ivan," *Enciklopedija Jugoslavije* V, 442-444.

472. *GPKH,* XXVI, 87, n. 1. See also Horvat, "Gaj," pp. 210-11.

473. For an example of the real enthusiasm with which *Danica* was received by the students, see the letter of Marcus Hallavanya to Ljudevit Gaj, February 22, 1838, *GPKH,* XXVI, pp. 189-91.

474. Letter of Stefan Herkalović to his brother Than Herkalović, November 30, 1837. *Ibid.,* 200. See pp. 205-06 for a brief biography.

475. Horvat, "Gaj," p. 211.

476. Herkalović stayed only a year in Serbia in this first position. Between

1838 and 1842 he travelled through Dalmatia, Bosnia and to Russia (1839) as Gaj's emissary. He then returned to Serbia in 1842 and became an important official in the War Ministry.

477. This is mentioned in a letter from Ljudevit Gaj to the Censor Stjepan Moyses, December 6, 1837, SKZ, *Spisi Zagrebačke cenzure*, R 3991 1.

478. *Ibid.*

479. Letter, L. Gaj to D. Rakovac *et al*, July 30, 1837, *GPKH*, III, 253-54.

480. Gaj, "Naš narod," *Danica*, August 29, 1835, p. 235.

481. *GPKH*, VI, 100 and *Ibid.*, XXVI, p. 260.

482. Letter, P. J. Šafařík to Jan Kollár, March 3rd, 1837, as cited in Šurmin, "Bilješke za hrvatski preporod," 474.

483. J. Horvat, "Gaj," p. 212.

484. Stjepan Moyses to Count Sedlnitzky, October 1, 1837. JAZU, *OFS*, XVIII B 172 8.

485. Count Sedlnitzky to Stjepan Moyses, December 21, 1837, *Ibid.*, 172 9.

486. Horvat, *Povijest novinstva*, p. 123.

CHAPTER VIII

487. For some reason the original contract with Haase and Sons was not kept in Gaj's personal papers. The inventory at the end of 1838, equipment, paper etc., totaled 8267 forints and 23 kreutzers. SKZ, *LG*, R 4704 II a.

488. Horvat, "Gaj," pp. 213-16.

489. Horvat, *Povijest novinstva*, p. 124.

490. R. Bićanić, *Doba manufakture*, p. 314. It is interesting that this contract included medical benefits. The 1839 contract can be found in SKZ, *LG*, R 4704 II a.

491. Horvat, *Povijest novinstva*, p. 124.

492. The Zagreb Reading Club, for example had business meetings on January 24th and June 24th each year. Officers were elected at the June meeting. Jakša Ravlić, "Ilirska čitaonica u Zagrebu," *Historijski zbornik*, XVI (1963), 164.

493. Letter, D. Kušlan to L. Gaj, February 23, 1838, *GPKH*, XXVI, 281.

494. Horvat, "Gaj," 218. List of the oldest members of the Zagreb Reading Club and other documents relating to the Club are in the personal papers of Vjekoslav Babukić, SKZ, R 3991 I 1.

495. Horvat, "Gaj," 218-19.

496. Count Janko Drašković, "Govor," *Danica*, IV (August 4, 1838), 122-23.

497. The text of this proposal is cited in full in Ravlić, "Ilirska čitaonica," 168-69.

498. *Ibid.*, 170.

499. Horvat, "Gaj," 245.

500. The best detailed study of the activities of the Zagreb Reading Club is: Ravlić, "Ilirska čitaonica," 159-214, which also includes, as an appendix, a list of its members and their professions. Another useful brief source which shows most clearly the role of the Club as a major initiator of national cultural

institutions is: Jakša Ravlić, "Ustanove i društva kulture u vrijeme hrvatskog narodnog preporoda," *Kolo,* new series IV (1966), 348-66.

501. Ravlić, *Ilirska čitaonica,* 174.

502. Josip Horvat, "Čitaonice: Hrvatske," *Enciklopedija Jugoslavije,* Vol. II, 606.

503. Horvat, "Gaj," 219-20.

504. Ljudevit Gaj, "Lectio pro Domino Carlo Rakovac die 9. Sept. 1838," SKZ, *LG,* R 4702a.

505. *Ibid.*

506. Wilhelm Landauer, the *faktor* for the printing press complained to Gaj soon afterwards that *Novine* was again late in coming to the press. Letter, Landauer to Gaj, September 19, 1838, *GPKH,* XXVI, 288-29.

507. See: Philip E. Mosely, ed., "Pan-Slavist Memorandum of Liudevit Gaj in 1838," *American Historical Review,* XL (1935), 715; and Gaj's memorandum of July 3rd, 1840 in Platon Kulakovskij, *Illirizm'* (Warsaw: Tipografija Varšavskago učebnago okruga, 1894), 84-85.

508. Frank Fadner, *Seventy Years of Pan-Slavism in Russia, Karazin to Danilevsky, 1800-1970* (Georgetown: Georgetown University Press, 1962, 20-30.

509. *Ibid.,* 29-30, 54.

510. *Ibid.,* 31.

511. "... Mr. Gaj requested him (Ozeretskovskii) to guarantee that what he, Gaj, has written shall remain absolutely secret and that the Russian government, now having in its hands the guarantee of his devotion, on which his life depends, shall preserve this document as a secret from the Austrian cabinet." Mosely, "Pan-Slavist Memorandum of Liudevit Gaj in 1838," 716.

512. This is Jaroslav Šidak's term and it seems an apt one. See Jaroslav Šidak, " 'Tajna politika' Lj. Gaja i postanak njegovih 'memorandumna' knezu Metternichu 1846-47," *Arhivski vjesnik,* XIII (1970), 397-434.

513. Ljudevit Gaj, "Memorandum of November 1, 1838," in Mosely, ed., "Pan-Slavist Memorandum," 708-16.

514. See Philip E. Mosely, *Russian Diplomacy and the Opening of the Eastern Question in 1838 and 1839* (Cambridge: Harvard University Press, 1934), and the general survey by M.S. Anderson, *The Eastern Question* (New York: St. Martin's Press, 1966), Ch. 4.

515. Mosely, "Pan-Slavist Memorandum," 707.

516. Gunther E. Rothenberg, *The Military Border in Croatia, 1740-1881* (Chicago: University of Chicago Press, 1966), 135-36.

517. He did begin to collect strategic military information on Bosnia and Serbia in the early 1840's, and may have begun in 1838 or 1839. See the list of questions he jotted down to ask the Bosnian Friar Stjepan Marijanovic. These were attached to a letter from Marijanovic dated July 21, 1843, *GPKH,* XXVI 307. See also the report on Turkish troop movements in the letter of P. Cavlovic to L. Gaj, March 17 5, 1844, *Ibid.,* 126.

518. Kulakovskij argues that Gaj turned to Russia because powerful Serbian groups had come out against the Illyrian Movement and he hoped that Russian support would win the Orthodox Southern Slavs over to support of the Illyrians. Kulakovskij, *Illirizm',* 235-36. Serbian opposition in 1838, however, was still mild. It began to gather momentum between 1839 and 1841. See Ilija Mamužić, "Ilirizam i Srbi," *Rad,* vol. 247 (1933), 91-92.

519. This fact is mentioned in a letter from S. Herkalović to L. Gaj, March 1839. *GPKH,* XXVI, pp. 209-10.

520. Letter from A. Vakanović to L. Gaj, March 26, 1839. *Ibid.,* p. 476.

521. It is not certain whether Matija reached Montenegro on his travels, but he mentioned in a letter to his brothers that he planned to go there. Letter of July 22, 1839, cited in T. Smičiklas, "Ivan Mažuranić," *Matica Hrvatska-spomen knjiga,* p. 125. Matija Mažuranić published his impressions of Bosnia in a short book, *Pogled u Bosnu* (Zagreb: Tipografija Ljudevita Gaja, 1842), which is considered to be a classic of Illyrian prose.

522. Antun Mažuranić as cited in T. Smičiklas, "Obrana i razvitak narodne ideje od 1790 do 1835 godine," *Rad JAZU,* 80 (1885), 52.

523. Milovoj Šrepel, ed. and trans., "Slika Zagrebačkoga života g 1841 i slavni pjesnik Jan Kollár," *Stari i novi Zagreb,* ed. by E. Laszowski, (Zagreb: Hrv. štamparski zavod D.D., 1925), 227.

524. Letter, L. Vukotinović to L. Gaj, December 6, 1840, *GPKH,* XXVI, 498.

525. This visit is described in detail in, Josip Buturac, *Povijest zbora duhovne . . .,* p. 24, and Izidor Škorjac, "Zagrebački bogoslovi prema Gaja, Slovencima i Srbima," *Izvještaji male realne gimnazije u Krapini* 1911, pp. 6-7.

526. Report of Stjepan Moyses to Count Sedlnitzky, July 26, 1839, JAZU, *OFS,* 84 B 20.

527. The Society would have several kinds of members: founders (those who contributed 50 forints); regular members (Illyrian writers); honorary members (men who had distinguished themselves in work toward national enlightenment); and corresponding members (others, including foreigners).

528. See J. Ravlić, "Povijest Matice Hrvatske," *Matica Hrvatska 1842-1862,* 18-19; and T. Smičiklas, "Povijest Matice Hrvatske," *Matica Hrvatska spomen-knijiga 1842-1892,* 5-7.

529. Ravlić, "Povijest Matice Hrvatske," p. 20.

530. T. Smičiklas, "Povijest Matice Hrvatske," p. 14.

531. Petition of Ljudevit Gaj, June 24, 1839, Miskolczy, *Horvát Kérdes,* I, No. 37 2, pp. 576-78.

532. Undated letter, written sometime in 1839, from Nikolaj Pavlivščev to L. Gaj, *GPKH,* VI, 148-50. In the memorandum dated St. Petersburg July 3, 1840, Gaj says: "In vorigen Jahre sandte ich meinen Plenipotentiaer Stefan Thadianovic Herkalović nach St. Petersburg mit dem Auftrage die bereits gemachten Vorstellungen dringend zu wiederholen. Nach 6 Monathen kehrte er ohne Result zurück." Kulakovskij, *Illirizm',* p. 085.

533. Horvat, "Gaj," 250.

534. The correspondence between Count Kolowrat and Count Majlath on this matter is highly interesting. See Miskolczy, *op. cit.,* I, No. 37 b c, pp. 579-80. The Emperor's statements on the matter are in Kolowrat's handwriting. Wien, Haus, Hof und Staats Archiv, *Acta Min. Kolowrat,* No. 100 839.

535. J. Neustaedter, *Le Ban Jelačić et les événements en Croatie depuis l'an 1848* (2 vols. Zagreb: Institut Français, 1940), Vol. I, 185-87.

536. Gaj, "Vjekopisni," p. XXVI.

537. Barac, *Hrvatska književnost,* I, p. 245.

538. Letter of H. Börnstein to L. Gaj, November 4, 1839, *GPKH,* XXVI, 60-61.

539. Šurmin, *Hrvatski preporod,* II, pp. 247-50.
540. Šišić, *Hrvatska povijest,* III, 224.
541. *Ibid.,* 238.
542. *Ibid.,* 221.
543. Cuvaj, *Gradja za povijest školstva,* III, 82. The elementary schools were the weakest part of the educational system. In 1840-1841 only thirty-seven percent of the children of school age attended elementary schools. The teachers were poorly trained, often retired actors or officers. They were paid by the local landlord or community usually in wood, wine and grain. Where there was no permanent teacher, the school would be taught by the local priest or an itinerant teacher who spent several months in one school, then moved on to the next. *Ibid.,* pp. 116-117.
544. Antun Mažuranić, *Temelj ilirskoga i latinskoga jezika za početnike* (Zagreb: Ljudevit Gaj, 1839). This text was designed for the first year language student in secondary school, but after 1840 it was used in the elementary schools as well. Cuvaj, *Gradja,* III, 82.
545. Letter of S. Vraz to D. Rakovac, January 30, 1840. Gradja III, 284.
546. The major sources for Gaj's trip to Russia are: Ljudevit Gaj, "Lisnica s različitim bilješkama" (Unpublished diary which runs from April to September, 1840), SKZ, *LG,* R 4701 B I 2; Kulakovskij, *Illirizm',* pp. 289-98, 083-086; V. Francev, "Za biografiju Ljudevita Gaja," *GPKH,* V (1907), 142-47; and J. Horvat, "Gaj," pp. 260-275.
547. Gaj, "Lisnica."
548. Václav Žaček, "Česka účast při pokusech o politické sblíženi Charvátů a Srbů v. 40. letech 19. století." *Slovanské historičke studie* (Prague), VI (1966), p. 61; and Václav Žaček, "Česko i poljsko učešće u postanku Garašinova 'Načertanija' (1844)," *Historijski zbornik,* XVI (1963), p. 38. See also: Jaroslav Šidak, "František Zach (1807-1892)," *Enciklopedija Jugoslavije,* vol. XIII, p. 564.
549. Kulakovskij, *Illirizm',* 290. For details on Gaj's stay in Warsaw see Francev, "Za biografiju Ljudevita Gaja."
550. The text of this petition is in Kulakovskij, *Illirizm',* 084-086.
551. Kulakovskij, *Illirizm',* p. 291.
552. Inna Ivanovna Leschilovskaía, *Illirizm* (Moscow: Nauka, 1968), 299. *Cf.* Kulakovskij, *Illirizm',* p. 292, where the author says Gaj received 5,000 rubles.
553. Kulakovskij, *'Illirizm',* 296; and Leschilovskaia, *Illirizm,* 299.
554. L. Gaj, "Lisnica."
555. Horvat, "Gaj," p. 273. Horvat believes that Šafařík was worried that Gaj might sell the manuscripts to some collector and that they would be lost to Slavic scholars.
556. Branko Vodnik, ed., "Ljudevit Gaj. Silhoueta iz dnevnika A. T. Brlića," *Jugoslavenska Njiva,* X (No. 2, 1926), 56-59.
557. SKZ, *LG,* R 4701 B A 7.
558. See L. Gaj, "Proglas," *Danica,* I (December 5, 1835), 292-93.
559. SKZ, *LG* R4701 B A 7.

CHAPTER IX

560. Letter, Vjekoslav Babukić to Ljudevit Gaj, April 2, 1841. *GPKH*, VI, pp. 13-15.

561. Gaj had paid Rakovac 30 forints a month plus housing, light and heat for editing *Novine* in 1840. Horvat, *Povijest novinstva*, 125. Babukić, on the other hand, received 10 forints a month in 1838, gifts totaling 45 forints in 1839, and a gift of 80 forints in 1840. Letter Babukić to Gaj, April 2nd, 1841, p. 14.

562. Letter, Babukić to Gaj, p. 15.

563. For a brief biography of Užarević, see *GPKH*, XXVI, 473-74, n. 1.

564. There is a brief autobiography of Šulek in his letter to Ljudevit Gaj, May 16th, 1841, *GPKH*, III, 276-77. For other biographical data: Rudolf Maixner, "Bogoslav Šulek," in Bogoslav Šulek, *Izabrani Članci*, ed. by Rudolf Maixner and Ivan Esih (Zagreb: Jugoslavenska akademija znanosti i umjetnosti, 1952), 7-28; and Jaroslav Šidak, Ljudevit Jonke and Stjepan Horvatić, "Bogoslav Šulek," *Enciklopedija Jugoslavije*, VIII, 273-74.

565. Vjekoslav Babukić, "Sabor čitaonica ilirske zagrebske," *Danica* VIG (February 6, 1841), 21-24.

566. Jakša Ravlić "Ustanove i društva kulture u vrijeme hrvatskog narodnog preporoda," *Kolo*, new series V (1966), p. 364.

567. See description of Karadžić's visit to Zagreb in 1838, in Viktor Novak, *Vuk i Hrvati* (Beograd, Naučno delo, 1967), p. 196.

568. Ravlić, "Ustanove i društva kulture," 363-65.

569. I. I. Sreznevskij, "Putevnja pis'ma," *Zhivaia Starina* (St. Petersburg) Vol. III (1893), p. 34. See also Horvat, "Gaj," p. 285.

570. Horvat, "Gaj," p. 330, n. 1.

571. *Ibid.*, pp. 285-86, and letters from Ambroz Vranyczany to Ljudevit Gaj, March 15th, 1841, March 30th, 1841 and a third which is undated but appears to have been written in March 1841, *GPKH*, XXVI, 486-87.

572. For a detailed study of Ambroz Vranyczany and his role in the Illyrian Movement see: Igor Karaman, "Ambroz Vranican lik jednoga hrvatskog trgovca i društvenog radnika u preporodno doba," in his *Privreda i društvo Hrvatske u 19. stoljeću* (Zagreb: Skolska knjiga, 1972), 23-37.

573. Šurmin, *Hrvatski preporod*, II, 255-56.

574. Jerome Blum, *Noble Landowners and Agriculture in Austria, 1815-1848*, The Johns Hopkins University Series in Historical and Political Science, Series LXV, No. 2 (Baltimore: The Johns Hopkins Press, 1948), pp. 132-44.

575. Horvat, "Gaj," 284.

576. Kedourie, Nationalism, 89-91.

577. For example: "Aristocracy is the opposite of democracy just as cream is the opposite of milk, but where would the cream be if there were not milk?" SKZ, *LG*R 4701 A II 22. There is also a longer anaology describing travelers on a hot day seeking shade in a field with only one big tree which cannot shade them all. It would be better, wrote Gaj, to cut down the big tree and plant many smaller ones so that all can be shaded. *Ibid.*

578. Ljudevit Gaj, unpublished fragment beginning, "Kad bi mogli izabrat izmedju ustava . . .," *Ibid.*

579. S. Urlić, *Pabirci o Ljudevitu Gaju po dalmatinskim listovima i koledarima za ilirskog doba* (Zadar: Brzotiskom Kat. Hrv. tiskarne, 1909), pp. 5-6, 28.

580. See Barac, *Hrvatska književnost*, I, pp. 106-108.

581. Anonymous, "Dvestoletna uspomena Ivana Gundulića," *Danica,* IV (December 22, 1838), p. 200.

582. Horvat, "Gaj," p. 294.

583. Letter, Antun Kaznačić to Ljudevit Gaj, January 14, 1843, *GPKH,* VI, 103.

584. Novak, *Vuk i Hrvati,* 244-48.

585. Horvat, "Gaj," 293.

586. Mirko Šandor de Gyala in 1837, while a student in Pest, announced that he planned to publish an almanac entitled *Zabavnik ilirski,* and a reprint of Zrinski's "Adrianskog mora sirena," and called for subscribers. Since the costs of subscription were quite low, five forints for the Zrinski work, Sandor got a great deal of money which he seems to have spent on himself in Pest, and the works never appeared. See *GPKH,* XXVI, 172-73, n. 5, and 446-67, n. 1.

587. Sreznevskij, "Putevnja pis'ma," pp. 155-56.

588. See Rade Petrović, *Nacionalno pitanje u Dalmaciji u XIX stoljeću,* (Sarajevo: Svjetlost, 1968), pp. 65-72; and Vinko Foretić, "Prva faza hrvatskog narodnog preporoda u Dalmaciji (do sredine 19. stoljeća)," *Kolo,* new series IV (1966), pp. 158-69.

589. Mamužić, "Ilirizam i Srbi" 51-67.

590. *Ibid.,* pp. 79-89. See Ljudevit Gaj, "Proglas," *Danica,* V (November 23, 1839), p. 187, in which he argues that the Cyrillic alphabet and the Latin alphabet are like the right and left hands, the one (Cyrillic) near the heart and the other (Latin) a link with the European world.

591. Ljudevit Gaj, "Proglas," *Danica,* V (November 23, 1839), 186.

592. Kulakovskij, *Illirizm',* p. 235.

593. Anton Slodnjak, "Ilirizam kod Slovenaca," *Enciklopedija Jugoslavije,* IV, 342-43.

594. *Ibid.*

595. The most vivid statement of Kopitar's views can be found in a letter to I. Kristijanović, September 11, 1838. I Kukuljević-Sakcinski, "Prinesci za povjest književnosti hrvatske," p. 101. For further elaboration see his letters to Kristijanović from 1838 to 1841. *Ibid.,* pp. 98-110.

596. The Franciscans were the most important preservers and transmitters of Christian culture and national identity in Bosnia-Hercegovina. See Kulakovskij, *Illirizm',* pp. 213-15, and the brief but useful article by O. Knezović, "Ilirizam u Bosni," *Hrvatska prosvjeta,* XIX (1931), 129-31.

597. Šišić, *Hrvatska povijest,* III, pp. 269-70. See also article by Ilija Kecmanović, "Rafo Barišić," *Enciklopedija Jugoslavije,* I, 368-69.

598. On the Magyarones see: Vaso Bogdanov, *Historija političkih stranaka u Hrvatskoj* (Zagreb: Novinarsko izdavačko poduzeće, 1958), ch. 5; Horvat, "Gaj," pp. 288-90; Šišić, *Hrvatska povijest,* III, pp. 239-43; and Jaroslav Šidak, "Prilozi historiji stranačkih odnosa u Hrvatskoj uoči 1848," *Historijski zbornik,* XIII (1960), pp. 167-206.

599. Šišić, *Hrvatska povijest,* III, 246.

600. None of the sources are explicit about exactly when the Party was formed, who was present when it was planned or where the first meeting was held. On the Illyrian Party see: Bogdanov, chs. 4 and 8: Šišić, *Hrvatska povijest,* III, pp. 246-44; Ferdo Šišić, "Hrvatski ilirizam, njegova politička strana," *Bratstvo,* XXVII (1921), pp. 134-75; and Šidak, "Prilozi historiji stranačkih odnosa."

601. Šišić, *Hrvatska povijest,* III, p. 247.

602. The letter from Baroness Sermage to Ljudevit Gaj authorizing him to represent her at the Varazdin election, dated October 17th, 1841, is in *GPKH,* XXVI, 422. For authorization by Abbott Krizmanić see Horvat, "Gaj," p. 311.

603. Branko Drechsler, *Stanko Vraz* (Zagreb: Matica Hrvatska i Slovenska, 1909), pp. 80-81. The reasons for the growing antagonism between Gaj and Vraz will be discussed below.

604. Milan Prelog, *Slavenska renesansa, 1780-1848* (Zagreb: Jugoslavenska štampa D.D., 1924), pp. 138-39.

605. Horvat, "Gaj," 301.

606. Prelog, *Slavenska renesansa,* p. 138.

607. Ivan Kukuljević, "Pozdrav Visokoučenomu Gospodinu Ivanu Kolaru." *Danica,* VII (18. Rujna, 1841), 153-54.

608. Milivoj Srepel, ed. and trans., "Slika Zagrebačkoga života g. 1841 i slavni pjesnik Jan Kollár," p. 229.

609. Jaroslav Šidak, " 'Tajna politika' Lj. Gaja i postanak njegovih 'Memoranduma' Knezu Metternichu 1846-47," *Archivski Vjesnik* Zagreb) XIII (1970), 407-08.

610. Letter, Stefan Herkalović to Ljudevic Gaj, October 1st, 1841, *GPKH,* XXVI, 212-13.

611. On the foreign policy of Prince Czartoryski see M. Kukiel, *Czartoryski and European Unity, 1770-1861* (Princeton: Princeton University Press, 1955), chs. 16 and 17; and Marceli Handelsman, *Czartoryski, Nicolas Ier et la Question du Proche Orient* (Paris: Editions A. Pedone, 1934), ch. 1.

612. Kukiel, *Czartoryski,* 209-13; and Handelsman, *Czartoryski,* 11-13.

613. See Václav Žaček, "Češke, i poljske učešće u postanku 'Načertanija,' " *Historijski zbornik,* XVI (1963), pp. 37-42, and Dragoslav Stranjaković, *Vlada Ustavobranitelja, 1842-1853* (Beograd: Narodna Štamparija, 1932), p. 32.

614. Bogoslav Šulek, *Šta naměravaju Iliri* (Beograd: Upraviteljstvenoi Knjigopečatniji, 1844), reprinted in Jakša Ravlić, ed., *Hrvatski narodni preporod Pet stoljeća hrvatske književnosti,* vols. 28 and 29 (Zagreb: Zora and Matica Hrvatska, 1965), II, p. 207.

615. Šišić, *Hrvatska povijest,* III, 250.

616. *Ibid.,* 251.

617. Šidak, "Prilozi historiji stranačkih odnosa," 167-68, 183-84.

618. See unpublished memoir by Ljudevit Vukotinović, "Magyaronstvo u Hrvatskoj," (1876), JAZU, Ostavština Ljudevit Vukotinovića, XV 17 c.

619. In fact in some areas in the first years of Party life the nobles were in the minority. This can be seen in a list drawn up in the early 1840's on the basis of class origin and political sympathy. In the town of Zagreb, for instance, and its immediate surroundings, there were 33 nobles and 65 non-nobles who supported the Illyrian Party. "Popis plemića i neplemića u Zagreb i okolici Varaždin i Karlovcu, po stranačkoj pripadnosti," SKZ, *LG*R4709 No. 70.

620. Šidak, "Prilozi historiji stranačkih odnosa," 184.

621. Dragutin Rakovac, *Mali katekizam za velike ljude* (Zagreb: Ljudevit Gaj, 1842), this is reprinted in Ravlić, *Hrvatski narodni preporod,* II, 85-97; Ljudevit Vukotinović, "Ilirizam i kroatizam," *Kolo,* II (1842), 109-115,

reprinted in Ravlić, II, 66-73; and Ivan Kukuljević, "Die Nationalität in Kroatien und Slavonien," *Luna*(1842), Nos. 77-78, 329-333, 338-344.

622. Rakovac, *Mali katekizam*, p. 91.

623. *Ibid.*, p. 96.

624. *Ibid.*, pp. 90, 96.

625. Vukotinović, "Ilirizam i kroatizam," in Ravlić, ed., *Hrvatski narodni preporod*, II, 69-71.

626. *Ibid.*, p. 67.

627. Ivan Kukuljević, "Die Nationalität in Kroatien und Slavonien," *Luna* II (1842), Nos. 77-78, pp. 329-33.

628. *Ibid.*, p. 330.

629. *Ibid.*, pp. 331-32. "Croatian" was too directly associated with Civil Croatia and might not appeal to Civil Slavonia, nor as he suggested in a footnote to the preceding page, to the people of the Military Frontier of Dalmatia. *Ibid.*, p. 330, footnote.

630. *Ibid.*, p. 339.

631. Rakovac, *Mali katekizam*, pp. 93-94; and Vukotinović, "Ilirizam i kroatizam," p. 72.

632. Rakovac, *Mali katekizam*, p. 93.

633. *Ibid.*, p. 94.

634. Miskolczy, *Horvát Kérdes*, I, p. 606.

635. Horvat, "Gaj," p. 314.

636. Letter, Maksimilijan Prica to Ljudevit Gaj, April 1st, 1847, *GPKH*, XXVI, 401.

637. Miskolczy, *Horvát Kérdes*, II, 1-10.

638. *Ibid.*, pp. 10-15.

639. JAZU, *OFS*, 84 B 26 (Copy).

640. JAZU, *OFS*, 84 B 27. Nesselrode carefully omitted from the dispatch any mention of the role Gaj suggested Russia should play in a Balkan uprising.

641. Šišić, *Hrvatska povijest*, III, pp. 272-73.

642. See reports of Stjepan Moyses, Karl Klobučarić, Bishop Haulik, and the Governor of Dalmatia, and the conclusions of the Austrian cabinet, in 1840-1842, JAZU, *OFS*, 84 26, 28, 29, 30, 31 (Copies).

643. Miskolczy, *Horvát Kérdes*, II, 16-20.

644. *Ibid.*, p. 22.

645. *Ibid.*, p. 25.

646. *Ibid.*, p. 27.

647. On this aspect of the Gaj-Vraz conflict see: Drechsler, *Stanko Vraz*, 80-86.

648. *Ibid.*, 93.

649. Horvat, "Gaj," 306.

650. *Ibid.*, 307.

651. See *Ibid.*

652. Horvat, "Gaj," 316, 318.

653. Ravlić, "Povijest Matica Hrvatske," 34.

654. Ravlić, "Ilirska čitaonica u Zagrebu," 198.

655. Horvat, "Gaj," 323.

656. Letters, Stefan Herkalović to Ljudevit Gaj, December 16, 1838; March 4, 1839; May 16 20, 1849; September 19 October 1, 1841; and December 11 27, 1842. *GPKH*, XVI, 206-13.

657. On the *Ustavobranitelji* see: Stranjaković, *Vlada Ustavobranitelja,* and Slobodan Jovanović, *Ustavobranitelji i njihova vlada* (Beograd: Gece Kon, 1933).

658. This is mentioned in the letter from Stefan Herkalović to Ljudevit Gaj, September 19 October 1, 1841, *GPKH,* XXVI, 213.

659. *Ibid.,* p. 206, n. 1.

660. *Ibid.,* p. 92, n. 1.

661. Letter, Ljudevit Gaj to Stefan Herkalović, November 23rd, 1842, as cited in Ljubomir Durković-Jakšić, *Branislav* (Beograd: Naučna knjiga, 1968), p. 14. See also Vojislav J. Vucković, "Učese Hrvata u pripremi Garašaninovog 'Načertanija,' " *Jugoslovenska revija za medjunarodno pravo* (Beograd), I (1954), br. 3, 49.

662. Đurković-Jakšić, *Branislav,* 14.

663. Žaček, "Češko i poljsko učešće," 45, 48.

664. Gaj's requests for gifts of money and Cyrillic type from the Serbs are discussed in detail in Ljubomir Durković-Jakšić, "Gajev pokušaj da izdaje 'Narodne Novine' ćirilicom," *Istoriski časopis* (Beograd) IV (1952-53), 95-129., and Šidak, " 'Tajna politika,' " 420.

665. Deželić, "Gaj o sebi," *Dragoljub,* 1895, p. 44. See discussion of this in Šidak, "Tajna politika," p. 411.

666. The Zach correspondence forms the basis of Žaček's two articles, "Česko i poljsko učešće," and "Česká účast při pokusech o politické sblížení Charvátů a Srbů v. 40 letech 19. století," *Slovanské historické studie* (Prague), VI (1966), 55-91. It is also used by Durković-Jakšić in his *Branislav,* together with material from the Serbian archives.

667. See *GPKH,* XXVI, p. 213.

668. Report of František Zach to M. Czajkovski of Februrary 24, 1844, as cited in Žaček, "Česko i poljsko učešće," p. 45; and his report of March 23, 1844, as cited in Durković-Jakšić, *Branislav,* 150. On Herkalović's testimony, see Letter, Ilija Garšanin to Stojan Simić, May 21, 1848, *Prepiska Ilije Garašanina,* edited by Grgur Jakšić, (Beograd: Srpske Akademije Nauke, 1950), I, 165.

669. Šidak, "Tajna politika," p. 410.

670. *Ibid.,* p. 409.

671. Ljudevit Gaj, "Proglas za prvu polovinu devetogodišneg tečaja 1843 Iliriskih Narodnih Novina i Danice Ilirske," *Novine,* VIII (December 7, 1842), flyer.

CHAPTER X

672. Miskokzy, *Horvát Kérdes,* II, No. 54, 31-33.

673. *Ibid.,* No. 72, 176-95.

674. *Ibid.,* p. 190. The criminal suit against Gaj was opened on May 21, 1843.

675. *Ibid.,* No. 71, 173-75.

676. *Ibid.,* p. 173.

677. The Croatian deputies were: Herman Bužan, Karlo Klobučarić and Metel Ožegović. See Šišić, *Hrvatska povijest,* III, 285-94.

678. Ivan Kukuljević, Speech to the Croatian *Sabor,* May 2nd, 1843, in Ravlic, *Hrvatski narodni preporod,* II, 158.

679. *Ibid.,* 161.

680. Horvat, "Gaj," p. 341. See also Šidak, "Pokret i Drašković," pp. 191-92; and letters, Janko Drašković to Metel Ožegović of 1843 and 1844, *GPKH,* I, 254-61.

681. Jaroslav Šidak, "Politička djelatnost Ivana Kukuljevića Sakcinskoga," in his *Studije iz hrvatske povijesti,* pp. 221-34.

682. For biographies of Kulmer see: Jaroslav Šidak, "Kulmer, Franjo," *Encikopedija Jugoslavije* V, 447-48; and Alfred Makanec, "Kulmerova pisma Banu Jelačiću 1848. (30. III.-29.XII.), *Narodna starina* IX (1937), 33, 33-43.

683. Šidak, "Kulmer," 447.

684. For others in this group see Ljudevit Vukotinović, "Magjaronstvo u Hrvatskoj," JAZU, *OLV,* XV No. 17 c; and Šidak, "Stranačko odnosi" 180.

685. See Šidak, "Tajna politika," 410-11.

686. For a variety of responses from Illyrians blaming Gaj see Šišić, *Hrvatska povijest,* III, pp. 275-78.

687. As cited in Horvat, "Gaj," 337.

688. Letter, Janko Drašković to Ljudevit Gaj, (1843), *GPKH,* XXVI, 143.

689. See for example Letters, Janko Drašković to Anton Vakanović; the one of October 27th, 1844, *GPKH,* III, 230; and the one from 1843 cited in Šišić, *Hrvatska povijest,* III, 230.

690. Jaroslav Šidak, "O uredniku" i značenju ilirskog "Branislava" (1844-45), *Historijski zbornik* IV (1961), p. 79.

691. Horvat, "Gaj," 341.

692. See, Letter, Ambroz Vranyczany to Ljudevit Gaj, March 4, 1844, *GPKH,* VI, 292-93. Nugent was active in Gaj's secret politics in Serbia. On Nugent see: Ferdo Hauptman, "Korespondencija grofa Alberta Nugenta iz god. 1848," *Arhivist* (Belgrade) I (1951), 21-23, and Neustadter, *Ban Jelačić,* I, pp. 191, 195.

693. Horvat, "Gaj," pp. 344-45. This is reflected in the Gaj correspondence from 1843-1845, in *GPKH,* XXVI.

694. Ljudevit Gaj, "Očitovanje," *Novine,* (March 19, 1844), p. 77.

695. Žaček, "Česko i poljsko učešće," pp. 42-44.

696. This letter is described in the January report of Zach to M. Czajkowski, Zach's immediate superior in the Czartoryski organization. Zach's report is reproduced as an appendix to *Ibid.,* pp. 55-56.

697. Žaček, "Česko i poljsko učešće," p. 45.

698. *Ibid.,* p. 46.

699. There is a wealth of literature on Garašanin's "Načertanija," and its relationship to the Croats and the Polish emigration. The most important articles are very well discussed in Niksa Stančić, "Problem "Načertanija" Ilije Garasanina u našoj historiografiji," *Historijski zbornik,* XXI-XXII (1968-69) 179-196. The texts of Zach's original plan and Garašanin's "Načertanija" are given in: Dragoslav Stranjaković, "Kako je postalo Garašaninovo 'Načertanije,' " *Spomenik SAN* (Belgrade) XCI (1939), pp. 75-102. See also the comparison of the two texts and analysis of the Greater Serb emphasis of "Načertanija" in: Charles Jelavich, "Garašanins Načertanije und das

grosserbisches Programm, *Südostforschungen* XXVII (1968) 131-47.

700. F. Zach, "Plan," in Stranjaković, "Kako je postalo," 92-96.

701. *Ibid.*, p. 92. See also Šidak, "Tajna politika," p. 409.

702. Šidak, "Tajna politika," pp. 409-10.

703. The many complaints from Zagreb about Mačhik's incompetence are discussed in Miskolczy, *Horvát Kérdes*, II, NO. 80, 256-59. The most detailed and amusing descriptions of his lack of language, skills are found in the article "Zagrebačka cenzura," *Branislav*, 11-14. *Branislav*, is reprinted in full as an appendix to Durković-Jakšić, *Branislav*.

704. "Uvod," and "Zagrebačka cenzura," *Branislav*, pp. 1, 11.

705. See *Spisi Zagrebačke Zenzure*, SKZ R 3991: 1843, No. 7, 9, 38, 539; 1844, No. 439, 480, 600.

706. Early in 1843, Čavlović was accused by some Magyarone students of plotting to kill the Emperor in revenge for the Imperial decree forbidding the use of the Illyrian name. Although charges could not be proven against him by the Investigating Commission, he was bitter about the affair, Buturac, *Povijest zbora duhovne mladeži*, "31-32; and Letter from Pavao Čavlović to Ljudevit Gaj, November 25th, 1843, *GPKH*, XXVI, p. 125.

707. Durković-Jakšić, *Branislav*, 29; and Šidak, "O uredniku i znacenju," p. 80.

708. Letter from Čavlović to Gaj of December 12th, 1843, *GPKH*, XXVI, 124.

709. (Bogoslav Šulek), *Šta nameravaju Iliri?* in Ravlić, ed., *Hrvatski narodni preporod*, II, 185-208. Date of publication from Durković-Jakšić, *Branislav*, 38.

710. Durković-Jakšić, *Branislav*, 34, 38.

711. Date for commencement of *Branislav* is taken from Durković-Jakšić, *Branislav*, p. 163; date of last issue is from Šidak, "O uredniku i znacenju," p. 87.

712. On the editorship of *Branislav* see Durković-Jakšić, *Branislav*, and Šidak, "O uredniku i značenju," and his "Još jednom o ilirskom 'Branislavu,' " *Historijski zbornik* XVII (1964), 381-92.

713. Šidak, "O uredniku i značenju," p. 83.

714. Šišić, *Hrvatska povijest*, III, p. 373, and Karaman, "Ambroz Vranjičan," 33.

715. Neustaedter, *Le Ban Jelačić*, I, 210-12.

716. Durković-Jakšić, *Branislav*, 34, 190.

717. These proposals were made in "Želja roduljuba," and "Šta valja Harvatom i Slavoncem ponajpre raditi, ako žele naprědovati," *Branislav*, 7-11, 34-36.

718. (Čavlović), "Očitovanje," *Ibid.*, 37. Kukuljević, however, was also involved in *Branislav*, see Šidak, "Politička djelatnost Sakcinskoga," p. 228.

719. Šidak, "Tajna politika," 413-14.

720. Date of arrival from Šidak, " 'Tajna politika,' " 411. Date of departure for Beograd from Durković-Jakšić, *Branislav*, 175. For a brief biography of Rieth Reiner see Durković-Jakšić, *Branislav*, 173-74.

721. On the reliability of Rieth Reiner's reports see: Šidak, " 'Tajna politika,' " 412-13; and Handelsman, *Czartoryski*, 89.

722. Šidak, " 'Tajna politika,' " 411-12.

723. *Ibid.*

724. Durković-Jakšić, *Branislav*, 175.

725. Miskolczy, *Horvát Kérdes,* II, No. 83, p. 267.

726. HHSA, *Informationsbüro,* Korrespondenz mit Engelshofer, 1844, VII-XII, No. 731.

727. This is discussed in a later report. See HHSA, Ad. Min. P.S. 95, *Berichte aus Belgrad,* October 19, 1847, No. 275.

728. HHSA, *Informationsbüro,* Korrespondenz mit der Polizeihofstelle, 1845, VIII-XII, June 15, July 7, July 26, 1845.

729. *Ibid.,* Metternich, Comments on the Report of July 26th, 1845.

730. Šidak, "Tajna politika," 412.

731. *Ibid.,* 411-12, based on Zach's report No. 5465 in Czartoryski's correspondence. Zach, is apparently the only source for Woronicz's visit and he was only partially informed of the reasons for the visit.

732. On Magyar reforms, those proposed and those accepted see C.A. Macartney, *The Habsburg Empire, 1790-1918* (New York: the Macmillan Company, 1969), 290-292; and Springer, *Geschichte Oesterreichs,* II, 59-90.

733. Šišić, *Hrvatska povijest,* III, 286-87.

734. Jaroslav Šidak, "Sabor Hrvatsko-Dalmatinsko-Slavonski," *Enciklopedija Jugoslavije,* VIII, 124.

735. For the full text of this law see Schlitter, Jans, *Aus Oesterreichs Vormärz,* (Wien: Amalthea Verlay, 1930), III, 89-90.

736. *Ibid.,* 25.

737. Macartney, *The Habsburg Empire,* 293.

738. On details of meetings between leaders of the National Party and members of the State Conference see letters from Ambroz Vranyczany to Ljudevit Gaj from Vienna between February and December of 1844. *GPKH,* VI, 283-98.

739. Anonymous Memorandum dated 1843, Miskolczy, *Horvát Kérdes,* II, 81 a, pp. 244-50; action on it, *Ibid.,* No. 81 b and 82, pp. 250-61. Horvat believes the authors were Klobučarić, Vranyczany and Kulmer. Horvat, "Gaj," p. 361.

740. Šišić, *Hrvatska povijest,* III, 373-74.

741. *Novine,* XI (February 12, 1845), p. 43.

742. Letter, Franjo Kulmer to Ljudevit Gaj, January 15, 1845. *GPKH,* VI, 111-13.

743. Although Kulmer's letter to Gaj was decisive in stopping *Branislav,* there were other contributing factors which are discussed in Durković-Jakšić, *Branislav,* 190-194.

744. See Tomislav Jakić, "Štamparstvo i knjižarstvo u Zagrebu za vrijeme ilirskog preporoda," *Kolo,* new series IV (1966), 370-71.

745. This can most clearly be seen if we examine the professions of the better known Illyrian writers: *Lawyers and government officials* —L. Vukotinović, T. Blažek, I. Mažuranić, A. Nemčić, I. Kukuljević (after 1841): *Military Officers:* P. Preradović, M. Bogović, O. Ostrožinski, I, Trnski: *Priests:* P. Stoos, M. Topalović, S. Marjanović, G. Martić, J. Tordinac; *Professors, teachers, editors, secretaries of cultural societies:* V. Babukić, S. Vraz, A. Mažuranić, D. Rakovac, L. Gaj, F. Kurelac, B. Šulek: *Doctors:* D. Demeter, A. Kaznačić.

746. Horvat, *Povijest novinstva,* p. 124.

747. See Barac, *Hrvatska književnost,* I, pp. 142-44.

748. On the problems of the writers see: Ljudevit Vukotinović, "Lětne

misli," *Danica,* IX (1843), pp. 153-33, 202-204.

749. Fedor Vassil'evitch Chizhov, "Puteshestvie po slavjanskim zemljam," ed. by E.I. Riabova with intro. by I.V. Kozemko, *Slavjanski Arhiv* (Moscow) IV-v (1958), 127-260.

750. *Ibid.*, pp. 149-51.

751. *Ibid.*, p. 151.

752. *Ibid.*, p. 161.

753. *Ibid.*

754. *Ibid.*, p. 163.

755. *Ibid.*, p. 164.

756. *Ibid.*, p. 171.

757. *Ibid.*, p. 177.

758. Horvat, "Gaj," 362-63.

759. Šišić, *Hrvatska povijest,* III, 411-19; and Horvat, "Gaj," 367.

760. Neustaedter, *Ban Jelačić,* I, 234-40.

761. *Ibid.*

762. For a description of the funeral see Šišić, *Hrvatska povijest,* III, 425-26. The draft copy of the announcement of the date and place of the funeral, in Gaj's handwriting with corrections by Ban Haller, is in SKZ, *LG* R 4709 36 a b.

763. *Novine,* XI (August 20, 1845), pp. 271-72.

764. Šišić, *Hrvatska povijest,* III, 429.

765. See letter from Vranyczany, who was a member of one of the delegations to Gaj reporting on their negotiations, August 13th, 1845. *GPKH,* VI, 300-01.

766. Šišić, *Hrvatska povijest,* III, p. 441. The most detailed coverage of the *Sabor* can be found in *Novine,* XI (1845), the September and October issues.

767. Šidak, "Sabor Hrvatsko Dalmatinsko-Slavonski," *Enciklopedija Jugoslavije,* VII, 124; and Šišić, *Hrvatska povijest,* III, 448-50.

768. Šišić, *Hrvatska povijest,* III, p. 455.

769. *Ibid.*, pp. 451-61.

770. Miskolczy, *Horvat Kerdes,* II, No. 91, 327-39.

771. Schlitter, *Vormärz,* III, 26.

772. Miskolczy, *Horvát Kérdes,* II, p. 555. Gaj's petition to Apponyi is reprinted in full on pages 555-56.

773. Ljudevit Gaj, "Dogodovština Ilirie Velike," *SKZ,* LG R 4701 A V.24; and (Bogoslav Šulek) Dr. L. Gaj, "Bibliotheca Illyrica sive Catalogus librarum impressorum et manuscriptorum de rebus Illyricus tractantium, ab Illyris concinnatorum, in typographiis Illyricis excussorum et lingua Illyrica quibusvis dialectis scriptorum," SKZ, *LG* R 4703 a.

774. Ljudevit Gaj, "Kratki uvod u dogodovščinu Velike Ilirie," *Danica,* II (May 30, 1836), pp. 70-72; "Tko su bili stari Iliri," *Ibid.*, V (March 9, through April 13, 1839), pp. 37-39, 41-43, 46-48, 49-51, 58-59.

775. Horvat, "Gaj," p. 360.

776. The most famous Magyar pamphlet is: Stephan von Horvat, *Über Croatien als eine durch Unterjochung erworbene ungarische Provinz und des Königreiches Ungarn wirklichen Theil* (Leipzig: Kohler, 1844). This work sparked a whole series of pamphlets on both sides and led the Croats to begin serious historical research. See Šišić, *Hrvatska povijest,* III, pp. 475-78.

777. Deželić, "Gaj," p. 191.

778. "Kakovi su bili pradavnji Iliri," and "Harvati obladavši Avare u Ilirii ureda dvie daržave medju Dravom i morem jadranskiem," Gaj, "Dogodov-

ština,'' I No. 3, and sec. 6. While Gaj does not cite Šafařík for the theory of Southern Slav immigration to the Balkans, he seems to refer in sec. 6 to Šafařík's recent work: Pavel Joseph (Šafařík) Schafarik, *Slawische Alterthümer* (2 vols., Leipzig: Wilhelm Engelsmann, 1843-1844), II, 226-30, 256-57.

779. Gaj, ''Dogodovština,'' date the manuscript passed the Vienna censor is on the concluding page.

790. Miskolczy, *Horvát Kérdes,* II, No. 114, 522-24.

781. SKZ LG R4701 A V 15.

782. *Ibid.*

783. Šišić, *Hrvatska povijest,* III, 466-67.

784. *Ibid.*, 468.

785. Springer, *Geschichte Oesterreichs,* II, 115.

786. Ljudevit Gaj, ''Proglas i pravac našega teženja,'' *Novine,* XI (December 13, 1845), pp. 416-18.

787. *Ibid.*, p. 417.

788. *Ibid.*, p. 418.

CHAPTER XI

789. Ljudevit Gaj, ''Odgovor gospodinu Kossuthu,'' *Novine,* XII (January 14, 1845), pp. 13-15.

790. *Ibid.*, p. 13.

791. *Ibid.*

792. This meeting is described in *Novine,* XI (December 17, 1845), pp. 442-44.

793. Gaj, ''Odgovor,'' pp. 13-14.

794. *Ibid.*, p. 14.

795. Letter of F. Kulmer to L. Gaj, January 19, (1846), *GPKH,* VI, pp. 113-15.

796. *Ibid.*, p. 115. The second part of Kossuth's article appeared in *Budapest Hirado* in January 1846. This is mentioned in *Novine,* XII (January 28, 1846), p. 32.

797. Lajos Kossuth, ''Odgovor na běsnito ilirske stranke u Križevačkoj varmedija,'' *Novine,* XII (January 24 to February 11, 1846), pp. 25-27, 49.

798. *Ibid.*, p. 26.

799. *Ibid.*, p. 27.

800. Ljudevit Gaj, ''Odgovor gospodinu Kossuthu na drugi njegov članak,'' *Novine,* XII (February 21 to February 28, 1846), pp. 63-64, 67-68, 71-72.

801. The original contract for the house is the first document in the collection of papers relating to Gaj's later bankruptcy: SKZ *LG*R4707 a 1.

802. Horvat, ''Gaj,'' pp. 380-81.

803. Ravlić, ''Ilirska čitaonica,'' p. 204.

804. Šidak, ''Tajna politika,'' p. 415.

805. Letter F. Kulmer to Minister Gervay, April 9, 1846. Miskolczy, *Horvát Kérdes,* II, p. 465.

806. *Ibid.*
807. Šidak, "Tajna politika," p. 416.
808. *Ibid.*, n. 98. Cf. Dragutin Stranjaković, "Srbija privlačna središte Jugoslavena, 1844-48," *Srpski književni glasnik*, LXI (1940), p. 518, who states that Gaj received this sum in March.
809. Žaček, "Česká účast," p. 82.
810. *Ibid.*, p. 419.
811. (F. Zach), "Einiges zur Bezeichnung der in Serbian zu verfolgenden Politik," is found in Gaj's *Ostavština*, SKZ, *LG*, R 4701 B I 6 and reprinted in Šidak, "Tajna politika," 423-28. Gaj's report to Metternich, "Memorandum ueber die vom 22. April bis 7 Mai in Serbien gemachte Reise des Dr. Ljudevit Gaj" is published in: Vladimir Čorović, "Jedan memorandum Lj. Gaja o prilikama u Srbiji iz 1846 g.," *Spomenik SAN* (Belgrade), 62 (1925), 71-77.
812. Gaj, "Memorandum," p. 74.
813. *Ibid.*
814. *Ibid.*, p. 76.
815. On the historiographical controversy over the "real" motives behind Gaj's Memorandum of 1846, see Šidak, "Tajna politika," pp. 397-403.
816. Gaj's comments on Zach would lead Metternich to write to the Austrian Consul in Belgrade the next year, explaining that he had received conflicting reports about Zach, some saying that he was the Belgrade representative of the Polish emigration, and another "reliable" source, quoting here the words of Gaj's Memorandum, as a man of moderate liberal ideas, in no way affiliated with the Poles. Letter, Metternich to Mayerhofer, October 12, 1847. HHSA, Politisches Arhiv Serbien, 1838-1847, 6 a.
817. Šidak, "Tajna politika," p. 418.
818. Žaček, "Česká účast," p. 85.
819. Šidak, "Tajna politika," p. 418.
820. Žaček, "Česká účast," p. 84, n. 59.
821. Metternich mentions only two trips made by Gaj to Serbia, one in 1846 and one in 1847, in his letter supporting Gaj's petition for Austrian financial support, which was written to Minister Kübeck on October 8, 1847, in Aleksa Ivić, *Arhivska gradja o jugoslovenskim književnim i kulturnim radnicima*, (Belgrade), III (1932), p. 67.
822. Horvat, "Gaj," p. 387.
823. Ljudevit Jonke, "Vrazova Korespondencija u 'Muzeju Kraljevine Češke,' " *GPKH*, XIII, pp. 138-51.
824. Ravlić, "Ilirska čitaonica," p. 208.
825. Jonke, "Vrazova korespondencija," pp. 138-39.
826. Ljudevit Gaj to Paulina Gaj, June 4, 1846. SKZ *LG* R 4702 a 8.
827. *Ibid.*
828. Letter, Stanko Vraz to František Palacký, August 4, 1846, in Jonke, "Vrazova korespondencija," pp. 141-48; and letter, Stanko Vraz to P.J. Šafařík, July 25, 1846. *Ibid.*, p. 150.
829. Ivo Frangeš, "Ivan Mažuranić," in *Ivan Mažuranić, Matija Mažuranić*, ed. Ivo Frangeš, *Pet stoljeća hrvatske književnosti*, XXXII, pp. 7-34.
830. Barac, *Hrvatska književnost*, I, 293.
831. "Parva izvorna ilirske opera . . ." *Danica*, XII (April 4 to 11, 1846),

pp. 53-56, 57-60. See also Nenad Turkalj, " 'Ljubav i zloba' Vatroslava Lisinskog — opera hrvatskog bidermajera," *Kolo,* IV, n.s. (1966), pp. 321-32.

832. "Parva izvorna ilirske opera . . .," p. 53.

833. On the role of *Zora Dalmatinska* see: Tade Čolak, " 'Zora Dalmatinska' i njen doprinos književnost ilirskog pokreta," *Kolo,* IV n.s., pp. 284-98.

834. On the square which is today known as Ilirski trg.

835. Ravlić, Ustanove i društva kulture," p. 354.

836. *Ibid.,* p. 365.

837. Ravlić, "Ilirska čitaonica," p. 207.

838. Ravlić, "Ustanove i društva kulture," p. 363.

839. "Svečano otvorenje dvorane zagrebačke u narodnome domu," *Danica,* XIII (February 13, 1847), pp. 27-28.

840. The Croatian text of the Hungarian Conservative Platform is reprinted in Šidak "Stranački odnosi," pp. 194-203.

841. Letter of Janko Drašković and Juraj Oršić to Ljudevit Gaj, February 10, 1847, *GPKH,* VI, 56-57.

842. Šidak, "Stranački odnosi," p. 189.

843. Both are reprinted in *Ibid.,* Vukotinović, "Program Narodne Stranke Ilirske od god. 1846," pp. 203-05; and Kušlan, "Nacrt Proglasa Hrvatsko-Slavonskih "Napredovaca," pp. 205-07.

844. Horvat, "Gaj," pp. 379-80.

845. Letter, Bogoslav Šulek to Ljudevit Gaj, December 14, 1845. *GPKH,* II, 282-84.

846. Letter, Bogoslav Šulek to Ljudevit Gaj, May 30, 1848. *Ibid.,* p. 285.

847. *Ibid.*

848. Letter, Stepan Pejaković to Ljudevit Gaj, March 23, 1847. *GPKH,* XXVI, pp. 382-85.

849. Pavel Suyer, "Ljudevit Gaj i obnova poslejednoga gradečkoga magistrata," *Historijski zbornik* IX (1956), 66.

850. *Ibid.*

851. Šidak, "Tajna politika," p. 420.

852. Durković-Jakšić, "Gajev pokušaj," p. 105.

853. Stranjaković, "Srbija privlačno središte," p. 518.

854. The text of this petition is in Durković-Jakšić, "Gajev pokušaj," p. 106.

855. *Ibid.,* p. 107.

856. *Ibid.,* p. 107-09.

857. Gaj as quoted by Zach in his report of July 12, 1844, from Žaček, "Česká účast," 88.

858. (F. Zach), "Skizze," SKZ *LG* R4701 B I 6. It is reprinted in Šidak, "Tajna politika," pp. 428-33.

859. In Gaj's petition for support dated September 4, 1847, Miskolczy, *Horvát Kérdes,* II, pp. 555-56; and in Metternich's letter to Kübeck on October 8, 1847, Ivić, *Gradja,* III, pp. 67-68.

860. Suyer, "Ljudevit Gaj," p. 64.

861. Horvat, *Povijest novinstva,* p. 145, and *GPKH,* XXVI, pp. 110-11, n. 2.

862. The purchase of a *Schnellpresse* is mentioned in a letter from Gaj's press manager Th. Claus, to Gaj, on November 8, 1847. *GPKH,* XXVI, pp. 109-10.

863. Letter, Ljudevit Gaj and L.L. Suppan to King Ferdinand, August 5, 1847. SKZ R 4704 22 — copy.
864. Šidak, "Tajna politika," p. 421.
865. Ljudevit Gaj, Petition of September 4, 1847. Miskolczy, *Horvát Kérdes,* II, 555-56.
866. The pressures from his wife are clearly revealed in her letters. She complains of the creditors, then asks for more for the house. She was already counting on how to spend the anticipated money and continually counseled her husband to think first of the needs of the family. See letters, Paulina Gaj to Ljudevit Gaj, October 8, and 19, 1847. SKZ, *LG,* R4702 b 174.
867. Ferdo Šišić "Knez Miloš u Zagrebu 1848," *Jugosloslovenska njiva,* VIII (1924), p. 52.
868. Documents relating to the action on Gaj's petition are published in Miskolczy, *Horvát Kérdes,* II, pp. 553-59; and Ivić, *Gradja,* III, pp. 65-73.
869. Letter, Metternich to Kübeck, October 8, 1847, Ivic, *Gradja,* III, pp. 67-68.
870. Miskolczy, *Horvát Kérdes,* II, p. 559.
871. Ivić, *Gradja,* III, p. 70.
872. Šišić, *Hrvatska povijest,* III, pp. 492-93.
873. *Ibid.,* p. 495.
874. Ferdo Šišić, "Hrvati i Madžari uoči sukoba, 1848," *Jugoslavenska njiva,* VII (1923), pp. 411-13.
875. *Ibid.,* p. 411.
876. See letter from Alexander Fodrocy to Ljudevit Gaj, December 24, 1847, *GPKH,* XXVI, p. 159.
877. Letter of November 30, 1847, and letter of December 3, 1847. SKZ, *LG* R4700 A 36-37.
878. SKZ *LG* R 4700 A 36.
879. SKZ *LG* R 4700 A 37.
880. Letter, Alexander Fodrocy to Ljudevit Gaj, December 24, 1847, *GPKH,* XXVI, p. 159.
881. This can also be seen in the letter of March 16, 1848 from the *Sabor* deputy Josip Bunyik to Gaj, asking for his advice now that Hungary was in revolution; *GPKH,* XXVI, p. 84.

CHAPTER XII

882. "Saborski věsti," *Novine,* XIV (January 22 through February 9, 1848), pp. 25-27, 29-31, 31-35, 41-42, 45-46.
883. Up to this time Magyar had not been taught in the primary schools.
884. This speech is reprinted in *Novine,* XIV (March 11-15, 1848), pp. 83, 87-88.
885. Neustaedeter, *Jelačić,* I, pp. 320-21.
886. *Novine,* XIV (March 18, 1848), p. 91.
887. Neustaedter, *Jelačić,* I, p. 314.
888. Ferdo Šišić, "Kako je Jelačić postao banom," *Jugoslovenska njiva,* VII (1923), pp. 174-75.

889. *Ibid.*, p. 175.
890. This proclamation dated March 21, 1848, is printed in *Novine,* XIV (March 27, 1848), p. 104.
891. This proclamation dated March 20, 1848, is printed in *Ibid.*, (March 25, 1848), p. 99.
892. Šišić, "Kako je Jelačić," p. 176.
893. *Ibid.*
894. Bogoslav Šulek, "Stampa je slobodna . . ." *Novine,* XIV (March 22, 1848), p. 95.
895. Neustaedter, *Jelačić,* I, p. 343.
896. Mijo Krešić, *Autobiografija* (Zagreb: Dionička tiskara, 1898), pp. 86-88.
897. *Ibid.*, pp. 88.
898. Neustaedter, *Jelačić,* I, pp. 359-60.
899. Krešić, *Autobiography,* p. 86.
900. Neustaedter, *Jelačić,* I, p. 360.
901. He tried to get them to include an article appointing a vice-Ban, but the others voted against it, fearing Gaj would be chosen for that post. *Ibid.*, pp. 347-48.
902. *Ibid.*, p. 344 and Horvat, "Gaj," p. 426.
903. This notebook is part of the collection of documents and bills "Računi hrvatske deputacije u Becu, 26. III-IV 1848," SKZ, *LG*R 4709 74.
904. Neustaedter, *Jelačić,* I, p. 349.
905. *Novine,* XIV (March 27, 1848), p. 100.
906. Neustaedter, *Jelačić,* I, p. 350.
907. The full text is printed in *Novine* as a flyer to the March 27, 1848 issue; and in Šidak, ed., *Hrvatska čitanka,* I, pp. 190-93. The original text with last minute revisions is in Gaj's papers, SKZ *LG*R4709 4.
908. Neustaedter, *Jelačić,* I, pp. 354-56.
909. *Ibid.*, p. 357.
910. As cited in Šišić, "Kako je Jelačić," p. 180.
911. Krešić, *Autobiografija,* p. 90.
912. *Ibid.*, p. 91.
913. Šišić, "Kako je Jelačić," p. 488.
914. The text of "Želje hrvatskog naroda," the revised Demands, dated Vienna, March 31, 1848, is in SKZ, *LG*R4709 42.
915. Šišić, "Kako je Jelačić," p. 181.
916. *Novine,* XIV (April 6, 1848), pp. 121-22.
917. Jaroslav Šidak, "Haulik, Juraj de Varallya," *Enciklopedija Jugoslavije,* III, pp. 664-65.
918. See Neustaedter, *Jelačić,* I, pp. 379-80.
919. Jurai Lahner, "Gajeva demonstracija protiv zagrebačkome biskupu Hauliku," *Croatia Sacra* (1944), pp. 61-63.
920. Neustaeder, *Jelačić,* I, p. 381.
921. *Ibid.*, p. 383.
922. Krešić, *Autobiografija,* p. 93.
923. *Ibid.*
924. Šišić, "Kako je Jelačić," pp. 181-82.
925. Neustaedter, *Jelačić,* I, p. 375.
926. Gaj's appointment is announced in a formal letter from Jelačić dated

April 22, 1848. It is printed in *Novine* XIV (April 22, 1848), p. 149. The appointment was made on April 14th.

927. The text of the April 25th decree is in *Novine,* XIV (April 27, 1848), p. 157.

928. Ferdo Šišić, "Knez Miloš u Zagrebu. 1848," *Jugoslovenska Njiva,* VIII (1924), p. 222.

929. Johann Franz Freiherr von Kempen, *Das Tagebuch des Polizeiministers Kempen von 1848 bis 1859,* J.K. Mayr, ed., (Vienna: Oesterreichischer Bundesverlag, 1931), p. 94.

930. Neustaedter, *Jelačić,* I, p. 368.

931. The text of this decree is reprinted as a flyer to the May 16th issue of *Novine.*

932. Ljudevit Gaj, "Idee der Erhebung," SKZ *LG*R4701 A V 10.

933. Gunther E. Rothenberg, "Jelačić, the Croatian Military Border and the Intervention against Hungary in 1848." *Austrian History Yearbook,* I (1965), pp. 51-52.

934. *Ibid.,* pp. 52-53.

935. *Ibid.,* p. 52; and Neustaedter, *Jelačić,* I, pp. 417-423.

936. Letter, Matija Ban to Stjepan Knjičanin, April 1848, as cited in Ferdo Šišić, *Jugoslovensko misao* (Belgrade: Balkanski institut, 1938), pp. 107-08.

937. See Jaroslav Šidak, "Austroslavizam i slavenski Kongres u Pragu 1848," *Historijski pregled* (Zagreb), 1960, pp. 204-19.

938. Letter, Ban Josip Jelačić to Prince Alexander Karadordević', May 16, 1848, SKZ *LG* R4709 55.

939. Arpad Lebl, *Revolucionarni pokret u Vojvodini 1848-1849 — nacrt studije,* (Novi Sad, Matica Srpska, 1960), pp. 43-44.

939. See Nikola Petrović, "Rajačić, Josif," *Enciklopedija Jugoslavije,* VII, pp. 32-33.

941. Documents used by the Special Commission (1848) and Zagreb Town Court (1848-49) to investigate the Miloš affair, as well as newly discovered documents relating to the case, are located in SKZ *LG*R4700 b. There are in all 72 documents; the majority of these, Nos. 1-40, are published in Đuro Šurmin, "Knez Miloš u Zagrebu 1848" *Spomenik SAN* (Belgrade), LIV (1922); letters to Gaj in *GPKH,* XXVI. For Knez Miloš's testimony see: Milenko Vesnić, "Knez Miloš u Ljubljani," *Delo* (Belgrade), I (1894), 64-76; and Milan Milićević, ed., "Knez Miloš prica o sebi," *Spomenik SAN,* XXI (1893) 37-42. A useful contemporary account is Neustaedter, *Ban Jelačić,* I, ch. XIII; on the judicial proceedings; Pavao Suyer, "Posao Milošiansko-Gajanski pred gradskim magistratrom," *Historijski zbornik,* V (1952), 85-101. For the diplomatic background: Ferdo Šišić, "Knez Miloš u Zagrebu," *Jugoslovenska Njiva,* VIII (1924), 49-53, 139-44, 188-94, 219-30, 265-75, 297-302, 341-46. The best general synthesis is Norvat, "Gaj," pp. 440-54.

942. Letter, Ljudevit Gaj to Ivan Kamauf, Zagreb town judge, May 23, 1848. SKZ LG R4700 b 13.

943. Letter, Stefan Herkalović to Ljudevit Gaj, 17 26 June, 1848. *Ibid.,* R4700 b 5. This letter is reprinted in Šurmin, "Knez Miloš," p. 7.

944. Letter, Ilija Garašanin to Stojan Šimić, May 21, April 20, 1848. Garašanin, *Prepiska,* I, pp. 165-67.

945. *Ibid.,* p. 166.

946. Herkalović then returned to Zagreb, handed 500 ducats over to Gaj and

went with the other 500 to Paris. This of course raises the question of whether Herkalović was a reliable representative of Gaj in 1848 and whether his testimony to Garašanin was tru in relation to Gaj's desire to create a Southern Slav kingdom with the Serbian dynasty at the helm. On Herkalović's return see: Jeustaedter, *Jelačić,* I, p. 441.

947. See the bitter attack on Haulik and his criticism of Church reform in *Novine* XIV (April 29, 1848), p. 161.

948. Horvat, "Gaj," p. 448. See description of the Patriarch's arrival on June 2nd and the festivities in his honor. *Novine,* XIV (June 3, 1848), p. 225.

949. Kempen, *Tagebuch,* p. 95.

950. Letter, Franjo Kulmer to Metel Ožegović, May 24, 1848, as cited in Horvat, "Gaj," p. 444.

951. See description in *Novine,* XIV (June 6, 1848), pp. 229-31.

952. *Novine,* XIV (June 8 and 10, 1848), pp. 233-34, 237-39.

953. SKZ *LG*R4700 b 16, reprinted in Šurmin "Knez Miloš," p. 9.

954. Neustaedter, *Jelačić,* I, p. 442.

955. *Ibid.*

956. Šuyer, "Posao Milošiansko-Gajanski," p. 84.

957. Šurmin, "Knez Miloš," p. 9.

958. SKZ *LG* R4700 b 26.

959. *Novine,* XIV (June 22, 1848), p. 258.

960. Šurmin, "Knez Miloš," p. 10.

961. Prince Mihail Obrenović, "Pro memoria," SKZ *LG*R4700 b 25.

962. Šurmin, "Knez Miloš," p. 28.

963. Suyer, "Posao Milošiansko-Gajanski," p. 92.

964. Prince Miloš's first accusation of June 8, 1848 is in SKZ *LG* R 4700 b 16, and the full one, made in Innsbruck on June 30, 1848 is in *Ibid.,* b 40.

965. There is a copy of this issue in SKZ *LG*R 4700 b 49.

966. The document referring to this debt dates from 1857, it was paid in three installments and this was, apparently, the last. Promissory note from Ljudevit Gaj to Prince Miloš Obrenović referring to a debt of 7,500 forints which would be repaid through Dr. Tkalac, June 3, 1857. SKZ LG R4700 b 70.

967. On Gaj's later life see Horvat, "Gaj," pp. 497-590; and Deželić, *Gaj,* pp. 176-93.

968. Đ. Šurmin, "Gaj o sebi," *Dragoljub*(1864), p. 34.

969. *Ibid.*

970. Horvat, *Povijest novinstva,* p. 177.

971. Horvat, "Gaj," p. 497.

972. This is now the Zagreb cemetary.

973. Horvat, "Gaj," p. 499.

974. Some documents relating to this arrest are found in SKZ, LG R4700 b 51-60, 67-69; others from the Vienna archives which are no longer extant — the originals were destroyed in World War II — are published in Ivić, *Gradja,* II, pp. 183-209.

975. SKZ *LG* R4700 b 59.

976. Horvat, "Gaj," p. 540.

977. *Ibid.*

978. Fran Kurelac, "Slova nad grobom Ljudevita Gaja . . ." (Zagreb: Narodne tiskarnica Lj. Gaja, 1872), reprinted in Ježić, ed., *Ilirska antologija,*

pp. 157-59.

979. "I.Z.". "Dr. Ljudevit Gaj," *Vienac,* IV (1872), p. 264.

980. Bogoslav Šulek, "Krive Mesije," in his *Izabrani Članci,* ed. R. Maixner and I. Esig, pp. 117-120. It was originally published in No. 102 of *Slavenski jug* in 1849. Šulek later wrote in a much different way about Gaj, see especially the article written after Gaj's death in 1872, "Ljudevit Gaj," in *Izabrani Članci,* pp. 223-232.

BIBLIOGRAPHY

Introductory Note to Bibliography

The bibliography is organized in the following manner:

I. *Archival Materials*
II. *Published Primary Sources*
  A. The Gaj Correspondence
  B. Other Selected Contemporary Correspondence
  C. Gaj's Posthumously Published Autobiographical Fragments
  D. Selected Contemporary Pamphlets, Articles, Books and Memoirs
  E. Contemporary Newspapers — Selected
  F. Published Documents and Collections of Primary Sources
  G. Statistics
III. *Selected Bibliography of Secondary Works*
  A. Unpublished Works
  B. Books
  C. Encyclopedias and Biographical Dictionaries
  D. Articles

There are four periodicals which are cited frequently in the bibliography. I will use the following abbreviated forms when referring to them:

JOURNAL	*ABBREVIATION*
Gradja za povijest književnosti hrvatske (1897)	*GPKH*
Ljetopis Jugoslavenske akademije znanosti i umjetnosti (1877-)	*Ljetopis*
Rad Jugoslavenske akademije znanosti i umjetnosti (1867-)	*Rad*
Spomenik Srpske Kraljevske akademije *Spomenik Srpske akademije nauka* (Belgrade, 1888-)	*Spomenik SAN*

All periodicals not published in Zagreb will have the place of publication given unless they are well known journals such as *The Slavonic and East European Review.*

I. ARCHIVAL MATERIALS

Sveučilišna knjižnica, Zagreb (Zagreb University Library)

Ostavština Ljudevita Gaja (Collected Papers of Ljudevit Gaj).

This collection was purchased from Velimir Gaj in 1896. It contains more than 10,000 documents: family papers, Gaj's unpublished poetry, prose, fragments and notes, material related to *Danica* and *Novine,* the remaining Gaj correspondence, Gaj's historiographical and political writings, copies and drafts of petitions to governmental officials and agencies, and financial records. Although rich in material about the Illyrian Movement, this collection was known only in part before World War II. In 1946, archivists began to sort and index the material, completing this project in the mid 1960's.

Pisma Julijane Gaj (Letters of Julijana Gaj).

This collection was discovered during the indexing of the Gaj papers in the late 1940's. It contains letters to Julijana Gaj from various members of her family, and letters from Julijana, the majority to her son Ljudevit.

Ostavština Vjekoslava Babukića (Collected Papers of Vjekoslav Babukić).

In addition to useful letters and manuscripts, this contains the archives of the Zagreb Reading Club.

Ostavština Antuna Mažuranića (Collected Papers of Antun Mažuranić).

Although relatively unknown, A. Mažuranić was a central figure in Illyrian cultural life and his Papers are especially useful for the early years of the Illyrian Movement.

Ostavština Antona Vakanovića (Collected Papers of Anton Vakanović).

Contains part of the Vakanović diary and several manuscripts written in later life about the first years of the Movement.

Societas culturae illyricae.

Documents relating to the establishment of an Illyian cultural society.

Spisi Zagrebačke Censure (Acts of the Zagreb Censor)

Includes lists of forbidden books, orders, copies of letters to and from Gaj about what could and could not be printed by his press, as well as detailed information about the number of copies of *Novine* and *Danica* to be submitted to the censor. This collection reflects the changing policy of the Hungarian and Austrian authorities toward the Movement and clarifies the role of Stjepan Moyses.

Državni Arhiv, Zagreb, (Zagreb State Archives).

Acta Gajana

A much smaller collection than that of the University Library, poorly indexed. It contains some of Gaj's German manuscripts, family pictures, family papers, bills, editions of *Danica* and *Novine* with corrections by the censor in 1845 and 1846, odes to Gaj, and copies of some of Gaj's published works.

Jugoslavenska akademije znanosti i umjetnosti (Yugoslav Academy of Sciences and Arts).

Ostavština Ljudevita Vukotinovića (Collected Papers of Ljudevit Vukotinović)

Contains some unpublished materials about the Illyrian period.

Ostavština Ferde Šišića (Collected Papers of Ferdo Šišić)

Šišić was, perhaps, the most prolific Croatian historian. His collected papers will serve as an important source and guide for future historians. The most important part for me of this enormous collections was B 84, which consisted primarily of the correspondance between Sedlnitzky, Kollowrat, Moyses and others about Gaj and the Illyrian Movement. Although many of these documents are copies, there are also some original documents. This collection assumes even more importance today because the Haus, Hof und Staatsarchiv in Vienna has either lost or misplaced several entire folios of this correspondence.

Haus, Hof und Staatsarchiv, Vienna.
Akta Min. Kollowrat (MKA)
Contains documents indicating that Kollowrat was, for a while a protector of the Movement.
Informationsburo, Korrespondenz mit der Polizeihofstelle. Karton 7-19 (1832-1848).
Although many of these documents have been published by Miskolczy and A. Ivić, this collection, consisting primarily of reports from local police agents, has much useful material on the spread of the Illyrian Movement and Austrian attitudes toward Gaj.
Informationsburo, Politisches Archiv Serbien (1838-1847).
Reports of Austrian consular and border officials on Serbia, and letters to them. This collection is quite small but contains some useful material on F. Zach and his Croatian contacts.

II. *PUBLISHED PRIMARY SOURCES*

A. THE GAJ CORRESPONDENCE

Deželic, Velimir, Ed. "Pisma pisana dru. Ljudevitu Gaju i njeki njegovi sastavci." with an introduction by the editor, *GPKH*, VI (1909).
The first collection of the Gaj correspondence, mostly letters written to Gaj by prominent figures in Illyrian cultural and political life, and foreigners. The transcriptions are occasionally inaccurate, notes are minimal, although the brief introduction discusses some of the letters.
Drechsler (Vodnik, Branko.), ed. "Iz ostavštine Frana Kurelca," *GPKH*, VIII (1910), 1-80.
Fancev, Franjo, "Iz prepiske Fra. Martina Nedića Ljudevitu Gaju," *Ljetopis*, XXXVII (1922), 96-101.
Horvat, Josip and Ravlić, Jakša, eds., "Pisma Ljudevitu Gaju," *GPKH*, XXVI (1956).
This completes the publication of letters found in the Gaj *ostavština*, primarily from less known people. It contains invaluable biographical notes, and the transcriptions are reliable.
Ježić, Slavko, ed. "Neka pisma Srba i o Srbima iz ostavštine Lj. Gaja," *Glasnik istorijskog društva* (Novi Sad), VIII (1935), 281-86.
Šrepel, M. ed. "Iz ostavštine D. Rakovca," *GPKH*, III (1901), 242-92.
Šrepel, M. ed. "Iz ostavštine B. Šuleka," *GPKH*, II (1899) 274-88.

B. *OTHER SELECTED CONTEMPORARY CORRESPONDENCE*

Brlić, Ignjat Alojzije. *Pisma sinu Andriji Torkvatu 1836-1855.* 2 vols. Zagreb: Hrvatskog izdavalačkog bibliografskog zavoda, 1942-43.

Garašanin, Ilija. *Prepiska Ilje Garašanina.* ed. by Grgur Jakšić. Belgrade: Srpska akademija nauka, 1950.

Hauptman, Ferdo, ed. "Korespondencija grofa Alberta Nugenta iz godine 1848," *Arhivist* (Belgrade), I (1951), 21-57.

Jonke, Ljudevit, ed. "Vrazova korespondencija u 'Muzeju kraljevine Česke'," *GPKH,* XIII (1938), 137-51.

Karadžić, Vuk. *Vukova prepiska.* 7 vols. Belgrade: Državna štamparija Kraljevine Srbije, 1907-1913.

Makanec, Alfred, ed. "Kulmerova pisma Banu Jelačiću 1848 (30. III.-29. XII), *Narodna starina,* XII (1937), 33-52; XIII (1938), 151-56; XIV (1939), 65-92.

Šafařík, Pavel Josef. *Korespondence Pavla Josefa Šafaříka: Th. I, Vzájemné dopisy P.J. Šafaříka s. Ruskými učenci (1825-1861).* Edited by Vl. Francev. 2 vols. Sbirka pramenú k poznáni literániho života v Čechách na Morave a v Slezsku. Prague: České akademie, 1927.

See especially Šafařík's letters to Pogodin in which he often discusses Gaj.

Sreznevskii, I.I. "Putevnya pis'ma," *Zhivaia Starına* (St. Petersburg), III (1893), 20-63, 139-79.

Vakanović, Antun, "Iz ostavštine A. Vakanovića," *GPKH,* II (1899), 213-33.

Vraz, Stanko. *Děla Stanka Vraza.* 2nd ed. Vol. V. Zagreb: Matica Hrvatska, 1877.

C. *GAJ'S POSTHUMOUSLY PUBLISHED AUTOBIOGRAPHICAL FRAGMENTS*

Gaj, Ljudevit. "Vjekopisni moj nacrtak," *Knjižnica Gajeva.* Ed. by Velimir Gaj. Zagreb: Narodne tiskare Gajeve, 1875, XVIII-XXX.

Dezelić, Duro Stj. ed. "Gaj o sebi," *Dragoljub ili upisnik kalendar za javne urede,* (1893), 53-57, (1894), 44-45.

Transcriptions of Gaj's comments about himself and his work, made when Gaj was an old man.

D. *SELECTED CONTEMPORARY PAMPHLETS, ARTICLES, BOOKS AND MEMOIRS*

I have not included any articles published in *Danica* or *Novine.*

Ban, Matija. "Ljudevit Gaj," *Vijenac,* IV (1872), 331-2.

Chizhov, Fedor Vassil'evitch. "Puteshestvie po slavjanskim zemljam," *Slavjanski Arhiv* (Moscow), IV-V (1958), 127-260. Ed. by E.I. Riabova, with an intro. by I.V. Kozmenko.

Derkoosz, Joanne. *Genius patriae super dormientibus suis filiis, seu folium patrioticum, pro incolis regnorum Croatiae, Dalmatiae, & Slavoniae in exitandum excolendae linguae patriae.* Zagreb: F. Suppan, 1832. Reprinted in *GPKH,* XII, 273-96.

(Drašković, Janko) *Disertacija iliti razgovor, darovan gospodi poklisarom zakonskim i budućem zakonotvorcem Kraljevinah nasih, za buducu Dietu ungarsku odaslanem, držan po jednom starom domorodcu Kraljevinah ovih.* Karlovac: Joh. Nep. Prettner, 1832. Reprinted in *GPKH,* XII, 297-315.

Drechsler (Vodnik, Branko.), ed. "Ljudevit Gaj. Silhoueta iz dnevnika A.T. Brlića," *Jugoslavenska njiva,* X (1926), 56-64.

G.,L.o. (Gaj, Ljudevit). *Kratka osnova horvatsko-slavenskoga pravopisana poleg mudrolubneh narodneh i prigospodarneh temelov i zrokov.* Buda: Kralevskoga Vseučilišča, 1830. Reprinted in *GPKH,* XII, 221-35.

Herder, Johann Gottfried. *Briefe zur Beförderung der Humanität: Erste Sammlung. Sämmtliche Werke.* Ed. by B. Suphan. Vol. VII. Berlin: Weidmannische Buchhandlung, 1881, 1-73.

Herder, Johann Gottfried. *Ideen zur Philosophie der Geschichte der Menschheit. Sämmtliche Werke.* Ed. by B. Suphan. Vol. XIV. Berlin: Weidmannische Buchhandlung, 1909.

(Hoić, S.) *Sollen wir Magyaren werden? Funf Briefe geschrieben aus Pesth an einen Freund an der Theis, von D.H.* Karlstadt: Joh. Nep. Prettner, 1833.

Horvát, Stepan von. *Über Croatien als eine durch Unterjochung erworbene ungarische Provinz und des Konigreichs Ungarn wirklichen Theil.* Translated from the Hungarian. Leipzig: Karl Franz Kohler, 1844.

Kempen von Fichtenstamm, Johann Franz. *Das Tagebuch des Polizeiministers Kempen von 1848 bis 1859.* Ed. with intro. by Josef Karl Mayr. Vienna: Oesterreichischer Bundesverlag, 1931.

Kollár, Jan. "O literarnéj vzájemnosti mezi kmeny a nářečimi slavskymi," *Hronka* (Prague), II (1836), 39-55. Reprinted in *Rozpravy o slovanské vzájemnosti.* Ed. by Miloš Weingart. Knihovna Slovanského ustavu, sv. l. Prague: Slovanské ustav. 1929, pp. 31-160.

Kollár, Jan. *Über die literarische Wechselseitigkeit zwishen den verschiedenen Stammen und Mundarten der slawischen Nation.* Pest: von Trattner, 1837. Reprinted in *Rozpravy o slovanské vzájamnosti,* pp. 32-166.

Kopitar, Bart. (Jernej.) *Grammatik der Slawischen Sprache in Krain, Kärnten und Steyermark.* Ljubljana: Wilhelm Heinrich Korn, 1808.

Kopitar, Jernej. *Spisov.* Ed. by R. Nahtigal. II, del. Ljublijana: Slovenska akademija znanosti in umetnosti, 1945.

Krešić, Mijo. *Autobiografija.* Zagreb: Dionicka tiskara, 1898.

Kurelac, Fran. *Slova nad grobom Ljudevita Gaja izgovorena Franom Kurelcom.* Zagreb: Narodna tiskarnica Lj. Gaja, 1872. Reprinted in Slavko Ježić, ed. *Ilirska antologija.* Zagreb: Minerva, 1934, 157-59.

Mažuranic. Antun. *Temelj ilirskoga i latinskoga jezika za početnike.* Zagreb: Ljudevit Gaj, 1839.

Mihanović, Antun. *Reč domovini od hasnovitost pisanja vu domorodnem jeziku.* Vienna: I. Schnirer, 1815. Reprinted in *GPKH,* XII, 118-123.

Nagy, Anton. *Novi i stari kalendar horvatski.* Buda: z vugerske mudrovućne kupčine Peštanske slovi, 1817. Reprinted in *GPKH,* XII, 124-29.

Neustaedter, Josip Baron. *Le Ban Jelačić et les événements en Croatie depuis l'an 1848.* 2 vols. Zagreb: Institut Français, 1940-42.

Memoirs of a German Field Marshal who served many years in the Military Frontier and was close friend of Jelačić.

Paton, A.A. *Highlands and Islands of the Adriatic.* 2 vols. London: Chapman and Hall, 1849. Vol. II, Chapter X.

Travel diary of an Englishman who visited Zagreb in 1847.

Rakovac, Dragutin. "Dnevnik (1842 i 1843)," ed. by E. Laszowski and Velimir Deželić, *Narodna starina*, I (1922), 62-72, 165-85, 283-312.

Rakovac, Dragutin. *Mali katekizam za velike ljude*. Zagreb: Ljudevit Gaj, 1842. Reprinted in J. Ravlic, ed. *Hrvatski narodni preporod*, II, 85-97. (For full citation see II F.)

Šafařík, Pavel Josef. *Geschichte der Slawischen Sprache und Literatur nach allen Mundarten*. 2nd ed. Prague: Friedrich Tempsky, 1869.

An exact reprint of the original.

Šafařík, Pavel Josef. "Über die neueste illyrische Literatur," *Ost und West* (Prague) II (1838), 70-721.

Although Šafařík wrote many articles about the new Illyrian literature, this one deals with Gaj's role.

Šafařík, Pavel Josef. *Slawische Alterthümer*. 2 vols. Leipzig: Wilhelm Engelsmann, 1843-1844, vol. II.

Šenoa, August. "Književna pisma," *Članci i kritike. Sabrana djela Augusta Šenoe*. Ed. by A. Barac. Vol. XIV. Zagreb: Binoza, 1934.

Vivid description of Gaj's personal magnetism as recalled by Šenoa from his gimnazium years.

Šrepel, Milovoj, ed. and trans. "Slika Zagrebačkoga života g. 1841. i slavni pjesnik Jan Kollár," *Stari i novi Zagreb*. Ed. by E. Laszowski. Zagreb: Hrv. štamparskog zavoda D.D., 1925, 227-31.

Section of Kollár's diary dealing with his trip to Zagreb in 1841.

Šulek, Bogoslav. *Izabrani članci*. Ed. by Rudolf Maixner and Ivan Esih. *Noviji pisci Hrvatski*, no. 8. Zagreb: Jugoslavenska akademija znanosti i umjetnosti, 1952.

See expecially "Krive mesije (1849), and "Ljudevit Gaj" (1872)."

Sulek, Bogoslav. *Šta namĕravaju Iliri?* Belgrade: Upraviteljstvena knjigopečatnja, 1844. Reprinted in Ravlić, ed. *Hrvatski narodni preporod*, II, 185-208.

Tkalac, Imbro. *Uspomene iz Hrvatske*. Trans. from the German by Josip Ritig, with notes by Stanko Dvoršak. Zagreb: Matica Hrvatska, 1945.

The Illyrian Movement from the viewpoint of a secondary school student in the 1840's.

Vukotinović, Ljudevit. "Ilirizam i Croatizam," *Kolo*, II (1842), 105-15. Reprinted in Ravlić, ed. *Hrvatski narodni preporod*, II, 66-73.

Vukotinović, Ljudevit. "Uspomena na godine 1833-1835," in Slavko Ježić, ed. *Ilirska antologija*, 154-64. (First published in *Narodne Novine* on January 5, 1885.)

Wilkinson, J. Gardner, Sir. *Dalmatia and Montenegro*. 2 vols. London: John Murray, 1848.

(Zerpak, Edward.) *Geschichte des Illyrismus oder des sudslawischen Antagonismus gegen die Magyaren*. Intro. by W. Wachsmuth. Leipzig: Gustav Mayer, 1849.

Bitter attack by a leading Magyarone.

(Z., I.) "Dr. Ljudevit Gaj," *Vijenac*, IV (1872), 264-6.

E. *CONTEMPORARY NEWSPAPERS AND JOURNALS — SELECTED*

Branislav (Belgrade). (October 1844 to February 1845). Reprinted as an appendix to Ljubomir Durković-Jakšić, *Branislav, prvi jugoslovenski ilegalni list 1844-1845*. Belgrade: Naučna knjiga, 1968, 192-251.

Anonymously edited by Pavao Čavlović.
Danicza Horvatzka, Slavonzka i Dalmatinzka (Jan. to July 1835), *Danica Horvatska, Slavonska i Dalmatinska* (July to Dec. 1835), *Danica ilirska* (1836-1843), *Danica horvatska slavonska i dalmatinska,* (1843-1849). Reprinted by Ivo Frangeš and Mladen Kuzmanović, *et al* eds., Series *Liber Croaticus,* Izdanja Instituta za znanosti o književnosti, Philosophical Faculty of the University of Zagreb. 5 vols. Karlovac: "Ognjen Prica," 1970-1972.
Ed. by Ljudevit Gaj.
Kolo: članci za literaturu, umětnosti i narodni život. 1842-present. Ed. by Stanko Vraz, Dragutin Rakovac and Ljudevit Vukotinović from 1842-1847, then in 1847 when *Kolo* was taken over by Matica ilirska, Vraz became the sole editor. I consulted *Kolo* for the years 1842-1848.
Luna. 1826-1858. Ed. by Franjo Staduar, 1826-1845. First published as a literary journal, *Luna* became the literary supplement of *Agramer Politische Zeitung* when it was founded in 1830. After 1841 *Luna* becaCe an organ of the Magyarone Party, but Illyrians continued to publish it in order to reach the German speaking public. I used *Luna* for 1826-1845.
Novine Horvatzke (1835), *Ilirske narodne novine* (1836-1843), *Narodne novine* (1843-1844), *Novine horvatsko, slavonsko i dalmatinsko* (1844-1849). Ed. by Ljudevit Gaj.
Ost und West: Blätter für Kunst, Literatur und geselliges Leben. Prague: 1837-1846. Ed. by Rudolf Glaser. This journal contains many articles, book reviews and discussions on Illyrian cultural life.

F. *PUBLISHED DOCUMENTS AND COLLECTIONS OF PRIMARY SOURCES*

Ćorović, Vladimir, ed. "Jedan memorandum Lj. Gaja o prilikama u Srbiji iz 1846 g.," *Spomenik SAN* 62 (1925), 71-77.
Despot, Miroslava, ed. *Privreda Hrvatske XVII-XIX. Izvor gradja.* Na izvorima historije, sv. 3. Zagreb: Skolska knjiga, 1957.
Fancev, Franjo, ed. "Dokumenti za naše podrijetlo hrvatskoga preporoda 1789-1832," with an introduction by the editor. *GPKH,* XII (1933).
Francev, Vladimir, ed. "Za biografiju Ljudevita Gaja," *GPKH,* V (1907), 142-47.
Ivić, Aleksa, ed. *Arhivska gradja o jugoslovenskim književnim i kulturnim radnicima.* (Belgrade) II (1931), 183-209; III (1932), 63-92.
Jelavich, Charles, ed. "Garašanins Načertanije und das grosserbisches Programm," *Sudostforschungen,* XXVII (1968), 131-47.
Ježić, Slavko, ed. *Ilirska antologija.* With an introduction and notes. Zagreb: Minerva, 1934.
Milićević, Milan, ed. "Knez Miloš priča o sebi," *Spomenik SAN,* XXI (1893), 37-42.
Miskolczy, Gyula, ed. *A horvát kérdés története és irományai a rendi állam korában.* With a long historical essay. 2 vols. Budapest: Kiadja a Magyar történelmi társulat, 1927-28.
Mosely, Philip E., ed. "A Pan-Slavist Memorandum of Liudevit Gaj in 1838," *The American Historical Review.* 40 (Oct. 1934-July 1935), 704-16.
Ravlić, Jakša, ed. *Hrvatski narodni preporod.* 2 vols. (Pet stoljeća hrvatske knjizevnosti, vols. 28 and 29.) Zagreb: Zora and Matica Hrvatska, 1965.

Stranjaković, Dragoslav, ed. "Kako je postalo Garašaninovo 'Načertanije'," *Spomenik SAN,* XCI (1939), 75-102.
Šidak, Jaroslav, ed. *Historijska čitanka za hrvatsku povijest.* Vol. I. Zagreb: Školska knjiga, 1952.
Šurmin, Duro, ed. "Knez Miloš u Zagrebu 1848," *Spomenik SAN,* LIV (1922), 1-40.
Vesnić, Milenko, ed. "Knez Miloš u Ljubljani," *Delo,* I (1894) (Belgrade), 64-76.

G. *STATISTICS*

Austria. Direction der administrativen Statistik im k.k. Handels-Ministerium. *Mittheilungen aus dem Gebiete der Statistik.* Vol. I (1851).
Austria. Direction der administrativen Statistik im k.k. Ministerium für Handel, Gewerbe, und öffentliche Bauten. *Tafeln zür Statistik der oesterreichischen Monarchie.* Vol. I (1846).
Brachelli, Hugo Franz. *Deutsche Staatenkunde.* Vienna: Wilhelm Braumüller, 1856.
Csaplovics, Johann von. *Gemälde von Ungern.* Two volumes in one. Pest: C.A. Hartleben, 1829.
Fényes, Alexius. *Ungarn im Vormärz.* Leipzig: Friedrich Ludwig Herbig, 1851. (The abridged German translation of *A Magyarország leirása.* Pest: 1847).
Hietzinger, Carl B. *Statistik der Militärgrenze des österreichisches Kaiserthums.* 3 vols. Vienna: Carl Gerold, 1817-23.
Mikhov, Nikola. *La population de la Turquie et de la Bulgarie au XVIIe et XVIIIe s.,* 4 vols. Sofia: Academie Bulgare de Sciences, 1915-1935. Vol. I.

III. SELECTED BIBLIOGRAPHY OF SECONDARY WORKS

Almost every major Croatian literary critic and journalist has at some time written about Gaj and the Illyrian Movement. I have included only those works which offer new facts or challenging interpretations. I have not included works in English or other Western European languages which are simply adaptations or translations of material available in more scholarly form in Croatian, such as the majority of the series of articles in *Le Monde Slave* in 1935.

Due to the difficulties of obtaining full runs of Yugoslav periodicals in this country, I have included reprints of articles in book form when available.

A. *UNPUBLISHED WORKS*

Horvat, Josip. "Ljudevit Gaj, njegov život, njegova doba." Unpublished manuscript, completed in 1959.
If this work is published, it will add much to the literature on Gaj and the Illyrian Movement. Horvat has drawn extensively from the Gaj papers, the correspondence, *Danica* and *Novine,* and other primary and secondary sources. He skillfully shows the interaction between Gaj and his con-

temporaries. This is primarily a biography, a medium in which Horvat excells. He does not analyse the political literature of the time, gives a chronological narrative which does not always follow a theme, nor does he trace the development of Gaj's ideas. What he does do is to give the mood, the setting of Gaj's life. It is inadequately footnoted, there are many small inaccuracies — all of which can be solved by careful editing. Mr. Horvat gave me a copy of this manuscript in 1962, as well as some of the notes he used for writing it.

Bonifačić-Rožin, Nikola. "Odnos Ljudevita Gaja prema narodnom stvaralastvu." A paper delivered on November 9, 1972, in Zagreb at the "Naučni skup o Ljudevitu Gaju," sponsored on the years of the centennial of Gaj's death by the Institute of Croatian History of the University of Zagreb.

B. *BOOKS*

Anderson, M.S. *The Eastern Question.* New York: St. Martin's Press, 1966.

Barac, Antun. *Hrvatska književnost.* Vol. I: *Književnost ilirizma.* Zagreb: Jugoslavenska akademija znanosti i umjetnosti, 1954.

Bićanić, Rudolf. *Doba manufakture u Hrvatskoj i Slavoniji.* (Hrvatska ekonomika na prijelazu iz feudalizma u kapitalizam, Vol. I.) Zagreb: Jugoslavenska akademija znanosti i umjetnosti, 1951.

Bićanić, Rudolf. *Počeci kapitalizma u hrvatskoj ekonomici i politici.* Zagreb: Školska knjiga, 1952.

Blum, Jerome. *Noble Landowners and Agriculture in Austria, 1815-1848.* (The Johns Hopkins University Studies in Historical and Political Sciences, LXV, 2.) Baltimore: The Johns Hopkins Press, 1948.

Bogdanov, Vaso. *Historija političkih stranaka u Hrvatskoj.* Zagreb: Novinarsko izdavacko poduzece, 1958.

Breyer, Blanka. *Das Deutsche Theater in Zagreb, 1780-1840.* Doctoral dissertation, German Department, University of Zagreb, 1937. Published in Zagreb, 1938.

Breyer, Mirko. *Fran Kurelac.* Zagreb: Tipografija, 1939.

Brozović, Dalibor. *Standardni jezik.* Zagreb: Matica Hrvatska, 1970.

Buturac, Josip. *Povijest zbora duhovne mladeži Zagrebačke, 1836-1838.* Zagreb: Dionička tiskara, 1937.

Chadwick, H. Munro. *The Nationalities of Europe and the Growth of National Ideologies.* Cambridge: University Press, 1945.

Cihlar-Nehajev, Milutin. *O stogodišnjici hrvatskoga preporoda.* Zagreb: Narodne novine, 1931.

Cuvaj, Anton. *Gradja za povijest školstva kraljevina Hrvatske i Slavonije.* 8 vols. Zagreb: kr. zemaljske tiskare, 1910-1913, Vols. II and III.

Deutsch, Karl Wolfgang. *Interdisciplinary Bibliography on Nationalism.* Boston: Technology Press of M.I.T., 1956.

Deželić, Velimir. *Dr. Ljudevit Gaj.* Zagreb: Anton Scholz, 1910.

Drechsler (Vodnik, Branko.) *Stanko Vraz.* Zagreb: Matica Hrvatska i Slovenska, 1909.

Durković-Jakšić, Ljubomir. *Branislav, prvi jugoslovenski ilegalni list, 1844-1845.* Belgrade: Naucna knjiga, 1968.

Fadner, Frank. *Seventy Years of Pan-Slavism in Russia, Karazin to Danilevsky, 1800-1879.* Georgetown: Georgetown University Press, 1962.

Fischel, Alfred. *Der Panslawismus bis zum Weltkrieg: Ein geschichtlicher Überblick.* Berlin: J.G. Cotta, 1919.

Gaj, Velimir, ed. *Knjižnica Gajeva.* Zagreb: Narodne tiskare Gajeve, 1875.

Gillies, A. *Herder.* Oxford: Blackwell, 1945.

Grafenauer, Bogo, *et al*, eds. *Historija naroda Jugoslavije.* 2 vols. Zagreb: Školska knjiga, 1953-1959.

Handelsman, Marceli. *Czartoryski, Nicolas Ier et la Question du Proche Orient.* Paris: Editions A. Pedone, 1934.

Hantsch, Hugo. *Die Geschichte Oesterreichs.* Vol. II: *1648-1918.* Graz: Verlag Styria, 1953.

Haumant, Emile. *La Formation de la Yougoslavie.* Institut d' Etudes Slaves de l'Universite de Paris. Paris: Editions Bossards, 1930.

Homan, Balint. *Geschichte des Ungarischen Mittelalters.* Vol. I. Berlin: Walter de Gruyter, 1940.

Horvát, Josip. *Ljudevit Gaj.* Biblioteka Portreti, No. 11. Belgrade: Nolit, 1961.

A popular biography which incorporates some of the insights but little of the substance of Horvat's unpublished biography of Gaj.

Horvát, Josip. *Politicka povijest Hrvátske.* 2 vols. Zagreb: Binoza, 1936-38. Vol. I.

Horvát, Josip. *Povijest novinstva Hrvátske.* Zagreb: Stvarnost, 1962.

Horvath, Michael. *Funfundzwanzig Jahre aus der Geschichte Ungarns.* 2 vol.s Leipzig: F.A. Brockhaus, 1867.

Jagić, Vatroslav. *Izabrani kraci spisi.* Edited by Mihovil Kombol. Zagreb: Matica Hrvatska, 1948.

Jelačić, Aleksije. *Socialni i načionalno-politicki momenti u hrvatskom pokretu god. 1848.* Lwow: Zaklade Narodwego imenia Ossolinskih, 1929.

Ježić, Slavko. *Hrvátska književnost od pocetka do danas, 1100-1941.* Zagreb: A. Velzek, 1944.

Jonke, Ljudevit. *Hrvátski knjizevni jezik 19. i 20. stoljeca.* Zagreb: Matica Hrvatska, 1971.

Jovanovic, Slobodan. *Ustavobranitelji i njihova vlada*(1838-1858) *Sabrana dela.* Vol. V. Belgrade: Gece Kon, 1933.

Kann, Robert A. *The Multinational Empire.* 2 vol.s New York: Columbia University Press, 1950.

Karaman, Igor. *Privreda i društvo Hrvátske u 19. stoljecu.* Vol. 1 of series: Rasprave i clanci, Institute of Croatian History of the University of Zagreb. Zagreb: Skolska knjiga, 1972.

Kedourie, Elie. *Nationalism.* 2nd ed. New York: Fredrick A. Praeger, 1961.

Kidric, France. *Zgodovina Slovenskega šlovstva od zacetkov do Zoisove smrti.* Ljubljana: Matica Slovenska, 1929-1938.

Kiraly, Bela K. *Hungary in the Late Eighteenth Century.* East Central European Studies of Columbia University. New York: Columbia University Press, 1969.

Kiszling, Rudolf. *Die Revolution im Kaisertum Österreich 1848-1849.* Vienna: Universum, 1948.

Klaić, Nada. *Povijest Hrváta u ranom srednjem vijeka.* Zagreb: Školska knjiga, 1971.

Klaić, Vjekoslav. *Život i djela Pavla Rittera Vitezovića* 1652-1713. Zagreb: Matica Hrvátska, 1914.

Kohn, Hans. *The Idea of Nationalism.* New York: Macmillan Co., 1944.

Kohn, Hans. *Pan-Slavism, Its History and Ideology.* Notre Dame, Ind.: University of Notre Dame Press, 1953.

Kombol, Mihovil. *Povijest hrvdtske književnosti do preporoda.* 2nd. revised edition. Zagreb: Matica Hrvátska, 1961.

Kozina, Antun. *Krapina i okolice kroz stoljeća.* Varaždin: Narodna tiskara, 1960.

Kukiel, M. *Czartoryski and European Unity* 1770-1861. Princeton University Press, 1955.

Kulakovskij, Platon. *Illirizm'.* Warsaw: Tipografija Varsavskoga ucebnago okruga, 1894.

Lebl, Arpad. *Revolucionarni pokret u Vojvodini 1848-1849 — nacrt studije,* Novi Sad: Matica Srpska, 1960.

Leschilovskaia, Inna Ivanovna. *Illirizm.* Slavic Institute of Akademie Nauk, SSSR. Moscow: Nauka, 1968.

Lorković, Mladen. *Narod i zemlja Hrvata.* Zagreb: Matica Hrvatska, 1939.

Lozovina, Vinko. *Dalmacija u hrvatskoj književnosti.* Zagreb: Matica Hrvatska, 1936.

Macartney, C.A., *The Habsburg Empire.* New York: The Macmillan Company, 1969.

Marczali, Henry. *Hungary in the Eighteenth Century.* Cambridge: University Press, 1910.

Marx, Julius. *Die Österreichische Zensur im Vormarz.* Vienna: Verlag für Geschichte und Politik, 1959.

Miskolczy, Julius (Gyula). *Ungarn in der Habsburger-Monarchie.* Vienna: Verlag Herold, 1959.

Mosely, Philip E. *Russian Diplomacy and the Opening of the Eastern Question in 1838 and 1839.* Cambridge, Mass.: Harvard University Press, 1934.

Novak, Grga. *Proslost Dalmacije.* 2 vols. Zagreb: Bibliografskog zavoda, 1944, Vol. II.

Novak, Viktor. *Vuk i Hrvati.* Belgrade: Naucno delo, 1967.

Ortner, Stjepan. *Dr. Ljudevit Gaj prvi hrvatski bibliofil.* Zagreb: F. Bogović, 1902.

Petre, F. *Poizkus ilirizma pri Slovencih (1835-1839).* Ljublijana: Matica Slovenska, 1939.

Petrović, Rade. *Nacionalno pitanje u Dalmaciji u XIX stoljecu.* Sarajevo: Svjetlost, 1968.

Petrovich, Michael Boro. *The Emergence of Russian Panslavism,* 1856-1870. New York: Columbia University Press, 1956.

Prelog, Milan. *Slavenska renesansa, 1780-1848.* Zagreb: Jugoslavenske stampe D.D., 1924.

Rothenberg, Gunther Eric. *The Austrian Military Border in Croatia, 1552-1747.* Illinois Studies in the Social Sciences, No. 8. Urbana, Ill.: University of Illinois Press, 1960.

Rothenberg, Gunther Eric. *The Military Border in Croatia, 1740-1881.* Chicago: University of Chicago Press, 1966.

Schlitter, Hans. *Aus Österreichs Vormarz.* Vol. III: *Ungarn.* Vienna: Amalthea Verlag, 1920.

Schwicker, Johann Heinrich. *Geschichte der Ungarischen Literatur.* Leipzig: Wilhelm Friedrich, 1889.

Skerlić, Jovan. *Istorija nove srpske književnosti.* 3rd. ed. Belgrade: Rad, 1953.

Slodnjak, Anton. *Geschichte der Slowenischen Literatur.* (Grundriss der Slawischen Philologie und Kulturgeschichte.) Berlin: Walter de Gruyter, 1958.

Smičiklas, Tade and Markovic, Franjo. *Matica Hrvátska od godine 1842. do godine 1892.- Spomen-knjiga.* Zagreb: Matica Hrvatska, 1882.

Smičiklas, Tade. *Povijest Hrvatska.* 2 vols. Zagreb: Matica Hrvatska, 1879-1882.

Smičiklas, Tade. *Život i djela Vjekoslava Babukića.* Zagreb: Narodne Novine, 1876.

Součkova, Milada. *The Czech Romantics.* 'S Gravenhage: Mouton and Co., 1958.

Springer, Anton. *Geschichte Oesterreichs seit dem Wiener Frieden 1809.* 2 vols. Leipzig: S. Hirzel, 1863.

Stojanović, Ljubomir. *Život i rad Vuka Stefanovića Karadžića.* Belgrade: Makarija, 1927.

Stranjaković, Dragoslav. *Vlada Ustavobranitelja, 1842-1853.* Belgrade: Narodna stamparija, 1932.

Şzekfü, Jules. *État et Nation.* Paris: Les Presses Universitaires, 1945.

Šidak, Jaroslav, *et al,* eds. *Spomenica u povodu proslave 300- godišnjice Sveučilista U Zagrebu.* 2 vols. Zagreb: Jugoslavenska akademija znanosti i umjetnosti, 1969. Vol. I.

Šidak, Jaroslav. *Studije iz hrvatske povijesti XIX. stoljeća.* Vol. 2 of series: Rasprave i članci, Institute of Croatian History of the University of Zagreb. Zagreb: Grafički zavod Hrvatske, 1973.

Šišić, Ferdinand von (Ferdo.) *Geschichte der Kroaten: Erster Theil.* Zagreb: L. Hartmann, 1917.

Šišić, Ferdo. *Hrvatska povijest.* 3 vols. Zagreb: Dionička tiskara, 1906-1913. Vol. III.

Šišić, Ferdo. *Jugoslovenska misao: istorija ideje jugoslovenskog narodnog ujedinjenja i oslobodjenja od 1790-1918.* Biblioteka Balkan i Balkanci, br. 3-4. Belgrade: Balkanskog instituta, 1937.

Šišić, Ferdo. *Pregled povijesti hrvatskoga naroda.* Edited with notes by Jaroslav Šidak. Zagreb: Matica Hrvatska, 1962.

Šurmin, Duro. *Hrvatski preporod.* 2 vols. Zagreb: Dionička tiskara, 1903-1904.

Tomasevich, Jozo. *Peasants, Politics and Economic Change in Yugoslavia.* Stanford: Stanford University Press, 1955.

Uhrlirz, Karl and Matilde. *Handbuch der Geschichte Oesterreichs und seiner Nachbarländer Böhmen und Ungarn.* Vol. II, 1 Theil. Vienna: Universitätsbuchhandlung Leuschner und Lubensky, 1930.

Urlić, S. *Pabirci o Ljudevitu Gaju po dalmatinskim listovima i koledarima za ilirskog doba.* Zadar: Kat. Hrv. tiskarne, 1909.

Zwitter, Fran, Šidak, Jaroslav and Bogdanov, Vaso. *Les problemes nationaux dans la Monarchie des Habsbourgs.* Belgrade: Comité National Yougoslave des Sciences Historiques, 1960.

C. *ENCYCLOPEDIAS AND BIOGRAPHICAL DICTIONARIES*

Krleža, Miroslav *et al,* eds. *Enciklopedija Jugoslavije.* 8 vols. Zagreb: Leksikografskog zavoda, 1955-1970.

An outstanding work whose contributors have been drawn from among the

most distinguished scholars in Yugoslavia. I especially recommend the articles by Jaroslav Šidak on "Ljudevit Gaj," and "Ilirski Pokret." as excellent introductions to the subject of this study.
Stanojević, Stanoje, ed. *Narodna enciklopedija srpsko-hrvatsko-slovenačka.* 4 vols. Zagreb: Bibliografski zavod d.d., 1925-1929.
Ujević, Mate, ed. *Hrvatska Enciklopedija.* 5 vols., incomplete. Zagreb: Naklada hrvatskog izdavalackog bibliografskog zavoda, 1941-45.
General encyclopedija of high quality, which goes only to *Elek.*
Wurzback, Constantin von. ed. *Biographisches Lexicon des Kaiserthums Oesterreich.* 60 vols. in 36. Vienna: K.K. Hof und Staatsdruckerei, 1856-91.

D. *ARTICLES*

Andrić, Nikola. "Hrvatski ilirizam i srpstvo," *Vienac,* XXVIII (1894), 4, 30-1, 46-7.
Andrić, Nikola. "Iz hrvatske književnost: "Putovanja Gajeva po Rusije," *Hrvatsko kolo,* IV (1908), 3-8.
Auty, Robert. "Jan Kollár, 1793-1852," *Slavonic and East European Review,* XXXI (1952-53), 74-91.
Auty, Robert. "The Formation of the Slovene Literary Language against the Background of the Slavonic National Revival," *Slavonic and East European Review,* XLI (1962-63), 391-402.
Barac, Anton. "Slom Ljudevita Gaja," *Ostvarenja,* I (1947), 227-41.
Cushing, G.F. "The Birth of National Literature in Hungary," *Slavonic and East European Review,* XXXVIII (1960), 459-75.
Čolak, Tade. "Zora Dalmatinska i njen doprinos književnost ilirskog pokreta," *Kolo,* n.s. IV (1966), 284-98.
Čupović, Aleksandar. "Dr. Ljudevit Gaj i odvjetništvo," *Odvjetnik,* XVIII (1968), 309-15.
Deželić, Velimir. "Gaj kao njemački pjesnik," *Ilustrovani Obzor,* II (1909), 432-40.
Diels, Paul. "Aus der Geschichte der lateinischen Schrift beu den Südslaven," *Sitzungsberichte der Bayerischen Akademie der Wissenschaften, Philosophisch- historische Klasse,* 1950, heft 10.
Drechsler (Vodnik, Branko.) "Istorije i politike," *Jugoslavenska njiva,* VII (1923), 21-31.
Durković-Jakšić, Ljubomir. "Gajev pokušaj da izdaje 'Narodne Novine' ćirilicom," *Istoriski časopis* (Belgrade) IV (1952), 95-129.
Fancev, Franjo. "Hrvatski ilirski preporod jest naš autohton pokret," *Hrvatsko kolo,* XVI (1935), 3-58.
Fancev, Franjo. "Ilirstvo u hrvatskom preporodu," *Ljetopis,* 49, (1937-38), 130-57.
Fancev, Franjo. "Postanak i historijska pozadina Gajeve pjesme 'Još Horvatska nij' propala," *Hrvatska revija,* II (1935), 617-33.
Foretić, Vinko. "Prva faza hrvatskog narodnog preporoda u Dalmaciji (do sredine 19. stoljeća)," *Kolo,* n.s. IV (1966), 158-69.
Georgijević, Krešimir. "Gajevo školovanje u tudjini," *Pitanja književnosti i jezika* (Sarajevo), II (1956), 23-44.
Hauptman, Ferdo. "Pregled povijest Rijeke do Bachova apsolutizma," in Jakša Ravlić, ed., *Rijeka-Zbornik.* Zagreb: Matica Hrvatska, 1953, 203-14.

Halecki, Oscar. "The Renaissance Origins of Panslavism," *Polish Review,* III (1958), 1-13.

Horák, Jiří. "Pavel Josef Šafařík," translated by Konstantin Jelinek, *Historica* (Prague), IV (1962), 289-302.

Ivšić, Stjepan. "Jezik Hrvata kajkavaca," *Ljetopis,* XLVIII (1934-35), 47-88.

Jakić, Tomislav. "Štamparstvo i knjižarstvo u Zagrebu za vrijeme ilirskog preporoda," *Kolo,* n.s. IV (1966), 370-74.

Jonke, Ljudevit. "Ideološki osnovi Zagrebačke filološke škole 19. stoljeća," Filologija, I (1956), 77-86. Reprinted in Jonke, *Hrvatski književni jezik . . .,* 85-96.

Jonke, Ljudevit. "Osnovni problemi jezika hrvatske književnosti u 19. stoljeću," *Radovi Slavenskoga instituta* (Zagreb University), II (1958), 75-90. Reprinted in Jonke, *Hrvatski književni jezik. .,* 97-120.

Jonke, Ljudevit. "Sporovi pri odabiranju govora za zajednički književni jezik u Hrvata u 19. stoljeću," *Radovi Slavenskoga instituta* (Zagreb University), III (1959), 5-33.

For other articles by Jonke related to the language question see his *Hrvatski književni jezik u 19. i 20. stoljeća* (listed under III B)

Klaić, Vjekoslav. "Priča o Čehu, Lehu i Mehu," in the author's *Slike iz Slavenske povijesti.* Zagreb: Matica Hrvatska, 1903, 5-17.

Knezović, O. "Ilirizam u Bosni," *Hrvatska prosvjeta,* XIX (1931), 219-21.

Kukuljević-Sakcinski, Ivan. "Prinesci za povijest književnosti hrvatske," *Arhiv za povjestnicu jugoslavensku,* XII (1875), 51-110.

Lahner, Juraj. "Gajeva demonstracija protiv Zagrebačkome biskupu Hauliku," *Croatia Sacra.* XIV (1944), 61-72.

Lekai, Louis J. "Historiography in Hungary, 1790-1848," *Journal of Central European Affairs,* XIV (1954), 3-18.

Lord, Albert B. "Nationalism and the Muses in Balkan Slavic Literature in the Modern Period." in Barbara and Charles Jelavich, eds. *The Balkans in Transition.* Los Angeles and Berkeley: University of California Press, 1963, 258-96.

Mamuzić, Ilija. "Ilirizam i Srbi," *Rad,* 247 (1933), 1-92.

Mažuranić, Vladimir. "Životpisna crta," introduction to D. Demeter, *Teuta.* Zagreb: Matica Hrvatska, 1891, I-XXI.

Milčetić, Ivan, "Hrvati od Gaja do godine 1850. Kulturno-istorijski i književni pregled," *Hrvatski dom,* III (1878), 152-217.

Milcetic, Ivan. "Gajev pravopis," *Vijenac,* XXV (1891), 614-18.

Murko, Matija. "Početak Gajevih 'Novin' i 'Danice'," *Spomen-Cvieće Matice Hrvatske.* Zagreb: Matica Hrvatska, 1900, 567-81.

Nemeth, Kresimir. "Zagrebačka akademija uoči narodnog preporoda," *Iz starog i novog Zagreba,* I (1957), 169-81.

Prpic, George. "French Rule in Croatia: 1806-1813," *Balkan Studies,* V (1964), 221-76.

Paul, Karel. "Ljudevit Gaj v Praze v letech 1834-1846," *Československo-Jihoslovanská Revue,* IV (1934), 179-83.

Paul, Karel. "P. J. Šafařik a Gajuv Ilyrismus," *Československo-Jihoslovanska Revue,* V (1935), 138-44.

Paul, Karel. "Štěpán Mojses a Gajuv Ilyrismus," *Československo-Jihoslovanska Revue,* V (1935), 147-8.

Patzl, Viktor. "Statistiká mapa Ilyrisma," *Československo Jihoslovanska Revue,* V (1935), 157-63.

Rački, Franjo. ''Nacrt hrvatske historiografije od 1835 do 1885 godine,'' *Rad,* 80 (1885), 246-313.

Ravlić, Jakša. ''Ilirska čitaonica u Zagrebu,'' *Historijski zbornik,* XVI (1963), 159-215.

Ravlic, Jaksa. ''Povijest Matice Hrvatske,'' in Jakša Ravlić and Martin Somborac, *Matica Hrvatska, 1842-1962.* Zagreb: Matica Hrvatska, 1963, 11-254.

Ravlic, Jaksa. ''Ustanove i društva kulture u vrijeme hrvatskog narodnog preporoda,'' *Kolo,* n.s. IV (1966), 348-66.

Rothenberg, Gunther E. ''Jelačić, the Croatian Military Border and the Intervention against Hungary in 1848,'' *Austrian History Yearbook,* I (1965), 45-68.

Smičiklas, Tade. ''Obrana i razvitak hrvatske narodne ideje od 1790 do 1835 godine,'' *Rad,* 80 (1885), 11-71.

Stančić, Niksa. ''Problem 'Načertanija'' Ilije Garašanina u našoj historiografiji,'' *Historijski zbornik,* XXI-XXII (1968-69), 179-96.

Steinacker, Harold. ''Das Wesen des madjarischen Nationalismus,'' in F. Walter and H. Steinacker, *Die Nationalitätenfrage im alten Ungarn und die Südostpolitik Wiens.* München: R. Oldenbourg, 1959, 29-67.

Stoianović, Traian. ''The Pattern of Serbian Intellectual Evolution, 1830-1880,'' *Comparative Studies in Society and History,* I (1959), 242-72.

Stranjaković, Dragutin. ''Srbija privlačna središte Jugoslavena, 1844-48,'' *Srpski književni glasnik,* LXI (1940), 508-24.

Sugar, Peter F. ''The Southern Slav Image of Russia in the Nineteenth Century,'' *Journal of Central European Affairs,* XXI (1961), 45-52.

Suyer, Pavel. ''Ljudevit Gaj i obnova posljednjega gradečkog magistrata 1847,'' *Historijski zbornik,* XI (1956), 61-68.

Suyer, Pavel. '' 'Posao Milošiansko-Gajanski' pred gradskim magistratom,'' *Historijski zbornik,* V (1952), 85-101.

Šidak, Jaroslav. ''Austroslavizam i Slavenski kongres u Pragu 1848,'' *Historijski pregled,* VI (1960), 204-218.

Sidak, Jaroslav. ''Hrvatski narodni preporod — ideje i problemi,'' *Kolo,* n.s. IV (1966), 137-57. Reprinted in Sidak, *Studije,* 95-111.

Sidak, Jaroslav. ''Hrvatsko pitanje u Habsburškoj monarhiji,'' *Historijski pregled,* IX (1963), 101-21, 175-94. Reprinted in Šidak, *Studije,* 3-44.

Sidak, Jaroslav. ''Hrvatski preporodni pokret i grof Janko Draskovic,'' Sidak, *Studije,* 181-194.

Šidak, Jaroslav. ''Još jednom o ilirskom 'Branislavu','' *Historijski zbornik,* XVII (1964), 385-92.

Šidak, Jaroslav. ''Južnoslavenska ideja u Ilirskom pokretu,'' *Jugoslovenski istoriski časopis,* (Belgrade) II (1963), 31-42. Reprinted in Sidak, *Studije,* 113-24.

Sidak, Jaroslav. ''L'Hotel Lambert et les Croates,'' *Annales de l' Institut français de Zagreb,* XVII (1942-43), 5-19. Reprinted in Šidak, *Studije,* 167-77.

Šidak, Jaroslav. ''O uredniku i značenju ilirskog 'Branislava' (1844-45),'' *Historijski zbornik,* XIV (1961), 75-87. Reprinted in Šidak, *Studije,* 153-65.

Šidak, Jaroslav. ''Odjeci Francuske revolucije i Napoleonova vladavina u hrvatskim zemljama,'' *Napoleonove Ilirske province.* Ljubljana: Narodni muzej, 1964, 37-45. Reprinted in Šidak, *Studije,* 87-94.

Šidak, Jaroslav. "Prilog razvoju jugoslavenske ideje do g. 1914," *Naše teme,* IX (1965), 1290-1317. Reprinted in Sidak, *Studije,* 45-64.

Šidak, Jaroslav. "Politička djelatnost Ivana Kukuljevića Sakcinskoga," *Radovi Instituta za hrvatsku povijest,* II (1972), 47-104. Reprinted in Šidak, *Studije,* 221-77.

Šidak, Jaroslav. "Prilozi historiji stranačkih odnosa u Hrvatskoj uoči 1848," *Historijski zbornik,* XIII (1960), 167-207. Reprinted in Šidak, *Studije,* 125-51.

Šidak, Jaroslav. "Seljačko pitanje u hrvatskoj politici 1848," *Jugoslovenski istoriski časopis (Belgrade), II* (1963), 3-30.

Šidak, Jaroslav. " 'Tajna politika' Lj. Gaja i postanak njegovih 'memorandumu' knezu Metternichu 1846-47," *Arhivski vjesnik,* XIII (1970), 397-434. Reprinted in Sidak, *Studije,* 195-220.

For other articles and essays by Šidak see his *Studije* and ed. *Spomenica . . .* I have cited the works as they appear in the text, therefore as I first used them.

Šišić, Ferdo. "Ban Josip Jelačić," *Savremenik,* IV (1909), 289, 371, 446, 512, 570, 625-36, 685.

Šišić, Ferdo. "Ime Hrvat i Srbin i teorije o doseljenju Hrvata i Srba," *Godišnjića Nikole Čupića* (Belgrade), XXXV (1923), 35-51.

Šišić, Ferdo. "Hrvati i Madžari uoči sukoba 1848," *Jugoslavenska njiva,* VII (1923), 409-19, 453-62.

Šišić, Ferdo. "Hrvatski ilirizam — njegova politička strana," *Bratstvo* (Belgrade), XXVII (1922), 134-75.

Šišić, Ferdo. "Kako je Jelačić postao banom," *Jugoslavenska njiva,* VII (1923), 169-183.

Šišić, Ferdo. "Knez Miloš u Zagrebu 1848," *Jugoslavenska njiva,* VIII (1924), 49-53, 139-44, 188-94, 219-30, 265-75, 297-302, 341-46.

Šišić, Ferdo. "O stogodišnjici ilirskoga pokreta," *Ljetopis,* 49 (1937-38), 99-130.

Šišić, Ferdo. "Podrijetlo Gajeva roda," *Jugoslovenski istoriski časopis* (Belgrade), V (1939), 150-66.

Šišić, Ferdo. "Školovanje Ljudevita Gaja u domovini," *Hrvatsko kolo,* XIX (1938), 53-81.

Šišić, Ferdo. "Une tentative pre-illyrienne: le journal de Sporer," *Le Monde Slave,* XII (1935), 374-83.

Škorjac, Izidor. "Zagrebački bogoslovi prema Gaja, Slovencima i Srbima," *Izvještaji male realne gimnazije u Krapini,* (1911), 3-32.

Šurmin, Đuro. "Bilješke za hrvatski preporod," *Vijenac,* XXXVII (1902), 424-5, 440-1, 474-6, 487-8, 503-04, 525-6.

Šurmin, Đuro. "Gaj kao novinar," *Zvono,* V (1911), 1-13.

Šurmin, Đuro. "Kulturne i književne prilike," *Savremenik,* VIII (1913), 102-6.

Šurmin, Đuro. "Početak Gajevih novina," *Rad,* 162 (1905), 110-34.

Šurmin, Đuro. "Književno-politička parodija Gajeva," *Savremenik,* VI (1911), 347-50.

Vince, Zlatko. "M. Bobrowski i A. Kuharski — svjedoci i suradnici reforme hrwatske (sic) latiničke grafije u 19. stoljeću," *Rocznik Slawistyczny Crakow) XXXXIII (1972), 47-57.*

Vodnik, Branko, "Istorija i politika," *Jugoslavenska njiva,* VII (1923), 21-31.

Vrbanić, Fran. "Jedno stoljeće u razvoju žiteljstva Hrvatske i Slavonije," *Rad,* 140 (1899), 17-58.

Wagner, Francis S. "Széchenyi and the Nationality Problem in the Habsburg Empire," *Journal of Central European Affairs*, 289-341.

Wollman, Frank. "Tchécoslovaques et Illyrisme," *Le Monde Slave*, XII (1935), 1-26.

Žáček, Václav. "Česká účast při pokusech o politické sblíženi Charvátu a Srbu v. 40. letech 19. stoleti," *Slovanské historičké studie* (Prague) VI (1966), 55-91.

Žáček, Václav. "Češko i poljsko učešće u postanku Garašaninova 'Načertanija' (1844)," *Historijski zbornik*, XVI (1963), 35-56.

INDEX